Monopoly of Force

Published by Books Express Publishing

ISBN 978-1-780399-22-5

Books Express publications are available from all good retail and online booksellers. For publishing proposals and direct ordering please contact us at: info@books-express.com

Monopoly of Force

The Nexus of DDR and SSR

Edited by Melanne A. Civic and Michael Miklaucic

With a Foreword by
General James N. Mattis, USMC

Published for the
Center for Complex Operations
Institute for National Strategic Studies
By National Defense University Press
Washington, D.C.
2011

Contents

Part II: Challenges of Reintegration

Part III: Managing DDR and SSR Programs

Foreword

If experience is any guide, it is safe to say that the next decade will be as full of surprises as the past decade. There is no doubt we will be surprised, so our job is to be prepared for the unexpected so that when it arrives, we have the fewest regrets. The Joint Operating Environment (JOE) is U.S. Joint Forces Command's review of possible future trends that present significant security challenges and opportunities for the next quarter-century. From economic trends to climate change, from cyber attacks to failed states, the JOE outlines future disruptions and examines the implications for our national security in general and for the joint force in particular. These implications, plus current operations, inform the concepts that drive our Services' adaptations and the environments within which they will operate.

Successful adaptation is essential if our leaders are to have the fewest regrets when future crises erupt. In our guardian role for the Nation, it is natural that we in the military focus more on the security challenges and threats than on emerging opportunities. Nonetheless, there are opportunities worthy of serious consideration, and it is our responsibility to reflect on those as well. This book, *Monopoly of Force*, highlights an area of opportunity we should all be interested in—one that, if done right, can save lives and resources and help short-circuit the cycle of violence in regions where conflict abounds.

All wars come to an end. Using all means possible, we attempt to end wars as quickly as possible and on the best possible footing for fostering stabilization and preventing (or at least discouraging) additional conflict. Successful disarmament, demobilization, and reintegration (DDR) are fundamental to enduring and equitable peace. For Afghanistan, the Bonn Conference established them as elements of success. DDR must be taken seriously if military or operational success is to gain strategic outcomes favorable to international order and American interests. Our security sector must embrace this thesis because there will most certainly be a next time, and we need to be ready to disarm, demobilize, and reintegrate combatants to achieve a stable environment for the establishment of economic prosperity and good governance.

DDR is not necessarily solely or even primarily a military effort. Once diplomacy or military force and persuasion have achieved adequate levels of security, a catalyst is required to focus effort and to create a DDR capability. Many actors could possibly play either leading or supporting functions in DDR. Organizations such as the United Nations (UN), the European Union (EU), and the World Bank potentially have parts to play in effective future DDR scenarios. Most importantly, a holistic effort is needed with the efforts of leadership focusing on the civil, political, economic, and diplomatic dimensions as well as the military dimension.

Our current North Atlantic Treaty Organization strategy in Afghanistan is ultimately based on reintegration of the *reconcilable* Taliban members into the body politic of the country. Persuading the Taliban to disarm, demobilize, and reintegrate will require various aspects of the military, diplomatic, and civil-societal-economic apparatus to be adjusted successfully. In short, full reintegration of former combatants requires a holistic approach.

Our security sector has recognized the importance of DDR even as we acknowledge that executing it is difficult. Why? Possibly for the United States, our difficulty with DDR is grounded in our argument with George III and our subsequent response to him that resulted in the Revolution, the *Federalist Papers*, and ultimately our system of government. Our way of governing is established to be inefficient, not integrated, requiring our various branches to compete, thus avoiding the centralization of power. So, while DDR requires a whole-of-government, and even a whole-of-society, response, America's cultural baggage may be a significant obstacle to the Nation playing a leadership role on the international stage in regard to DDR.

Accordingly, the United States may be better suited to act as a catalyst or in a supporting role for DDR. Our history, our form of government, and our cultural baggage *combined* lead me to suggest this is an area where America's partners might take the lead, although being a meaningful participant in an international effort still requires significant work on America's part.

This is part of the challenge. DDR should not be viewed as an orphan in the U.S. Government, but to be successful, it requires an international, integrated effort rather than just being left to the United States. For instance, the initial attempt to perform DDR in the "Afghanistan New Beginnings Program" from 2003 to 2006 was a Japanese-led effort under the banner of a UN program development project. Successful DDR may require the help of nongovernmental organizations.

We need to recognize that in an imperfect world, we cannot blame a man for wanting to maintain his arms for the protection of his family, land, and community when all around him is chaos, lawlessness, and corruption, with little or no opportunity. As in most societies, it is no stretch to say the average Afghan seeks a base level of security in which to live, educational opportunities for his children, and the chance to provide for his family and prosper economically. Unfortunately, because those conditions have not yet prevailed in Afghanistan, there is evidence that some combatants who previously turned in their arms during the New Beginnings program are now rearming.

Clearly, "good intentions" alone cannot suffice for successful DDR. The road to international Hades is paved with good intentions. We must *never* confuse emotion with progress, and we must follow through on our commitments—that is, providing timely and relevant benefits for disarmament—for we will generally get the behavior we reward.

So how should we approach DDR in our planning? First, the complexity of conflict resolution and the role of DDR demand clarity. Clarity means we must focus initially on problem-setting versus problem-solving. Often referred to as *problem definition*, in today's military we call this *campaign design*, and the U.S. Army has done some of the best thinking on this line of effort. Elements of design include taking the situation for what it is, not what we would like it to be; ensuring we are focused on the right problem; and performing continuous assessment and structured learning. We should break down the challenges of DDR into a set of clear problem statements. Preplanned, one-size-fits-all templates simply will not suffice for successful DDR because every scenario is different.

Once the "problem" is defined with the greatest fidelity possible and derived from an inclusive process that brings together the right people with real experience, we will find that the time spent framing the problem was not wasted. Without a clear and shared view of the problem seen on its own terms, problem-solving is futile and more likely to create adversarial relations among the problem solvers. Possessing clarity and a shared understanding of the problem through effective design is more likely to incite a spirit of effective collaboration among the host of organizations and peoples involved.

Secondly, as seen recently in South Africa, Sierra Leone, Northern Ireland, Bosnia, Iraq, and Afghanistan, it is clear that DDR requires a long time, certainly longer than Western election cycles. Again, clarity must be stressed if we are to hold the support of our democracies, for over the long term, with the usual good and bad associated with such efforts, we need our citizens to understand that these wars are complex. They are really nothing new, because as a human endeavor, the essential nature of war has never changed. Only its specific characteristics have. The challenge, issues, and goals must be clear if we expect to keep our populations and our legislative bodies committed over the duration of such complex operations.

And in an age when some Western political leaders doubt the concept of victory, we may be forced to initiate the DDR process from the unenviable position of no political commitment to the decisive defeat of the enemy—that is, to defeat his armed forces and, more importantly, to create in his mind and spirit a sense of defeat. So in some instances, we may lack a level playing field for the effort of DDR. Without forcing an irreconcilable enemy to accept defeat and cease fighting, you do *not* possess a viable disarmament, demobilization, and reintegration situation—you have a war.

So knowing when to start DDR is critical to its chance for success—especially in a nonlinear, irregular environment. We must also be open to the possibility that DDR may not be able to proceed in the prescribed order and that there may be cases in which the *R*—reintegration—may have to precede disarmament or demobilization. We must understand that successfully ending wars is as important as successfully fighting them. The complex operations that characterize modern conflict and our contemporary national security challenges require new procedures, such as whole-of-government approaches, and new attitudes that lead to better collaboration, cooperation, and coordination. What we cannot permit is the assumption that the end of war will take care of itself, and that DDR is somebody else's problem. Whether or not the United States takes a leading role in a specific DDR environment, it needs to take the challenges of DDR very seriously, develop better understanding of its dynamics, and above all establish institutional knowledge of DDR and the end of wars so it will be better prepared for the surprises of the future. *Monopoly of Force* is an important step in the right direction.

General James N. Mattis, USMC
Commander, U.S. Central Command

Acknowledgments

Every book has a beginning. This book began as a conversation during a conference organized by the Stanley Foundation entitled "Forging a U.S. Strategy for Strengthening Fragile States," which was held October 15–17, 2009, at the Airlie Center in Warrenton, Virginia. For that original conversation, we thank the Stanley Foundation, Airlie Center, and our colleagues Sean McFate (also a contributing author to this volume) of the College of International Security Affairs at the National Defense University (NDU) and Robert Perito of the U.S. Institute of Peace (USIP).

The conversation evolved into another conference held at NDU on March 5, 2010, in Washington, DC, which was coorganized by the Center for Complex Operations (CCO) and USIP. From USIP, we thank Dan Serwar, Robert Perito, and Liz Panerelli. We also thank Will Imbrie and John Gastright of DynCorp International for their support. We thank all of the conference panelists for their participation and contributions to a robust and stimulating discussion of Disarmament, Demobilization, and Reintegration, Security Sector Reform, and the state's Monopoly of Force. We wish to express special appreciation to Ambassadors Thomas C. Krajeski and Jacques Paul Klein and to General James N. Mattis for their inspirational keynote remarks.

This second conference, in turn, evolved into the present volume. For this, we thank the authors who contributed their time, experience, and insights voluntarily and enthusiastically to build this book. Dr. Hans Binnendijk, Vice President for Research and Applied Learning at NDU, and Ambassador John E. Herbst, Director of CCO, gave us ongoing support and encouragement. The CCO intern core, specifically Joshua Jones, Heather Rehm, and Amanda Boak-Riggs, supported our work steadfastly and professionally before, during, and after the conference and throughout the book preparation process.

Finally, in producing the volume itself, we thank the team at National Defense University Press—in particular Mr. Calvin Kelley, Dr. Jeffrey D.

Smotherman, and Dr. Thomas F. Lynch III—who turned a series of essays into this book.

Every book has a beginning, but we hope this book will not be an end.

Melanne A. Civic
Michael Miklaucic
May 2011

Introduction

The State and the Use of Force: Monopoly and Legitimacy

By Melanne A. Civic and Michael Miklaucic

In the immediate aftermath of war or in the midst of violent conflict, there is everything to be done. The urgency of anything can be overwhelming and can lead to paralysis. Sequencing and prioritizing seem unrealistic luxuries, and confusion often reigns. Studies show that of the countries emerging from conflict, 40 percent return to it within 10 years.[1] Indeed, immediate past conflict is the single most highly correlated predictive factor for future conflict. When the window for peace consolidation opens, robust efforts must be directed toward reinforcing and broadening the peace to ensure that combatants do not return to arms; the window shuts all too rapidly. The timeframe for consolidating peace is compressed. This will often—perhaps inevitably—require some extremely difficult decisions, choices, and compromises. However, if human life is to be protected, certain important public goods may have to be deferred to ensure against a rapid return to violence.

In the "golden moment" when recent belligerents have agreed on peace terms—before the ensuing enthusiasm has dissipated—there is often a multitude of donors, sponsors, and other benefactors ready to help. This is both a blessing and a curse. The blessing is in the resources, both human and capital, brought to the peace consolidation process. The curse comes in the form of the multiple agents offering those resources and their expertise, each with its own agenda, objectives, expectations, and methods. The topography of peace can be crowded, confused, and conflicted.

Writings on complex operations, development, and peace-building are permeated by optimism and a can-do attitude. All problems can be solved if only the right techniques are applied and the "political will" is present.[2] Indeed, it is tempting to suppose that all good things go together. In the high-pressure environment of complex operations, we want to believe that with enough consultation and coordination, all efforts to establish equitable and durable peace can be harmonized and deconflicted. Unity of command and unity of effort will ensure that all parts contribute optimally to the shared ultimate objective. As comforting as this vision might be, it is not plausible, and even agendas with similar ultimate goals (such as durable peace) may have conflicting intermediate objectives.

In his classic formula, Max Weber distinguished the state as an institution by its monopoly of the legitimate use of force. Although the state may delegate the legitimate use of force, it remains the unique owner of that prerogative. Other institutions, agencies, or elements within society may exercise force, but without delegation from the state, any such exercise is unsanctioned and is thus illegitimate.[3] In reality, no modern state, strong or weak, has an absolute monopoly on the use of force; however, the legitimacy of the use of force is central to the modern concept of governance. Today, many states are threatened by the loss of the monopoly of force and its legitimate use.

In his seminal study of state formation in Europe, Charles Tilly argued that the state as we know it—what he refers to as the "national state"—is the product of the interplay between the accumulation of capital in cities and the concentration of coercion by sovereigns. This interplay intensified as the development of national capacity for warfare became structurally endemic in the 16th to 20th centuries, with *structurally endemic* defined as a permanent part of national life requiring permanent institutions and standing armies. These institutions and militaries, in turn, required a full spectrum of support institutions. Standing armies and the associated institutional support architecture enabled European sovereigns to exert dominance over competing power centers, including, critically, the class interests of the owners of capital concentrations.[4]

The unique role of the institutions of force in society, particularly in the formation and identity of the state—as suggested by both Weber and Tilly—has gained renewed focus in recent decades. The new polities of Iraq and Afghanistan are being built upon national security forces and institutions that are the recipients of unprecedented levels of resourcing, for it is widely acknowledged that the futures of these two countries depend on the successful development of their respective security forces.

The relevance of both Weber and Tilly with respect to state formation and identification is enduring, but recent changes have been dramatic. Thus, the insights of these theorists should be continually reexamined and revalidated in light of these changes. To modernize Weber's formulation, we must acknowledge the global political awakening of the late 20th and early 21st centuries, which was catalyzed by epic advances in information, communication, and transportation technologies. Nearly universal awareness and interconnectivity have awakened previously nascent or dormant desires for identity and equity. The ensuing struggles challenge state legitimacy and demand recognition of those multiple equities and actions to ensure they are realized. Zbigniew Brzezinski writes, "For the first time in history almost all of humanity is politically activated, politically conscious and politically interactive. Global activism is generating a surge in the quest for cultural respect and economic opportunity."[5] Within any state, there are inevitably and naturally competing equities held dear by groups with conflicting interests and social objectives. The state must mediate these competing equities and interests in a nonviolent fashion while retaining the ultimate right and prerogative of representing the various constituencies as a whole. This has become vastly more difficult. What has emerged is a condition of fragmented and contested legitimacy in which the assumption of legitimacy on the part of state leaders cannot be taken for granted. It remains true that only through a monopoly of the legitimate use of coercive force can a state effectively exercise its mediating role, but both the monopoly and the legitimacy have become more difficult to attain.

The central role of violence and war in state formation as Tilly describes it must be measured against the astounding increase in the lethality of conflict and war, as well as the decline over the past half century in the global acceptance of violence and mass killing. Extensive weapons proliferation and the widespread availability of significant force both to private individuals and to nonstate groups have irreversibly altered the cost/benefit equation. The exercise of coercive authority has become an extremely violent competition even in well-established states. One need only consider Mexico—a member of the Organisation for Economic Co-operation and Development (OECD)—where over 35,000 have died in the narcotics wars since 2006.[6] While no state has an absolute monopoly of force, to be accountable for actions taken within its borders a state must have at least a preponderance of force; it must be able to prevent hostile acts toward other states. This is a minimum assumption of effective sovereignty. As a self-protective measure, therefore, helping states attain that minimum level is an appropriate aim of U.S. foreign and national security policy. Secretary of Defense Robert Gates argues, "Building the governance and security capacity of other countries must be a critical element of U.S. national security strategy."[7]

These dramatic changes condition the state formation dynamics described by Weber and Tilly. It is sovereignty itself—the foundation of the Westphalian and post–World War II interstate system—that is at issue here. In a strictly legal sense, sovereignty is recognized in many cases in which the state does not exercise a monopoly of the legitimate use of force. Of the 193 state members of the United Nations in 2010, no fewer than 20 and as many as 50 exercise sovereignty only in terms of legal recognition.[8] That is to say, they are recognized legally as sovereign states by other states and interstate organizations but can neither effectively protect their borders from military, migratory, or subversive intrusion nor enforce the rule of law and orderliness within their borders. They are sovereign in legal terms only.[9] This condition poses serious challenges to U.S. national security, as states unable to exercise effective sovereignty in the practical (not strictly legal) sense cannot meaningfully be held accountable for hostile or threatening activity taking place within their borders.

The erosion of sovereignty in large swaths of the world is already the stuff of numerous wargames, military experiments, intelligence scenarios, and contingency plans. We are not speaking of a distant future but of the present, in many cases. The 2002 *National Security Strategy of the United States* stated, "America is now threatened less by conquering states than we are by failing ones."[10] Ten years later, we find failing states not only in Central and South Asia, but also throughout Africa (for example, Somalia and Democratic Republic of the Congo), Latin America (Guatemala and Honduras), and the Middle East (Yemen). The threats emanating from these "undergoverned" spaces do not respect borders; they strike across borders, oceans, and continents, often with impunity.[11]

Traditional development approaches such as "modernization," private sector and civil society empowerment, and democratization have been applied by the United States and other national and interstate powers over the past 60 or so years to establish robust sovereign states out of the detritus of the colonial world. Some of the postcolonial territories have indeed become robust states, but many have not. Many states such as Nepal, Burundi, and the Philippines have been recipients of billions of dollars in official development assistance over the past decades, yet they remain poor and caught up in conflicts.[12]

DDR and SSR have emerged in recent years as promising though poorly understood tools for consolidating stability and establishing meaningful sovereignty after conflict.[13] The chapters in this book reflect the diversity of experience in DDR and SSR. Yet, with the considerable experience we have acquired, our ability to use these tools with consistent success remains less than optimally developed. By anointing a complex set of relationships with an acronym—Disarmament, Demobilization, and Reintegration (DDR) or Security Sector Reform (SSR)—we endow it with a misleadingly singular character, and significant tensions within the component elements are obscured.

It is tempting to view DDR as a linear and sequential process beginning with the disarming and demobilizing of ex-combatants, followed by their peaceful reintegration into postconflict society. This is alluring because of its optimistic simplicity, but it is an ideal case and not necessarily a natural, necessary, or normative template for accomplishing the objective of returning combatants, society, and the state to "normal" civilian life.

In reality, DDR contains substantially distinct and separable operations, often involving different people, organizations, motivations, and modalities. The assumption that disarmament should precede reintegration may seem logical but may not be politically feasible. And while we may wish to demobilize ex-combatants prior to reinserting them into the civilian population, it may be their solidarity that permits them to avoid the early alienation and disenchantment that might return them to arms. Though we know that ex-combatants who retain their weapons constitute a loaded gun aimed at state and society, and that only by disarming them can the state regain the preponderance, let alone its monopoly, of coercive power, we must understand that ex-combatants may view their weapons as their only means of survival. Despite the risks, and although disarmament must ultimately succeed in order for the state to attain a preponderance of force, this process will often require great flexibility and the setting aside of preconceived assumptions or formulas.

DDR is further complicated by the occasional addition of a fourth R—Reinsertion. Some practitioners and scholars presume reinsertion within reintegration, while others, depending on the circumstances, consider it a distinct intermediate phase. Various other related processes may be included in the overall concept: for example, repatriation, resettlement, rehabilitation, and redeployment. While no formal consensus definition of *DDR* has emerged, the United Nations (UN) Integrated Disarmament, Demobilization and Reintegration Standards (IDDRS) offers the most systematic set of guidelines and procedures for implementing DDR programs, as well as a set of operational definitions, all developed by UN DDR practitioners at the headquarters and country levels.[14]

Successful DDR theoretically removes at least the instruments and peer pressure to resume violence. But how can the state reclaim the lost legitimacy that led combatants to violence? State security forces are often predatory, repressing rather than protecting society. Hosni Mubarak's Egypt and Zine El Abidine Ben Ali's Tunisia are merely the latest in a long stream of regimes kept in power by oppressive security services, following in the footsteps of the Shah's Iran, the military dictatorships of South America in the 1980s, Suharto's Indonesia, Mobutu Sese Seko's Zaire, and many others. Citizens throughout the developing world have good reason not to trust coercive force in the hands of the state. Reform of the security sector is a step toward that trust, though only time and experience will consolidate it.

Like DDR, the acronym SSR conceals in its simplicity a highly complex system of systems. As Secretary Gates writes, "The United States now recognizes that the security sectors of at-risk countries are really systems of systems tying together the military, the police, the justice system, and other governance and oversight mechanisms."[15] The acknowledgment by state authorities that reform is required, the inclusiveness and transparency of the reform process, and of course the substance of the reform are key factors in establishing legitimacy. The inclusion of representatives of the population affected by a given reform is a well-established principle of development.[16] Without inclusion of those affected and well-grounded in local conditions, the reform will not possess organic staying power and is unlikely to be adopted or internalized by the local population. Such foreign-designed and -implemented reforms rarely endure the departure of the foreign designer. Transparency will reinforce legitimacy by reducing the mystery and remoteness of governmental processes and will encourage the participation that is the basis for local ownership. That interaction within the parameters of a mutually accepted social contract is a source of legitimacy and an opportunity for citizens and officials to engage and build trust.

What should a reformed security sector look like? The answer is, of course, context-specific. *SSR* is defined by the UN as "a process of assessment, review and implementation as well as monitoring and evaluation led by national authorities that has as its goal the enhancement of effective and accountable security for the State and its peoples without discrimination and with full respect for human rights and the rule of law."[17] Some practitioners find this definition inadequate and favor the OECD's integrated and operational approach. According to the OECD Development Assistance Committee (DAC) publication *Security System Reform and Governance*,[18] the security sector is seen as more than merely the security forces as a system of interacting core or state security forces; governance, justice, and law enforcement institutions; and nonstate actors who contribute to or alternatively undermine security. SSR through the OECD lens involves the "transformation of the 'security system' which includes all the actors, their roles, responsibilities and actions—working together to manage and operate the system in a manner that is more consistent with democratic norms and sound principles of good governance, and thus contributes to a well-functioning security framework."[19]

According to the U.S. Government, the ultimate objective of SSR "is to provide (security) services in a way that promotes an effective and legitimate public service that is transparent, accountable to civilian authority, and responsive to the needs of the public."[20] According to the Geneva Centre for the Democratic Control of Armed Forces, security sector reform should aim to "enhance Security Sector Governance through the effective and efficient delivery of security under conditions of democratic oversight and control."[21] Perhaps most widely accepted is the statement of the Development Advisory Committee of the Organisation for Economic Co-operation and Development: the "overall objective of security system reform is to create a secure environment that is conducive to development, poverty reduction and democracy."[22] These statements constitute at least a Western consensus on how SSR can serve as a tool the state can use to attain legitimacy.

Again, definitions are elusive and can be misleading. No template is likely to serve in all or even many cases. What the authors in this volume suggest is the complexity and amorphousness of these concepts, their essentially political nature, and the elusiveness of precise definitions. These concepts should not be interpreted rigidly as fixed or unchanging principles or processes, but rather as flexible tools for restoring to the state the monopoly of force that has been lost—or not yet achieved.

The recognition of SSR linkages to DDR and other transitional activities has gained momentum over the past decade. In 2000, the pivotal Report of the Panel on United Nations Peace Operations (Brahimi Report),[23] through its review of all aspects of peacekeeping operations, advocated for a holistic approach to peacekeeping and preventing the resurgence of conflict. The report highlighted the impact of disarmament, demobilization, and transitional justice to the overall peace process, and recommended linking these to security sector reform and long-term development. In 2008, the Security Council, in its report on the Role of the UN in Supporting Security Sector Reform[24] further identified good governance and the consolidation of state power through disarmament, demobilization, and other reconciliation processes as critical to building sustainable peace. In 2009, the UN Development Program (UNDP), through the UN Inter-Agency Working Group on DDR, added SSR to the operational guidelines of the IDDRS designed for DDR practitioners.[25]

Working in concert with UN efforts, the Geneva Centre for the Democratic Control of Armed Forces in 2009 published an analysis of lessons from complex multinational peacekeeping missions.[26] Among the recommendations, the authors advocated for the UN to delve more deeply into all aspects of SSR and explore linkages with related activities such as DDR and transitional justice.

A significant coordinated governmental effort to develop SSR linkages with DDR and other related and cross-cutting sectors is found in Sweden. The government created a Steering Committee on SSR to bring together the Ministries of Foreign Affairs, Justice, and Defense, and a National Contact Group for SSR that includes military, justice, police, and academic collaboration. The Folke Bernadotte Academy, a member of the Contact Group, conducts research on justice, police security, SSR, and other areas of common concern, informing government policy.

Within the U.S. Government, both DDR and SSR are orphans, with no single agency claiming ownership of either. There are aspects of each that are primarily military, and other aspects that are diplomatic and/or developmental. Individual offices in various agencies—or just individuals—may be interested in either or even both. There is no true interagency policy or doctrine dealing with either. Secretary Gates concedes, "For all the improvements of recent years, the [U.S.] interagency tool kit is still a hodgepodge of jury-rigged arrangements constrained by a dated and complex patchwork of authorities, persistent shortfalls in resources, and unwieldy processes."[27] The closest thing to interagency policy or doctrine is the February 2009 publication *Security Sector Reform*, which "provides Department of State, Department of Defense, and United States Agency for International Development practitioners with guidelines for planning and implementing Security Sector Reform programs with foreign partner nations."[28] With no agency parent and no governmental policy or doctrine, these programs would take luck to succeed. They inherently require the diverse elements of national power as housed in the various agencies of the U.S. Government. They are thus complex operations by nature.

This volume specifically explores the interface between DDR and SSR. The assumption that they contribute to the same ultimate goal—enduring peace—seems valid; however, the associated assumption that they are complementary or coordinated in practice is not justified by experience. With the aim of examining the nexus between the two, the volume examines the politics of DDR and SSR, the challenges of reintegration, problems related to implementing DDR and SSR programs, and lessons and recommendations on how SSR and DDR programs can establish or restore the monopoly of the legitimate use of force to the state and thereby support sustainable peace. Hopefully, these chapters will serve to excite further thought on how these two processes—DDR and SSR—can be implemented effectively and complementarily to better accomplish the shared ultimate goal of enduring peace.

In Part I, Véronique Dudouet focuses on the politics surrounding reintegration of nonstate actors and the state providing an alternative to rebel violence through the development of a legitimate and democratic political order. Michelle Hughes advances a theory of a symbiotic relationship between SSR and DDR and argues that the restoration of the monopoly of force requires political buy-in of a whole-of-government approach to planning and operations with coordinated military and interagency civilian engagement. Paul R. Williams and Matthew T. Simpson provide an assessment of the Doha Agreements on the peace process in Darfur and identify the missed opportunities and thwarted momentum for peace-building as a result of politics leading to abbreviated SSR and DDR programs.

In Part II, Mark Knight explains the relationship between unsuccessful reintegration and failed peace, proposing that incomplete, poorly structured reintegration programs actually undermine peace-building efforts. Jacqueline O'Neill and Jarad Vary argue that failing to engage women in negotiations of peace accords and in the formation of parameters of SSR and DDR results in a multitude of essential issues being ignored and a tendency to omit women from reintegration and rehabilitation. Jennifer M. Hazen proposes that DDR must be construed more narrowly, rather than comingled with long-term development and societal reforms, and that reinsertion should be an intermediary, distinct step preceding reintegration. Courtney R. Rowe, Eric Wiebelhaus-Brahm, and Anne-Tyler Morgan analyze the special challenges of DDR, especially the rehabilitation and reintegration of former child combatants. Judith Burdin Asuni utilizes a case study of the Niger Delta to link the lure of the profitable conflict economy, the lack of political will to reform the security sector, and the failure to reintegrate combatants, which have resulted in the perpetuation of armed conflict.

In Part III, Jacques Paul Klein and Melanne A. Civic describe the chaotic circumstances and pressing nature of the DDRR program in Liberia that are demonstrative of many postconflict environments and lead to seemingly contrary but necessary decisions for the DDRR program. G. Eugene Martin shows that a vague and ambiguous peace agreement lends support to political backsliding and subverts progress in both DDR and

SSR. Adriaan Verheul exposes DDR in the Sudan Comprehensive Peace Agreement as a misnomer, incomplete, and lacking the capacity to reintegrate, and argues the importance of coordinated planning and management of the SSR and DDR processes.

In Part IV, Sean McFate consolidates theories on the DDR–SSR nexus and demonstrates how the monopoly of force through DDR and reform of the complex security system are the underpinnings of a strong and peaceful state. Alan Bryden expounds on the security system approach to stabilization and peace-building, sets DDR and SSR within the broader context of good governance, and emphasizes the importance of engaging nonstate actors. Mark Sedra illustrates the DDR–SSR nexus through a case study on Afghanistan and argues for an integrated approach. Through a concluding case study, Josef Teboho Ansorge and Nana Akua Antwi-Ansorge highlight the link between the monopoly of force and government legitimacy in Liberia.

It is the intention of the editors that these chapters serve to excite further thought on how DDR and SSR can be implemented effectively and holistically to better accomplish the shared goals of peace and stability. The contributors are dedicated and experienced professionals who form a community of practice and of interest. We wish to expand that relatively small community and bring to it not only the additional resources required to implement effective DDR and SSR, but also the additional innovation and intellectual creativity needed to turn these processes into effective tools of statecraft to meet the challenges of the 21st century.

Notes

[1] Paul Collier, Anke Hoeffler, and Måns Söderbom, *Post-Conflict Risks* (Oxford: Centre for the Study of African Economies, 2006).

[2] Lant Pritchett, Michael Woolcock, and Matt Andrews, *Capability Traps? The Mechanisms of Persistent Implementation Failure*, Working Paper 234 (Washington, DC: Center for Global Development, December 2010).

[3] Max Weber, *Politics As a Vocation* (Munich: Munich University, 1918).

[4] Charles Tilly, *Coercion, Capital, and European States, AD 990–1992* (Malden, MA: Blackwell Publishers, 1990).

[5] Zbigniew Brzezinski, "The Global Political Awakening," *The New York Times*, December 16, 2008.

[6] Bob Killebrew and Matthew Irvine, *Security Through Partnership: Fighting Transnational Cartels in the Western Hemisphere* (Washington, DC: Center for a New American Security, 2011).

[7] Robert M. Gates, "Helping Others Defend Themselves," *Foreign Affairs* (May–June 2010).

[8] The Fund for Peace identifies 37 states in the "Alert" category of failed or likely to fail states in its 2010 "Failed States Index."

[9] For an interesting discussion of sovereignty, see Stephen D. Krasner, *Sovereignty: Organized Hypocrisy* (Princeton: Princeton University Press, 1999).

[10] *The National Security Strategy of the United States of America* (Washington, DC: The White House, September 2002).

[11] For a discussion of ungoverned spaces, see Angel Rabasa, ed., *Ungoverned Territories: Understanding and Reducing Terrorism Risks* (Santa Monica, CA: RAND, 2007).

[12] The World Bank, *Breaking the Conflict Trap: Civil War and Development Policy* (Washington, DC: The World Bank, 2003).

[13] The term *security sector reform* was coined only in 1998, according to the Geneva Centre for the Democratic Control of Armed Forces. See *Security Sector Governance and Reform* (Geneva: Geneva Centre for the Democratic Control of Armed Forces, 2009).

[14] Available at <www.unddr.org/whatisddr.php#8>, 15.

[15] Gates.

[16] Andrew Natsios, "The Nine Principles of Reconstruction and Development," *Parameters* (Autumn 2005). According to Natsios, the first principle of reconstruction and development is "ownership." Inclusion is not one of the nine principles he articulates, but it is implied in several references.

[17] UN Report of the Secretary-General on Securing Peace and Development: The Role of the United Nations in Supporting Security Sector Reform, A/62/659-S/2008/39, January 23, 2008.

[18] Available at <www.oecd.org/dataoecd/8/39/31785288.pdf>.

[19] Available at <www.oecd.org/dataoecd/15/54/1886146.pdf>.

[20] U.S. Agency for International Development, U.S. Department of Defense, and U.S. Department of State, *Security Sector Reform*, February 2009.

[21] Geneva Centre for the Democratic Reform of Armed Forces.

[22] Organisation for Economic Co-operation and Development (OECD), *Security System Reform and Governance* (Paris: OECD, 2005).

[23] UN Report of the Secretary-General on a Comprehensive Review of the Whole Question of Peacekeeping Operations in All Their Aspects, A/55/305-S/2000/809.

[24] UN Report of the Secretary General on Securing Peace and Development.

[25] Available at <www.unddr.org/iddrs/06>. A summary of the DDR–SSR guidelines is appended to this book.

[26] H. Hänggi and V. Scherrer, eds., *Security Sector Reform and UN Integrated Missions: Experience from Burundi, the Democratic Republic of Congo, Haiti, and Kosovo* (Geneva: Geneva Centre for the Democratic Control of Armed Forces, 2008).

[27] Gates.

[28] The World Bank.

Part I
The Politics of Disarmament and Security Sector Reform

Chapter 1

Nonstate Armed Groups and the Politics of Postwar Security Governance

By Véronique Dudouet

Introduction

"Conventional security promotion efforts such as DDR [Disarmament, Demobilization, and Reintegration] and SSR [Security Sector Reform] are widely considered a *sine qua non* of contemporary peace support operations and state-building."[1] However, the vast majority of such programs tend to be externally run, biased, short-sighted, and implemented in artificial isolation from each other and from other arenas of structural transformation. In particular, postwar security transition should be understood as a politically driven undertaking, the implementation of which is heavily conditioned by the parties' political will and the general political climate throughout the peace process.

This chapter provides an overview of the processes of restoration of state monopoly of force as well as the democratization and legitimization of state structures from the specific perspective and interests of (former) nonstate armed groups (NSAGs). It seeks to demonstrate that combatants aspire to play an active part in peace- and state-building, and that to ensure that they maintain the political will to undergo war-to-peace transitions, they should feel that the process will address their structural grievances and empower them as a sociopolitical force rather than weaken their capacity to effect change.

To support these arguments, some information will be drawn from an ongoing participatory research project carried out in cooperation with local researchers and leading members from nine former NSAGs, namely, the African National Congress (ANC) in South Africa, Movimiento 19 de

Abril (M19) in Colombia, Sinn Fein in Northern Ireland, the Communist Party of Nepal–Maoist (CPN–M) in Nepal, Gerakan Aceh Merdeka (GAM) in Aceh, the Kosovo Liberation Army (KLA), Farabundo Martí Liberation Front (FMLN) in El Salvador, the Sudan People's Liberation Movement/ Army (SPLM/A), and the National Council for the Defense of Democracy–Forces of Defense of Democracy (CNDD–FDD) in Burundi. The findings were also correlated with ongoing consultation by the author with members or "proxies" from active NSAGs in the Philippines, Colombia, the Basque country, Turkey, and Sri Lanka.

The chapter starts with a short overview of the role and nature of politically motivated NSAGs, also labeled "rebel opposition movements," in contemporary armed conflicts, as well as processes of war termination and postwar peacebuilding and security transformation. It then discusses some of the terminological, conceptual, and political challenges that underpin the implementation and sequencing of disarmament and demobilization schemes. This is followed by some analysis of the (re)conversion of NSAGs into civilian entities and the integration of their members in the security, political, and socioeconomic systems of governance. Particular attention is given to the factors that influence the various trajectories pursued by former combatants, including their individual attributes but also the nature and root causes of the conflicts. Finally, these dynamics at the agency level are linked to the structural processes of security sector transformation as well as broader state reform, seen as a reciprocal guarantee to ensure fairness and political will throughout the processes of stabilization and peace consolidation.[2]

1. Nonstate Armed Groups, Major Stakeholders in Contemporary Conflicts

The patterns of contemporary conflicts indicate that states' monopoly of legitimate coercive force has become seriously eroded from below. According to a comprehensive statistical database on armed conflicts, most major armed conflicts in the past decade (30 out of 33) were fought within the borders of single states, between governments and one or several nonstate rebel movements engaged in armed struggles over issues of territory (9) or governmental power (21).[3]

Such asymmetric conflicts are often rooted in the state's inability and/ or unwillingness to provide security and welfare for all its citizens, leading to the adoption of violent strategies on the part of societal forces who feel discriminated against or oppressed. Their armed resistance is often based on collective grievances recognized under international law, such as the right to self-determination[4] or the right to fundamental freedoms.[5] It tends to build on the support of large segments of society that consider the groups to be legitimate defenders of their interests. NSAGs therefore represent influential stakeholders who have the effective capacity to either impede or promote constructive social change.

If political violence is a tool of both state and nonstate actors, reaching peace settlements also needs the active involvement and cooperative engagement of all concerned parties. Since the end of the Cold War, a growing number of conflicts have been resolved through negotiated settlement rather than military victory,[6] and NSAGs have thus become central stakeholders in peace processes, recognized by their opponents as legitimate negotiation interlocutors and core partners in peace consolidation and state-building.

The political role of NSAGs has become increasingly recognized by the international community as well. Governments that do not adhere to basic universal standards of human and minority rights are no longer protected by the principle of state sovereignty under international law. As an expression of this, the "responsibility to protect" is gradually evolving from a moral imperative into a globally recognized legal norm. Although this trend does not imply political or even legal absolution for the use of organized force outside the norms of international law, it does lend more political authority to organized nonstate actors vis-à-vis their governments. It also increases their obligation to enter a reform process which aims at a just and participatory society based on the rule of law.

Definition and Features of NSAGs

As implied by their name, NSAGs are characterized by their independence from state control and their use of violent strategies against political opponents. Among the vast universe of armed actors operating beyond state control, the scope of this chapter is restricted to armed movements that have primarily political objectives—thereby excluding groups that chiefly pursue private agendas, such as warlords, criminal organizations, and private security and military companies. For the sake of clarity, one could also refer to the label *rebel opposition groups*, conventionally defined as being "engaged in a political struggle . . . to redefine the political and legal basis of the society through the use of violence."[7] Therefore, state-sponsored actors such as paramilitaries are also excluded from this analysis.

For politically motivated rebel groups, challenging the state's monopoly of force strictly represents a means to an end in the pursuit of flexible and adaptable objectives that are constantly reassessed and adjusted in the light of an evolving environment. Therefore, any attempt at defining their features should encompass an understanding of their goals and aspirations. They often have clearly articulated political or socioeconomic objectives. Some are revolutionary (often Marxist-influenced) or prodemocracy movements launched by members of social groups experiencing blocked social mobility (e.g., M19, FMLN, ANC, CPN–M, CNDD–FDD). Others have been engaged in national liberation struggles on behalf of oppressed ethnic minorities or disempowered majorities (e.g., GAM, Sinn Fein, KLA).

The recourse to violence is justified by such groups as a legitimate form of self-defense employed as a last resort in the face of acute human rights abuses and denial of democracy, as a carefully considered means to an end, and as one form of (rather than the opposite of) political intervention.[8] For instance, in South Africa, the ANC adhered to nonviolent forms of struggle until the end of the 1950s and established its armed wing in 1961 following a campaign of violent repression and the banning of the organization in 1960, which prevented it from operating peacefully or even legally existing. In Northern Ireland, the violent repression of the civil rights movement in the 1960s and the introduction of internment without trial in 1971 convinced Sinn Fein members that only armed struggle could accomplish the end of British rule on the Irish island. Official Republican declarations (such as the 1994 Peace Proposal) define armed struggle as "an option of last resort" and "a legitimate part of a people's resistance to foreign oppression."[9]

Additional defining features of armed opposition movements, recognized by the Geneva Conventions,[10] include their clear hierarchy and command structure, as well as their readiness to assume political responsibilities in the territories under their control. Given their preponderant role in armed conflicts as well as their political aspirations, NSAGs often play core governance and security functions vis-à-vis their constituencies, and have the potential to play vital leadership roles in implementing postwar political reforms, community peacebuilding, and the provision of (human) security.

Inclusive Approach to Postwar Security Governance

"Local ownership" and the empowerment of "peace constituencies" have become buzzwords of international peacebuilding and development agencies, NGOs, and researchers alike. State actors are no longer recognized as the sole interlocutors or partners for international peacebuilding agencies, and national ownership is now increasingly recognized as encompassing nonstate actors as well, including civil society organizations but also former combatants.[11]

However, peacebuilding approaches and agencies often fail to adequately include NSAGs and their (former) combatants in their attempts to stabilize war-torn societies and build democratic institutions. They tend to look on them as passive recipients or "target groups" of assistance programs who have to become "educated" and "socialized," or else as "spoilers" who should disband and disappear once peace has prevailed. A recent review of SSR missions by regional organizations (European Union [EU], North Atlantic Treaty Organization [NATO], African Union [AU]) in postconflict environments has shown that their mandates make no explicit references to nonstate armed groups, even when these were primary signatory parties to the peace accords.[12] Although several United Nations (UN) reports have pointed to an appreciation of the significance of armed groups as actors for positive change in postconflict peacebuilding[13] and a few mission mandates recognize the need to engage constructively with rebel movements (e.g., Liberia), the implementation of UN peacebuilding missions often looks quite different from what was envisioned. The tendency is for "outside experts" to work solely with their state-labeled partners without questioning who they represent and what legitimacy they can claim, or to "follow technocratic blueprints informed by normative assumptions about what the [new] state should be" without consulting local actors about the dynamics at play in the host country.[14]

However, it can be logically assumed that when reforms or power-sharing provisions are externally imposed, local stakeholders will not feel genuinely committed to the process and will fail to comply if they see that the strategy is failing. This brings into question the need for an inclusive approach to conflict transformation: the broader the ownership, the greater the chances that the root causes of the conflict will be placed on the peacebuilding agenda and that the parties will generate and maintain the political will to bring about necessary reforms to democratize, demilitarize, develop, and reconcile the country.

In all cases mentioned in this chapter, rebel leaders as well as governmental actors were centrally involved in negotiating, planning, implementing, and monitoring DDR and SSR provisions, resulting in sustainable conflict transformation outcomes. None of these countries have yet returned to war. The purpose of the project on which these findings are based aims to include former NSAGs in assessing past peacebuilding processes and designing innovative frameworks that take their specific needs, perspectives, lessons learned, and potential contributions into account.

2. The Challenges of Disarming and Demobilizing Nonstate Armed Groups

This section focuses on the terminological, conceptual, and political challenges that underpin the implementation and sequencing of reciprocal security measures by state and nonstate conflict parties throughout peace processes: cessation of hostilities and unilateral or bilateral ceasefires, prisoners' release, amnesties, registration, cantonment, disarmament, and demobilization of combatants.

Since the legal recognition of sovereign states as the guiding principle for establishing the current (post-1945) world order, states have been considered the monopolists of legitimate coercion in the Weberian tradition. It follows that the international community has usually looked upon NSAGs as "spoilers" to be fought and eliminated. The restoration of the monopoly of force is considered a legitimate aim of acting state rulers to bring an end to an internal violent conflict. However, as argued earlier, the ultimate aim of politically motivated NSAGs is not to challenge state authority and develop parallel security structures. Restoring the monopoly of force might actually be in their interest as long as certain guarantees are met. In most cases, they are ready to accept (or might even be struggling for) a genuine integration into transformed and democratic state structures. An external indication of their readiness to assume political responsibility and restore state monopoly over the use of legitimate force lies in the effective transition "from bullets to ballots" by most rebel movements under scrutiny (see below). When they are accepted as legitimate or at least unavoidable stakeholders and are invited to the negotiation table on the basis of relative parity, NSAGs become ready to adopt constructive policies, moderate their goals, and demobilize their militants. However, such transitions cannot be imposed as preconditions for engagement. Rather they should be accompanied by reciprocal concessions to address their claims to political, structural, and socioeconomic reforms.

Security Dilemma and the Right-timing of Disarmament

Local state actors and their international sponsors usually call for the renunciation of force by nonstate actors right at the beginning of a peace process as a prerequisite for reaching political agreements, transforming state structures, and redressing the conflict's root causes. For instance, in the security sector, most current missions treat DDR completion as a precondition for commencing a future SSR strategy.

A major caveat in such an approach is that it fails to take into account the "security dilemma" encountered by combatants. When disarmament takes place in the absence of a broader political solution, it creates safety hazards for the individuals going through such programs if the government or another armed group chooses to renege on a ceasefire or peace accord. In postwar situations characterized by extreme interparty mistrust, mere promises under the auspices of confidence-building talks or even signed peace agreements do not offer sufficient guarantees for combatants to disarm unilaterally.

For NSAGs, possessing and using arms are not ends in themselves but instruments that serve vested political, societal, security, economic, and symbolic interests. As long as conflict parties consider the use of force to be the best choice for serving their interests, a transition from armed conflict to nonviolent politics can hardly be achieved. To put it bluntly, while governments consider the existence of armed nonstate actors as such to be a serious threat to the security of the state, nonstate armed actors consider the possession and use of arms to be an indispensable prerequisite for the security of the people they represent.

During the first peace process in Aceh (2000–2003), premature demands by the Indonesian government for GAM to disarm caused the talks to break down, because the rebel forces felt that handing over their weapons would leave them unprotected in the absence of a reciprocal commitment by the state to reduce its armed forces on the ground and address Acehnese grievances. Even in the aftermath of the 2005 Comprehensive Peace Agreement, GAM leaders were reluctant to abide by the government's request to provide a list of their demobilized combatants until they were confident that they could guarantee their security.[15] For their part, members of the M19 in Colombia unanimously agreed to dispose of (i.e., melt) their weapons as a result of a bilateral peace accord with the government in 1990 but could not secure their own safety because other armed groups and paramilitaries were still operating in the country, and the state's unreformed security personnel (who were supposed to protect the lives of demobilized guerrillas) were infiltrated by "criminal organizations opposing the peace process."[16] Consequently, up to 18 percent of M19 veterans were assassinated between 1989 and 2005.

In view of such risks, NSAGs see the retention of armed forces during political negotiations as a necessary form of leverage or "security fallback" to appease their constituencies and as a physical guarantee that might be used should the negotiation process falter or fail.[17] Therefore, beyond the usefulness of early ceasefire declarations, transitory weapons storage, and other confidence-building measures that help to convince their opponents to put reciprocal concessions on the negotiation table, rebel troops will usually only agree to formally disarm once they are confident that they can insure the safety of their demobilized combatants, that comprehensive agreements have been reached over the substantive conflict issues, and that their political aims will be achieved or at least that they will be able to pursue them effectively by nonviolent means. "Governance incentives" such as power-sharing provisions in the political, economic, territorial, or security arenas represent "the promise that an armed group will be allowed to accomplish at least some of the objectives that motivated it to fight in the first place . . . [and] help to cement and institutionalize their survival and their capacity to help and protect themselves and those whom they purport to represent."[18] In other words, security is both an outcome and a precondition for demobilization.[19]

In contrast to the Aceh and Colombia examples cited above, the ANC in South Africa only disbanded its armed force in December 1994 once it was in control of the state and army, 8 months after the first democratic elections and 4 years after the peace accord. In Northern Ireland as well, where decommissioning represented the most contentious issue in the negotiation, Republicans only became ready to relinquish their right to armed resistance through political progress, with the creation of an interim power-sharing executive and a new all-island political dispensation (through the institution of cross-border bodies). In July 2005, 8 years after the peace agreement, the Irish Republican Army (IRA) leadership formally announced an end to its armed struggle and instructed all members to "assist the development of purely political and democratic programs through exclusively peaceful means." They confirmed in September that the decommissioning process had been completed.[20] The case of Burundi represents another interesting example of concomitant DDR/SSR processes, as the various armed groups only proceeded to disarming their troops after isolating combatants who would go for civilian reintegration programs; those judged apt to join the security services kept their weapons with them and did not go through any demobilization schemes.

The terminology surrounding DDR programs is also judged highly problematic by NSAG members; in particular, the emphasis on the "disarmament" of nonstatutory troops wrongly suggests that they have been defeated or forced to surrender, whereas in reality peace agreements are typically signed between parties who find themselves in situations of relative power parity, having often reached a "mutually hurting stalemate." Alternative terms that were judged more appropriate in such contexts include decommissioning (Northern Ireland, Aceh) and arms management (Nepal). The term "putting arms beyond use" (Northern Ireland) also suggests that such processes are much less concerned with depriving fighters access to weapons[21] than demonstrating the political will to relinquish their use.

Beyond formal decommissioning programs, studies of small arms and light weapons (SALW) reduction have also highlighted the limitations of approaches which emphasize disarmament as a technical endeavor isolated from its structural or cultural environment. The proliferation of weapons in many postwar contexts cannot be solely tackled by short-term decommissioning schemes, but rather is closely connected with broader micro-and macro-level determinants such as individual and cultural security perceptions, socioeconomic development and creation of jobs, or dynamics in the regional geopolitical environment.[22]

Challenges of Registration and Cantonment

According to former NSAG members, the registration of weapons and combatants represents not only a security risk, but also a sensitive political act with decisive consequences on the success of the reintegration process. The "official" numbers of combatants declared by the movements often tend not to reflect their "real" size and capacity for various reasons. When NSAGs are immersed in their communities (see below), the actual size of the movement—which comprises combatants in arms but also those carrying support or logistics roles, sympathizers, etc.—can be much higher than is officially agreed at the negotiation table. For instance, GAM veterans contend that although their movement had 20,000 to 30,000 combatants, the official number of troops going through the DDR process was declared to be only 3,000, since they would have been unable to hand over a sufficient number of weapons to provide evidence for their actual size. With the same logic, other movements underestimate the number of troops in order to keep some weapons on hold (e.g., in hidden caches) in case of negotiation breakdown. By contrast, in other contexts, the numbers of combatants were inflated during negotiations (e.g., through late recruitments) in order to increase the parties' bargaining power, integrate more people into the security services, or increase the scale of reintegration benefits.

In parallel to registration processes, the cantonment of combatants in temporary assembly areas is typically viewed as an indication of commitment by NSAGs to pursue nonviolent means. However, to avoid the pitfalls of unilateral demobilization mentioned earlier, the measures should either be applied to all armed formations that have taken part in the conflict (both regular and irregular), or at least be paralleled with reciprocal demilitarization measures by the state. They should also be compounded to short-term, interim measures. In Nepal, where Maoist combatants have been stationed in barracks since the signature of the 2006 peace agreement, the lack of progress on the political front regarding their fate and the modalities of security sector reform have resulted in deteriorating conditions and unspecified timelines within cantonment camps, creating growing resentment and disillusions and affecting the ability of the command structures to maintain control.[23] This brings into question the role of NSAG leadership and structures during postwar security transitions.

Dismantlement versus Maintenance of Combatant Support Structure

The typical view within international DDR programs that demobilization requires "breaking down the command and control structures operating over rebel fighters . . . thus making it more difficult for them to return to organized rebellion"[24] is challenged by local researchers and NSAG veterans in recent postwar contexts. They argue that abrupt demobilization leads to disorder and disorientation among former combatants, whereas in highly volatile transitional situations it is important to retain (at least temporarily) coordination and communication channels through cohesive structures, at the very least to instruct members about their reintegration options. Thus, in Northern Ireland, IRA command structures (i.e., Army Councils) have remained more or less intact since the 1994 ceasefire including after IRA leadership declared a formal end to armed campaigns in 2005. Even their political opponents have accepted the pragmatic logic that maintaining a leadership structure was required to oversee the transition and demobilization of the organization and prevent frustrated people from joining dissenting factions. Today the IRA seems to be functioning more as an association of old comrades than a fighting force.[25] In Aceh, the 2005 peace accord did not contain any provisions regarding the dissolution of GAM's military wing; instead, it was transformed into a civilian Transitional Committee in charge of supervising the demobilization of its combatants and maintaining a cohesive structure until the formation of a political party. In parallel, the movement also formed a longer term Reintegration Board, mandated by the central and provincial government to supervise the reintegration and reparation schemes. In Kosovo as well, the KLA chief of staff insisted on the removal of the word "dissolution" from the negotiations agenda; instead, the guerrilla faction was transformed into a civilian security entity, the Kosovo Protection Corps.

The concept of "interim stabilization measures" has been recently introduced in the DDR literature to encompass temporary schemes that prevent the creation of security vacuums in the early stages of postwar transition, keep combatant cohesiveness intact within a military or civilian structure, and improve real and perceived security during the negotiation or planning of long-term conventional security promotion activities. Such measures include civilian service corps, transitional military integration arrangements, transitional security forces, or differentiated forms of transitional autonomy.[26] They offer combatants not only a welcome opportunity to use their wartime skills and experience for peacekeeping purposes during volatile war-to-peace transitions, but they are also useful confidence-building and social cohesion exercises that help prepare their members for the sociopsychological transformation from combatant to civilian identity. As examples, one could cite the deployment of armed components from the various parties to the negotiations as an integrated peacekeeping force during the South African peace process in the early 1990s, or the establishment of Joint Integrated Units comprised of equal numbers of troops from the Sudanese Armed Force and the Sudan People's Liberation Army (SPLA) in South Sudan. These units are deployed in selected areas of the ceasefire zone until a referendum scheduled for 2011 will decide on the South Sudanese status and the future of the two armed forces.

3. Security, Socioeconomic, and Political (Re)integration in Perspective

This section turns to the necessary counterpart to disarming, demobilizing, and dismantling NSAGs, namely, the inclusion of their members into the security, political, and socioeconomic system of governance, and the transformation of militant structures into functioning and sustainable organizations that pursue the "struggle" through nonviolent means. Scholars and practitioners alike tend to examine the various "career (re)conversion" paths followed by former rebel fighters in artificial isolation from each other; in other words, security experts focus on military/police integration while the development approach is applied to socioeconomic reintegration and political scientists/organizations turn to the transition from rebels to politicians. By contrast, this chapter adopts a holistic approach encompassing multisectorial reintegration paths in the broader sense of reskilling for postconflict life and careers. In fact, there is an acute need for more systematic research on the factors that influence the different postwar trajectories of NSAG members, from the nature and goals of the movement (and of the conflict) to the features (e.g., age, gender, prewar education and skills, position occupied within the movement) of individual combatants.

Security Sector Integration: A Crucial Guarantee for Stability and Reconciliation

As indicated by the emerging literature on "rebel-military integration,"[27] the integration of nonstatutory forces into the national defense and security apparatus (e.g., army, police, intelligence) represents a primary means for former ANSAs to take part in democratic state-building and a convenient reconversion path for their combatants. From the point of view of national governments, this might also be an effective way to convert potentially destabilizing threats into support for new structures, as well as a demonstration of fair employment practices by the new administration.

The process of selecting combatants apt to join the statutory security apparatus represents a real challenge given the clash between a collective sense of entitlement and limited career opportunities. This disparity is currently felt most strongly in Nepal, between the Maoists' maximalist claims to bulk integration and the army's readiness to opt only reluctantly for very limited integration on an individual basis and at basic entry level (below officer ranks). In Kosovo, out of the 20,000 estimated KLA members, 17,000 applied for positions in the KPC, which was limited to only 5,000 members.[28] Even in a very "liberal" case such as South Africa, where all declared armed factions were invited to join the new army on a voluntary basis, only 17,000 combatants from the liberation forces (out of 28,000) integrated into the army.

Selection criteria are partly based on a needs assessment of the absorption capacity of the security apparatus (where DDR is concomitant with SSR planning, see below), as well as on the competencies, age, and physical aptitudes of the candidates. For instance, in Sudan the current DDR process is proceeding in two phases, with first a demobilization of approximately 35,000 combatants belonging to a "special needs group" (child soldiers, elders, disabled, "women associated with armed forces"), followed by some 55,000 "nonessential soldiers," according to the required gender, ethnic, and geographical balance.[29]

Vetting systems represent additional selection tools for former state or rebel forces prior to their incorporation into the new security forces. It is important that all forces equally take part in such a screening process overviewed by independent commissions in order to redress past human rights abuses, increase public confidence in the new security apparatus, and foster cohesion and harmony among former enemy armies so they become comrades in arms. In the contexts under scrutiny in this chapter, most human rights abuses were in fact committed by state or parastate forces, and NSAGs themselves insisted on the need for judicial accountability. For instance, in El Salvador, where 85 percent of killings during the civil war were attributed to the state or its allies as opposed to the rebels,[30] all the generals and more than half of the colonels were dismissed from the army during the "purification" component of SSR.[31] This was seen as a productive measure to avoid the country relapsing into military domination, and also because it was accompanied by broader institutional reform (see further below).

The first stage of army/police integration usually consists of reconversion and reskilling schemes to harmonize the various profiles, experience, and technical skills gained by the members of the new security forces during the conflict as well as to ensure appropriate professional standards. This is a particularly sensitive issue in some contexts, where political or army leaders oppose rebel-military integration on the grounds that non-state armed movements have untrained combatants who are unfit for conventional warfare. Insurgency troops are indeed largely volunteer-fed and typically trained for guerrilla combat, although this does not mean they cannot be trained to professional norms and standards—nor does it imply that wartime army and police forces, often ill-trained and perhaps indoctrinated by years of repressive counterinsurgency warfare, should be exempt from such reskilling processes. In order to avoid their becoming too highly politicized, decisions over training and integration technicalities (e.g., reranking systems) have typically been handed over to a joint technical committee. The participation of international experts (e.g., assistance by French and Belgian armies in Burundi and by the British army in South Africa) also helps to guarantee internationally-agreed standards and compensates for the lack of state capacity in this domain.

It should be noted, finally, that the nature of the conflict has a strong impact on the relevance of security sector integration. In identity-based conflicts, former liberation troops (unless their secession claims have been granted, which is a very rare occurrence, e.g., Kosovo and East Timor) tend to show no interest in joining an army still controlled by the "imperialist forces" or ethnic majority. This is particularly the case in Northern Ireland and in Aceh, where GAM fighters have unanimously refused to integrate with the Indonesian security forces which they have fought for several decades, as a matter of principle and dignity.[32] Alternative security sector transformation options in such contexts will be explored further below.

Socioeconomic Reintegration: Community-based Approach

Regarding the fate of combatants who do not join the security apparatus, the term "reintegration" is widely used in international academic and policy circles to refer to the process of facilitating their transition to civilian status and access to the social and labor worlds. Unfortunately, both the label itself and the assumptions that underpin it fail to reflect the reality of postwar trajectories by NSAGs. Indeed, in many contexts the specificities of insurgency warfare mean that combatants are not cut off from their social milieu but are embedded in their communities at all times as "citizen soldiers, farmers or fishermen mobilized to fight as required."[33] As argued earlier, it might even be difficult to clearly distinguish combatants from noncombatants in social or regional contexts where large parts of the population are involved in the insurgency in various ways even if they do not carry weapons. In the case of guerrilla troops or political prisoners who do undergo periods of relative isolation from their constituencies, the term reintegration is also challenged by NSAGs because it seems to imply a process of reconciliation with the population, obscuring the fact that upon their return, most combatants are "considered as freedom fighters, and are looked upon like heroes, which are accepted easily into society based on their constituencies."[34]

Alternative terminology used to refer to the process of preparation for civilian life and imparting demobilized combatants with new skills includes rehabilitation (Nepal), inclusion in social life (Kosovo), economic facilitation (Aceh), and socioeconomic support (Burundi). These processes typically include programs for housing, social security, education, support for those incapacitated by war, vocational training, or financial assistance to start urban productive projects or acquire land. However, the individual needs and challenges of the beneficiaries may be different depending on their status within the movement (military leader or "foot soldier," male or female, long-term or short-term combatants) and their pre-war experience (e.g., whether they already have qualifications or professional experience). Thus, the means of assisting them need to be differentiated too.

Although short-term financial or technical reinsertion packages at an individual level are helpful to prevent the relapse of former combatants into political or criminal armed activities, such schemes are doomed to failure if they exclusively target registered NSAG members at the expense of their broader social base given the specificities of insurgency warfare indicated above. They may trigger negative reactions in the needy population, who might see these support programs as an unfair privilege granted to ex-combatants since the return of combatants is often less of a problem than rebuilding the community as a whole. Moreover, if socioeconomic provisions within peace agreements only deal with the interests of major armed factions while neglecting the needs and grievances of other groups and social forces, they might also risk spawning potential new "spoilers." These problems were felt particularly acutely in Aceh, where the end of the armed conflict closely followed the devastating 2004 tsunami, and where the main challenge for GAM members was less "how to reintegrate" them than "reintegrate them into what?" The cash amounts distributed as part of the economic facilitation scheme were intended for registered combatants only, but the movement attempted to redistribute them equally among a wider range of families, which did not prove sufficient to help them start new activities (e.g., small businesses). In Northern Ireland, a local trust was set up to manage EU reintegration assistance to ensure that the funds would be disbursed to collective projects rather than individual combatants. Another community-wide approach to reintegration was the education scheme put in place in Colombia after the 1990 peace agreement with the M19: 50,000 noncombatants were invited to take part in the primary and secondary school certification programs offered to demobilized guerrillas.

Political Integration: Transition to the Electoral Battleground

The third integration arena concerns the career shifts by NSAGs' political cadres from underground leadership to the conventional political arena, e.g., to becoming members of parliamentary bodies and national or local governments. At the organizational level as well, given the political nature and aspirations of most rebel movements, the transformation of militant structures into functioning and sustainable civilian entities such as political parties or veteran associations helps to convince their members that they can effectively protect their interests through nonviolent politics.

Most movements mentioned in this chapter have achieved remarkable long-term or recent success in their postwar conversion "from bullets to ballots," from the outstanding performance of the ANC in South Africa, which gained 63 percent of the votes in 1994 and has been confirmed in power in all subsequent elections, to the recent election of an FMLN candidate as President of El Salvador and the unexpected Maoist victory in the 2008 constituent assembly elections in Nepal. In fact, with the exception of the M19 in Colombia, all nine NSAGs under scrutiny are presently either in control of the national or regional (in the case of separatist conflicts) legislative or executive powers or participating in power-sharing governments.

The growing literature on the postwar political development of insurgency movements has identified a number of factors which might explain the success or failure of their transitions from the battleground to the electoral arena,[35] including the degree of separateness between political and military wings during the struggle. Indeed, some rebel movements start off as political parties before establishing armed branches and maintain very distinct dual (political/military) structures during the conflict (e.g., ANC/MK, CPN-M/PLA, Sinn Fein/IRA, CNDD/FDD, SPLM/SPLA). Their engagement and expertise in conventional politics in parallel to armed campaigns helps explain their swift reconversion into nonviolent political entities in the postwar environment. For their part, most Latin American guerrillas (such as the M19 or FMLN) define themselves as "political-military organizations" with a combined structure of command, which might be part of the reason the M19 was unable to sustain itself as a strong and cohesive political party in the posttransition era. Despite its early achievements in the immediate postagreement phase (constituent assembly, presidential, local, and parliamentary elections in 1990–1991), it steadily lost its initial electoral support and has remained a minor political force ever since.

Although most NSAGs aspire to participate in democratic politics, they are not always sufficiently qualified for—or experienced in—political organization. Indeed, reskilling and training are as crucial for rebel leaders turned politicians as for their former comrades who join the security apparatus or the private sector, and international agencies thus have a welcome role to play by offering specialized and focused capacity building support in administrative skills, good governance, (legal) financing, campaigning, etc.

4. Security Sector Reform and Democratic State-Building Imperatives

This final section turns to the interactions between the transformation of rebel forces and broader state reform in a postwar setting. For rebel movements to generate and maintain the political will to demobilize their troops, and to avoid the resumption of violence by splinter groups feeling excluded by, or uncommitted to, the negotiated agreements, there must be parallel planning and implementation of their claims to structural reform, which often lie at the roots of the conflict. These include a genuine democratization of the political system and structural transformation of the security, socioeconomic, and justice sectors.

DDR/SSR Linkages

The conventional approach to peacebuilding tends to emphasize the restoration of the primacy and integrity of state structures through DDR at the expense of necessary reforms of the security apparatus. For instance, an overview of UN peacebuilding guidelines highlights a lack of parity in their treatment of statutory and nonstatutory forces. On the one hand, the UN Integrated DDR Standards indicate that "UN peacekeeping forces can pressurize armed forces and groups into disarming voluntarily through military operations aimed at achieving specific results. Such operations aim to break the hold of armed forces and groups and weaken their structures."[36] By contrast, "influential members of the UN Security Council as well as much of the General Assembly have been reluctant to endorse explicitly support for SSR in postconflict or other contexts. Efforts to influence or re-shape countries' security institutions have raised concerns about implications for 'sovereignty.'"[37] As a result, a recent comparative research project found that "the failure of previous DDR initiatives to lead into or incorporate elements of SSR had been widely seen as a problem, often leading to renewed tensions or conflict, with an unreformed military or police repeating the mistakes of the past."[38] Based on these discrepancies, NSAGs tend to view the generic terminology and concepts of DDR and SSR with suspicion, perceiving them as biased and imbalanced and chiefly concerned with dismantling nonstatutory forces and removing their capacity to engage in armed rebellion, whereas statutory forces can get away with minor reforms.

In contrast to the prevalent model of "DDR before SSR," recent reports on the DDR/SSR nexus calls for early negotiation and planning of the modalities of postwar security governance, if possible, through direct and inclusive talks between respective commanders and military leaders.[39] In South Africa, the formation of a joint technical committee comprised of military leaders from all sides represented in itself the first act of postwar military integration and a model for the future merging of the old army and liberation forces. These security talks provided highly inclusive platforms where all armed formations, irrespective of their size, could take part in decisionmaking regarding the future defense and security strategy.[40] Accordingly, the talks helped to prevent the sidelining or radicalization of some factions, which could have led them to engage in "spoiling behavior" during the implementation of the peace accords.

Moreover, the content of peace agreements should clearly and explicitly address the commitments of all parties with regard to postwar security transformation, at the very least by spelling out core principles and timeframes to guide further technical negotiations. In Aceh, the 2005 Memorandum of Understanding included detailed agreements concerning on the one hand the demobilization and reintegration of GAM combatants, and on the other hand the withdrawal of Indonesian army ("nonorganic troops") from the province, other than a small contingent to be kept strictly for external defense purposes. The perceived fairness and symmetry between these reciprocal arrangements partly explains their swift and effective implementation.[41] In Colombia, however, the peace accord between the government and the M19 did not include any provisions regarding necessary reforms within the army and police. That shortcoming has discouraged former guerrillas from joining the state security apparatus.

Modalities of Security Sector Transformation[42]

The transformation of national defense and security architectures (army, police, intelligence) in the aftermath of violent internal conflicts represent crucial components of peacebuilding and reconciliation and are essential means of ensuring that the newly reestablished state monopoly of force is exercised in a democratic manner. In fact, a recent statistical study found that the presence or absence of an SSR process is the single most significant factor in explaining the durability of peace settlements.[43]

According to the context and specific interests of the parties, such restructuring might take various forms. First, demilitarization measures encompass the removal of occupation/nonindigenous armed forces from newly independent or autonomous territories (e.g., Aceh, Northern Ireland, Kosovo) or the downsizing of unnecessary troops in compliance with new strategic security assessments. In El Salvador, although its maximalist demand for a security system without any army was rejected by the government, the FMLN obtained a more than 50 percent reduction in the size and budget of the military. Secondly, SSR might also imply the merging of former enemy armies into a new security sector, as opposed to the absorption of insurgency troops into unreformed structures. To avoid a resurgence of violence, such integration schemes should be genuinely democratic and inclusive, e.g., open to all armed formations irrespective of their size, and more representative of society. The Burundian case is illustrative, as the control of the state by an exclusive armed force dominated by the Tutsi ethnic minority was seen by the rebel group CNDD as the primary root cause of the conflict; hence, SSR was perceived as the most crucial component of peacebuilding and included the restoration of ethnic, regional, political, and gender parity in a heavily reformed army and a new police force.[44]

As argued earlier, SSR can be problematic in identity-based conflicts where NSAGs are not concerned with the democratization of security forces but seek the formation of their own sovereign entities. What type of security sector transformation might be envisaged which would recognize such aspirations? An alternative reform path that has been considered in South Sudan consists of permitting former liberation movements to keep their own autonomous security forces. Kosovo represents a unique case, where in parallel to the formation of a separate state, the KLA underwent a dual conversion into first a civilian security force and then back into a military force—the new national army. Therefore, the former NSAG is not concerned with restructuring the Serbian security forces, but rather with transforming its guerrilla army into a smaller but professional and democratic security apparatus on its own. However, the ongoing challenge of integrating minority (e.g., Serbian) communities within the new security structures shows that the challenge of building inclusive state structures (whether within the former Serbian entity or the new Kosovo state) has failed to be resolved so far.

Additional components of security sector transformation include the restoration of rule of law, accountability, impartiality, noninterference in political matters, and civilian oversight and control (through the role of the government, the parliamentary defense committee, and media and civil society institutions). In the aftermath of violent conflicts, there is also a broader need to redefine the purpose and societal role of security forces, and their members need to understand their role as protecting citizens and defending national sovereignty, as opposed to defending the party in power or acting against the population. In El Salvador, for instance, the FMLN insisted on the new national police being immersed in the community rather than living in isolated barracks as a reconciliation measure.[45]

Linkages with Political, Socioeconomic, and Justice Reform

Beyond the security sector, the success of DDR is also dependent on the implementation of power-sharing and state reform in the other areas of governance so combatants feel that their collective grievances have been (or will be) addressed.

In the political arena, peace agreements and their implementation need to facilitate organizational shifts toward conventional politics by offering incentives for political participation. A necessary prelude to the "demilitarization of politics"[46] is a democratic transition opening up the political system to opposition groups that were previously denied representation. In immediate postwar contexts, transitional democratization measures usually take the form of multilateral consultative mechanisms and joint decisionmaking bodies, interim power-sharing governments, election of a constitutional assembly, establishment of a new constitution and bill of rights introducing institutional and electoral reforms, or devolution of power and competencies to local/regional institutions. According to the proponents of "institutionalization before liberalization,"[47] including such provisions in peace agreements helps to institutionalize the role of former combatants within state structures prior to competitive electoral processes. Once they do take place, the first (and subsequent) postwar elections represent a crucial test for the success of resistance/liberations movements' transition to conventional politics.

In the socioeconomic sector, the limits to reintegration schemes exposed above call for embedding support programs for former combatants into more structural reforms (e.g., land redistribution, decentralization, reconstruction, and rehabilitation programs) in order to address postwar development needs and transform the structures of inequality and exploitation that triggered the conflict. This might not only help to maintain the political will of transformed NSAGs, but can also contribute to intercommunity reconciliation by rehabilitating regions affected by conflict as a whole. The lack of linkages between agency and structural approaches to postwar reconstruction was felt in Aceh, where international assistance programs created a disconnection between small reintegration programs and larger post-tsunami development work.

Finally, in the judiciary domain, a UN Secretary-General Report from 2004 recalls that sustainable peace "cannot be achieved unless the population is confident that redress for grievances can be obtained through legitimate structures for the peaceful settlement of disputes and the fair administration of justice."[48] Rule of law or justice sector reform programs in postagreement environments thus focus on (re)establishment of fair and transparent judiciary institutions, training of legal professionals, improvement of physical infrastructure, strengthening of oversight agencies and civilian control, and promotion of human rights. These activities are core elements of security sector reform both in terms of institutions they address and aims they want to achieve, such as building trust in public institutions and promoting security. On the ground, a malfunctioning justice sector can push people to "take the law into their own hands," thereby undermining arms management efforts. Some authors thus call for putting human rights violations and justice mainstreaming at the heart of SSR programs.[49]

Implementation Monitoring and Oversight

Successful peace- and state-building do not depend only on the design of fair and reciprocal security, political, and socioeconomic reforms, but obviously also on the effective implementation by all parties of their respective commitments. Reciprocity can serve as a powerful guarantee to maintain parity, mutual trust, and political will to pursue the necessary reforms, as well as power-sharing arrangements. When the former conflict stakeholders have access to power, it increases their leverage and confidence that peace agreements will be implemented.

Additional institutional guarantees and oversight mechanisms should be put in place as well, for instance through a monitoring body comprised of all relevant political stakeholders. In Colombia, broader multiparty structures were set up to monitor the implementation of the 1990–1991 peace agreements, including a Consulting Committee for Reinsertion, with participation from demobilized groups. In order to avoid such mechanisms being jeopardized by likely blockages and hindrances in the political sphere, international actors might also be called on to take the lead in monitoring the implementation of security provisions. Past cases include, for instance, the EU-led Aceh Monitoring Mission supervising the demobilization process in Aceh, the UN (UNUSAL) mission verifying the reduction and restructuring of the armed forces in El Salvador, and the role of UN and NATO troops in screening the registration, training, and civilian reconversion of KLA fighters in Kosovo.

Conclusion

In closing, it might be useful to summarize the main arguments raised in this chapter and briefly illustrated through examples from nine recent conflicts. First, state actors can no longer be considered the sole interlocutors or partners for international peacebuilding agencies; postwar security governance must include all stakeholders who have the ability to assist in the effective implementation of peace agreements. Second, the restoration of state monopoly of force through the disarmament and demobilization of nonstate actors can only take place once they are confident that their own safety is guaranteed and that they will be able to effectively pursue their political goals through peaceful means in a legitimate and democratic security and political order. For its part, reintegration should be approached in a holistic yet context-specific way by identifying the collective and individual factors that influence the divergent trajectories pursued by former combatants and their various capacity-building needs. Consequently, a necessary counterpart to the demobilization and decommissioning of rebel troops should be the support of their political, army/police, or civilian (re)integration. This includes assisting the transformation of militant structures into functioning and sustainable legal entities in the political and civil society spheres. Finally, in order to guarantee the sustainability of reintegration programs, they should be complemented with reforms aimed at transforming the state (rather than reestablishing the prewar status quo) through political capacity-building and democratization, security sector transformation, and socioeconomic regeneration and development.

Notes

[1] Nat Coletta and Robert Muggah, "Rethinking Post-War Security Promotion," *Journal of Security Sector Management* 7, no. 1 (2009), 3.

[2] This chapter is partly based on a conceptual framework cowritten with my colleagues Hans J. Giessmann and Katrin Planta for the purpose of the above-mentioned project; I would thus like to gratefully acknowledge their contribution to this text.

[3] See Stockholm International Peace Research Institute, *SIPRI Yearbook 2008: Armament, Disarmament and International Security* (New York: Oxford University Press, 2008), 72. The criteria used for listing "major armed conflicts" are described as "a contested incompatibility concerning government and/or territory over which the use of armed forces between the military forces of 2 parties—of which at least one is the government of a state—has resulted in at least 1,000 battle-related deaths in a single calendar year."

[4] "All peoples have the right to self-determination." *United Nations International Covenant on Economic, Social and Cultural Right*, part 1, article 1(1). According to the Geneva Conventions (Protocol 1, part 1, article 1.4), such a right applies to cases of colonial domination, alien military occupation, and where a distinct racial group is denied equal access to government (so called "racist regimes").

[5] "It is essential, if man is not to be compelled to have recourse, as a last resort, to rebellion against tyranny and oppression, that human rights should be protected by the rule of law. . . . Member States have pledged themselves to achieve, in co-operation with the United Nations, the promotion of universal respect for and observance of human rights and fundamental freedoms." United Nations, *Universal Declaration of Human Rights*, Preamble.

[6] According to the Human Security Brief 2007, 58 armed conflicts were terminated through a negotiated settlement in the period 1990–2005, in comparison with 28 conflicts ended by the military victory of one party. See Human Security Center, *Human Security Brief 2007* (Burnaby, British Columbia: Simon Fraser University, 2008), 35, available at <www.humansecuritybrief.info>.

[7] Claude Bruderlein, *The Role of Non-State Actors in Building Human Security: The Case of Armed Groups in Intra-State Wars* (Geneva: Center for Humanitarian Dialogue, 2000), 8.

[8] According to a former Irish Republican negotiator, "there was . . . political armed struggle and there was political nonarmed struggle." Bairbre De Brun, *The Road to Peace in Ireland*, Berghof Transition Series No. 6 (Berlin: Berghof Research Center for Constructive Conflict Management, 2008), 6.

[9] Ibid., 25.

[10] See the Geneva Conventions Protocol II, available at <www.icrc.org/ihl.nsf/FULL/475>.

[11] See, for instance, Liz Panarelli, "Local Ownership of Security Sector Reform," Peace Brief No. 11 (Washington: United States Institute of Peace, 2010).

[12] Albrecht Schnabel, "Working with Armed Non-State Actors in Security Sector Reform and Governance," paper presented at the conference "Governing Private Security" (Geneva: Geneva Centre for the Democratic Control of Armed Forces, November 3, 2009). According to the author, the only exception is the EU Monitoring Mission in Aceh/Indonesia, which does contain references to the implementation of DDR programs in cooperation with the Free Aceh Movement (GAM).

[13] For instance, the UN Security Council recognizes that "in the aftermath of recent internal conflict peace agreements may allocate parallel legitimate roles . . . also to some nonstate security actors such as former rebel forces or militias." UN Security Council (UNSC), *UN Security Council Report, Update Report—Security Sector Reform* (New York: UN Secretary General, 2007).

[14] Andreas Mehler, "Hybrid Regimes and Oligopolies of Violence in Africa: Expectations on Security Provision from Below," in *Building Peace in the Absence of States: Challenging the Discourse on State Failure*, Berghof Handbook for Conflict Transformation, ed. Martina Fischer and Beatrix Schmelzle (Berlin: Berghof Research Center for Constructive Conflict Management, 2009), 59.

[15] Aguswandi and Wolfram Zunzer, *From Politics to Arms to Politics Again: The Transition of the Gerakan Aceh Merdeka* (GAM), Berghof Transition Series No. 5 (Berlin: Berghof Research Center for Constructive Conflict Management, 2008).

[16] Otty Patiño, Vera Grabe, and Mauricio García, "The M19's Reinsertion Process in Colombia: Challenges and Lessons Learnt," in Veronique Dudouet, Katrin Planta, and Hans-Joachim Giessmann, eds., *Post-war Security Transition Processes: Participatory Peacebuilding after Asymmetric Conflicts* (London: Routledge, 2011).

[17] Nat Coletta, ed. *The Cartagena Contribution to Disarmament, Demobilization and Reintegration* (Cartagena, Colombia: DDR International Congress, 2009), available at <http://cartagenaddr.org/>, 75. See also Mark Knight, "International Approaches to Post-war Security Transition and Their Implications for Resistance and Liberation Movements," in Dudouet et al.

[18] Chandra Lekha Sriram, *Peace as Governance: Power Sharing, Armed Groups, and Contemporary Peace Negotiations* (New York: Palgrave Macmillan, 2008), 183.

[19] Terrence Lyons, "Peacebuilding, Democratization, and Transforming the Institutions of War," in *Conflict Transformation and Peacebuilding: Moving from Violence to Sustainable Peace*, ed. Bruce W. Dayton and Louis Kriesberg (New York: Routledge, 2009), 91–106.

[20] De Brun, 16.

[21] The capacity will always be there. For instance, former Irish Republican combatants also argue that they "can [still] produce homemade explosives and mortars. [One] cannot decommission that knowledge. What is more important is [their] commitment to peace and politics." Danny Morrison, "An Issue of Trust," *Andersonstown News* (August 16, 2004), available at <www.nuzhound.com/articles/Irelandclick/arts2004/aug16_an_issue_of_trust_DMorrison.php>.

[22] Colletta and Muggah, 7–8.

[23] Kiyoko Ogura, *Seeking State Power: The Communist Party of Nepal (Maoist)*, Berghof Transition Series No. 3 (Berlin: Berghof Research Center for Constructive Conflict Management, 2008).

[24] Joanna Spear, "Disarmament and Demobilization," in *Ending Civil Wars: The Implementation of the Peace Agreements*, ed. Stephen J. Stedman, Donald Rothchild, and Elizabeth M. Cousens (Boulder, CO: Lynne Rienner, 2002), 141.

[25] Kieran McEvoy, "Ex-prisoners, Ex-combatants and Conflict Transformation in Northern Ireland," in Dudouet et al.

[26] Colletta and Muggah.

[27] Matthew Hoddie and Caroline Hartzell, "Civil War Settlements and the Implementation of Military Power-Sharing Arrangements," *Journal of Peace Research* 40, no. 3 (2003), 303–320. See also Mark Knight, *Security Sector Reform: Post-conflict Integration* (Birmingham, UK: Global Facilitation Network for Security Sector Reform, 2009).

[28] Ramadan Qehaja, Kosum Kosumi, and Armend Bekaj, "Demobilising and Integrating a Liberation Army in the Context of State Formation: Kosovo's Perspective on Security Transition," in Dudouet et al.

[29] William Deng Deng, "Security Sector Reform, DDR and Transitional Justice in Southern Sudan," in Dudouet et al.

[30] El Salvador Truth Commission, *From Madness to Hope: The 12-year War in El Salvador: Report of the Commission on the Truth for El Salvador* (San Salvador: El Salvador Truth Commission, 1993).

[31] Ruben Zamora and David Holiday, "The Struggle for Lasting Reform: Vetting Processes in El Salvador," in *Justice as Prevention: Vetting Public Employees in Transitional Societies*, ed. Alexander Mayer-Rieckh and Pablo De Greif (New York: Social Science Research Council, 2007), 80–119.

[32] Aguswandi, "Guns, Soldiers and Votes: Lessons from DDR in Aceh," in Dudouet et al.

[33] Colletta, 76.

[34] Ibid., 73.

[35] See Mimmi Soderberg Kovacs, *From Rebellion to Politics: The Transformation of Rebel Groups to Political Parties in Civil War Peace Processes* (Uppsala, Sweden: Uppsala University, 2007); Jeroen De Zeeuw, ed., *From Soldiers to Politicians: Transforming Rebel Movements after Civil War* (Boulder, CO: Lynne Rienner Publishers, 2008).

[36] Elaborated by the UN Interagency Working Group on DDR between 2004 and 2006, they represent the most comprehensive guidelines on DDR. See UN Working Group, *Integrated Disarmament, Demobilisation and Reintegration Standards (IDDRS)*, 2006, available at <www.unddr.org/iddrs/>.

[37] Owen Greene and Simon Rynn, *Linking and Coordinating DDR and SSR for Human Security after Conflict: Issues, Experience and Priorities* (Bradford, UK: Centre for International Cooperation and Security, 2008), 8.

[38] Guy Lamb, *Current Approaches to Disarmament, Demobilisation, and Reintegration (DDR) Programmes Design and Implementation* (Bradford, UK: Centre for International Cooperation and Security, 2008).

[39] See for instance Michael Brzoska, "Embedding DDR Programmes in Security Sector Reconstruction," in *Security Governance in Post-Conflict Peacebuilding*, ed. Alan Bryden and Heiner Hänggi (Münster: Lit Verlag, DCAF, 2005), 95–114; Sean McFate, *The Link between DDR and SSR in Conflict-Affected Countries*, United States Institute of Peace, Special Report No. 238 (Washington: United States Institute of Peace, 2010).

[40] Gavin Cawthra, "South Africa's Political and Security Negotiations and Security Sector Transformation," in Dudouet et al.

[41] However, the agreement did not contain any provisions relative to broader reforms in the Indonesian security sector. This was not seen as a priority by the GAM negotiators, who were primarily concerned with gaining self-governance in the Aceh province.

[42] The term "security sector reform" has been judged inappropriate in certain contexts and replaced by other labels such as "security sector restructuring" in Nepal, "security sector development" in Kosovo, and "security sector transformation" in South Africa.

[43] Monica Duffy Toft, *Securing the Peace: The Durable Settlement of Civil Wars* (Princeton, NJ: Princeton University Press, 2010).

[44] Julien Nimubona and Joseph Nkurunziza, "Transitional Security and Reintegration Challenges in Burundi," in Dudouet et al.

[45] Julio Martinez, "Security Guaranty: Political Transformation of the FMLN in El Salvador," in Dudouet et al.

[46] Lyons, 93.

[47] Roland Paris, *At War's End: Building Peace after Civil Conflict* (Cambridge: Cambridge University Press, 2004), 179–211.

[48] UN Secretary General, *Report of the Secretary General on the Rule of Law and Transitional Justice in Conflict and Post-Conflict Societies* (New York: UN Security Council, 2004).

[49] Laura Davis, *Transitional Justice and Security System Reform* (New York: International Center for Transitional Justice, 2009).

Chapter 2

The Relationship Between SSR and DDR: Impediments to Comprehensive Planning in Military Operations

By Michelle Hughes

Introduction

In early 2006, the Office of the Under Secretary of Defense for Policy informally asked the U.S. Joint Forces Command (USJFCOM) Joint Experimentation Directorate to experiment with a concept called the Comprehensive Approach to Security Sector Reform (SSR) to determine whether it had operational utility for military planners. Disarmament, Demobilization, and Reintegration (DDR) was a recognized component of the Comprehensive Approach, but the relationship between DDR and SSR was unclear from the perspective of military support. Over the following 4 years, a team of consultants working on behalf of USJFCOM experimented with the Comprehensive Approach to SSR in war games, limited objective experiments, and field tests in eight countries on four continents. The team also collaborated with more than forty U.S. Government agencies and bureaus; the United Nations (UN); international organizations including the European Union, the Organization for Economic Cooperation and Development, and the African Union; NATO allies; coalition partners; numerous Nongovernmental Organizations; and the International Committee of the Red Cross.

The SSR work on behalf of USJFCOM officially concluded with a set of joint capabilities recommendations in March 2010, but a number of issues arose along the way that remain unresolved. One was the nexus between military support to SSR and military support to DDR, and how a joint force commander can effectively operationalize the two in a way that supports a more holistic, whole-of-government approach. From a defense perspective, the linkages are not always clear, implementation timelines are disconnected, and the absence of an institutionalized approach to facilitate comprehensive planning at the operational level for each presents a significant impediment to understanding and coordination.

This article focuses on the relationship between the two from a military planner's perspective, highlights some DDR-specific challenges, and recommends approaches that planners can use to overcome planning and coordination gaps. Ultimately, however, the nexus between SSR and DDR, and effective military support to both, is a complex operational problem that requires interagency solutions.

Drawing the Lines for Military Planners

The Comprehensive Approach to SSR is not a U.S. idea. Until recently, with the rewrites of the Army's Field Manual on Stability Operations, FM 3–07, and its joint counterpart, Joint Publication 3–07, *Joint Doctrine for Military Operations Other Than War*, it was not even cited in U.S. military doctrine. Instead, it represents international consensus on good development practice. As a concept, the Comprehensive Approach to SSR addresses the challenge of insecurity and conflict as a barrier to political, economic, and social development, and recognizes that security, justice, and governance are inextricably linked. It offers a way to more closely synchronize donor activity across multiple lines of effort, with a focus on building capable, accountable, and sustainable capacity within the host nation.

From a donor perspective, SSR is an umbrella term that includes integrated activities in support of defense and armed forces reform; civilian management and oversight; administration of justice; police; corrections; intelligence reform; national security planning and strategy support; border management; DDR; and/or reduction of armed violence through conflict resolution strategies.[1] Although DDR is included as an SSR "activity," the relationship between military support tasks in one and military support tasks in the other is less than clear. Furthermore, the absence of common, repeatable, and transparent processes for either SSR or DDR creates a series of impediments to comprehensive, collaborative planning and coordination. This represents a gap that needs to be filled.

As defined by the principal U.S. Government agencies involved in SSR programming:

> SSR involves policies, plans, programs and activities that a government undertakes to improve the way it provides safety, security, and justice. The overall objective of such reform is to provide an effective and legitimate public service that is transparent, accountable to civilian authority, and responsive to the needs of the public.[2]

One of the immediate challenges that the USJFCOM J9 effort faced was that the military planners with whom the team was working had to first be introduced to the ideas and practices embedded in the Comprehensive Approach to SSR before the question of its applicability to military operations could be explored. The definition itself was not particularly helpful because under this definition, it would appear that the predominant focus of SSR is security sector governance rather than the day-to-day activities involved in administering justice or providing internal and external security. Developing host nation governance capacity is not generally thought of as a military task, and under the Foreign Assistance Act, responsibility for governance assistance rests with the civilian agencies.[3] Therefore, the connections between normal defense-related security assistance activities and the Comprehensive Approach to SSR were not immediately apparent to the planners.

Along with the governance focus, the definition also implies that SSR development is a long-term undertaking for both donors and recipients. In fact, both the Organisation for Economic Co-operation and Development (OECD) guidelines and U.S. Government publications reinforce this idea. Most security assistance, however, is conducted within relatively short 1- to 2-year timeframes, so again the issue of relevance arose.

DDR, on the other hand, is described as:

> a process that follows a peace accord, ceasefire agreement, or other negotiated settlement of an armed conflict. Depending on the nature of the conflict, and the subsequent settlement, DDR processes can include options that allow for some former combatants to remain in the armed forces, or be reconstituted into civilian security forces. In such instances, vetting should become a major element of the process, and integration with an overall strategy for Security Sector Reform (SSR) will

> become key. Ultimately, however, the objective of DDR is to re-establish order and the authority of the state by disarming and demobilizing combatants and reintegrating them into society.[4]

Unlike SSR, the DDR process is generally finite, with fixed negotiated activities, timelines, and objectives. Governance is something that is enabled or strengthened by an effective DDR process, but it is not the focus that it is in SSR. And while DDR may contribute to SSR, neither one is a prerequisite for the other; comprehensive SSR strategies do not even exist in many DDR situations.

Although both definitions refer to each other, it is tough to see how the two activities coincide on the ground from a military operational perspective that tends to focus on near-term implementation tasks. In SSR, for example, much of the military enabling activity encompasses training and equipping armed forces, mentoring military leaders, and providing opportunities for constructive partnering through real world operations, exercises, and professional military education. In DDR, the enabling tasks that a military force would undertake tend to be short term with very limited objectives, such as running a cantonment area or weapons collection site for newly demobilized forces. Planning is usually more tactically focused and, as it is currently conducted, does not generally include consideration of a long-term SSR development strategy. In fact, in the fast-paced environment of military planning for support to DDR, SSR can appear to be an irrelevant distraction.

To make the linkages more apparent for experimentation, USJFCOM J9 recharacterized the two concepts by placing them into a common rule of law framework based on the definition of rule of law that is used in U.S. Foreign Assistance planning,[5] so both activities could be seen as having a common objective of restoring or strengthening the partner nation rule of law. Once a common context is established, it becomes easier to identify the rule of law-related effects to which both SSR and DDR contribute, and from there, an operational staff can create a plan for military support to both SSR and DDR that encompasses near, mid-, and long-term tasks, all of which have a common goal.

Under the USJFCOM J9 umbrella planning framework for military support to rule of law, SSR is identified as its own line of effort, and because the military role in SSR is focused primarily on supporting the reform, restructuring, or reestablishment of the host nation's armed forces and the defense sector,[6] the perspective that USJFCOM J9 used is codified in the statement, "When the Joint Force Commander is building host nation capacity to restore and strengthen the rule of law, his activities should be nested in a comprehensive strategy for SSR."[7]

DDR is also identified as a specific line of effort within the rule of law framework with the following military problem statement: "How can the [Joint Force Commander] support DDR in a way that results in the successful reintegration of former combatants as productive members of society, and precludes them from becoming a factor that contributes to the resumption of conflict?"[8]

With this framework as a start point, USJFCOM J9, in collaboration with civilian interagency experts, multinational experimentation partners, and NGOs, examined best practice in DDR, and directly supported SSR planning at the Combatant Command and Joint Task Force levels in the USSOUTHCOM, USEUCOM, USCENTCOM, and USAFRICOM areas of responsibility through its Unified Action and Deployable Security Sector Reform programs. In the end, the work succeeded in broadening the aperture on SSR among military planners, many of whom are becoming very familiar with the lexicon even if they don't understand the full depth and breadth of the Comprehensive Approach. Additionally, as a result of operations in both Afghanistan and Iraq, there is greater awareness of DDR as a critical component in conflict mitigation and management as well as postconflict stabilization and reconstruction. But the two still aren't linked operationally, in particular because there is no institutionalized means to achieve effective DDR interagency planning and coordination at the level where military theater campaign planning occurs. There are a number of other impediments to a coordinated approach to DDR in particular, and in addition to the problem of the definitional disconnect discussed above, the USJFCOM J9 experimentation supports the following observations:

1. Because DDR involves transforming former combatants into productive members of a community pursuant to a political settlement, it is a complex process with political, military, security, humanitarian, and socioeconomic dimensions. The complexity of the problem means that, in the compressed timeline normally faced by a military planner, it is unlikely that the average staff officer will be able to tap into the full spectrum of expertise and experience necessary to conduct a comprehensive mission analysis. Many critics will say the military should leave such planning to the civilian agencies, who have the requisite expertise and mandate. However, as first responders, the military must be able to engage in this level of analysis quickly and comprehensively, preferably with those in the civilian interagency who have the expertise and are routinely charged with doing comprehensive DDR planning. But who exactly those agencies are and where the real experts can be found is a problem in and of itself. This leads to the second impediment.

2. The U.S. Government does not have centralized capacity for implementing DDR programs. Within the government, responsibilities for DDR component activities are disaggregated, there is no commonly understood process for DDR planning, and the expertise and experience is dispersed throughout the interagency. The U.S. Agency for International Development (USAID) has, in certain cases, engaged in DDR reintegration programs, but there are legal restrictions on how closely USAID can engage with related activities that are defense focused. To illustrate, the military may be responsible for detainee operations, which can include reintegration for those detainees that are subsequently released. However, the military is unlikely to be responsible for job training, reconciliation processes, and other reintegration-focused activities in the communities to which a detainee is returned. These are likely led by USAID, but there is a common perception on the ground among USAID practitioners that they cannot engage directly in facilitating this type of military-led detainee reintegration. This perception has been reinforced by legal opinions issued in Afghanistan and elsewhere, and creates a practical impediment to coordination for a military operational planner.

Other agencies that engage in DDR include the Department of State's Bureaus for Political-Military Affairs (PM), International Organizations (IO), and International Narcotics and Law Enforcement Affairs (INL), and the relevant regional bureaus coordinate overall policy. The Office of the Coordinator for Reconstruction and Stabilization, as the agency responsible for whole-of-government planning and coordination in stabilization operations, has a significant role as well when directed by the Secretary of State. However, no one agency or bureau has the lead for all DDR-related issues, and the actual expertise is limited, scattered throughout the government, and unfortunately often not in the agency or bureau that appears to be the coordination lead. It wasn't until the USJFCOM J9 experimentation had been underway for almost 2 years, for example, that the Department of Labor (DoL) surfaced as a key DDR stakeholder. Other principal agencies and bureaus questioned why USJFCOM included DoL in its experiments. It was explained that while analyzing operational lessons learned, USJFCOM J9 discovered that DoL had planned and implemented significant reintegration programs focused on job training, small business development, and commercial enterprise in Bosnia, Afghanistan, and Iraq, and had other activities throughout Africa that were targeted at the reintegration of child soldiers. All of these had a direct relationship to ongoing DDR processes.

3. ***Critical coordination partners for a military planner can be different from those of the lead civilian agencies, so where collaboration does take place, the relevant actors that are necessary to address the Commander's immediate security imperatives are often absent.*** Ultimately, the Joint Force Commander is addressing a set of security as opposed to governance imperatives, acting as an implementer rather than a policymaker. The civilian departments and agencies that tend to share this focus in the field, and those that have the most operational overlap, are the bureaus and agencies within the Departments of Justice and Homeland Security, acting in an extension of their domestic law enforcement missions. However, neither department is a significant stakeholder in DDR, and their role in the nascent interagency SSR planning processes has been secondary to that of the Department of State and USAID. This may be logical from a civilian agency perspective, but for the joint force commander, it creates another coordination gap that the theater level planner must understand and overcome.

4. ***Where SSR and DDR planning and coordination efforts do exist within an agency, they seldom seem to occur in the same office, and the individuals involved are different as well.*** This not only exacerbates the disconnect between SSR and DDR strategies, but combined with the absence of common planning frameworks for either SSR or DDR and from a planner perspective on an operational military staff, there appears to be no place to go to achieve a coordinated response.

5. ***The multilateral nature of DDR poses further coordination challenges.*** Experience has shown that the military's role is generally one of support to a civilian-led DDR process with multiple international donors, and the two major international institutions that support DDR programs are the United Nations and the World Bank. These are not organizations with which a Joint Task Force (JTF) or Combatant Command staff has a habitual relationship. In fact, the authorization to directly coordinate with either organization is often prohibited or severely constrained. DDR programs also generally garner support from a large number of nongovernmental organizations (NGOs) and aid groups. Again, these are communities of interest with whom the military does not usually engage. For example, the largest DDR program in Africa, a multicountry initiative in the Great Lakes region run by the World Bank, drew on the contributions of forty Western and African governments, NGOs, and regional organizations, and

supported approximately 455,000 ex-combatants. No one is proposing that the military become involved in direct coordination with all of these as a matter of course, but at some point, the planner has to at least have a way of identifying and understanding the major stakeholders that supporting military forces are likely to encounter. In the absence of a coordinated, centralized process for operational planning, much of that analysis is left to blind research and a lot of luck.

6. The absence of military doctrine that defines DDR, its component activities, and the military supporting, enabling, and condition-setting tasks, means that every planning process that involves DDR is essentially ad hoc. While lessons learned from prior operations do exist, they are not readily accessible to military planners who are operating under tight timelines dictated by exigencies on the ground. During the course of experimentation, the USJFCOM J9 support team examined a number of DDR planning efforts that had taken place over a 20-year period. In each case, the military planning staff had conceptually started from scratch, researching the basics of DDR and sending out wide-ranging general inquiries in an effort to understand potential stakeholders both within and outside of the U.S. Government. This level of "ad hocery" wastes time and energy and does not engender a sustainable, repeatable, or transparent process.

Planning Frameworks and Best Practice

As discussed earlier, to support experimentation and field testing with the Combatant Commands and JTFs, USJFCOM J9 developed a rule of law framework in which to shape both SSR and DDR concepts. As implementation gaps subsequently emerged, checklists and processes were created to help planners identify issues and locate the stakeholders they would need to coordinate with to align their operations with larger civilian strategies.

One of the first issues that had to be resolved was answering the "so what" of DDR—from a strategic perspective, what does DDR contribute to restoring or strengthening the rule of law in the host nation? These effects were generically summarized and aligned with a list of related effects that can be achieved through successful SSR:

- The host nation is able to control its sovereign territory.
- The host nation's government gains monopoly control over the use of force within its territory.
- All parties fulfill their obligations under the peace agreement that settled the former conflict.

- Opposition armed forces that were involved in the conflict are dissolved or, if reduced or reintegrated into legitimate postconflict security forces, are subject to government control.
- Demobilized combatants are accepted by their communities and become productive members of society.

From there, the essential elements of a DDR line of effort were identified (again, generically) as:

- formal agreements for disposition of combatants
- areas of cantonment for former combatants and/or weapons
- designated responsibilities for monitoring former combatants
- designated responsibilities for receiving and maintaining/disposal of weapons
- agreements specifying rights/responsibilities former combatants may or may not retain
- agreements specifying former combatants' rights of return and/or rights to reclaim property
- formal programs of economic and resettlement assistance for former combatants
- formal programs for economic, medical, resettlement, and protection assistance for women and children associated with demobilized forces.

Applying these two lists—strategic effects and essential elements—to the specific operation enables a military planner to develop a focused set of critical information requirements during the mission analysis phase of joint planning so the DDR provisions of a negotiated settlement can be translated into operational terms. The DDR planning construct that results from such a "translation" can then be further integrated into plans for SSR or even stability operations as a whole. As a result of experimentation, USJFCOM J9 developed the following template for Critical Information Requirements:

- What are the governing documents, principles, and/or agreements that control the DDR process?
- How is the DDR process linked to SSR, directly or indirectly?
- Under the governing peace agreement or other negotiated settlement to the conflict, who is eligible to take part in a DDR program? Does it include vulnerable populations such as child soldiers, women, and their dependents, etc.?

- How is DDR supposed to be administered? Which agencies and organizations have the lead for what issues, and how will medical care, accommodations, food, and other special humanitarian needs be managed? How is coordination between the military and other lead agencies or organizations accomplished?
- What are the responsibilities of the host nation and/or transitional government, and how is its role coordinated?
- Does the military have a specified role in supporting the DDR, and what are the constraints or restraints on that role?
- What weapons are in the possession of combatant forces, both state and nonstate, and in what quantities?
- What are the main sources of the weapons in the country/region, and what are the main supply lines?
- Who are the groups, factions, or other spoilers that would want to block implementation of DDR? Is there a strategy already in place to deal with them?
- How will the DDR process dissolve the command and control structures of ex-combatants to ensure groups do not reform as criminal organizations?
- What unresolved questions may have an impact on the success of DDR, such as the status of military or police pensions?
- Is there an agreed information strategy or message for informing former combatants of program details? Is that strategy sufficient to preclude future misunderstandings and the possibility that participants will perceive that program administrators are changing the rules to cheat the former combatants out of benefits they were promised?
- How are the DDR phases linked so disarmament and demobilization processes can effectively transition participants into reinsertion and reintegration programs?

Armed with a comprehensive list of relevant questions, planners will have the tools they need for more constructive coordination with external actors, regardless of whether they are U.S. Government agencies, host nation partners, international organizations, or NGOs.

Other Key Planning Considerations

Finally, in addition to creating the framework for DDR mission analysis, USJFCOM J9 experimentation identified a number of other planning considerations. If military planners take these into account, the joint force commander will, at a minimum, have a more comprehensive understanding of the environment, the interests and motivations of key actors, operational risks and opportunities, and the roles and responsibilities of interagency colleagues and principal donors. This in turn will drive decisions toward a synchronized, collaborative approach and should force discussion of the linkages between SSR and DDR. Important planning considerations include:

DDR planning must be grounded in a thorough interagency conflict analysis. What are the agendas of the contending actors and forces? Do DDR reintegration measures address grievances that fueled the conflict? Will power-sharing arrangements motivate the leaders of armed factions to demobilize forces and pursue their agendas politically, thereby potentially undermining the legitimacy and stability of the host nation? Conducting conflict analysis in close collaboration with interagency colleagues and experts on the ground will enable the joint force commander to adapt DDR support in a way that supports sustainable or "viable" peace as opposed to one-off activity.

Decisions on the appropriate levels of security forces that will exist after SSR and the number and type of ex-combatants to be integrated into them should be made prior to demobilization. Establishing the framework for SSR will facilitate DDR by determining how many ex-combatants reformed or reconstituted security forces can or should absorb. The symbiotic relationship between SSR and DDR programs means that the two are often best considered as interdependent parts of comprehensive security and justice development.

DDR and SSR programs should be planned to clearly distinguish both donor and host nation roles and responsibilities, codify them in legislation, and raise general awareness of the objectives. Achieving this level of synchronization will require close collaboration with policy-level planners and a carefully coordinated communications strategy, but the payoff in host nation buy-in and sustainability will be well worth the time and effort and may be the difference between mission success and mission failure.

All security forces are not alike, and DDR must take their differences into account. DDR usually involves downsizing armed forces, with some ex-combatants frequently integrating into police or private security companies. However, clear criteria should be developed for the entry of ex-combatants into the civilian security system prior to launching a DDR program. Not only are different training and skills required for military and police, but the roles of police and the military may have become blurred during the conflict. Hasty or "generic" integration from one type of security force to another may create unanticipated capability gaps in the newly reconstituted forces.

The integration of ex-combatants into either the national armed forces or a police force must include a strict vetting process to ensure that known human rights abusers or criminals do not become part of the new security forces. The inclusion of such individuals may subvert the legitimacy of the new security forces or otherwise discredit them, instill corruption, and provide apparent exoneration and impunity for wrongdoers.

Implementation of DDR and SSR programs should be closely aligned to prevent emergence of a security vacuum. State law enforcement agencies, legitimate nonstate actors, or foreign civilian police should be prepared to provide security for local communities during periods in which the military and armed groups are being demobilized.

Where host nation governments are responsible for disarmament of former combatants, international organizations and foreign partners should encourage national DDR commissions to work closely with government agencies and NGOs responsible for women's issues to ensure that DDR programs are sensitive to the needs of female participants. In this regard, UN Security Council Resolution 1325, adopted unanimously in 2000, called on all actors "to adopt a gender perspective, including inter alia during repatriation and resettlement and for rehabilitation, reintegration and post-conflict reconstruction" when negotiating and implementing peace agreements. Efforts to this end in the DDR process should address the problems of abducted, raped, or abused women, female combatants, female support workers, and the wives and children of former combatants.

Nongovernmental organizations are very active in DDR, and there are well-established networks and communities of interest among international practitioners that military planners should consult if possible. NGOs operate both independently in niche areas such as women's issues or agricultural development, and as implementing partners funded by government donors. Creating both formal and informal opportunities for dialogue and consultation, such as donor conferences, town hall meetings, workshops, and site visits, should be incorporated into both planning and implementation whenever time and circumstances permit.

Understand the linkages between DDR programs and more general reconciliation and humanitarian reintegration processes. All three impact each other, and an imbalance or failure in one can adversely affect not only the others, but also the ultimate goal of reestablishing the order and authority of the state.

The Way Forward

So after 4 years of experimentation, what can be said about the nexus between SSR and DDR from a military perspective? First, there is absolute consensus that the military is in a supporting role in each. These are complex undertakings that require a coordinated, whole-of-government approach to succeed. In the absence of a sustainable, repeatable, and transparent interagency process for coordination, the joint force commander can conduct theater level planning in a way that facilitates constructive collaboration with his civilian counterparts and better informs his mission analysis, but ultimately, interagency solutions are required. In particular, agency roles, responsibilities, and limitations need to be clarified, with a common lexicon adopted by all. The Concept of the Comprehensive Approach to SSR and the role of DDR as a component activity have to be reconciled with more specificity than current guidance provides.

Within DOD, the Combatant Commands have demonstrated demand for SSR and DDR constructs, and, in the absence of doctrine or clear planning guidance, have developed creative solutions to achieve mission success. The USJFCOM J9 effort codifies best practices and a way of approaching the planner's problem, but more work is required to achieve an institutionalized approach that can be understood by all.

Notes

[1] USAID, Department of Defense, and Department of State, *Guidance on Security Sector Reform*, January 15, 2009, available at <www.ausa.org/news/2009/Pages/SecuritySectorReform%E2%80%9D>.

[2] Ibid.

[3] Title 22 U.S.C., Ch. 32—Foreign Assistance, available at <uscode.house.gov/download/pls/wwC32>.

[4] U.S. Joint Forces Command, *Military Support to Rule of Law and Security Sector Reform*, available at <www.dtic.mil/doctrine/doctrine/jwfc/ims_hbk.pdf> (definition derived from presentations and discussions at the *Workshop on Military Support to Rule of Law—Reconciliation and Reintegration* conducted by the Joint Futures Lab, U.S. Joint Forces Command, on February 25–26, 2009, at Arlington, VA).

[5] See U.S. Department of State, U.S. Foreign Assistance Framework, available at <www.state.gov/documents/organization>.

[6] USAID, Department of Defense, and Department of State.

[7] U.S. Joint Forces Command.

[8] Ibid.

Chapter 3

Drafting in Doha: An Assessment of the Darfur Peace Process and Ceasefire Agreements

By Paul R. Williams and Matthew T. Simpson

In the spring of 2010, in Doha, Qatar, the major parties to the Darfur conflict signed a series of framework and ceasefire agreements. The Doha Agreements comprise the Justice and Equality Movement (JEM) Framework, the Liberation and Justice Movement (LJM) Framework, and the LJM Ceasefire Agreements. These accords served two principal purposes. The first and more obvious was to establish a cessation of hostilities and lay the foundation for the negotiation of a comprehensive peace agreement. Critical to each are provisions relating to Security Sector Reform (SSR) and the Disarmament, Demobilization, and Reintegration (DDR) of combatants. Well drafted SSR and DDR provisions, even at the very early stages of a peace process, encourage stabilization in the conflict region and the implementation of the agreement in a sustainable manner. The Doha Agreements, though including occasional language relating to SSR and DDR, largely missed the opportunity to set the framework for mechanisms that would bind the parties to the sustainable deescalation of the conflict.

The second and less obvious purpose was to create momentum. From the perspective of the international community, the hope was for momentum to salvage a faltering peace process. From the perspective of the Darfurians, the hope was for momentum to construct a final negotiated settlement that would heal the humanitarian scars of the conflict and generate a level of power-sharing consistent with that enjoyed by Southern Sudan under the Comprehensive Peace Agreement. For the government of Sudan, the hope was for momentum to gain the upper hand in the April elections, legitimize the regime of President Omar Al-Bashir, and complete the process of transforming the Darfur conflict into a "humanitarian matter" that would solidify the status quo, in which they held a superior position, and limit the active engagement of the international community.

The competing and highly political interests of the three stakeholders affected the nature and quality of the agreements negotiated in Doha. This chapter examines the collective development and impact of the Doha Agreements, seeking to place them in their appropriate political context, analyze the momentum and political slant of the negotiating processes, and consider the missed opportunities of the abbreviated DDR and SSR programs.

For purposes of this analysis, Security Sector Reform is understood to include cessation of hostilities, DDR, combating the spread of small arms and light weapons, prohibiting the use of landmines and undertaking demining, establishing mechanisms for transitional justice, strengthening the rule of law, combating trafficking in people, weapons, and drugs, and creating a framework for imbedding best practices throughout the security sector.

Historical Context

The current Darfur conflict began in the spring of 2003 when two Darfurian rebel movements—the Sudan Liberation Movement (SLM) and Justice and Equality Movement (JEM)—launched attacks against government military installations as part of a campaign to fight against the historic political and economic marginalization of Darfur.[1] The government of Sudan responded swiftly, often through a hired militia known as the Janjaweed, brutally attacking the movements and anyone affiliated with them. The government targeted the SLM's and JEM's predominant ethnic groups, and millions of civilians were forced to flee their homes. An immense humanitarian crisis resulted, and in September 2004, U.S. President George W. Bush declared the crisis in Darfur a "genocide."[2]

In May 2006, the government of Sudan signed the Darfur Peace Agreement (DPA) with one of the SLM groups, but this brought about little in terms of peace.[3] The two movements that refused to sign (JEM and SLM–Wahid) continued fighting the government and at times each other. This internal fighting and discord led to the fragmentation of the movements, and many leaders broke off to form their own groups. At one point, upwards of 27 rebel groups claimed legitimacy as the representatives of the people of Darfur.[4]

As of this writing, the fighting continues, and the United Nations estimates that 300,000 people have died and 2.7 million have been displaced.[5]

The Doha Peace Talks

The United Nations (UN) and the African Union (AU) have led efforts to resolve the conflict, with the United States and other countries providing support. To enhance their ability to mediate a resolution, the UN and AU created a Joint Mediation and Support Team (JMST) and appointed former Burkina Faso Foreign Minister Djibril Bassole as the joint AU/UN mediator. Mr. Bassole's tenure was preceded by a number of failed attempts at mediation by AU and UN cochairs of the peace process.[6]

To create a suitable venue for the peace talks, the JMST turned to the state of Qatar, which agreed to host and underwrite the talks in its capital city of Doha. The JMST and the Qatari government launched a new round of talks in July 2009 between the government of Sudan and the JEM, which have continued to some extent since that time.[7] Initially, the other Darfurian rebel movements refused to join the talks, citing the choice of an Arab state as the venue and the perceived lack of good faith by the government of Sudan as their primary rationale.

Over time though, most of the other Darfurian rebel movements joined the talks in Doha. In February 2010, several of the predominantly Fur rebel movements affiliated previously with the SLM united to form LJM. In late April, SLA–Abdel Shafi, SLM–Unity, and several other Fur rebel movements joined the LJM.

In an effort to broaden Darfurian input into the peace process and, according to some observers, to possibly dilute the influence of the Darfurian rebel movements, the JMST also hosted a large civil society "workshop" in Doha. The workshop resulted in a statement of principles agreed to by the civil society representatives referred to as the Doha Declaration.[8] Many observers noted that the "civil society" delegation included numerous representatives appointed by or affiliated with the government and could therefore not serve as a legitimate voice of civil society. As a result, the JMST later undertook a more extensive effort to travel throughout Darfur to consult with and seek to incorporate the voice of traditional civil society.

As for the government, it actively participates in the Doha peace process through a moderately high-level delegation. For signing ceremonies, Sudan has been represented by President Al Bashir and Vice President Ali Osman Taha. Government delegations come and go from Doha at will;

their presence often dictates when talks will be held rather than the other way around.

As for structure, the JMST has adopted an approach of proximity talks between the parties. Under this approach, the mediation team creates an initial draft and then shops it separately to each of the parties in an effort to create a consensus document. The mediation does accept documents produced by the parties, but seems to rely on them only as an expression of the interests of the groups and not as actual negotiating texts.

In February and March 2010, two key milestones were reached in Doha. On February 23, the government and the JEM signed the Framework and Ceasefire Agreement (JEM Framework). The JEM Framework set forth a general roadmap for future negotiations. It also included guiding principles relevant to a cessation of hostilities.

On March 18, the government and the LJM signed two documents. The first, a Framework Agreement to Resolve the Conflict in Darfur (LJM Framework), provided a roadmap for future negotiations, and the other, a ceasefire agreement (LJM Ceasefire), provided for the temporary cessation of hostilities and the formation of a Ceasefire Commission.

Pre-agreement Momentum

Collectively, the Doha Agreements sought to provide a framework for lasting peace. The desire to conclude the agreements was spurred by a sense of urgency on the part of the parties, the Qataris, and international political actors. In particular, the government of Sudan and the international community were interested in shifting their focus to the pending referendum in South Sudan. Yet the singularly political approach of the internationals and their narrow and short-term focus on elections compromised success and sustainability of the process from the start.

In the winter of 2010, both the Qataris, as the host nation and financier of the peace process, and the JMST as the mediation team, had a strong interest in seeing the peace process gain momentum. Many in the international community were getting impatient with what was viewed as a drawn-out process that yielded limited deliverables. The international donor community was also under pressure from their governments and funders to justify the millions of dollars in expenditures. The JMST and Qataris were well aware of this impatience, and it could be sensed that they felt a significant urgency to generate an initial agreement to maintain the viability of the JMST as a credible vehicle for mediation, and Doha as a suitable venue.

The mediation team was also under pressure from other important international players. Both General Muammar Qhadafi of Libya and former South African President Thabo Mbeki publicly and privately expressed interest in playing a greater role. Libya's desire to reestablish itself as a key player in the peace process and Mr. Mbeki's wish to interject himself into the effort were not welcome by Mr. Bassole or at least initially by the Qatari hosts.[9]

Another political actor who played a significant role in moving the agreements forward, especially the signing of the JEM Framework, was President Idriss Deby of Chad. Several weeks prior to the JEM signing ceremony, he made significant headway on the normalization of the previously contentious relations between Chad and Sudan over their shared border.[10] As part of the process of normalization with Sudan, President Deby sought to use his influence over JEM to promote the negotiation of a framework agreement and ceasefire between the government and the JEM (which reportedly utilized territory within Chad as a safe-haven). He hosted the negotiations in N'djamena and prepared the initial draft of the JEM Framework. Some observers have noted that the legally imprecise terminology of the framework agreement and its rather disjointed organization are the result of it being appropriately and primarily a political document penned by President Deby himself. It was originally written in French and then poorly translated into Arabic and English, the languages of the negotiations.

The U.S. commitment to the April 2010 elections in Sudan, and the perceived crucial role of the elections in the implementation of the North-South Comprehensive Peace Agreement, contributed to the momentum for concluding the agreements. U.S. Special Envoy General Scott Gration had long made it known that it was a priority of Washington to support the elections, with little regard to whether they were free and fair.[11] To this end, Envoy Gration was a strong proponent of a temporary cessation of hostilities that would allow the elections to occur with limited violence and interruption.

In parallel with this international pressure, the parties themselves were also individually motivated to sign peace documents with each other. The government of Sudan was looking for the political benefits of peace. Through the first elections in 24 years, it sought to legitimize the regime and counterbalance the negative publicity resulting from the indictment by the International Criminal Court of President Bashir on war crimes and crimes against humanity. The government was clearly focused on holding the elections with minimal disruption and was therefore eager to sign an agreement with the Darfur movements that would provide for the temporary cessation of hostilities, hoping that would be enough to allow the elections. Possibly for that reason, President Bashir personally attended the signing ceremony of the JEM Framework in Doha. Indeed, it was said that the government was only interested in reaching a temporary cessation of hostilities before the elections using the ceasefire as a political tool, and that it was unwilling to negotiate any of the more substantive proposals the Darfurian rebel movements tried to place on the agenda.[12]

The government's avoidance of the substantive proposals may also have reflected its desire to stall comprehensive negotiations until after the elections in the hope that the results would produce an alternative Darfurian delegation for future talks. Almost immediately after the elections, the government began to argue that the newly elected representatives from Darfur, who came primarily from President Bashir's dominant National Congress Party, were now the legitimate, democratically endorsed representatives of the region and should therefore represent the people of Darfur in future negotiations. This claim, on its face, lacks credibility given the nearly universal criticism of the Sudanese elections, and of the election process in Darfur in particular. The government likely reasoned, however, that the international community, which validated the elections to a certain degree, may feel compelled to allow participation of an additional NCP-dominated delegation. Even if the delegation were not added to the talks, the assertion of an alternative "elected" delegation would suit the interests of the government to undermine the validity of the claims that the Darfurian movements represent the whole of Darfurian society.

The timing for an agreement was also right between the JEM and LJM. For the Darfurians, the vast majority of the prior year was spent addressing the unification of the movements. Pressure from the mediators and international community was strong for the Darfurians to do away with the fragmentation that plagued them during prior negotiations and to present a united front against the government. Intensive resources and time were spent on meetings in Addis Ababa, Tripoli, and various parts of Darfur, encouraging the movements to crystallize into a single negotiating block. The U.S.-led effort in Addis saw many of the most powerful Fur groups join together. Similarly, a program led by General Qhadafi formed a separate alliance of Fur fighters in Kufra, Libya. Many of these efforts were successful. The Addis and Tripoli groups, along with a handful of others, merged through a series of shifts and realignments to form the LJM. This intensive engagement generated results, as the once highly-fragmented movements consolidated into fewer than a half dozen. To this end, much of the international community's attention up to and even after the signing of the Doha Agreements was focused on bringing the movements together around common leadership.

The staging of the signing ceremonies revealed the political motivations of the various stakeholders. Reflecting the Qataris' desire to highlight the progress made in their peace process, the ceremonies were held in Doha at the opulent Sheraton and Ritz Carlton hotels.[13] To demonstrate the perceived breakthrough and the hopes for a reinvigorated process, the guest lists included heads of state from neighboring countries, the Secretary Generals of the Arab League and African Union, and representatives from still other countries. As noted above, President Bashir attended the signing ceremony with the JEM and made a concerted effort to highlight his engagement with the other Presidents and dignitaries including many from Western Europe.

President Deby of Chad sat immediately to the right of the Emir of Qatar during the signing of the JEM Framework. The event was also used to demonstrate the Qataris' commitment to the peace process and to highlight the fact that they were willing and able to put substantial resources into the effort. This sent a positive signal to both participants and observers, giving hope that there was strong support for the process. However, as will be discussed below, the signal was not backed by substance or operational support through security sector reform.

The Doha Agreements and Consequences

While the Doha Agreements appeared at the time to achieve their objective of reinvigorating the peace process, there was immediate concern that they might not have succeeded in setting forth an adequate foundation for sustainable SSR. This section will introduce the three agreements and provide a general analysis. The next section will examine the substantive provisions of the agreements in detail. Given that all peace processes are naturally fluid, the following critique will focus on the key elements of SSR covered in the agreements and note which additional elements are necessary for future accords.

The JEM Framework and Limitations for SSR

The JEM Framework and Ceasefire Agreement (JEM Framework), which as noted above was initially negotiated under the auspices of President Deby of Chad, was designed to bring about a cessation of hostilities, set forth a preliminary substantive agenda for future talks, acknowledge and address in principle the pressing issues of internally displaced persons

(IDPs) and refugees, and initiate a process of Security Sector Reform, with primary emphasis on DDR. The document, which was only three pages, was intended to express agreement between the parties and define the process for moving the peace talks forward at the highest level of generality. The parties' and mediation's motivation to see a document signed took priority over including details and specifics that would presumably prolong and complicate the negotiations.

The substantive agenda for talks embedded within the JEM Framework contained commitments to negotiate issues relevant to both parties including the participation of the JEM at all levels of government, the administrative restructuring of Darfur, resource sharing, and land reform. The agreement also contained commitments relating to IDPs and refugees including recognition of their right to voluntary return, the provision of fair compensation, the creation of adequate social infrastructure, and the guarantee of a dignified life in their places of origin. The agreement, however, failed to address several issues that were of particular importance to the Darfurians including borders, transitional security, the disarming of the Janjaweed, economic reconstruction and rehabilitation of Darfur, national wealth sharing, and reconciliation and justice mechanisms.

With respect to cessation of hostilities, the JEM Framework provided rather opaquely that the parties "proclaim a cease-fire and engage in immediate discussions to reach an agreement for its observation." This wording almost immediately led to a dispute as to whether the parties had in fact agreed to a ceasefire or merely to negotiate one.[14] As of mid-June 2010, the parties had not yet negotiated an agreement to implement the framework provisions relating to the proclamation of a ceasefire, although the draft agreement circulating around Doha did include provisions for implementation.

The JEM Framework also failed to establish a clear timeline for the initial cessation of hostilities. The agreement, consistent with all parties' desire to build momentum through quick results, did provide a March 15, 2010, deadline for final peace negotiations, but this date was unrealistic given the capacities of the parties and the complexity of the issues. The passing of the deadline for a final agreement led many to conclude that the ceasefire had expired on that deadline as well.

In addition to establishing a cessation of hostilities, the JEM Framework was intended to serve as a precursor to a full-fledged Ceasefire Agreement and therefore contained a number of very specific SSR and DDR principles. Significantly, these provisions did not carry over to the actual agreement.

The JEM Framework Agreement started with a general release of prisoners of war by both parties and included amnesty for combatants. This amnesty provision was particularly important for JEM as over 50 of its combatants were held by the government and otherwise were scheduled for execution after allegedly taking part in a raid on Khartoum.

As part of SSR, the agreement included a provision for the disbandment of JEM forces and their integration into the ranks of the state armed forces and other Sudanese military and police groups. It did not include an option for creating a separate police or military force for Darfur comprised of former JEM members, as is commonly found in similar agreements. Interestingly, the agreement also included a commitment by the government, rather than the international community, to fund JEM's daily operations, cantonment, and training through the abbreviated DDR process. Given the preliminary nature of the agreement, it is likely that disbandment was chosen by JEM over more thorough DDR as a hedge against its belief that their forces would be needed to defend against government attack in the near future.

Finally, the agreement provided at an early stage for the political reformation of JEM, through the transformation of JEM back into a political party. This provision was important for returning JEM to its roots as a political organization. It also set a positive precedent for other movements with regard to integration into the political process, which will be critical to the future stability of the government of Sudan. Importantly, although the JEM was willing to consider returning to the status of a political party, it insisted on a lengthened process for disarmament and demobilization with integration into the Sudan Armed Forces preferred over a quick disbandment and return to civilian life for its combatants. Notably, the interest in reintegration was consistent with the general trend to reestablish the monopoly of force by states instead of preservation of a separate post-conflict police or security force.

In short, the initial JEM Framework, despite its brevity and the absence of disarmament or demobilization, paid considerable attention to SSR provisions. Unfortunately, when the mediation later developed and circulated a subsequent draft comprehensive ceasefire to implement the JEM Framework, none of these SSR provisions was expressly present. While it is possible that SSR could be included in another portion of a final peace agreement, established practice indicates that these provisions should have been provided for expressly in the comprehensive ceasefire. For instance, recent ceasefire agreements in the Democratic Republic of the

Congo, Liberia, and Burundi have all expressly provided for SSR provisions rather than leaving them to incorporation in subsequent documents.[15]

Within weeks of signing the Framework Agreement, JEM and the government exchanged accusations of ceasefire violations, and renewed violence erupted between the parties. From late April to early May 2010, renewed clashes between JEM forces and the government intensified, resulting in the deaths of over 100 Darfurians in the Jebel Mara region.[16] On May 4, JEM announced that it was suspending its participation in the Doha peace talks to protest the government attacks on its forces and "a lack of seriousness from the part of the Government of Sudan regarding a peaceful resolution to the conflict." JEM also accused the international community, and the AU in particular, of failing to assert sufficient pressure on the government, thereby allowing it to turn the peace process into "political theater" designed to rehabilitate the image of newly reelected President Bashir.[17]

After the breakdown of talks in Doha, tensions between JEM and the government escalated further. In May 2010, government leadership insisted that Interpol apprehend JEM leader Dr. Khalil Ibrahim on terrorism charges.[18] Additionally, later that month, upon his return from a series of meetings in Cairo and Doha, the once-supportive government of Chad denied Dr. Khalil access to Darfur through Chad, his customary route into the region, and he was forced to take refuge in Libya.[19] The government of Sudan concurrently issued statements ruling out future negotiations with JEM in Doha.[20]

The LJM Agreements and the Absence of DDR

The signing of an agreement between the government and JEM created a sense of urgency for the other movements. With advance warning that the agreement was to be signed the evening of February 23, 2010, the fragmented Fur movements conducted intense internal negotiations on unification for the several days prior to that event. Likely to prevent the JEM from getting too far ahead in the talks, and with the goal of presenting a unified face for the Fur movements, the LJM was formed only a few hours before the JEM signing ceremony.

Then, as noted above, the LJM signed a separate framework agreement and ceasefire. The Framework Agreement was much more detailed than the framework signed by JEM. The Ceasefire Agreement reflected both the aspiration of a cessation of hostilities and a detailed set of standards and procedures for implementing the cessation, as well as a minimal degree of SSR. However, no components of DDR other than an amnesty provision were carried over, with other SSR, transitional justice, and governance issues left to a future time. The agreements were lacking in certain areas of substance and failed to account for important contextual realities. As a result, they failed to create an adequate incentive for the Darfurians to disarm and reintegrate, and thus limited the utility of the agreements for restoring the monopoly of force to the state.

The LJM Agreements accomplished a great deal on the political front and set out an initial foundation for cessation of hostilities, DDR, and SSR by providing initial treatment of several topics that routinely appear in ceasefire and peace agreements. Accordingly, the agreements provide a workable basis for a more comprehensive ceasefire. Their signing also generated momentum in the peace process and created the political space for future negotiations.

LJM Framework. The LJM Framework began by setting out an eclectic mix of general principles that included respect for Sudan's territorial sovereignty, a reaffirmation of democracy, fair and equitable power and wealth sharing, alleviation of suffering of the people of Darfur, provision of humanitarian assistance, and a commitment to an efficient federal system of government.

Importantly, the general principles section did not clearly indicate whether these were principles that a subsequent peace agreement should incorporate as goals of an agreement or simply affirmed the status quo. It is likely the parties would argue differently: the government of Sudan would probably insist the general principles are a reflection of the status quo, while LJM could well see the section as calling for their enforcement, calling for the creation of competent mechanisms to ensure their implementation. Such ambiguity was no doubt necessary to secure the agreement of both parties, but it can have a destabilizing effect during the negotiation of a full peace agreement unless it is addressed clearly at that time.

The LJM Framework then turned to some preliminary principles. The agreement broadly provided for a ceasefire and cessation of all hostilities, effective upon the signing of the agreement and the final ceasefire. Both parties also committed themselves to permitting the African Union-United Nations Hybrid Operation in Darfur (UNAMID) to monitor the ceasefire.

Like the framework signed by JEM, the LJM Framework provided for a general amnesty for civilian and military members of the LJM and the release of prisoners of war by both sides. However, it did not include the other SSR and DDR provisions that were contained within the JEM framework for the disarmament of fighters, the reconfiguration of the movement as a political party, and the reintegration of former combatants into civil society.

After the initial ceasefire provisions, the LJM Framework set out a detailed list of issues for subsequent negotiation, including the administrative status of Darfur, wealth and natural resource sharing, democratic reform, security arrangement, and reconciliation and "issues of justice."

Interestingly, the LJM Framework also included a provision that all disputes arising under the agreement were to be resolved by the AU/UN Joint Mediation Support Team. This provision is both unusual and problematic, as disputes under the agreement are likely to arise long after the mediators have concluded their work. Most agreements provide for a more formal and regularized body or mechanism to resolve disputes relating to implementation.

Just as the agreement between JEM and the government set March 15, 2010, as the deadline for final negotiations, the LJM Framework provided that the "Final [peace] agreement and its additional implementing protocols shall be prepared, negotiated and signed in Doha before the end of March 2010." This deadline, less than 3 weeks after the initial agreement was signed, seemed to confirm the motivation of the government to secure a peace agreement, no matter how limited, to build momentum for the elections. Unfortunately, previous experience in Sudan demonstrates that setting unrealistic deadlines can in fact erode momentum for a peace process and breed mistrust among the parties and with the mediators.[21]

The LJM Framework concluded with an agreement on the role of civil society, which is a relatively recent addition to framework agreements in general and a call for the parties to work in political partnership. Given the need for substantial public participation in the implementation of certain SSR provisions, the inclusion of genuine civil society representatives in the peace process, if done appropriately, could have a long-term positive impact on both the development and implementation of security sector reform.

The reference to political partnership, while seemingly innocuous, is reminiscent of the Comprehensive Peace Agreement between the government and the SPLM in South Sudan, and is generally seen as an attempt to bind each party to the implementation of the agreement once the rebel movements have transformed into political parties. It is also odd in the context of DDR to provide for the transformation of the movement into a political party but not for the reintegration of movement soldiers. It begs the question what will happen to combatants once the movement is established as a political party.

LJM Ceasefire. The LJM Ceasefire sought to accomplish the four main objectives of bringing about a cessation of hostilities, creation of a ceasefire commission, DDR of LJM combatants, and DDR of child soldiers. However as noted above, DDR of adults was abbreviated and limited to disbandment. DDR of child soldiers was far more expansive, with considerable specificity and even innovation.

The LJM Ceasefire began with a typical commitment to the prior obligations of both parties under international law, and then turned to an agreement to observe an immediate and complete cessation of hostilities between the two parties both on land and in the air. Providing for a cessation of hostilities in the air was a major victory for LJM, who sought to curb the government's aerial bombardments of military and civilian positions within Darfur and had no planes or helicopters of its own.

The LJM Ceasefire spelled out the parties' disbandment and other peace commitments in more detail than the JEM Ceasefire, including agreement to cease and refrain from acts of hostility, military or other armed activity, recruitment or military activity within proximity of the IDP camps, acts of violence against UNAMID or other humanitarian personnel, acts of gender-based violence, and hostile propaganda.

While the LJM Ceasefire generally included many of the provisions necessary for an effective ceasefire and peace promotion, two major weaknesses may prove problematic in its implementation and support for sustainable peace. First, the agreement is overly broad and vague in parts, lacking in essential specificity and precision. Second, it inadequately addresses SSR and DDR other than DDR for child soldiers. Third, it fails to account adequately for the political and historical context of the Darfur conflict. Fourth, it does not address provisions for renewal or modification.

The first major concern with the LJM Ceasefire is that it lacks specificity on numerous issues. For instance, in an effort to be comprehensive, it contains a general prohibition against all "military or other armed activity in Darfur," and any "retaliatory action . . . against any armed groups. . . ." These overbroad statements would, if interpreted strictly, prohibit legitimate policing activities as well as self-defense against attack from a nonsignatory.

Similarly, though the ceasefire contains a list of prohibited acts, the document fails to clearly define many of them. The agreement prohibits "actions that impede humanitarian access," all "acts and forms of gender based violence," "recruitment and other activities" near IDP and refugee camps, and even "[o]ther activities that could endanger or undermine their commitment to a complete and durable cessation of hostilities." Such catch-all prohibitions are dangerously broad and subjective, and without further expansion and definition they are virtually guaranteed to raise allegations of violation and cause dispute.

Moreover, the ceasefire uses the term "offensive action" without providing a clear definition. It is customary to clearly specify a positive, exemplary list of actions that constitute offensive actions under the agreement. In defining offensive and prohibited actions, it is also customary to clarify which acts are considered to be within the scope of the military. Defining prohibited actions and military/nonmilitary distinctions makes it easier to identify violations of the agreement, and provides for more effective and efficient dispute resolution. Failing to do so is cause for substantial confusion and potential lack of implementation.

An obvious example of the LJM Ceasefire's lack of specificity and precision is its creation of a Ceasefire Commission (CFC). The agreement provided for the establishment of a body responsible for the implementation and monitoring of the agreement but did not provide any detail on its mandate or composition. Likely as a result of the speed at which the negotiations progressed, and the political motivations to get the LJM Ceasefire signed as soon as possible, the drafters referenced, but failed to include, an annex which would set out the mandate and procedures for the CFC. The lack of an annex defining its role is particularly troubling because it leaves the LJM Ceasefire without a clear process to address violations. Given the frequent violations in prior ceasefires,[22] any ceasefire in Darfur would require robust monitoring and verification mechanisms as well as meaningful penalties.

The LJM Ceasefire, furthermore, did not obligate the parties to refrain from reprisals in response to violations of the agreement, nor did it clearly distinguish acts that constitute retaliatory actions or reprisals (violations) from defensive acts (not violations).

The ceasefire also suffers from a failure to set out clearly affirmative and restrictive obligations. For instance, it restricts acts of hostility and violence toward the civilian population in Darfur but does not specify an affirmative obligation for the parties to protect civilians. An affirmative obligation would require additional specificity that obligates the parties to not only avoid hostilities and violence but also provide a safe environment for civilians, typically in accordance with international standards. Similarly, with the parties not obligated, it becomes difficult to identify responsibilities, which will hamper the monitoring of implementation and violations.

The agreement also failed with regard to holding the parties accountable not only for their own troops and their direct actions, but also those groups that are engaged in the conflict on their behalf. Armed groups affiliated with the parties play a prevalent role in the conflict. Thus, the ceasefire should have provided that the parties are affirmatively responsible for communicating the provisions of the ceasefire and any other agreement to affiliated groups and are fully responsible for any affiliated group's violations. Furthermore, particular provisions on affiliated groups should list identifiable affiliated groups to the conflict such as Chadian forces, fighters under the control of Mini Minawi, border guards, and Janjaweed.

The LJM Ceasefire would have benefited from much greater attention to the core elements of a traditional ceasefire agreement, including SSR and DDR. The separation of forces should be provided for on a detailed level, including the disengagement of troops, establishment of security zones, troop and weapons verification, and the withdrawal of foreign and proxy forces.

Notably, considerable attention is paid to the DDR of child soldiers, including provisions obligating the parties to adhere to several international conventions on the protection of children, and to turn over all children associated with the armed forces soldiers to the UN. The specificity on this issue likely is the result of the active involvement of the United Nations Children's Fund (UNICEF) in Doha and its work with the movements. UNICEF deployed its people to the Doha talks to advocate for the greater inclusion of child protection provisions and clearly have had an impact.

The LJM Ceasefire fails to account adequately for the political and historical context of the Darfur conflict. For instance, the agreement reaffirms the territorial integrity and sovereignty of Sudan but fails to reiterate the customary corollary, which is right to internal self-determination and self-government. The agreement thus focuses more heavily on the prerogatives of the government rather than mutually agreed goals. An agreement based on the needs and interests of one party is less likely to yield lasting peace on the ground than an agreement where both parties' needs have been equally addressed.

Similarly, the agreement prohibited offensive action against any party signatory to the Darfur Peace Agreement (DPA) signed on May 5, 2006. While the DPA created an obligation on the government not to use force against the other signatory to the DPA, the LJM was not bound by any such obligation. Under the new ceasefire, the LJM is banned from using force against those who signed the DPA, but those groups are not bound by a reciprocal agreement. Under strict interpretation of the agreement, the LJM is thus exposed to attack, while the government is protected. The LJM was also burdened with an additional obligation, while the government gave up nothing to maintain its prior obligation under the DPA. Considering the DPA's lack of implementation, this was a missed opportunity to accomplish forward progress in SSR and DDR, and created an asymmetrical relationship between the DPA signatories and the LJM.

Given the government's poor track record on the implementation of previous ceasefire and peace agreements in Darfur, and the international community's expressed interest in achieving a sustainable solution to the conflict there, the ceasefire should also have empowered the international community to monitor and enforce the security provisions of the agreement by providing a clear mandate for international participation in the CFC, as well as establishing mandates for other international organizations. The enforcement of these provisions, including the obligation to grant unimpeded access to humanitarian agencies, and the prohibition of military activity within the IDP camps, was a ripe opportunity to involve the international community and increase the likelihood that the security provisions would indeed be respected.

Conclusion

The story of the Doha Agreements is one of complicated relationships and political motivations. For some stakeholders like the government, they accomplished their goals; temporary documents with limited substance that advertise their participation in the process without actually binding parties to firm commitments. LJM arguably accomplished its goal of establishing itself as a legitimate negotiating block in the process. Other stakeholders accomplished less; the JEM Framework was repeatedly violated early on, and its March 15 deadline for final negotiations seemingly came and went without notice. What cannot be lost in the frenzy of these constantly changing relationships, and what this article has endeavored to establish, is that words matter. Though they were no doubt a positive step in the peace process, the substantive weakness of the Doha Agreements limited their ability to be sustained and implemented in any meaningful way. In particular, the parties and the mediators missed a real opportunity to set the foundation for significant security sector reform and DDR. Greater specificity, more consistency with international state practice, and an increased role for the international community would all have contributed to the likelihood that the agreements would be meaningfully implemented in a sustainable way. Going forward, those responsible for negotiating and drafting subsequent agreements must recognize that the words, when drafted well and in a manner consistent with international state practice, work to bind the parties to the document and its principles in a way that self-interest and motivation cannot break apart.

Notes

[1] Ted Dagne, *Sudan: The Crisis in Darfur and the Status of the North-South Peace Agreement*, Congressional Research Service, May 12, 2009, available at <http://www.fas.org/sgp/crs/row/RL33574.pdf>.

[2] George W. Bush, President's Statement on Violence in Darfur, Sudan, Office of the Press Secretary, September 9, 2004, available at <http://georgewbush-whitehouse.archives.gov/news/releases/2004/09/20040909-10.html>.

[3] Laurie Nathan, "No Ownership, No Peace: The Darfur Peace Agreement," Crisis States Working Papers No. 5, September 2006, available at <http://www.crisisstates.com/Publications/wp/WPseries2/wp5.2.htm>.

[4] Kelly Campbell, "Peace Brief: Negotiating Peace in Darfur," U.S. Institute of Peace, January 2008, available at <http://www.usip.org/resources/negotiating-peace-darfur>.

[5] "Mbeki's Panel Flirting with Failure in Darfur," *Sudan Tribune*, March 13, 2010, available at <http://www.sudantribune.com/spip.php?page=imprimable&id_article=34424>.

[6] International Crisis Group, *Darfur's New Security Reality*, Africa Report No. 134, November 2007, 21–22, available at <http://www.crisisgroup.org/~/media/Files/africa/horn-of-africa/sudan/Darfurs%20New%20Security%20Reality.ashx>.

[7] "Darfur Peace Talks Begin in Doha," *Al Jazeera*, February 11, 2009, available at <http://english.aljazeera.net/news/middleeast/2009/02/200921013551771791O.html>.

[8] "Civil society urges cease-fire and peace in Darfur," *Sudan Tribune*, November 21, 2009, available at <http://sudantribune.com/spip.php?article33189>.

[9] "Rift Emerges Between Mbeki and Bassole over Darfur Peace Process," *Sudan Tribune*, May 14, 2010, available at <http://www.sudantribune.com/spip.php?page=imprimable&id_article=33134>; "Mbeki Meets Libya Leader for Talks on Darfur," *Sudan Tribune*, February 14, 2010, available at <http://www.sudantribune.com/spip.php?article34125>.

[10] "AU Chief Hails Sudan, Chad Normalization Engagement," *Sudan Tribune*, January 21, 2010, available at <http://www.sudantribune.com/spip.php?article33848>.

[11] After meeting with election representatives in Sudan on April 3, 2010, a week before the elections were scheduled to begin, Special Envoy Gration endorsed the process, stating that the elections would be "as free and fair as possible." "Sudan Vote Free and as Fair as Possible: U.S. Envoy," Associated Foreign Press, April 3, 2010, available at <http://www.google.com/hostednews/afp/article/ALeqM5g3Rs2XJOVOUm5BQtvWgt0XBKWcGg>.

[12] Enough Project, "The Darfur Peace Process: Recipe for a Bad Deal?" April 5, 2010, available at <http://www.enoughproject.org/publications/update-doha>.

[13] "Sudan Parties Sign Darfur Cease-fire," *Al Jazeera*, February 24, 2010, available at <http://english.aljazeera.net/news/africa/2010/02/2010223618950368.html>; "Sudan Signs Cease-fire Deal with Main Darfur Rebels," Reuters Africa, February 23, 2010, available at <http://uk.reuters.com/article/idUKTRE61M5XB20100223>.

[14] "JEM Rebels Urge Sudanese Army to Stop Attacks on Jebel Marra," *Sudan Tribune*, March 1, 2010, available at <http://www.sudantribune.com/spip.php?article34274>; "Darfur Rebels Threaten to Quit Peace Talks," Reuters Africa, March 3, 2010, available at <http://af.reuters.com/article/sudanNews/idAFHEA33245820100303?sp=true>.

[15] Democratic Republic of Congo, Cease-fire Agreement for Democratic Republic of Congo, August 31, 1999, available at <http://www.usip.org/library/pa/drc/drc_07101999_toc.html>; Liberia, Agreement on Cease-fire and Cessation of Hostilities Between the Government of the Republic of Liberia and Liberians United for Reconciliation and Democracy and the Movement for Democracy in Liberia, June 17, 2003, available at <http://www.usip.org/library/pa/liberia/liberia_cease-fire_06172003.html>; Burundi, Arusha Peace and Reconciliation Agreement for Burundi, Protocol III, Peace and Security for All, chapter III, "Permanent Cease-fire and Cessation of Hostilities," August 28, 2000, available at <http://www.usip.org/library/pa/burundi/pa_burundi_08282000_toc.html>.

[16] "US Condemns Darfur Attacks, Urges Resumption of Talks," *Sudan Tribune*, May 18, 2010, available at <http://www.sudantribune.com/spip.php?article35126>.

[17] "African Union Undermined Peace Process—Rebels," *Sudan Tribune*, May 5, 2010, available at <http://www.sudantribune.com/spip.php?article34991>.

[18] "Sudan Asks Interpol to Arrest Rebel Chief," Reuters Alert, May 10, 2010, available at <http://www.alertnet.org/thenews/newsdesk/LDE6492RQ.htm>.

[19] "Libya Receives Former Rebel Leader After Chad Denies Entry," *Sudan Tribune*, May 19, 2010, available at <http://www.sudantribune.com/spip.php?article35137>.

[20] "Sudan Shelves Peace Talks with JEM," *Al Jazeera*, May 26, 2010, available at <http://english.aljazeera.net/news/africa/2010/05/2010526203549379729.html>.

[21] See Laurie Nathan, *No Ownership, No Peace: The Darfur Peace Agreement, Crisis States Working Papers*, no. 5, September 2006, available at <http://www.crisisstates.com/Publications/wp/WP-series2/wp5.2.htm>, which explains how the use of deadline diplomacy in the DPA negotiations undermined both parties' trust in the mediation and ultimately led to the collapse of the agreement. See also Alex de Waal, "I Will Not Sign," *London Review of Books* 17, 18–19 (2006), available at <http://www.lrb.co.uk/v28/n23/alex-de-waal/i-will-not-sign>. According to Alex de Waal, the rebel movements were only given 5 days to review the final version of the 100+ page peace agreement, and the mediators refused their request to extend the signing deadline thus leading to several key rebel leaders refusing to sign the agreement.

[22] See International Crisis Group, *Darfur's New Security Reality, Africa Report* No. 134, November 2007, 22 (detailing multiple violations of prior ceasefire agreements).

Part II
Challenges of Reintegration

Chapter 4

Military Integration and War Termination

By Mark Knight

Introduction

This chapter provides a synthesis of key issues and lessons drawn from academic and policy papers focused on the integration of rebel and government military forces as part of a wider peace settlement following civil war. Besides drawing on existing studies, it synthesizes themes by examining the data from eight primary case studies: Bosnia, Burundi, Democratic Republic of the Congo (DRC), Mozambique, Namibia, South Africa, Zimbabwe, and Philippines. It also looks at fifteen secondary case studies: Angola, Azerbaijan, Cambodia, Chad, Chechnya, Djibouti, El Salvador, Eritrea, Ethiopia, South Ossetia, Haiti, Lebanon, Nicaragua, Rwanda, and Uganda.[1]

Of particular importance were the online quantitative data sets related to the Hartzell and Hoddie[2] and Glassmyer and Sambanis[3] papers. This data and information gathered from other sources have been collated and summarized in the primary and secondary case studies and form the data upon which the analysis within this chapter is based.

Approaches to RMI

A key conclusion of this study is that rebel military integration (RMI) does not lead to peace. The study finds that peace initiatives are more likely to fail where there was an attempt at RMI, but suggests that this is because incomplete, poorly structured RMI within peace agreements increases the risks of the failure of the wider peace process. Successfully implementing RMI aspects of peace agreements positively supports the wider peace.

The Mozambican case is instructive as a fully implemented RMI. Mozambique's peace settlement required government troops and the

Mozambican National Resistance (RENAMO) rebel forces to integrate in order to form a new national army. Because RENAMO delayed sending students for officer training for the new joint army, demobilization of both the RENAMO and government troops was not completed until nearly 2 years after the peace agreement was signed. Ultimately, however, demobilization by both groups proved so successful that in 1995 President Joaquim Chissano announced that conscription would be necessary to get the new, integrated Mozambique Democratic Armed Forces up to full strength.

Partial implementation is also a common outcome of RMI endeavors, as the two accords intended to end the civil war in Angola highlight. The Bicesse Accords, signed in 1991, called for the creation of a new national army totalling 40,000 men, which was to be evenly divided between government and National Union for the Total Independence of Angola (UNITA) troops. Although UNITA did send some of its troops to assembly points to be disarmed and demobilized, tens of thousands of guerrillas and their arms were concealed in remote areas. By the time elections were held in September 1992, only 45 percent of government troops had been demobilized and only 24 percent of the forces assembled by UNITA had given up their weapons. The subsequent Lusaka Protocol, signed in 1994, also called for the creation of a unified national army, this time with approximately 90,000 troops. Although the integration process was deemed to have concluded in 1998, with UNITA claiming to have fully completed the demobilization process, it was reported that UNITA still had 25,000–30,000 fully equipped and mobilized troops.

Cases of failed RMI, often leading to or constituting an element of a wider failure of the peace process, are also a common theme within the literature. The Cambodian peace settlement provides a case of failed implementation of military measures. The Paris Agreement, signed in 1991, called for the regrouping, cantonment, and disarmament of at least 70 percent of the forces of each of the four warring factions—the State of Cambodia, the faction headed by Son Sann, the Royalist faction led by Prince Norodom Ranariddh, and the Khmer Rouge—with the remaining 30 percent to be incorporated into a new national army. Although the State of Cambodia government and the two noncommunist factions cooperated to varying extents, the Khmer Rouge refused to regroup and disarm its forces (Hoddie and Hartzell, 2003).[4]

One + One = Three

There are as many approaches to RMI as there are contexts in which it has been attempted. Judging success within any given context requires a detailed understanding of the requirements of a given conflict resolution process. No universal concept or approach to RMI exists, although Licklider suggests that "Integration means that individuals are brought into the new military in positions similar to the ones they occupied in prior organizations which were in combat with their own."[5]

Two distinct contexts, military defeat and political defeat, can be identified. South Africa, Zimbabwe, and Namibia are examples of political defeat, whereby undefeated militaries were required to merge into a single entity. Within the context of political defeat, the approach that has achieved the most recognizable success is defined as the "*1 + 1 = 3*" approach. This highlights the requirement for two separate military structures and cultures to merge. Success is achieved when no single structure or culture dominates the merged force. Instead, a "third force" results from the RMI process: hence the 1 + 1 = 3 formula. The second scenario, where one group is militarily defeated or a national military incorporates a much smaller regional secessionist military group, often results in the smaller (or defeated) force being subsumed in the existing structures and culture of the national military.

The case of the Moro integration within the Filipino military highlights the problems of cultural assimilation and the need to create new programs and approaches as problems arise. The South African, Zimbabwean, and Namibian case studies highlight the advantages of utilizing the existing military structures and personnel of a politically defeated military within the RMI process. In South Africa, the process included programs to upgrade the capacity of ANC (African National Congress)/MK (Spear of the Nation) personnel through education and staff training so they could assume senior ranks within the new South African National Defence Force (SANDF).

Bosnia saw a phased approach that resulted from significant international support. The first step was to bring the Croat and Bosniak forces together. This process went fairly smoothly. The major instrument was a $250 million Train and Equip program, developed by the United States and funded by the U.S., Saudi Arabia, Kuwait, United Arab Emirates, Malaysia, and Brunei with the aim of establishing military parity between the Federation Army and the Republik Serbska forces. In return, the United States required that the Bosnian and Croatian forces be integrated at the upper levels, although initially not at the lower levels. The program involved substantial amounts of equipment and training and joint planning at high levels. Subsequent phases of planning called for integration at the lower levels. There were to be three regiments, one each made up of Serbs, Croats, and Bosniaks, and each consisting of three battalions. However, the regiments would not be operational units.[6]

The approach adopted in Burundi consisted of demobilizing forces, creating a constitution for the National Defence Force, and wider security sector reform. The Burundian government signed agreements with the different rebel forces stipulating that they would be brought in, jointly disarmed, and then integrated into what would be a transformed army and police force. The process was hindered by the government's delay in producing a budget and financing the integration process. Although the army was supposed to be working with the rebels to create new security forces, it was still deployed fighting the rebel National Liberation Front (FLN). Eventually, the Demobilization, Disarmament, and Reintegration (DRR) process moved forward.

The RMI approach in the DRC required the immediate mixing of different ethnic groups that comprised the forces, with little additional training for senior positions. This process was not fully successful for a number of reasons. Rank alignment in terms of officer ranks was based on seniority within militia groups. Retraining and training did not take into consideration issues such as human rights, the rule of law, and civil oversight. While both unit and single combatant integration took place, soldiers moved towards leaders and brigades of their own ethnicity, thus polarizing the new National Military (FARDC). One consequence was that soldiers were reluctant to accept postings in regions where their ethnic group was not seen to be in charge. Old rivalries from the civil war remain and have led to an escalation in tensions between different brigades. Officers were not immune from this ethnic rivalry. Some leaders who were made senior ranking officers within the army on account of their previous militia seniority have simply built a personal support base of soldiers within the FARDC.

In Namibia, the integration process faced language barriers, hostility, and distrust between former enemies, as well as lack of infrastructure. The British Military Advisory Training Teams (BMATTs) in Namibia drew on lessons learned in Zimbabwe, concentrating advice and training at a more senior level and "training the trainers." The training course included both South African and Soviet-bloc techniques that had been employed by ex–SWATF (South West Africa Territory Force) and ex–PLAN (People's Liberation Army of Namibia) members, respectively. However, British Army methods were given precedence, which helped to integrate the Namibian Defence Force (NDF) and foster a sense of Namibian identity. The Namibian RMI is an instructive case of the 1 + 1 = 3 process with external assistance. Neither of the two militaries' structures or cultures gained ascendancy; instead, the RMI resulted in a third force and new military culture.

The South African approach entailed training and education of ex-rebels. Initially, former South African Defence Force (SADF) officers continued to occupy senior command and staff positions within the new SANDF, especially while ex–ANC/MK officers were involved in extensive training programs. By 1998, there were shifts in the balance of power in the SANDF, and the integration process began in earnest. After a failed power play by General George Meiring, he and other ex–SADF officers were compelled to retire from the SANDF, which opened the door to integration in the higher ranks. A cohort of ex–ANC/MK officers who had completed their compulsory training were promoted into senior command and staff positions.

The RMI process in Zimbabwe welcomed all wishing to launch military careers into the Zimbabwe National Army. The plan was to fully train between 30,000 and 35,000 troops by the end of 1980 and ultimately reach a total of 45,000, which represented a compromise between a larger ideal strength of more than 60,000 and the need to contain costs. From the Zimbabwe African National Liberation Army (ZANLA) and the Zimbabwe People's Revolutionary Army (ZIPRA), 9,500 members were expected to join the army. The remaining 23,000 guerrillas were to become reservists. Rather than relying on former Rhodesian Army officers, the new Zimbabwe government called on the United Kingdom to take a leading role in training the Zimbabwe National Army (ZNA) and for financial assistance. In June 1980, the British government responded by sending a BMATT to assist in creating and integrating the ZNA. At the BMATT's request, former ZANLA and ZIPRA commanders provided 300 leaders and 400 rank-and-file members for each of the 15 planned battalions. BMATT trained senior officers, middle-ranking officers, and noncommissioned officers and soldiers. After 6 weeks of basic infantry training, segments were combined before deployment to remote areas. By July 1980, battalions were being formed at the rate of two per month. However, plans to divert a large number of demobilized guerrillas to development work failed, and they had to be integrated into the ZNA as well, further accelerating the formation of battalions.

The Philippines' RMI in Mindanao adopted a two-track approach, for police and military forces. The settlement, signed in September 1996, called for the integration of 7,500 members of the Moro National Liberation Front (MNLF) rebels' military wing into the national army and security forces and the establishment of a regional security force in Mindanao. Implementation of the measures proceeded apace, with at least 6,750 MNLF members integrated into special and auxiliary units of the Armed Forces of the Philippines (AFP) and the Philippine National Police (PNP) 4 years after the settlement was signed.

The Government of the Philippines' order in October 1997 to integrate over 4,000 members of the MNLF into the AFP and the PNP took place without disarming the combatants. Retrospectively, a number of incentives were offered, such as modest cash allowances, but that made little difference to the proliferation of weapons. The integration process into the AFP took 3 years, while integration into the PNP took 5. The integration began with processing followed by individual training and then on-the-job training and deployment. The training for integration into the AFP was carried out separately from the original AFP forces. Once completed, combatants would merge into existing AFP units. A quota system was set up for different ranks, with quotas for officers, soldiers, and auxiliaries being filled by selection and testing.

With MNLF combatants leaving a highly politicized and religious movement, there were initial problems between the "integrees" and their new colleagues. The recruits felt they were misunderstood. Moreover, they were not used to the rigid hierarchical structures of the AFP and PNP since their movement emphasized equality between trainer and teacher. An "internalization" program was then established for ex-combatants, which included counseling to counter their previous political beliefs and a psychocultural program to harmonize the relationships between the ex-combatants and their new colleagues.

The case studies clearly suggest that in contexts of political defeat, where neither military force achieved a decisive victory, a 1 + 1 = 3 formula should be applied to the process of rebel-military integration. This formula indicates that two separate forces integrating should result in a new third force; neither of the existing militaries' structures, personnel, or cultures should dominate the integrated force.

RMI Defined by the Political Situation

Hoddie and Hartzell highlight how RMI is often used in conjunction with political power-sharing agreements.[7] Power-sharing is understood within the context of a wider peace agreement and entails any formal arrangement for the distribution of political positions (cabinet posts, legislative seats, etc.), as well as sharp departures from previous exclusionary systems if the new system formally includes minority groups and allows factions associated with the rebels to participate in elections. A common conclusion, supported by the case studies, argues that pursuing RMI outside of the context of a political settlement is unlikely to work and that RMI should be promoted as a peacekeeping strategy only as a part of a multidimensional approach to peace-building.

Some cases provide evidence on the ways power-sharing might work together with RMI. In some peace-building success stories, the rebel army transformed itself into a political party and engaged in nonviolent political competition, while also being integrated into the military or police (El Salvador, Mozambique, Djibouti). But in other cases, political competition led to more instability (Angola, Rwanda, Chad). Power-sharing and RMI seemed to be mutually reinforcing in several cases, as in Tajikistan and Uganda, where commanding officers from both sides were heavily involved in the design of the peace process. In Mali, high-ranking Tuareg officers were integrated into the high command of the army and were also appointed to key nonmilitary government positions. In cases such as Bangladesh and Papua New Guinea, where power-sharing amounted to increased regional autonomy for the rebels, there should be less of a need for RMI if the autonomous regions are given the authority to self-police. In most of the cases that were reviewed, RMI preceded and supported political reforms, including power-sharing.

It is a clear lesson from past RMI processes that the political solution to ending the conflict is the most pressing contextual factor in which the RMI will be implemented. The RMI process will more likely be successful if it closely reflects the prevailing political solution and neither party to the conflict attempts to gain an undue advantage through the RMI outcome.

RMI as "Credible Signs of Intent"

Hoddie and Hartzell develop a theory to explain why peace settlement implementation is important for building an enduring peace in states emerging from violent civil conflict.[8] By implementing the provisions of an agreement, it is suggested that leaders of the compromising groups are unambiguously signalling their genuine commitment to peace. These signals are understood to be credible because they are associated with heavy costs to the implementing parties in terms of both an immediate loss of political power vis-à-vis their competitors in the war and the likely loss of support among the more militant members of their own groups. It is argued that it is the willingness to endure these costs in an effort to demonstrate a preference for stability that allows former antagonists to surmount security concerns and move toward a self-sustaining peace.[9]

Implementation thus serves as a concrete signal of a genuine commitment to peace as signatories to an agreement prove willing to endure the costs associated with both compromising their original war aims and withstanding challenges from within their own groups.

Prior to the signing of a settlement, an army provides the greatest degree of security for a group as well as the most obvious source of leverage vis-à-vis adversaries. In most cases, the implementation of a RMI arrangement requires that organizations and individuals forgo the capacity to protect their own interests and instead entrust their security to the newly established institutions of the postwar state. Therefore, intense feelings of insecurity and resistance are likely to emerge around this issue, especially if the implementation of provisions limits a group's capacity to provide for its own security.

Glassmyer and Sambanis's examination of case studies suggests that overcoming mistrust is very difficult and that constant reassurance is needed throughout a peace process.[10] RMI can help build trust, but integration must be deep and well structured. A good example is Tajikistan, where the armies were integrated into the national army unit by unit. There was no within-unit integration, and planning for RMI involved the military command from both sides, which helped address the mistrust that built up during the war.

However, if RMI is poorly structured or incomplete, these studies suggest that it is associated with increased risk of peace failure. Delays create suspicion, and implementation delays can cause a return to violence. But more frequently, RMI implementation delays are a symptom of a failing peace process rather than a cause of it. In Sierra Leone, the RMI specified under the Abidjan agreement of 1996 was never implemented, but the ceasefire leading up to Abidjan had broken down soon after signing and before substantive implementation was initiated. Angola in 1994 is another example. RMI was an integral part of the peace process, with a plan to create a new national army split evenly between rebels and government troops. With an inflow of foreign assistance and 7,000 UN peacekeepers, the process could move fast, but at least 15,000 of UNITA's troops were never demobilized, and this undermined the entire demobilization process. The rebel leader, Savimbi, stalled at each turn of the peace process, and by mid-1997 only a small percentage of the rebels had been integrated. Fighting recommenced in 1998. UNITA demonstrated a general lack of commitment to the peace, and this was not due to the failure of RMI.

The cases reviewed and the consensus of the studies show that there was not a clear causal chain: sometimes failure to implement RMI can lead to peace failure, but at other times it is a general deterioration of the peacebuilding environment that can explain RMI failure. An RMI process requires parties to a conflict, and individuals engaged in the conflict, to forgo the instruments that are seen to provide for their security. Therefore, intense feelings of insecurity and resistance are likely to emerge around the RMI issue. Progress on integration greatly enhances the wider process of reconciliation. RMI constitutes credible signals of conciliatory intent among former enemies.

Individuals' Economic Imperatives

Glassmyer and Sambanis explore the relationship between RMI serving a primarily security and an economic objective.[11] Their discussions are based on the premise that the RMI security guarantees are credible. RMI cannot offer credible security guarantees if there are severe imbalances in the numbers of rebels and government soldiers that are integrated into a new national army, since large power asymmetries imply that the stronger side can easily unilaterally defect from the agreements. If the cases show evidence that RMI is used despite large power asymmetries, that would be evidence more consistent with the economic mechanism than the security mechanism.

The case studies suggest that RMI rarely results in the integration of equal numbers of rebels and government soldiers, though in some cases the army is expanded substantially and absorbs many rebels. In Uganda, Museveni's National Resistance Army (NRA) expanded from 15,000 in the late 1980s to over 100,000 by 1992 as it absorbed fighters from other groups. In many other cases, rebels agreed to integrate even when the government forces would far outnumber them, as in South Africa, where the former government army constituted nearly 80 percent of the new army.

Cases of RMI after military victory also do not fit the security mechanism. In Nigeria, after the Biafran war (1967–1970), Biafran rebels were reintegrated into the army from which they had broken away to start their rebellion. Their military defeat clearly implied that integration would not provide them with a security guarantee, and it could only be seen as a political or economic strategy by the government to foster stability by restoring those soldiers to their jobs. After military mutinies in the Central African Republic, rebel leader Lieutenant Parfait Mbaye insisted that his men be permitted to return to barracks rather than be demobilized. The 200 defeated mutineers did not pose a significant security threat to the government, so reintegrating them in the army was not intended to resolve a security dilemma, but rather was a low-cost way to decrease the rebels' incentives for continued fighting.

Glassmyer and Sambanis conclude that in most cases that were reviewed, economic incentives seem to drive the process.[12] This was evident even where the military was carefully balanced between government and rebel soldiers, as in Mozambique. Likewise, the 1999 peace accord in Congo-Brazzaville describes the parties' concerns over "the reconstitution of [their] careers" through reintegration into the military. In Angola, Jonas Savimbi highlighted the importance of economic concerns, saying that warfare had become the rebels' "raison d'être": these men had no homes and families, let alone jobs, to which they could return. The critical economic function of RMI can explain why it is often pursued even when it cannot offer security guarantees.

A well supported conclusion is thus that the RMI process is often viewed by individual combatants primarily from a livelihood perspective. In cases where RMI could not provide a security guarantee, it was successful by achieving an economic objective.

Police Reform and RMI

The case studies highlight the requirement within any RMI process to pay equal attention to the police force. At the conclusion of internal conflicts, the national police are often viewed as the state's instrument of repression, as was the case in many southern African examples. The ability to transfer individuals from a military organization to a police force is not as straightforward as military integration. The skills and education and professional aptitudes required for effective policing are radically different from those favored within militaries. A comprehensive RMI process should therefore include planning for the individual selection, education, and training of personnel for the police.

A common theme in the case studies is the use of the police, as a uniformed service, serving as a political safety valve for ex-combatants not required or selected by the RMI process to join the military. In Mozambique, a seemingly deliberate policy of the government was to bolster the police force with loyalists, hence creating a political police force. In Namibia, the failure of the civilian reintegration process created pressure on the government from "ex-liberation fighters," which it tried to deal with by creating an auxiliary police force (SFF). This auxiliary force is widely viewed as a political force outside the control of the legitimate state structures.

The police integration process in Burundi was carried out with some difficulty due to poor logistics and the training and reorientation of new elements. The necessity of training newcomers—former guerrillas or ex-government soldiers—for police work posed serious problems. In response, the government appealed to the international community for assistance in police training. By 2007, the integration process had made considerable progress, as evidenced by Burundi's pledge of 1,800 personnel from the integrated security forces to the African Union Mission in Somalia.

In 1994, a Civilian Police (CIVPOL) mission deployed to Mozambique to observe policing activities during the transition and helped to reassure RENAMO. During the demobilization and disarmament processes, CIVPOL officers found that government military troops and equipment were being transferred to the police, especially to the presidential guard. The CIVPOL confirmed that the Liberation Front of Mozambique (FRELIMO) government appeared to be preparing a police force that was loyal to the party. The integration process thus faced problems that included low standards of education and training, a lack of objective criteria in the selection of police candidates, a predisposition among police officers to take bribes, and a lack of resources. The police grew from an estimated 18,000 in 1994 to more than 21,000 in 1998. A UNDP mission in the late 1990s helped to assess and upgrade the police. As a consequence of the assessment and upgrade, more than 300 officers were expelled, corruption was curbed, and crime-fighting potential was increased.

In Namibia, the South West Africa People's Organization (SWAPO) government consolidated its hold on its core supporters and the state security apparatus by employing ex-combatants in public service, especially the uniformed services. The Special Field Force (SFF) branch of the Namibian Police (Nampol) most clearly exemplifies the strategic and volatile position of the ex-combatants. Since the late 1990s, it has incorporated thousands of ex-combatants and now outnumbers the Namibian Police personnel by nearly three to one. The SFF mainly patrols the borders but also supplements other Namibian Police branches elsewhere. It is widely seen as a SWAPO, even presidential, force, while government officials maintain it is a neutral part of the police. The role and mode of operation of SFF has been continually controversial. The media and human rights organizations regularly report on the heavy-handed measures by the SFF against civilians. It has a reputation for casual beating of suspected offenders, has a mandate to use violence beyond official rules and procedures, and operates in the territorial, social, and political margins of the state.

In apartheid-era South Africa, the police were notorious for controlling and suppressing the black population and for widespread human rights abuses. Consequently, the Interim Constitution of April 1994 provided for the creation of a unified South African Police Service (SAPS). The new service inherited more than 140,000 personnel from the SAP and began the process of transformation into a representative and effective crime-fighting and public-protection force. The door was opened to ANC/MK security personnel and others to join, be trained, and rise through the ranks. The process was guided by a white paper, the ANC's Reconstruction and Development Program, and a new national police commissioner. While progress in building an effective national police force was slow and painstaking, it eventually became a positive influence for peace-building, justice, and stability.

Past examples of RMI have shown that police forces and other uniformed services can be misused as a political safety-valve for ex-combatants not required or selected by the RMI process to join the military. A comprehensive RMI process should include planning for the individual selection, education, and training of personnel for the police as a separate process from the formation of the military.

RMI and Civilian Reintegration

As highlighted previously, there exists a strong economic incentive for individuals to take part in an RMI process and gain employment in a reconstituted military. With such a link established, the RMI process should not be conceived or planned separately from any civilian reintegration (CR) processes, but the two should form part of a wider integrated process of transition. In Mozambique, a fairly generous civilian reintegration program made it difficult to staff the new, integrated national army. Intended to be 30,000 strong and drawn equally from FRELIMO and RENAMO, the actual post-war integrated Mozambican army was less than half that size. The CR program ended up with 20,000 more participants than anticipated.

Mali's successful peace process similarly offered both civilian and military integration opportunities. While fewer than 2,000 ex-combatants ended up integrating into the military, more than 9,000 participated in CR, which involved a cash payment and either a small monthly stipend or enrollment in a UNDP credit program, depending on whether they turned in their weapons, plus vocational training and educational scholarships. Of those who took the CR option, about a third opted for the plan that paid more generous benefits yet required turning in a weapon, while 6,000 took the less lucrative plan that did not require handing over a weapon.

Like the program in Mozambique, Mali's CR program reduced the demand for RMI and offered tangible economic benefits to keep the peace.

Several of the cases that were reviewed suggest that CR and RMI are substitutable, and CR is often used to accommodate an "excess supply" of ex-combatants. In Angola's most recent peace process, UNITA combatants who had been formerly integrated into the government army and demobilized were paid 5 months of back pay and given an integration allowance and a reintegration kit of household and farming items. Likewise, in Cambodia in 1998 and Iraq in 1972, former rebel combatants who could not be integrated in the national army were provided with cash payments. This also happened informally in Namibia, where most of the 21,000 or so demobilized soldiers from SWATF (the largest Namibian force to fight for the South African side) continued to take their pay well after the peace process concluded.

While Disarmament, Demobilization, and Reintegration (DDR) is viewed as an essentially civilian project, and army reform as a military initiative, there is nevertheless a fundamental link between their successes. This inherent link is recognized in the DRC through the national documents and operational plans governing the DDR and Army Reform programs, which set out a *tronc commun,* or combined core, for the two programs. The process under the *tronc commun* requires all fighters, whether they are to enter the DDR program or be recruited into the new army, to follow identical procedures that involve awareness-raising, disarmament, identification, and orientation. On November 12, 2004, a law regulating and organizing the unified army (FARDC) came into force. Article 45 of the *Loi portant organisation générale de la défense et des forces armées* (Law on the General Organisation of Defence and the Armed Forces) recognized the key national military entities that were to take part in the process of integration into the FARDC.

Namibia is an example of the RMI succeeding while the civilian reintegration failed. Neither the United Nations nor the new government planned any reinsertion or reintegration assistance to ex-combatants. After independence, many former soldiers of both sides failed to reintegrate economically. In response to protests from disaffected veterans, the government hastily designed a number of ad hoc activities. Consequently, the Namibian demobilization and reintegration program resembles a patchwork of well-intended program responses rather than a strategic government policy and planned program response.

With no coherent targeting mechanism in place and uneven registration to link ex-combatants to the benefits safety net, targeting leakages were numerous and substantial at all stages of the process. The objective of this policy was to address the basic needs of the ex-combatants. The Ministry of Defence estimated that up to 40 percent of eligible ex-combatants did not benefit from severance pay. The Development Brigade (DB), established in 1991 to address the needs of the many ex-combatants who had been unable to secure employment after repatriation, also proved unsuccessful, leading eventually to the establishment of the SFF, as discussed above.

In light of the evidence from the case studies examined, the RMI process should be conceived and planned with a specific Civilian Reintegration component for those individuals not selected for military service. The CR programs should be planned and managed by the same body responsible for RMI to ensure cohesion and equity for all personnel.

Conclusions

This chapter has highlighted the complex and diverse nature of Rebel Military Integration processes. There exist as many approaches and solutions as there are contexts in which it has been attempted. An examination of the available case study material has, however, provided some consistent themes summarized here.

A clear lesson from past RMI processes is that the political solution to ending the conflict is the most pressing contextual factor in which the RMI will be implemented. The political solution to ending the conflict should therefore be the defining framework in which the RMI process is designed and implemented. The case studies indicate that a RMI process will more likely be successful if it closely reflects the prevailing political solution.

Within the context framework where a conflict ended in political defeat, with neither military force achieved a decisive victory, a "1 + 1 = 3" formula should be applied to the RMI process. This formula indicates that two separate forces integrating should result in a new third force; neither of the existing military structures nor their personnel nor cultures should dominate the new integrated force. This formula should guide all external support to RMI processes. Furthermore, external support to RMI should adopt the 1 + 1 = 3 formula as an indication of success if the belligerent parties accept and work towards achieving the concept summarized in this formula.

A key conclusion of this study is that Rebel Military Integration does not lead to peace. The study finds that peace initiatives are more likely to fail where there was an attempt at RMI, but suggests that is because incomplete, poorly structured RMI within peace agreements increases the risks of the failure of the wider peace process. Successfully implementing RMI aspects of peace agreements positively supports the wider peace. Progress on RMI greatly enhances the wider process of reconciliation, as RMI constitutes credible signals of conciliatory intent among former enemies. Implementation serves as a concrete signal of a genuine commitment to peace as signatories to an agreement prove willing to endure the costs associated with both compromising their original war aims and withstanding potential challenges from within their own groups.

RMI should be viewed as an element of wider postconflict peacebuilding and state-building processes; as such, the outcome is rarely predictable. An effective and sustainable solution from one context cannot be assumed to represent a template for a different context. Formulating external support should be based on a comprehensive analysis of the context and the parties and should remain flexible to react to the evolving needs of the parties and the process. An effective strategy for external assistance has been seen to be support directed at the decisionmaking bodies established to implement the RMI process, which are comprised of the belligerent parties. An overarching and consistent theme throughout all case studies examined is the requirement that external support to the RMI process operates on the understanding that "process is outcome"; support to the parties that must make decisions and understanding their capacities to implement their decisions are more effective than supporting "template" solutions.

An RMI process requires parties to a conflict, and individuals engaged in the conflict, to forgo the instruments that are seen to provide for their security. Therefore, intense feelings of insecurity and resistance are likely to emerge around the RMI issue. A well-supported conclusion is that the RMI process is often viewed by individual combatants primarily through an economic or livelihood perspective. In cases where RMI could not provide a security guarantee, it was successful by achieving an individual's economic objectives.

Past examples of RMI have shown that police forces and other uniformed services can often be misused as a political safety-valve for ex-combatants not required or selected by the RMI process to join the military. A comprehensive RMI process should include a second element focused on planning for the individual selection, education, and training of personnel for the police as a separate process to the formation of the military.

The third element of a comprehensive RMI process is the Civilian Reintegration (CR) component for those individuals not selected for military or police service. The CR programs should be planned and managed by the same body responsible for RMI to ensure cohesion of implementation and equity for all personnel.

Notes

[1] This article is a composite version of "SSR: Post-conflict Integration," available at <www.ssrnetwork.net/publications/postconfl.php>, where full details of the case studies can be found.

[2] C. Hartzell and M. Hoddie, "From anarchy to security: Comparing theoretical approaches to the process of disarmament following civil war," *Contemporary Security Policy* 27, no. 1 (2006), 155–167.

[3] K. Glassmyer and M. Sambanis, "Rebel Military Integration and Civil War Termination," *Journal of Peace Research* 45 (2008), 365.

[4] Hartzell and Hoddie.

[5] R. Licklider, "New Armies from Old: Merging Competing Military Forces after Civil War," unpublished, Rutgers University, 2009.

[6] Regiments are purely ceremonial organizations and unlike brigades have no operational, training, or administrative roles. Brigades are the "business organizations." A regimental system embodies the historical military lineage of the component from which it is descended. It reflects symbols and accomplishments with which soldiers identify and maintains the regimental heritage.

[7] M. Hoddie and C. Hartzell, "Arrangements, Civil War Settlements, and the Implementation of Military Power-Sharing," *Journal of Peace Research* 40 (2003), 303.

[8] Ibid.

[9] Ibid.

[10] Glassmyer and Sambanis.

[11] Ibid.

[12] Ibid.

Chapter 5

Allies and Assets: Strengthening DDR and SSR Through Women's Inclusion

By Jacqueline O'Neill and Jarad Vary

Following the signing of the Lusaka protocol in 1994, President Bill Clinton's Special Assistant for African Affairs Donald Steinberg proclaimed proudly that the agreement was "gender neutral." There was not a single provision in it that discriminated against women, he declared.[1]

Steinberg supported the negotiations that brought an end to 2 decades of war that killed half a million people in Angola. As he transitioned to a new role as U.S. Ambassador to the country, he was optimistic that the comprehensive peace agreement would usher in an era of national reconciliation and reconstruction.

Only weeks into his new post, however, Ambassador Steinberg realized that "a peace agreement that is gender neutral is, by definition, discriminatory against women and thus far less likely to be successful." He explains, "The exclusion of women and gender considerations from the peace process proved to be a key factor in our inability to implement the Lusaka protocol and in Angola's return to conflict in late 1998."[2]

Ambassador Steinberg's experiences in Angola are emblematic of those of well-meaning people around the world. Presumably, they don't want to isolate women through targeted or exclusive language and initiatives. They likely feel that identifying women as a group with special needs and interests would create a perception of them as burdensome or distinct from the rest of their communities. They may be concerned that addressing gender-related issues would bring the international community inappropriately close to the private rather than public affairs of the state.[3] Most likely, they also simply assume that women would be included in the services and programs outlined in the peace agreement and that specifying otherwise is unnecessary.

In the case of Angola, however, these approaches and assumptions led directly to profoundly negative consequences. Women were absent from the formal process from the outset. Not one delegation to the peace talks—including those from the United Nations (UN) and the United States—included a single woman. Their absence contributed to a lack of women's perspectives on issues addressed at the negotiations. It also marginalized, and in some cases fully excluded, issues women were more likely to raise, such as sexual violence, abuses by government and rebel security forces, and the provision of key social services. The peace agreement was even based on 13 amnesties that prevented prosecution for atrocities committed during the conflict. Although not specified, these included acts of sexual violence and the use of rape as a weapon of war. As Ambassador Steinberg expressed it, "the amnesties meant that men with guns forgave other men with guns for crimes committed against women."[4]

Challenges stemming from a lack of women's inclusion became clear as parties implemented the agreement. The peace accord proclaimed that military and rebel leaders had exclusive authority to identify combatants. As Disarmament, Demobilization, and Reintegration (DDR) programs began, leaders were asked to produce lists of combatants eligible to participate. Presumably to privilege male colleagues and ensure women remained dependent, most excluded women from their lists. Donors had to scramble to provide support to the vast majority of Angolan women associated with the forces.

When it came time to clear more than a million landmines planted during the conflict, planners prioritized demining roads. The planners consulted almost exclusively with men, so they didn't consider that fields, wells, and forests also needed demining. As the more than two million refugees and internally displaced persons returned to their homes, newly resettled women faced a new wave of landmine accidents as they went out to plant fields, fetch water, and collect firewood.

Ambassador Steinberg claims that the exclusion of more than half of the population of Angola was a major reason the process was viewed as serving the interests of the combatants and warriors and not the general population. Subsequent attempts to build public trust in justice and security sector institutions including the police and military were largely futile, and the opportunity to lay a foundation for sustainable peace was lost.

In short, the cautionary tale of Angola highlights that parties to war are not the same as parties to peace. To exclude women and others with an enormous stake in lasting peace from security sector reform (SSR), DDR, and related programs is to fundamentally hinder the likelihood of success and sustainability. Compelled by lessons in Angola and beyond, Ambassador Steinberg has become one of the world's most effective, committed, and respected advocates for women's inclusion.

Explaining Women's Exclusion from Full and Consistent Participation in DDR and SSR

Rhetoric in the fields of DDR and SSR has no doubt evolved towards greater recognition of the importance of women's inclusion. Operational guidelines are now following rhetorical commitments, with the United Nations, World Bank, Organisation for Economic Cooperation and Development (OECD), North Atlantic Treaty Organization (NATO), civil society, and others issuing guidance aimed at closing the gap between policy and practice.

Yet despite these important advances, women are still not fully and consistently included in DDR and SSR. There are three primary reasons for the absence of a more fundamental shift in approaches to DDR and SSR. First, those driving the underlying processes fail to acknowledge the extent of women's agency during and after conflict, considering them almost exclusively as passive victims. Second, there is a severe lack of awareness of the operational benefits of women's inclusion; it is not yet widely understood or accepted that their involvement is critical to the long-term success of DDR, SSR, and other attempts at stabilization. Third, women remain largely barred from formal peace negotiations where the foundations for stabilization and reconstruction are laid. Critical provisions and considerations related to women's participation in DDR and SSR are therefore often absent from "gender blind" peace agreements.

Exclusion from DDR

Women continue to be underrepresented in DDR initiatives both as ex-combatants participating in programs and as community members advising on program design and supporting reintegration. Reasons for their exclusion vary. Often, planners underestimate the extent and misunderstand the nature of women's participation during conflict. As a result, they design programs that are not prepared to include and serve them adequately. In Liberia in 2003 and 2004, planners expected no more than 2,000 women.[5] Ultimately, the UN disarmed over 22,000[6] and, by some estimates, excluded 14,000 others.[7]

Eligibility criteria for participation are sometimes biased against females. During the first two phases of Sierra Leone's DDR program that began in 1998, adult combatants had to present, disassemble, and reassemble a weapon to be eligible. As in conflicts around the world, serving in combat was but one of many roles women in Sierra Leone filled within the fighting forces. They were also cooks, medics, porters, spies, translators, medical assistants, and forced sex slaves. Not considered "primary" fighters, they typically shared guns with male colleagues and were consequently unable to surrender a weapon. Many women were ordered to give their weapons to men before demobilization.[8] Eligibility in other processes has depended on unit commanders supplying names, leaving the process ripe for manipulation. In some instances, women were not assigned formal ranks in the fighting forces and depended on male colleagues to confirm their roles and ranks.[9] When allowances for ex-combatants are calculated based on rank, the process again leaves women's inclusion in men's hands.

Women who do participate in DDR face unique challenges. For a woman in Sierra Leone to access microcredit as part of the DDR program, she had to be accompanied by a man who was willing to identify her as his wife. This requirement not only disregarded her agency as an adult, but also perpetuated abuse and enslavement in cases where women had been forced into marriage during conflict and sought independence afterwards. In some cases, cantonment sites failed to provide facilities for mothers with infants or even to secure the areas in which women were housed, exposing them to sexual and physical abuse.

Negative stigmas associated with participating in DDR further compound the challenges of serving women. These are often dramatically more severe for females. Returning men may be welcomed as heroic defenders while women are sometimes shunned as likely survivors of rape. In some reintegration programs such as Eritrea's, women are trained in traditional livelihoods for which there is little demand, despite having gained leadership experience in command positions as well as medical, mechanical, and other practical skills.[10]

Finally, as providers of key services related to education and healthcare, heads of households, and moral leaders, women bear a heavy burden for supporting the reintegration of ex-combatants even though they are rarely drawn into reintegration processes as consultants or partners.

Exclusion from SSR

Overwhelmingly, SSR initiatives emphasize narrow descriptions of the security sector, focusing on the traditionally male-dominated spheres of the military, police, intelligence, and judiciary. They normally devote scant time and resources to other areas of the security sector in which women are more commonly active, such as oversight to ensure transparency and accountability by civil society, the media, and parliaments.

When planners do act on the need to recruit women as uniformed police and military, they are often unsuccessful. Recruitment campaigns have tended to fail to grasp women's unique motivations and interests in joining security forces. Many emphasize the physical and aggressive aspects of service instead of components that more commonly appeal to female candidates, such as the opportunity to serve their communities meaningfully, contribute practically to stabilization and lasting peace, and ensure that marginalized survivors of crime can access justice.[11]

At the same time, reforms often do not address the structural issues, policies, and practices that limit women's retention and advancement within security forces. They frequently result in pigeonholing them in support, clerical, noncombat, and other roles deemed less integral to the core of the security service.

In oversight roles, female ministers of defense are a small minority. Few chair parliamentary committees on defense, police reform, and related topics. Women-led civil society organizations are seldom called upon to help shape recruitment and other campaigns or to train military and police personnel directly.

As frustrating as initiatives that fail to engage women in countries undergoing SSR is the lack of training and political commitment by international advisers deployed to provide support. A significant component of modern SSR includes the coaching and advising of local actors by members of security forces from other countries through international advisory missions organized bilaterally or through the United Nations and other multilaterals. While virtually all nations providing SSR advisers profess their commitment to women's full inclusion in peace-building,[12] only a small minority adequately train personnel on the subject. These nations remain ill-equipped to support women's recruitment into security forces and, equally important, to consult and engage them on key security issues within the theater of operations. In some cases, the training is even counterproductive.

Significant numbers of U.S. military personnel report, for example, that prior to deployment to Afghanistan, the only component of their training that refers to women is a section on cultural awareness. Men are told that it is offensive to make eye contact with an Afghan woman and in the interest of preserving women's honor and safety, they should avoid any type of contact or outreach altogether. Many report deploying for 6-month missions, realizing 3 or 4 months into the term that it is indeed possible to engage Afghan women on security issues in culturally appropriate ways. They return home a month or two later and have no mechanism for transferring their contacts and lessons. Similarly, Iraqi women have expressed frustration with U.S. military personnel arriving in their country having been told that Iraqi culture prohibits women from participating in political and public spheres. They note that training fails to acknowledge the significant roles women played in politics and government in Iraq prior to Saddam Hussein's rule and assert that their attempts to regain these advances are jeopardized by outside forces.[13]

Widely varying predeployment training for peace and stability operations is compounded by inconsistent and unchecked levels of top-level political commitment. A 2009 study on UN Security Council Resolution (UNSCR) 1325 on Women, Peace, and Security in Afghanistan examined Provincial Reconstruction Teams (PRTs) led by Italy, the Netherlands, New Zealand, Norway, and Sweden. Researchers determined that despite the proven benefits to the PRTs' operational effectiveness from incorporating UNSCR 1325, the initiative remained entirely with the leadership of the PRTs rather than constituting a systematic approach. Adherence to principles of women's inclusion and engagement depended on the will of individual commanders.[14]

Nevertheless, there are some positive practices that have enabled greater women's engagement in DDR and SSR. In DDR, for instance, when the North Atlantic Treaty Organization (NATO) commenced Operation *Essential Harvest* in 2001 to disarm ethnic Albanian groups in Macedonia, officials deliberately solicited women's participation in NATO's public education and information strategy. According to a branch chief in the UN Department for Disarmament Affairs, the operation was highly successful.[15]

The paradigm for NATO's strategy in Macedonia was an earlier weapons collection initiative in Gramsch, Albania. With support from the UN Development Fund (UNIFEM) and the UN Development Programme (UNDP), women raised public awareness about the disarmament initiative with a variety of rallies and workshops, as well as a call-in program on a local TV station.[16] Women's groups called on all citizens to "stop guns" and sponsored tapestry design competitions under the slogan, "Life is better without guns." Where the project was implemented, 6,000 weapons and 150 tons of ammunition were collected.[17] Analysts noted that many weapons were turned in explicitly as a result of women's participation.[18]

In the Democratic Republic of the Congo, Burundi, and elsewhere, organizers rightfully separated males from females in demobilization camps. In Liberia, they provided gender appropriate medical screening.[19] Colombia is taking important steps towards collecting gender-disaggregated data on the success of reintegration efforts.

Responding to the shortage of female applicants able to meet literacy and educational requirements, in 2007 the Liberian National Police, the United Nations, and the Government of Liberia instituted a program in which young women receive scholarship funds to enroll in an accelerated educational program that qualifies them for police recruitment.[20] In parts of the Royal Netherlands Army, and increasingly in other NATO militaries, Afghan women are engaged to help train and interact with soldiers in pre-deployment training.[21]

Yet significant challenges persist. Innovative approaches adopted in one context are often not transferred to others, while operational guidance can be slow to disseminate and often lacks specificity. Overall, the extent to which DDR and SSR fully include, consult, and serve women depends enormously on the commitment of specific individuals. Without strong and innovative champions for women's inclusion, there is little progress.

Challenge One: Planners and Policymakers Fail to Acknowledge Women's Agency

It would be unfair to assert that women are excluded from systematic, full, and meaningful participation in DDR and SSR because planners and policymakers simply don't care enough about them. Although still insufficient, there is significant and growing attention placed on the horrible and disproportionate impacts of war on women, including the abhorrent and increasing use of rape as a weapon of modern warfare. Rhetoric and responses are focusing on the need to protect women, deliver services to them, and enable them to access justice.

Discourse, however, overwhelmingly emphasizes women's victimhood. Often lumped into the infantilizing category of "women and children," they are widely perceived as submissive victims of the tragedies of war rather than capable agents who are combatants and activists during conflict and peace-builders and even spoilers following it. As a result, they are often viewed primarily as passive recipients of DDR and SSR, not as partners who could assist in design and support implementation. Dutch Major General Patrick Cammaert (Ret.), former UN Force Commander in Eastern Congo and in Ethiopia and Eritrea, described the need to move beyond considering women as security beneficiaries and see them as valuable security providers who bring needed comparative operational advantages.[22]

To appreciate the extent of women's agency and potential contributions to DDR and SSR, it is important to understand the nature and extent of their roles during and after conflict.

Women as Combatants

Women fight in virtually every conflict. They engage in combat, operate weapons, spy on enemies, and direct men and women within their command. Their presence is often sparsely acknowledged, however, and their roles are poorly documented.

Rates vary, but women are thought to account for between 10 and 33 percent of most fighting forces.[23] In El Salvador, for instance, 25 percent of combatants in the Frente Farabundo Martí para la Liberación Nacional (FMLN) were women.[24] They were roughly 30 percent of Sandinista fighting forces in Nicaragua[25] and as much as 20 percent of fighting forces in Peru's Shining Path.[26] Within Sri Lanka's Liberation Tigers of Tamil Eelam (LTTE), they made up a third of all fighters, and in some cases were organized into distinct women-led battalions.[27] In Sierra Leone, a third of women in some forces said they had fighting experience.[28] They accounted for between a third and half of Viet Cong troops.[29]

Women also assume leadership positions. They have been senior commanders in Sudan's People's Liberation Army (SPLA), the Afghan national army, Spain's Basque separatist organization (ETA), and the Revolutionary Armed Forces of Colombia (FARC).[30] A woman served as deputy commander of the entire Viet Cong insurgency operation in South Vietnam.[31]

Women combatants participate with notable frequency in national liberation struggles. They fought in the Bolshevik Revolution,[32] the Communist Revolution in China,[33] and Castro's Cuban Revolution.[34] Eritrean rebels[35] and Sri Lanka's Tamil Tigers[36] are among several groups said to have attracted women fighters in part because they espoused an ideology of women's equality. In Guinea-Bissau, "Women were recruited before their husbands on many occasions, because they were so totally absorbed by the ideas of the revolution."[37]

Technological innovations and the changing nature of combat have led to new roles. Terrorists in particular have taken advantage of commonly held perceptions that women are nonthreatening and unlikely to commit acts of violence. In Sri Lanka, the LTTE pioneered the use of female suicide bombers and deployed them on key missions, including the assassination of former Indian Prime Minister Rajiv Gandhi in May 1991. A suspected LTTE female suicide bomber blew herself up at a busy railway station in Colombo in 2008, killing at least 14 and injuring 100. In 2002, women bombers emerged in the Middle East, when the military wing of Fatah took responsibility for a suicide bombing by a Palestinian woman that killed one Israeli civilian and approximately 140 others.[38] Later that year, women made up a significant portion of the Chechen rebels who invaded a Moscow theater, reportedly wearing suicide bombs. In several instances, women have planted bombs under their clothing and feigned pregnancy, gaining access to crowded areas and evading searches.[39]

The threat of women suicide bombers has become so significant that in 2008, the U.S. Department of Homeland Security and Federal Bureau of Investigation issued a Joint Homeland Security Assessment that noted, "The enlistment of women from Chechnya, India, Iraq, Pakistan, the Palestinian territories, Sri Lanka, and Turkey for suicide attacks may well represent a growing phenomenon internationally. Female suicide bombers have been especially effective in Sri Lanka and Iraq."[40]

Women as Activists and Peacebuilders

In all parts of the world, women spearhead efforts for peace and mediate between warring factions. Following conflict, they work to build reconciliation.

In 2002, the Colombian government broke off formal negotiations with the FARC and initiated a major armed offensive. Women's groups, united across the ideological spectrum, responded with a protest march 40,000 strong against the war and the growing militarization of society. The organizers roused the desire for peace in the female population and built the women's coalition into leaders of the movement in Colombia.[41]

In 1999, women from Sierra Leone, Liberia, and Guinea banded together to fight for an end to the brutal conflict in their countries. Facing intransigence from three Presidents who had vowed to never talk to one another, the Mano River Women's Peace Network used unorthodox tactics including threatening to lock the President of Guinea in a room until he agreed to attend negotiations.[42] Thousands of women came together again in Liberia in 2004 to nonviolently force a resolution to stalled peace talks.[43]

Naga women used innovative approaches to mediate among armed actors and mobilize for peace and reconciliation in northeastern India in 1997. As the ceasefire faltered, they began to negotiate successfully with Indian security forces, underground armed opposition forces, and a variety of tribal factions and groups to sustain it. Women also led intercommunity and intertribal events and ceremonies considered key to promoting long-term peace and reconciliation.[44]

Rwandan women are widely credited with leading reconstruction and reconciliation after the 1994 genocide. Following the conflict in East Timor, women's groups helped establish the Truth Commission within the Commission for Reception, Truth, and Reconciliation.[45]

In Sri Lanka, Women Waging Peace Network member Visaka Dharmadasa, founder of the Parents of Servicemen Missing in Action and the Association of War-affected Women, designed and facilitated track two dialogues, bringing together influential civil society leaders from both sides of the conflict. In 2002, as peace talks were faltering, the LTTE refused direct contact with the government, accusing it of noncompliance. LTTE leaders conveyed their concerns to the government through Ms. Dharmadasa, foreign diplomats, and Norwegian negotiators. She remained an impartial bridge between the parties for years.[46]

In Uganda, minister of state Betty Bigombe negotiated unprecedented access to the leader of the Lord's Resistance Army (LRA), Joseph Kony. Her work culminated in 1994's "Bigombe" peace talks. From 2004 until 2006, she served as the Ugandan government–named chief mediator for talks with the LRA.[47]

Women as Service Providers

The task regularly falls to women to maintain public services during and after crises. In the course of the Taliban reign in Afghanistan, for example, it was primarily they who continued to educate girls, organizing secret schools, invariably in the face of enormous personal risk.[48] During a decade of civil war in Bougainville, clandestine women's organizations ensured the delivery of critical social and humanitarian needs, including food, clothing, medicine, and educational services. "At the time," according to Sister Lorraine Garasu of the Bougainville Interchurch Women's Forum, "movement restrictions meant that these clandestine networks were the only source of emergency assistance."[49]

The extent of women's leadership in restoring communities following natural disasters also demonstrates their commitment and capacity to rebuild. After Hurricane Mitch devastated the flood-prone Bajo Lempa region of El Salvador in 1998, they led the recovery, organizing community meetings to rebuild levees and pressuring the government and industry for aid.[50] As Haiti struggled to rebuild after the crippling January 2010 earthquake that affected more than three million people, UNIFEM's Country Programme Director Kathy Mangones reported that there, too, women and women-headed organizations led the way.[51]

Challenge Two: Women's Contributions to Effectiveness Not Widely Understood

Among practitioners of DDR, SSR, and other areas of stabilization, there is a growing interest and openness to including women throughout the process. Individuals express willingness to "mainstream gender" because it advances human rights, contributes to a broad notion of justice, is felt to be "the right thing to do," is a new global standard, and/or is understood to be an operational directive. Rarely, however, is full inclusion throughout DDR and SSR linked directly to mission mandates and desired operational outcomes. Simply put, it is seldom cited as an effective way to reach broader and more fundamental goals.

Consultations with women community leaders, demobilization of female combatants, partnerships with women-led organizations, recruitment into the police and military, and other actions are not peripheral activities to add on only after a process is designed and extra funding appears available. They are core to the effectiveness, legitimacy, and sustainability of DDR, SSR, and other stabilization and reconstruction efforts.

Acknowledging the operational, not just ethical, imperatives of including women strengthens commitment and resolve. It can bring about genuine partnerships and collaboration. In the long run, it saves money and time and lays a stronger foundation for sustainable peace.

Contributions to DDR

Disarmament. Women have proven effective partners in efforts to disarm combatants despite being brought into the process late and at times never formally invited at all. They often assert that they are the most committed and natural allies for international actors in the disarmament process. They want hostilities to end and peace and stability to return. They also generally want fewer weapons in their communities and homes. The authors of *Sexed Pistols: The Gendered Impacts of Prolific Small Arms* note that the presence of a gun in the home increases the likelihood that domestic violence will result in death.[52] As rates of domestic violence often increase in postconflict communities, disarmament can take on a unique imperative for women.

Women's organizations around the world have led planned and spontaneous initiatives to disarm fighters and remove small arms from communities. In Mali, women organized a public burning of more than 3,000 weapons, the "Flame of Peace," in 1996.[53] During Bougainville's civil war, they went into the jungle to disarm and demobilize rebel fighters.[54] After a peace treaty was signed in 2001, they insisted on the destruction of all weapons on the island.[55] In Liberia in the late 1990s, they pressed for disarmament as a precursor to elections. They advertised for women to join the movement across the country and stationed at least one woman at every arms collection point. They encouraged fighters to hand in their weapons and offered them water and food. Estimates indicate that some 80 percent of weapons were collected in 1996 prior to the election.[56]

Liberian women were again at the center of disarmament efforts 7 years later. In December 2003, after several years of horrific violence ended in a peace treaty and the removal of President Charles Taylor, the UN Mission to Liberia (UNMIL) planned to disarm combatants by offering U.S. $300 for weapons. The UNMIL site in Monrovia had space for 1,000 combatants, but over 12,000 arrived for the promised money. Riots ensued at the disarmament site.[57] Without training or equipment, Liberian women helped the well-armed UN peacekeeping troops do what they could not do alone: put an end to the chaos. As mothers and moral leaders, they appealed directly to ex-combatants to cease rioting and surrender their weapons.[58]

Reintegration. Through organizations and as individuals, women provide services and support essential for the reintegration of male and female former combatants. When researchers in Sierra Leone asked ex-combatants to identify those who played a significant role in helping them reintegrate, 55 percent named women in the community. Only 20 percent cited traditional leaders while 32 percent named international aid workers.[59]

The reasons given in Sierra Leone echo those cited by ex-combatants around the world. They noted the moral influence women have in families and communities, namely the power they hold as heads of households and village leaders to determine whether returning fighters will be ostracized or welcomed back. Without genuine acceptance within social structures, prospects for sustainable reintegration in economic, professional, and virtually all other areas are significantly decreased. Women in Sierra Leone helped shape attitudes towards ex-combatants, while many, including mothers whose children were killed during the war, opened their homes to former child soldiers. Ex-combatants also said women shared meager resources and delivered childcare—a service not provided through official DDR programming and without which many would not have been able to participate in education and training.[60]

Local organizations led by women play equally important roles in facilitating reintegration. They provide support, training, and economic opportunities that are essential complements to formal DDR programs. In some cases, they wholly replace inadequate or failed initiatives.

Women-led organizations, for example, help vulnerable ex-combatants gain economic self-sufficiency. In El Salvador, the organization "Las Dignas" trains low-income women and single mothers in trades that have traditionally been dominated by men, such as carpentry, masonry, and auto mechanics.[61] In Cambodia, the "Help the Widows Association" provides microcredit for trade and agriculture.[62] In Sierra Leone, women's groups were central to reintegrating male and female child soldiers, and many organized themselves to care for children coming out of fighting forces.[63]

Women-led organizations also focus on social issues. When conflicts end, for example, and men return to their families, many find their home lives have changed. Women who stayed behind acted as heads of household and in many cases began earning their own incomes. Dealing with the trauma of war and unfamiliar roles in the home, many men have difficulty adapting to civilian life. Gender based violence often escalates in the period after conflict.[64] Organizations such as the Leitana Nehan Women's Development Agency (LNWDA) in Bougainville work with men to ease this transition back to society. As Helen Hakena of LNWDA explains, "Our anti-violence workshops help men and boys understand that the guns and violence of their childhood are not a necessary part of their futures."[65] LNWDA programs bring hardened former guerilla fighters to talk to younger males in the community about the social impact of violence against women. Other groups, such as "The Women's Rehabilitation Centre" in Nepal, address the aftermath of gender-based violence, providing psychosocial assistance and counseling for traumatized survivors.[66]

Groups of women ex-combatants fill another niche in the reintegration process. These groups, some including men and some not, organize their fellow ex-fighters to support each others' peaceful reentry into society. They are sources of empathy and acceptance, in particular for women who find mainly fear and rejection in their communities. In Mozambique, former soldiers and disabled veterans worked together to form ProPaz, an organization that provides peace education in the community, conducts interventions in violent outbreaks at the local level, and promotes the reintegration of women combatants locally and nationally.[67]

Recommendations for Strengthening DDR

1. Set Accurate Targets for Women's Participation

a. Prioritize ascertaining the number and percentage of women and girls in armed groups as well as their ranks, training, roles, and responsibilities. Seek to determine how and why women joined, directly interviewing women to the greatest extent possible.

b. To guard against the most harmful outcomes when accurate data is unattainable, adopt a conservative expectation that women will account for 15 percent of combatants.

2. Adopt Nondiscriminatory Eligibility Criteria

a. Adopt a broad definition of combatant that accounts for the range of duties women assume in most conflicts.

b. Ensure eligibility criteria are not limited to requirements that women are least able to fulfill.

c. If a disarmament program does require a gun for access, allow women to enter DDR at the demobilization stage.

d. Ensure trained female staff are present to interview and assess women combatants. Train male staff on gender sensitivity in interview and assessment processes.

3. Design Gender-Sensitive Assembly and Cantonment Facilities

a. Enable men and women to register separately. Issue each combatant his or her own identity card as opposed to issuing one card per couple or family.

b. Create and secure separate housing for women and men in the cantonment site.

c. Create a separate health facility for women, girls, and young children staffed by trained female doctors or nurses. Provide birth kits, voluntary HIV testing, and vaccinations.

d. Provide women with separate latrines, washing, and kitchen facilities in well-lit and open areas to prevent sexual violence and harassment.

e. Provide fuel, food, and water so women do not have to leave the security of the site.

f. Provide childcare and mandate a balance of domestic duties between men and women to ensure all have equal access to briefings, retrainings, and other benefits.

g. Aim for strong female representation among program staff and leadership at all assembly and cantonment sites.

4. Facilitate Women's Full Participation in Training

a. Conduct a thorough labor market assessment to determine the current range of options for employment, cognizant that communities can support only a limited number of professionals in any particular trade. Assess a participant's eligibility based on his or her skills and interests, not on assumptions about appropriate roles for men and women.

b. Promote a balance of long-term professional training and short-term, quick income-generating activities to provide women with the means to quickly prove their economic self-sufficiency.

c. Supply women with tangible proof such as certificates and accreditations upon completion of training.

d. When possible, design and conduct training in close collaboration with family and community leaders.

e. To reduce potential resentment by male family members, consider including the husbands of women ex-combatants in training programs. Offer training for couples interested in creating family-owned small businesses, for example.

f. Provide childcare or encourage communal childcare. Ensure the delivery of training programs is flexible. Schedule training around women's availability and conduct it near homes. Requiring travel and extended periods away from home will exclude many women.

5. *Create Support Systems for Women's Social Reintegration*

a. Provide medical support, counseling, and rehabilitation to wounded, disabled, and traumatized male ex-combatants so the burden of unpaid care-giving work does not deter women from obtaining education and employment.

b. Consult with women combatants to assess their desire to participate in community mental health practices, including cleansing rituals, which may erase stigma and promote the long-term psychological rehabilitation of ex-combatants, but may also reinforce demeaning gender stereotypes or encourage impunity for sexual abuse.

c. Support associations of women ex-combatants.

d. Create a transitional safety net for those women who are rejected by their original communities or who do not wish to return home. Provide housing, healthcare, counseling, and education.

Contributions to SSR

As with DDR, there is no single group more vested in achieving the goals of SSR, nor able to help achieve them, than women. They are natural allies in the pursuit of effective, legitimate, and accountable security for all citizens.

Often traumatized by members of security forces during conflict and unable to access justice afterwards, women have a distinct and first-hand understanding of the consequences of an illegitimate and unaccountable security sector.

Reform that emphasizes women's full inclusion helps increase local ownership as men and women begin to perceive security institutions and forces to be genuinely representative. Moreover, women's inclusion throughout the sector increases legitimacy and at least the perception of reduced corruption. Nicaraguan police, for example, credit massive reforms aimed at increasing the number of women officers in its ranks as a primary driver of a dramatic turnaround in levels of public confidence.[68]

Military and police services. One of the most strikingly undervalued aspects of women's participation in the security sector is the immense and important contribution they make as uniformed police and military. They improve the operational effectiveness of police and military organizations, contribute to achieving core mandates, and improve forces' capacities to serve not just other women, but the needs of the community more broadly.

There is increasing evidence that uniformed women are more likely than their male colleagues to deescalate tensions and less likely to use excessive force. In the United States, the National Center for Women and Policing released a study in 2002 on excessive force and citizen complaints.[69] While women comprised nearly 13 percent of sworn personnel in big city police agencies, only 5 percent of citizen complaints for excessive force and 2 percent of the sustained allegations of excessive force in large agencies involved female officers. The study found that they accounted for only 6 percent of the money paid out in court judgments and settlements for excessive force among these large agencies. It determined that the average male officer is over eight and half times more likely than a female officer to have an allegation of excessive force sustained against him and costs the force up to five times more than the average female officer in lawsuit payouts.[70] Sergeant Marty True, a 16-year veteran of the Special Weapons and Tactics Team (SWAT) of the Fresno, California, Police Department, explains, "I think [female officers] recognize their physical limitations and don't rely on strength to control suspects; they primarily rely on talking their way through situations. In addition, I have never had a situation where force was required to resolve an incident and a female officer was reluctant to use it."[71]

Female police and military officers can perform functions that may be impossible for men. In Afghanistan, for example, a shortage of female officers at border checkpoints has posed serious problems. Male officers are unable to perform physical searches on women, exposing personnel and civilians to risks posed not only by women carrying weapons, bombs, and contraband, but also by male militants disguising themselves as women to avoid searches.

The unique intelligence and knowledge women are often able to gather can be enormously useful. Those traumatized by crimes during conflict are often reluctant to speak candidly with male officers but are willing to communicate with female officers. Violence against women, in particular, is one of the most prevalent crimes in postconflict societies, yet experts believe it remains dramatically underreported. The Liberian National Police credit increases in the number of female police officers patrolling Monrovia with significant increases in reports of domestic vio-

Afghan Women and Provincial Reconstruction Teams: A Model for Collaboration[1]

When presented with arguments for the inclusion of women in security matters, many argue that recruiting women and engaging with women in the community are simply not possible in certain contexts. They assert that cultural norms prohibit female participation in discussions about security.

In every part of the world, however, there are women who want their opinions heard by those making decisions that affect them and their families. It is the responsibility of those driving such decisions to find a way to reach out appropriately.

Almost nowhere is this cultural argument more present than in Afghanistan. However, the experience of NATO forces collaborating with Afghan women in the southern province of Kandahar shows that cultural norms are not immutable, nor do they necessarily represent the ideas and aspirations of all members of society.

The southern provinces are among the most conservative and restrictive in the country. At the Canadian-led NATO base in Kandahar in 2008, military personnel were leading large-scale security and reconstruction efforts, yet their direct contact with citizens was limited almost entirely to barely half the population—Afghan men.

As part of an independent economic empowerment initiative, a Kandahari woman leader arranged for women in the program she coordinated to sell their handicrafts to personnel at the PRT base. As she left the base one day, a female Canadian civil affairs officer approached her and expressed an interest in meeting other Afghan women. The leader offered to convene a small gathering. The groups agreed on a safe, neutral meeting space—the city airport. Female civil affairs officers began meeting regularly with Afghan stay-at-home mothers, farmers, businesswomen, and others. The Canadians began discussions with neutral questions like, "What are your concerns for your children?"

Before long, the Afghan women began sharing information that was highly relevant to the NATO mission. They talked about their pri-

Continued

orities for development, corruption in projects NATO was funding, and regions that were too insecure for NATO to travel through. What they shared was different from what the military was hearing from many Afghan men. Through these informal meetings, NATO benefited from useful information, more representative priorities for reconstruction, and an increased sense of local ownership. People who previously had little understanding of the goals of the NATO mission now felt engaged and committed. Some women even reported discouraging their sons from joining insurgencies.

In June 2008, there was an insurgent attack on the Kandahar prison, leading to the escape of more than 600 Taliban detainees. One of the women participants of the NATO discussion groups lived near the prison and, as the attack began, heard a series of explosions. Wanting information about what was happening, she picked up her mobile phone and called her contact at NATO Civil Affairs. Because of her actions, the Canadian officer learned of the attack a full 10 precious minutes before anyone else at the PRT base was notified. This collaboration was possible because there were women in the Canadian military who could initiate contact with Afghan woman, and because these women appreciated the value of engaging other women in their theater of operations.

Note

[1] Based on *Afghan Women and Provincial Reconstruction Teams: A Model for Collaboration* (Washington, DC: The Institute for Inclusive Security, 2009).

lence. As is true in the United States today, complaints of domestic violence are now the single largest category of calls to police agencies in Liberia.[72]

Through the singular abilities of female officers to reach out and communicate with women in the general community, police and military forces are able to gain a more full and representative picture of the community's security needs. They can learn about the nature and extent of gang violence and recruitment, human trafficking, intimidation and extortion by organized crime, drug use in schools, and much more.

Enrollment increases as women perceive police and military forces as legitimate institutions through which they can contribute to their communities and build careers. Experience shows that women often need to see other women active within their forces to consider service to be an option. In the month after the UN deployed an Indian all-female peacekeeping unit to Liberia in 2007, the Liberian national police received triple the usual number of female applicants. Since that time, as Indian women continue to be visible throughout the capital, recruitment has increased to the point that women make up about 15 percent of the national police.[73]

Finally, the presence of women in security forces—particularly a critical mass of 30 percent or more—can positively impact the way men behave within the community and as colleagues in the police and military. A 2009 study of five provincial reconstruction teams in Afghanistan noted that Dutch military officers had the impression that many Afghan men found the women officers to be interesting. Informants were prone to be more open and even more accepting of female staff, according to the commander of police trainers. According to the PRT commander, talking to a female officer even "loosened men's tongues," which provided the PRT with very useful information.[74]

There is not yet a proven correlation between the presence of a critical mass of women in security forces and the reduced occurrences of sexual exploitation and abuse by those forces, but anecdotal evidence abounds. Gerard J. DeGroot, a history professor and scholar of women in the military at the University in St. Andrews in Scotland, says, "When female soldiers are present, the situation is closer to real life, and as a result the men tend to behave. Any conflict where you have an all-male army, it's like a holiday from reality. If you inject women into that situation, they do have a civilizing effect."[75] As women account for an increasing number of uniformed peacekeepers, police, and military members, rates of sexual abuse and exploitation in those forces are sure to be an area of future research.

Women in oversight capacities. From within parliaments, the executive branch, civil society, the media, and elsewhere, women oversee the reform and continued operations of the security sector. With unique approaches and priorities, they help ensure the sector remains transparent, effective, and responsive to all citizens.

National parliamentarians are able to ensure inclusivity within security forces, introduce codes of conduct, and review human resource policies for discriminatory practices. They authorize the deployment of military forces and draft gender-sensitive legislation. In 2000, parliamentarians in Israel amended the Security Service Law to open all military professions to women.[76] In Uganda and Colombia, parliamentarians are actively engaged in demobilization, in some cases visiting camps to investigate conditions and raising concerns on behalf of constituents.[77] In Rwanda, women parliamentarians drove the creation of legislation criminalizing domestic violence.[78]

Parliamentarians are also able to conduct gender budgeting. The analysis of police, military, and other budgets is identified, addressed, prioritized, and resourced with an eye to ensuring the unique needs of women, men, girls, and boys. The executive is able to initiate the development or modification of a security policy, ensuring review processes are inclusive and gender sensitive.

Within civil society, women and women-led organizations provide input and advice on improving transparency, accountability, and responsiveness to parliamentary committees, in defense review committees, through the media, and to political parties and actors. They also monitor high-level commitments to and implementation of legislation and international commitments including UN Security Council resolutions on women, peace, and security. In Malaysia, for example, the Women's Aid Organization monitors the enforcement of national legislation on domestic violence. Their recommendations have led to modifications to the content and implementation of the legislation.[79] In Cambodia, civil society and women's rights groups are working with government agencies to investigate claims of abuse of the Law on the Prevention of Domestic Violence and the Protection of Victims.[80]

South Africa's 1996–1998 national review of defense policy exemplifies the contributions women make in this field and the benefits of cooperation among civil society, parliament, the executive branch, and the media.[81] In the last decades of apartheid, South Africa's white rulers built a society that was highly militarized and a military that was unaccountable to the majority. The transformation into a representative democracy in the early 1990s would have been incomplete without a new, more democratic and representative security sector.

In the 1980s, anticonscription groups led by women first highlighted the costs of the militarized society. Women academics helped build the theoretical architecture of reform. In the early 1990s, the Military Research Group, founded by influential male and female academics, elaborated the doctrine of human security that laid a foundation for future reforms.

The national review process itself showcased women making important contributions to security sector reform. The insistence of female parliamentarians ensured that the national review was consultative and inclusive. During public consultations, women's groups raised awareness of important issues including gender discrimination and the link between security and the environment.

South Africa's defense reviews encouraged the participation of actors at every level. Public forums drew women's organizations, religious leaders, academics, and defense leaders into informed discussions about priorities for the defense of South Africa as well as methods to replace discrimination with openness in the military. The democratic and participatory nature of the process built national consensus around security issues. The result was increased public confidence and ownership of an institution that was a symbol of repression only a few years earlier.

Recommendations for Strengthening SSR

1. Recruit Women into the Police and Military

a. Set clear and ambitious targets related to the recruitment of women. Communicate these targets widely.

b. Design recruitment campaigns that accurately portray recruits' likely roles and responsibilities. Profile diverse aspects of police and military service; don't focus exclusively on physical aggression.

c. Where necessary, recruit men and women on different days, or create separate sign-up areas when recruitment is happening at the same time so women are not directed or pushed out of the line by male candidates.

d. Offer childcare during recruitment drives.

e. Identify and remove barriers to women's recruitment, including unnecessary physical qualifications.

f. Provide accelerated training and education programs to ensure that women can meet entrance requirements.

g. Include women in teams focused on recruitment and on interview panels. Provide all members of both groups with gender training. Establish review committees to enforce gender-sensitive recruitment and training practices.

h. When appropriate, conduct joint physical and academic training for women and men as a means of promoting force cohesion and respect for female servicemembers.

2. Retain and Promote Qualified Women

a. Ensure men and women receive equal compensation for equal work.

b. Implement mentoring programs and encourage the development of associations of women officers.

c. Develop maternity and paternity policies. Create adapted uniforms for pregnant officers and establish and communicate policies related to the deployment and functions of pregnant women.

d. Ensure that all staff- and servicemembers of every rank undergo mandatory sexual harassment and gender-awareness training. Ensure that senior leaders establish and enforce a culture in which sexual harassment is not tolerated.

e. Include an assessment of gender sensitivity in performance evaluations. Incentivize gender analysis and the inclusion of women by evaluating individuals based on their approaches and results.

f. Base advancement on transparent and objective criteria that reflect actual job requirements. Reward skills such as problem solving, cooperation, and crime prevention. Ensure male and female representation on all panels determining promotion, taking care that panelists are of similar seniority and influence to avoid inserting "token" individuals.

g. Minimize the power of "old boy networks" by relying on independent interviewers and assessments for advancement decisions.

h. Promote women's participation in positions and departments that are regarded as valuable prerequisites to promotion.

i. Avoid concentrating women in domestic violence units and other functions with an emphasis on women's security where they may be marginalized within the larger force and their potential for advancement may be limited.

j. Where appropriate, create different uniforms for men and women.

3. Elevate Inclusion in Oversight and Evaluation

a. Increase women's representation in parliament and government by instituting constitutional or legislative quotas.

b. Use parliamentary prerogatives including budget audits and high-level inquiries to monitor female recruitment and retention in security forces.

c. Encourage the development of a cross-party women's caucus in legislative bodies. These bodies have demonstrated willingness to work across party lines on legislation to promote women's security, including laws to criminalize domestic and sexual violence.

d. Encourage female legislators to sit on defense and other security-related parliamentary committees. Promote women's leadership in interior, defense, and related ministries.

e. Conduct a transparent, consultative, and comprehensive review of national defense and policing. Solicit the input of local and national NGOs, women's organizations, lawyers, academics, media, and citizens.

f. Create national and local-level police liaison boards and other forums for ongoing cooperation between civilians and security actors.

g. Insist that all data collected and evaluated be disaggregated by gender.

h. Ensure that implementation indicators include targets for men and women and that strategies for ongoing monitoring and evaluation of these indicators include, if necessary, differentiated approaches for collecting data related to men and women beneficiaries.

i. Support academic institutions and research programs to promote women's scholarship on security issues.

4. Ensure Women in the Community Experience the Peace Dividend of Greater Security

a. Through training and leadership, ensure that security forces understand their mandate to serve and protect the community and nation as a whole including women and underrepresented groups.

b. Train both genders of all ranks on how and why to engage women in all aspects of the design, delivery, and evaluation of security initiatives. Emphasize contributions to operational effectiveness.

c. Integrate gender perspectives into all training curricula. Do not consign training and discussions on women's engagement to vague sessions on gender, human rights, or diversity. Ensure curricula exist for topics such as human trafficking, domestic and sexual violence, and hate crimes.

d. Consider establishing special police units dedicated to gender-based violence, but beware that such units may be targets for marginalization. Ensure that they possess sufficient authority and credible leadership and are thoroughly integrated within the larger police structure.

e. Adopt a zero-tolerance policy toward sexual abuse and exploitation by security forces.

f. When implementing "community-based policing," ensure women's equal access to justice and security by guaranteeing their representation on community advisory boards by creating close ties to local women's organizations and by holding regular meetings at times and locations that do not impede attendance.

g. Involve women in the community in vetting processes to screen out candidates with a history of perpetrating gender-based violence or atrocities against civilians.

Challenge Three: Women Remain Largely Excluded from Formal Peace Negotiations

Most commonly, it is during peace negotiations that the foundations for DDR and SSR are laid. When women are absent, they miss opportunities to shape the emphasis and approach to these processes and to advocate their own inclusion within them. Their exclusion from formal peace negotiations can kick off a series of miscalculations and oversights that fundamentally undermine the design and implementation of successful DDR and SSR programs, ultimately jeopardizing the sustainability of the entire peace agreement.

Nearly 10 years have passed since the UN Security Council passed SCR 1325, calling for more women to be involved in decisionmaking at every level of peace processes. Yet, UNIFEM reports that since 1992, only 2 percent of the signatories to peace agreements have been women—which includes not only negotiators, but also international mediators and observers. Within negotiating delegations, women averaged about 7 percent of the membership.[82] The UN has never appointed a female chief or lead mediator in UN-sponsored peace talks to date.

When it does occur, women's inclusion in peace negotiations has positive effects on the content as well as the process through which the agreements are negotiated and implemented.[83] Research indicates that when present at negotiations, they broaden the set of issues addressed.[84] They expand the debate beyond military action, power, and wealth-sharing to incorporate social and humanitarian matters.[85] When parties to the talks between the Lord's Resistance Army and the Government of Uganda addressed DDR, for example, Ugandan women urged the parties to prioritize heath and education for ex-combatants. They also expanded the definition of "ceasefire" to include the cessation of gender-based violence committed by combatants.[86] In Guatemala, women ensured the inclusion of unaddressed human rights issues related to police power and civilian oversight of the security sector, maximum working hours for laborers, and indigenous rights.[87]

In Darfur, women played an active role in the seventh round of negotiations of the Darfur Peace Agreement. Although key parties refused to sign the accord, and negotiations did not end the conflict, the agreement remains one of the most gender-sensitive to date. Through a structure called the Gender Expert Support Team, women infused gender perspectives in all three official commissions—wealth sharing, power sharing, and security arrangements. They also gained attention for property ownership, economic empowerment, and a range of other topics.[88]

As participants at peace negotiations, women also influence sensitive group dynamics. The Institute for Inclusive Security reports that female negotiators help establish positive relationships and steer talks away from zero-sum games over political domination. A Canadian observer of the Darfur negotiations, Senator Mobina Jaffer, noted that women raised previously neglected issues that all the parties could agree on, such as food security. These topics served as confidence-building measures. She described the issues as shifting the dynamics of the peace table.[89] In Uganda, U.S. observers to the talks claimed women delegates "greased the wheels," facilitating communication between the parties.[90] In Sri Lanka, women "drew on social roles to create a congenial atmosphere in which delegates could talk and generate trust."[91]

Evidence indicates that women are also prone to advocate for more broadly participatory processes related to peace negotiations. In Guatemala, they proposed and organized consultations with displaced men and women, infusing their voices into formal processes. In Northern Ireland, they drove the creation of a civic forum that enabled civil society to provide input into negotiations and remain up-to-date with the progress of negotiations.[92]

Recommendations for Elevating Women's Inclusion in DDR and SSR Negotiations and Planning

Having a critical mass of women (at least 30 percent) involved in peace negotiations could fundamentally alter traditional approaches to DDR and SSR and increase the likelihood that these programs will more meaningfully serve all members of conflict-affected communities. In the absence of this critical mass, however, there is a great deal that planners and implementers can do to lay a foundation for more gender-sensitive DDR and SSR programs.

1. From the Outset, Involve Women in Program Planning[93]

a. Analyze the extent of women's inclusion in all stages of the peace process, including top-level peace negotiations, needs assessments, constitutional assemblies, and donor conferences.

b. As an incentive, offer negotiating teams extra seats at the table, but only if they are filled by women.

c. Enable women to participate in negotiations as civil society observers, particularly when they do not make up at least 25 percent of negotiating delegations. Fund their participation and ensure they have access to the same resources as negotiators. Ensure they stay in the same hotels as other delegates as negotiations often happen between formal sessions.

d. Guarantee equal funding to negotiators, mediators, and observers regardless of gender for airfare, hotel, meals, and incidental expenses.

e. Establish an advisory group or appoint a dedicated gender adviser in the office of the facilitator or mediator.

f. Hire senior-level gender experts to work hand in hand with planners from the beginning.

g. Work closely with civil society, including women's organizations, at all stages of planning and designing security programs.

2. Profile Senior-Level Male Champions

a. Cultivate influential men in senior positions within a range of organizations to promote the importance of women's inclusion in security issues. Target men with moral and formal authority. Include male negotiators and leaders in the police, military, defense ministries, and other traditionally male-dominated bodies.

b. Regularly provide male champions with data and information on good practices from within the country and around the world.

c. Encourage male champions to be spokespersons on issues of women's inclusion. Profile them in the media and within their own organizations.

d. Ensure training with gender components delivered as part of DDR and SSR are not delivered exclusively by women. Aim for a mixed team of trainers.

3. Target and Engage Women in Community Sensitization and Awareness Raising

a. Engage female leaders and women-led organizations in community sensitization and awareness-raising campaigns. They can help ensure materials are appropriate and meaningful to their target audiences as well as assist in ensuring they are received by women combatants and other potentially hard-to-reach groups.

b. Target female combatants using, if appropriate, radio, posters, and word of mouth to inform them of the availability and advantages of participation in DDR and SSR programs.

c. Ensure visuals used in recruitment and awareness campaigns feature images of women.

d. Prior to reinsertion, hold awareness-raising meetings and consultations with a broad range of actors, including female leaders and women-led organizations, to prepare community members to receive ex-combatants and involve communities in the design of reintegration programming.

e. Disseminate the results of civilian commissions overseeing security sector reforms and DDR initiatives to the public via radio, newspapers, and other media.

Conclusion

Some recommendations put forward in this chapter can be implemented with little or no additional resources. Others imply major changes and require high-level political commitment and transformations in thinking, practice, and sometimes power structures.

Relatively small changes can be integrated into existing DDR and SSR initiatives and lead to concrete improvements in the lives of men and women. Practitioners gain experience and exposure to new approaches, and the resulting successes build the case for why women's inclusion matters.

Marginal changes, however, aren't likely to result in anything more than marginal improvements. Dramatic improvements in the long-term success, sustainability, and cost-effectiveness of DDR and SSR initiatives require fundamentally modified approaches.

The more minor changes can come about because planners and practitioners are obligated by UN Security Council and other resolutions, operational guidance, and/or an inherent sense of justice and equality. The most meaningful changes require individuals with a firm conviction that fully including women in DDR and SSR makes operational good sense. They must consider women's inclusion a security issue, not a soft issue. Fortunately, women are working hard to make this point.

Notes

[1] Donald Steinberg, "Failing to Empower Women Peacebuilders: A Cautionary Tale from Angola," April 25, 2007, available at <http://www.crisisgrouorg/en/regions/africa/southern-africa/angola/failing-to-empower-women-peacebuilders-a-cautionary-tale-from-angola.aspx>.

[2] Ibid.

[3] Louise Olsson describes this idea in "The Namibian Peace Operation in a Gender Context" in *Gender, Conflict and Peacekeeping*, ed. Mazurana, Raven-Roberts, and Parpart (Lanham, MD: Rowman & Littlefield Publishers, 2005).

[4] Steinberg.

[5] C. Coulter, M. Persson, and M. Utas, "Young Female Fighters in African Wars: Conflict and Its Consequences" (Uppsala: Nordic Africa Institute, 2008), 24.

[6] Ibid.

[7] I. Specht, "Red Shoes: Experiences of Girl-combatants in Liberia" (Geneva: International Labour Organization, 2006), 83.

[8] D. Mazurana and K. Carlson, "From Combat to Community: Women and Girls in Sierra Leone" (Washington, DC: Women Waging Peace Policy Commission: Hunt Alternatives Fund, 2004).

[9] N. De Watteville, "Addressing Gender Issues in Demobilization and Reintegration Programs," *Africa Region Working Paper Series* (Washington, DC: The World Bank, May 2002), 3.

[10] A. Mehreteab, "Veteran Combatants Do Not Fade Away: A Comparative Study of Two Demobilization and Reintegration Experiences in Eritrea," Paper 23, Bonn International Center for Conversion, Bonn, 2002, 25.

[11] "Recommendations from Consultation on Recruitment of Uniformed Women for U.S. Police Missions Overseas," developed at a workshop convened by the Initiative for Inclusive Security and the Woodrow Wilson Center for International Scholars, with support from the Bureau of International Narcotics and Law Enforcement Affairs (INL) of the U.S. Department of State, June 20, 2007, Washington, DC, available at <http://www.huntalternatives.org/download/835_policing_consultation_final_recommendations.pdf>.

[12] The UN Security Council unanimously passed Resolution 1325 on October 31, 2000. The resolution reaffirms "the important role of women in the prevention and resolution of conflicts and in peace-building," and stresses "the importance of their equal participation and full involvement in all efforts for the maintenance and promotion of peace and security, and the need to increase their role in decision-making with regard to conflict prevention and resolution."

[13] Remarks by Yanar Mohammed, President of the Organization for Women's Freedom in Iraq, at "The International Gender Justice Dialogue," convened by the Nobel Women's Initiative and Women's Initiatives for Gender Justice, April 20, 2010, Puerto Vallarta.

[14] L. Olsson and J. Tejpar, eds., with B. Andreassen et al., *Operational Effectiveness and UN Resolution 1325—Practices and Lessons from Afghanistan* (Stockholm: Swedish Defence Research Agency [FOI], 2009).

[15] A. Marcaillou, "Gender Perspectives on D, D and R," presented at the United Nations Development Fund (UNIFEM) Seminar, "Gender Perspectives on DDR," New York, March 9, 2004, conference notes.

[16] UNIFEM, "Project Report: Public Awareness Campaign for Voluntary Weapons Collection in Elbasan and Diber," *United Nations Development Fund for Women—Regional Programme for Central and Eastern Europe*, UNIFEM, n.d., available at <http://www.unifem.sk/?module=Project&page=Project&ProjectID=16>, May 10, 2010.

[17] S. Anderlini and C. Conaway, "Disarmament, Demobilisation, and Reintegration" in *Inclusive Security, Sustainable Peace: A Toolkit for Advocacy and Action* (Washington and London: Hunt Alternatives Fund and International Alert, 2004), 6.

[18] V. Farr, "The Importance of a Gender Perspective to Successful Disarmament, Demobilization, and Reintegration Process," *Disarmament Forum*, no. 4 (2003), 29.

[19] Amnesty International, "Liberia: A Flawed Post-War Process Discriminates Against Women and Girls" (London: Amnesty International, 2008).

[20] T. Denham, "Police Reform and Gender" in Megan Bastick and Kristin Valasek, eds., *Gender and Security Sector Reform Toolkit* (Geneva: DCAF, UN-INSTRAW, OSCE/ODIHR, 2008), 17.

[21] Remarks by Captain Stefanie Groothedde of the Royal Netherlands Army, former deputy commander of the Dutch-led provincial reconstruction team in Tarin Kowt, Afghanistan, at the "Consortium Workshop on Gender and Security Sector Reform" convened by Geneva Centre for the Democratic Control of Armed Forces (DCAF) Partnership for Peace Consortium of Defense Academies and Security Studies (PfPC), February 8, 2010, Geneva, Switzerland.

[22] Remarks submitted by Major General Patrick Cammaert (Ret.), former Commander of the Eastern Division of the UN Mission to the Democratic Republic of the Congo and the UN Mission to Ethiopia and Eritrea, to "Engaging Women in the Security Sector," convened by the United States Institute of Peace, January 28, 2010, Washington, DC.

[23] T. Bouta, "Gender and Disarmament, Demobilization and Reintegration: Building Blocs for Dutch Policy" (Clingendael: Netherlands Institute for International Relations, 2005), 5. A number of recent scholarly accounts provide excellent documentation of women's roles in modern combat. See especially Bouta, 5–7, and L. De Pauw, *Battle Cries and Lullabies: Women in War from Prehistory to the Present* (Norman: University of Oklahoma Press, 1998), 263–302.

[24] Ibid.

[25] Ibid.

[26] Foreign Policy Association, "Commentary: Women and Terrorism," Foreign Policy Association: Terrorism/Terrorism, Foreign Policy Association Newsletter, January 15, 2003, available at <http://www.fpa.org/newsletter_info2478/newsletter_info.htm>, May 10, 2010.

[27] De Pauw, 292.

[28] Mazurana and Carlson.

[29] De Pauw, 271.

[30] For example, Anne Itto served as a colonel in the Sudan's People's Liberation Army (SPLA); Khatol Mohammad Zai is a general in the Afghan National Army; Eldaneyis Mosquera was a senior leader in the Revolutionary Armed Forces of Colombia (FARC), Foreign Policy Association, "Commentary: Women and Terrorism."

[31] De Pauw, 271.

[32] M. Stockdale, "'My Death for the Motherland Is Happiness': Women, Patriotism, and Soldiering in Russia's Great War," *The American Historical Review* 109, no. 1 (2004), 78.

[33] C. Gilmartin, *Engendering the Chinese Revolution: Radical Women, Communist Politics, and Mass Movements in the 1920s* (Berkeley: University of California Press, 1995), 169.

[34] Haney, R., *Celia Sánchez: the Legend of Cuba's Revolutionary Heart* (New York: Algora Publishing, 2005), 69.

[35] Bouta, 7.

[36] De Pauw, 292.

[37] Ibid., 6.

[38] Foreign Policy Association (2003) "Commentary: Women and Terrorism."

[39] On May 1, 2007, a woman pretending to be pregnant detonated her explosives in the town center of Balad Ruz, Iraq, killing 29 people and wounding 52, available at <http://www.npr.org/templates/story/story.php?storyId=90367974>, May 10, 2010.

[40] Department of Homeland Security, "Female Suicide Bombers Threat," *Joint Homeland Security Assessment*, Department of Homeland Security Office of Intelligence and Analysis and Federal Bureau of Investigation, February 11, 2008, available at <http://nefafoundation.org/miscellaneous/FeaturedDocs/JHSA_Femalesuicidebombers.pdf>, 2, May 10, 2010.

[41] C. Rojas, S. Anderlini, and C. Conaway, "In the Midst of War: Women's Contributions to Peace in Colombia," Women Waging Peace Policy Commission, Hunt Alternatives Fund, Washington, DC, (2004), 24.

[42] M. Fleshman, "African Women Struggle for a Seat at the Peace Table," *Africa Renewal* 16, no. 4 (2003).

[43] Gini Reticker, director, Abigail Disney, producer, *Pray the Devil Back to Hell*, Fork Films LLC, 2008.

[44] R. Manchanda, "Naga Women Making a Difference: Peace Building in Northeastern India," Women Waging Peace Policy Commission: Hunt Alternatives Fund, Washington, DC, (2005).

[45] S. Anderlini, C. Conaway, and L. Kays, "Transitional Justice" in *Inclusive Security, Sustainable Peace: A Toolkit for Advocacy and Action* (Washington and London: Hunt Alternatives Fund and International Alert, 2004), 6–9.

[46] S. Anderlini, "Peace Negotiations and Agreements" in *Inclusive Security, Sustainable Peace: A Toolkit for Advocacy and Action* (Washington and London: Hunt Alternatives Fund and International Alert, 2004), 20.

[47] A. McLaughlin, "Africa's peace seekers: Betty Bigombe," *Christian Science Monitor*, September 13, 2005, available at <http://www.csmonitor.com/2005/0913/p01s04-woaf.html>, May 10, 2010.

[48] For example, Sakena Yacoobi founded the Afghan Institute of Learning. During the Taliban era, Yacoobi's institute operated 80 underground schools for girls, available at <http://womensenews.org/story/the-world/091127/afghan-women-would-rather-talk-about-recovery> or <http://afghaninstituteoflearning.org/imports/AIL_Programs.pdf>.

[49] Available at <http://www.c-r.org/our-work/accord/png-bougainville/women-peace-reconciliation.php>.

[50] C. Conaway and S. Martinez, "Adding Value: Women's Contributions to Reintegration and Reconstruction in El Salvador," Women Waging Peace Policy Commission, 22.

[51] Remarks by Kathy Mangones, UNIFEM country program director for Haiti, at "Lessons from the Frontlines: Afghanistan, Haiti and the Path to a More Secure World," second annual International Women's Day breakfast hosted by Women Thrive Worldwide and UNIFEM, Washington, DC, May 4, 2010.

[52] Vanessa Farr, Albrecht Schnabel, and Henri Myrttinen, eds., *Sexed Pistols: Gendered Impacts of Small Arms and Light Weapons* (Tokyo: United Nations University Press, 2009).

[53] C. Conaway, "Small Arms, Light Weapons and Landmines," in *Inclusive Security, Sustainable Peace: A Toolkit for Advocacy and Action* (Washington and London: Hunt Alternatives Fund and International Alert, 2004), 22.

[54] Sarah Douglas et al., "Getting It Right, Doing It Right," International Knowledge Network of Women in Politics, 2004, 22.

[55] Ibid., 20.

[56] S. Anderlini and C. Conaway.

[57] Douglas, 14.

[58] Reticker and Disney.

[59] Mazurana and Carlson.

[60] Ibid.

[61] Conaway and Martinez.

[62] S. Anderlini and J. El-Bushra, "Civil Society," in *Inclusive Security, Sustainable Peace: A Toolkit for Advocacy and Action* (Washington and London: Hunt Alternatives Fund and International Alert, 2004), 9.

[63] Mazurana and Carlson.

[64] M. Vlachova and L. Biason, eds., *Women in an Insecure World* (Geneva: Geneva Centre for the Democratic Control of Armed Forces [DCAF], 2005), 119.

[65] H. Hakena et al., *NGOs and Post-Conflict Recovery: the Leitana Nehan Women's Development Agency* (Canberra: Asia Pacific Press, 2003), 20.

[66] Anderlini and El-Bushra, 9.

[67] Anderlini and Conaway, 7.

[68] K. Valasek, "Security Sector Reform and Gender," in Megan Bastick and Kristin Valasek, eds., *Gender and Security Sector Reform Toolkit* (Geneva: DCAF, UN–INSTRAW, OSCE/ODIHR, 2008), 5.

[69] K. Lonsway et al., "Men, Women and Police Excessive Force: A Tale of Two Genders: A Content Analysis of Civil Liability Cases, Sustained Allegations and Citizen Complaints" (Los Angeles: National Center for Women and Policing, 2002).

[70] Ibid., 3.

[71] K. Foster, "Gender and Excessive Force Complaints," *Law and Order* 54, no. 8 (2006), 95–99.

[72] Cammaert.

[73] Doreen Carvajal, "A Female Approach to Peacekeeping," *The New York Times*, March 5, 2010, A12.

[74] L. Olsson and J. Tejpar, eds., "Operational Effectiveness and UN Resolution 1325—Practices and Lessons from Afghanistan" (Stockholm: FOI, Swedish Defence Research Agency, 2009), 42.

[75] Carvajal.

[76] I. Luciak, "Parliamentary Oversight of the Security Sector and Gender" in Megan Bastick and Kristin Valasek, eds., *Gender and Security Sector Reform Toolkit* (Geneva: DCAF, UN–INSTRAW, OSCE/ODIHR, 2008), 4.

[77] Ibid., 13.

[78] E. Pearson, "Demonstrating Legislative Leadership: The Introduction of Rwanda's Gender-Based Violence Bill" (Washington, DC: Initiative for Inclusive Security, Hunt Alternatives Fund, 2008).

[79] P. Albrecht and K. Barnes, "Civil Society Oversight of the Security Sector and Gender" in Megan Bastick and Kristin Valasek, eds., *Gender and Security Sector Reform Toolkit* (Geneva: DCAF, UN-INSTRAW, OSCE/ODIHR, 2008).

[80] Ibid.

[81] S. Anderlini, "Negotiating the Transition to Democracy and Reforming the Security Sector: The Vital Contributions of South African Women," Women Waging Peace Policy Commission: Hunt Alternatives Fund, 2004.

[82] "Women's Participation in Peace Negotiations: Connections between Presence and Influence," United Nations Development Fund for Women, New York, 2009.

[83] M. Page, T. Whitman, and C. Anderson, "Strategies for Policymakers: Bringing Women into Peace Negotiations" (Washington, DC: The Institute for Inclusive Security, 2009).

[84] Ibid., 2.

[85] Ibid.

[86] Ibid.

[87] Ibid., 5–8.

[88] Ibid., 9–13.

[89] Ibid., 11.

[90] Ibid., 2.

[91] Ibid.

[92] Ibid., 13–16.

[93] For additional recommendations on increasing women's inclusion in peace negotiations, see M. Page, T. Whitman, and C. Anderson, "Strategies for Policymakers: Bringing Women into Peace Negotiations" (Washington, DC: The Institute for Inclusive Security, 2009).

Chapter 6

Understanding "Reintegration" within Postconflict Peace-building: Making the Case for "Reinsertion" First and Better Linkages Thereafter

By Jennifer M. Hazen

Introduction

Disarmament, Demobilization, and Reintegration (DDR) have become commonplace programs in postconflict settings and "a well-established feature of post–cold-war peacekeeping."[1] Despite years of practice in implementing DDR in a number of contexts, there remains little knowledge about whether it works, why it works, and its impacts on achieving broader peace-building goals. In large part, this is the result of the failure to establish clear goals and related benchmarks, and to measure DDR as an outcome rather than merely a mechanism for returning combatants to civilian life. The lack of clarity on its definitions, goals, and measurement ensures ongoing debate about its focal constituency, the breadth of activities contained within the program, and its relationship to the broader peace-building process.

DDR as a concept has grown too large. As a result, there remains confusion about what it entails and how it should be implemented in any given context. Despite an understanding of its limitations, and that DDR "should not become the societal vehicle for post-conflict peacebuilding,"[2] DDR has become an umbrella term encompassing activities that, while important, are no longer specific to it, and which have timelines that far exceed its own. DDR marks an important step forward in the peace-building process, but the road is long, and too much focus on DDR as a program, and not on the broader goals of peace-building, economic development, and government reform, threatens to hinder progress on all of these goals.

This chapter puts forward an argument for a focus on ex-combatants during the DDR process, a circumscription of activities to focus on disarmament, demobilization, and *reinsertion*, and the need for much greater thought as to how DDR can contribute to the broader peace process. The R of DDR has in practice represented "reinsertion," not "reintegration." Acknowledging reinsertion as the third phase of DDR enables a targeting of short-term programming at ex-combatants, which is the first step in the long-term reintegration process. The next step is to determine the links that need to be made in practice between DDR and reintegration, and how reintegration fits into broader programs aimed at economic development, peace-building, and governance reform.

The argument for focusing on *reinsertion* for ex-combatants and *reintegration* for communities is not entirely new. However, this chapter pushes this position further by arguing for a finite DDR process that focuses on combatants and whose sole purpose is to disarm combatants, demobilize them from active combat, and reinsert them into civilian life. These steps are essential to marking the end of the war and the return of combatants into society in a postconflict setting. However, DDR is a necessary but insufficient process for achieving reintegration, economic development, and sustainable peace. It must therefore be carefully situated within broader ongoing economic and peace initiatives. While this has been widely recognized, little has been done to achieve it in practice, as implementing agencies have found it difficult to translate principles into action.

This chapter is divided into five sections. The first presents a number of lessons learned over the past 2 decades of DDR practice. It highlights shifts in the conceptualization of DDR and its implementation. The second identifies both what DDR can and cannot achieve, dispelling some misperceptions about its role in postconflict processes. The third section makes the case for why the R in DDR should stand for *reinsertion*, not reintegration. The fourth turns to address reintegration and makes the case for implementing *both* reinsertion (individual ex-combatants) and reintegration (community) programs. It also emphasizes the need to link reinsertion to reintegration efforts while situating reintegration within broader peace-building, economic development, and governance reform strategies. While the need to link DDR to these longer term programs and processes has been widely recognized, it has not been achieved in practice. The chapter ends with a number of conclusions about the future steps needed to enhance the practice of DDR, and in particular to ensure that both reinsertion and reintegration achieve positive results.

Evolution of DDR: Lessons Learned

The Disarmament, Demobilization, and Reintegration of ex-combatants have become a standard practice in postconflict countries since the 1990s.[3] There have been more than two dozen DDR programs conducted over the past 2 decades.[4] At its core, DDR aims to return combatants mobilized during a civil war to civilian life. The process involves combatants handing in their weapons, being formally discharged from combat service, returning to their community of origin (or choice), and receiving short-term benefits to assist them in reestablishing a civilian life (see sidebar). DDR can contribute to building stability and security in a country by marking an end to war, removing weapons from circulation, and reducing the number of combatants in society, thereby providing a platform for peace-building, economic development, and political reform.

United Nations Definitions

Disarmament is the collection, documentation, control, and disposal of small arms, ammunition, explosives, and light and heavy weapons of combatants and often also of the civilian population. Disarmament also includes the development of responsible arms management programs.

Demobilization is the formal and controlled discharge of active combatants from armed forces or other armed groups. The first stage of demobilization may extend from the processing of individual combatants in temporary centers to the massing of troops in camps designated for this purpose (cantonment sites, encampments, assembly areas, or barracks). The second stage of demobilization encompasses the support package provided to the demobilized, which is called reinsertion.

Reinsertion is the assistance offered to ex-combatants during demobilization but prior to the longer term process of reintegration. Reinsertion is a form of transitional assistance to help cover the basic needs of ex-combatants and their families and can include transitional

Continued

safety allowances, food, clothes, shelter, medical services, short-term education, training, employment, and tools. While reintegration is a long-term, continuous social and economic process of development, reinsertion is a short-term material and/or financial assistance to meet immediate needs, and can last up to one year.

Reintegration is the process by which ex-combatants acquire civilian status and gain sustainable employment and income. Reintegration is essentially a social and economic process with an open timeframe, primarily taking place in communities at the local level. It is part of the general development of a country and a national responsibility, and often necessitates long-term external assistance.

Source: Disarmament, Demobilization and Reintegration, Report of the Secretary-General, UN Document A/60/705, March 2, 2006, 8.

The design and implementation of DDR have evolved over the past 2 decades.[5] Reviews of DDR programs in postconflict contexts have produced a number of lessons learned that inform the conceptualization, design, and implementation of current-day DDR programs. This section reviews a number of these lessons and their implications for future practice. This is not a comprehensive assessment of lessons learned, as they can be found elsewhere,[6] but instead it is intended to lay the groundwork for the identification of what DDR can and cannot achieve, a discussion of reinsertion and reintegration, and the proposal of next steps in the practice of DDR that follow in this chapter.

DDR is not a linear process. Early versions of DDR tended to emphasize the process as linear, wherein combatants would move from one phase to the next in synchronization. Implementation led to the widespread understanding that such a linear approach is not always possible, and that DDR can in fact take a variety of forms. This is true for a number of reasons. In some instances, not all combatants can move through the process at the same time, and thus some will be ahead or behind in the process. In other instances, the sequencing might be changed, with demobilization and/or reinsertion taking place before disarmament. In a small handful of cases, disarmament has not been tried, but instead the process has emphasized the demobilization of combatants and their reinsertion into society.

Each approach has its pros and cons, as well as inherent difficulties in implementing any particular sequencing of the process. Different countries are experimenting with sequencing or omitting elements of the process, and these cases should provide important insights into the potential for formulating new modes of implementing DDR programming.[7]

Reintegration cannot be an afterthought.[8] Planning for reintegration needs to begin early in the process to avoid long gaps between combatants completing the demobilization phase and entering the reintegration phase. This includes financial, technical, logistical, and programmatic planning. Reintegration has been the most difficult phase to conceptualize, fund, and implement. While assessed contributions can be used for the disarmament and demobilization phases, funding for reintegration is based on voluntary contributions. This has often resulted in large funding gaps for reintegration programming and delays in providing reintegration opportunities to former combatants. This poses security challenges if disgruntled combatants become "spoilers" to the peace process, but it also impedes the return of combatants to civilian life.

DDR is not a simple technical exercise. Early versions of DDR were largely seen as technical exercises designed to manage large numbers of ex-combatants at the end of conflict. An emphasis on the technical and logistical aspects of the exercise encouraged a bifurcation between the DD and the R, whereby the military retained responsibility for the former, but the R was largely viewed as a civilian task. The distinction between military and civilian tasking enhanced the division between the steps in the process and made linking the R to the D difficult in practice. Increasingly, DDR is viewed not as a technical procedure, but as an important process within postconflict peace-building[9] that has far-reaching political, security, economic, and social dimensions.

DDR must be country-specific. DDR is now "part of the standard post-conflict package" for war-torn countries. It is seen as an "essential element" in "the success of an entire peace process."[10] It has also become a standard component of many UN peacekeeping operations.[11] Despite its standardization within postconflict operations, there is recognition that DDR cannot be applied in the same fashion in every country, but instead needs to be adapted to the characteristics and dynamics of the country itself.[12] Nevertheless, standard approaches often prevail,[13] resulting in a technical, almost automatic implementation of DDR that fails to acknowledge and address alternate perspectives or the particular needs on the ground.[14]

Regional dynamics matter. No civil war today takes place solely within the national borders of a country. Regional and international factors have contributed to both prolonging conflicts and ending them. Regional dynamics have been emphasized in West Africa and in Central Africa. DDR programs have adjusted to this reality, and efforts have been made to acknowledge the role of regional factors during DDR campaigns. This includes the presence of combatants from neighboring countries, the circulation of arms and combatants among countries in conflict, the role of regional sponsors of armed groups, weak border controls and porous borders, and the presence of peacekeeping missions in contiguous countries.

DDR targets combatants but cannot omit noncombatants. DDR should focus on combatants.[15] Women and children have been largely ignored in early versions of DDR programs. As information surfaced of the roles of women and children in conflict, from war wives to cooks to porters to actual combatants, a general understanding emerged that programs must address the needs of these noncombatants and nontraditional combatants. However, this remains difficult under traditional DDR programs. These programs remain focused on individual combatants, and that should continue because former combatants do require assistance in leaving their military life.[16] However, community-based programs are also necessary outside of the formal DDR process to address the special needs of these noncombatant and nontraditional combatant groups, prepare communities for the return of combatants, facilitate the reintegration of combatants, and provide opportunities for community development activities. This requires a variety of programs to run in parallel with DDR.[17]

Combatants are not all alike. Increasingly, it is recognized that it may not be possible or even desirable to treat all ex-combatants alike.[18] In situations where clear command structures exist, senior commanders may possess more reasons for continuing a conflict and face higher stakes in ending one. Consideration should be given to creating different incentive structures for senior and mid-level commanders versus foot soldiers, with the understanding that additional incentives may be required for commanders, though their provision could also lead to intra-group tensions.

DDR is finite. DDR programs last 5 years or less on average. They are finite in their resources, often with most of the available funding being used for the first two D's. Although the expectations of what DDR can achieve are often expansive, most DDR programs have specific mandates to complete certain tasks (e.g., collect arms, repatriate combatants to their communities). In completing these tasks, DDR can lay the foundation for working on longer term goals. For example, economic development and peace-building are long-term processes to which DDR can contribute by providing the groundwork for stability and security but which it cannot achieve on its own.

Security and development are inherently interlinked. DDR was traditionally seen as a stand-alone program "largely unconnected conceptually or institutionally to broader projects of development, arms control or security sector reform."[19] This traditional security-first approach, which emphasized physical security in terms of collecting arms and dismantling armed groups, has proven an important first step in reestablishing stability, but insufficient in ensuring long-term peace and development. As a result, there is increasing recognition of the need to incorporate economic concerns earlier in the postconflict process and to recognize economic development as an important element of security. This requires linking DDR to development programming.

Coordination is essential, but integration might be difficult. DDR poses important challenges for coordination. While disarmament and demobilization can be straightforward exercises, they nevertheless require substantial logistical preparations. Reintegration is often managed by a central and often national commission but implemented by numerous independent organizations. The thousands of participants moving through various programs across a country make implementation and tracking progress extremely difficult. Such complexity has led many to propose greater coordination of efforts and others to argue for an integrated approach to DDR.[20]

While it is true that a coordinated approach among the various actors is necessary for enhancing the effectiveness of programming and linking DDR to broader development programs, it is not clear that a fully integrated approach is the solution. The development by the United Nations of the Integrated Disarmament, Demobilization and Reintegration Standards (IDDRS) provides a model for an integrated solution.[21] The IDDRS is still in its testing phase in the UN peacekeeping missions in Haiti and Sudan. However, early evidence suggests total integration is extremely difficult to achieve.[22] Complexity results from various actors being involved at each stage of DDR, in particular the reintegration phase.[23] Each actor has its own set of organizational rules, regulations, and mandates[24] that do not necessarily correspond to one another or promote collaboration. A review of the integrated missions suggests that given the different nature of involved organizations, "it is not possible to insist on complete operational/administrative integration" and "instead the goal should be to complement each other in a mutually reinforcing way" in order to integrate planning and coordinate implementation.[25]

Rising Expectations and Expanding DDR Programs

As DDR has evolved over the past 2 decades, it has grown into a much larger and broader program than originally anticipated or designed. In fact, expectations of what it can do have quickly outgrown its capacity to achieve concrete results on the ground. This has led to unrealistic and largely unfulfilled expectations by donors, implementing agencies, and recipients. Reintegration originally referred to economic assimilation of ex-combatants back into the economy through vocational training and job creation schemes.[26] However, the expansion of activities included under the reintegration umbrella, and a shift in focus from short-term economic activities to an emphasis on full economic and social integration, have widened the concept and blurred the meaning of reintegration.[27]

Reintegration has come to be "seen as a societal process aiming at the economic, political, and social assimilation of ex-combatants and their families into civil society."[28] Such long-term goals are not achievable in the short timeframe of a DDR program. The proliferation of R's has only added to the confusion. DDR has been called DDRR, DDRRR, and even DDRRRR. The multiple R's have stood for reinsertion, reintegration, repatriation, resettlement, and rehabilitation. The trend has been to incorporate a number of objectives that are not possible to achieve through DDR, including "fundamentally transforming social relations, achieving reconciliation, solving structural economic imbalances or helping countries to achieve significant development leaps."[29] Reintegration now seems to refer to "*all* activities after demobilization" even though ex-combatants have mostly received reinsertion benefits.[30] This has led to contradictory impulses: on the one hand is the push to make DDR "comprehensive,"[31] but on the other is the realization that "DDR should not be overburdened with all post-conflict demands."[32]

Today there is ongoing debate about expectations and which activities should be part of DDR. Some see it as a short-term security program, while others view it as part of a long-term development approach.[33] While this division is often found between military officers who support the former view and development agents who support the latter view, the two sides are not so easily defined. In late 2007, a range of experts from various fields acknowledged the need "for a clear definition of what DDR should incorporate and the boundaries of expected outcomes."[34] The approach taken has important implications for practice. Those favoring a more limited approach see the purpose of DDR as addressing the immediate needs of ex-combatants while supporting broader community-based programs outside of the DDR umbrella. By contrast, those in favor of a broader approach see community-based reintegration as the platform for the reintegration of ex-combatants, not as a complement to their integration.

Table: Tempering Expectations

DDR can . . .	DDR cannot . . .
build confidence between former warring factions	completely eliminate small arms from armed groups and private hands
reduce the number of weapons in circulation by encouraging combatants to give up their weapons	result in total disarmament
offer combatants the option to lay down their arms without surrendering	reduce demand for small arms if security is not provided
provide a short-term safety net	prevent combatants from picking up a gun again
start the process of changing habits and identities as combatants	provide instant security and stability
provide a transition period between war and civilian life	reform the military or police
offer the opportunity to begin to reintegrate into civilian life	save a failing peace process
provide an important symbolic indication of the end of war	substitute for political will to end a war
provide the basis for security and stability	create economic development
contribute to security and stability, which in turn provides the basis for economic development, peace-building, political reform, and SSR	generate sustainable employment opportunities
	reestablish the rule of law
	drive military or political change
	demilitarize politics
	address root causes of the war

At the core of this debate should be a discussion of what DDR can and cannot achieve (see table), as well as how DDR can link to broader programs that can achieve governance reforms, economic development, and a reduction in the root causes of the war. This requires taking a step back to rethink the goals of DDR and how best to use such programming to contribute to stability and security. This is likely to require acknowledging the finite nature of DDR, circumscribing ambitions for the program, and then targeting the program appropriately. This requires a shift in perspective from seeing DDR as a comprehensive program (under which many things fall under the umbrella) to seeing it as a first step in a comprehensive approach to peace-building, economic development, and security. Yet even for those who have already argued that "DDR should be embedded in a broader post-conflict reconstruction and development framework,"[35] it is not at all clear what this means in practice. Even where this linked approach is acknowledged as necessary, it has yet to be implemented on the ground. Importantly, linking DDR to broader peace-building and development programs and to goals is not the same as an integrated approach to conducting DDR.

DDR is not a solution to all postconflict problems.[36] It can lay the groundwork for peace if it is well designed and implemented, but it can likewise contribute to the return of conflict if poorly done. DDR programs are most successful when they are coordinated with and linked to broader reforms, including reforms of the security sector, governance, and the judiciary, and to economic development.[37] DDR "should have backward and forward linkages to the broader peace process (including peace agreements) and peace-building programs. DDR should always be accompanied by parallel relief, resettlement and rehabilitation efforts for all war-affected populations, especially in the context of local communities, as well as security sectors reforms."[38]

An Argument for "Reinsertion"

"Technically speaking, the first two components of the [DDR] process are finite, while reintegration is ongoing, complex and its success dependent on a number of interconnected issues that go beyond the formal end of war."[39] Yet in practice, the reintegration phase has been designed to fit within the short-term timeframe of DDR programming. While there is a widespread understanding now that reintegration cannot be completed within this timeframe, and that the reintegration phase could last substantially longer than the DDR program or the presence of a UN peacekeeping mission, reintegration, in name at least, continues to constitute the third component of DDR programs. Yet what is often called reintegration is in practice reinsertion. The difference is substantial.[40] Acknowledging the practice of "reinsertion" may provide an avenue for discussing real reintegration programming and the links among reinsertion, reintegration, and broader development and peace-building programs.

Reinsertion has been defined as "short-term material and/or financial assistance to meet immediate needs."[41] It has also been called a "transitional safety net" which "enables the combatant to survive, take care of his/her family and cope while adjusting to his/her new status as a productive member of society."[42] This safety net often includes "a mix of in-kind and cash entitlements covering a basket of basic needs such as food, shelter, clothing, health and education requirements."[43] The primary purpose of reinsertion is to provide short-term benefits to "keep ex-combatants off the streets"[44] and deter them from returning to conflict or turning to crime as a means of making ends meet. The reality is that what is happening on the ground is reinsertion,[45] with ex-combatants receiving short-term benefits and vocational skills training. The result is many identifying reinsertion as the first phase of reintegration, the short-term phase, whereas what has been called reintegration actually focuses on the long-term phase.[46] In other words, DDR is not doing reintegration, but is instead providing reinsertion benefits.

Along with the fact that it is what is actually being implemented on the ground, there are a number of other reasons why *reinsertion* should be the third element of DDR programming. First, addressing reinsertion needs enables a focus on achievable results in the short term, while acknowledging reintegration as a long-term process with an open timeframe. Reinsertion is a finite activity involving the return of the former combatant to his/her community of origin (or to a chosen community) and the provision of materials to address basic needs in the short term. Reinsertion is the first step to reintegration. The combatant must first return to a civilian life in a community before reintegration can take place. Yet emphasis on the status of the individual as an "ex-combatant" after his/her return can pose obstacles to reintegration. Thus reinserting the former combatant, ensuring that he/she is not a drain on community resources, and then turning to a community-based reintegration strategy may have the best chance of success.

Second, it allows the reinsertion program to target ex-combatants specifically, thereby providing a means for meeting the widely acknowledged special needs of ex-combatants when returning to civilian life. The assistance is necessarily limited in duration, with an established timeline for distributing and terminating it. Targeted programming helps make it clear to ex-combatants and communities what benefits ex-combatants are receiving, which reduces the likelihood of creating unrealistic expectations by either group.[47] This can aid in reducing perceptions that ex-combatants are being favored or rewarded.

Third, clearly identifying the target group and the goals of the program makes it easier to assess progress on achieving these goals. Most argue that measuring the success of reintegration efforts is not possible for several years after the implementation of reintegration programs due to the complexity of reintegration and the fact that it often takes years (if not generations) to achieve. Reinsertion, on the other hand, has much more limited goals: providing the means for ex-combatants to reenter civilian life. It is therefore possible to identify a number of indicators for successful reinsertion and to monitor and evaluate programs as to whether they are effective in achieving progress on these indicators.

Fourth, reinsertion programming can allow for flexibility and a focus on the immediate economic needs of the country (e.g., reconstruction). Attention to short-term economic opportunities is often necessary in the early stages of postconflict recovery when economies are weak and employment opportunities extremely limited; it also provides time for a detailed economic assessment to determine potential future options and to design reintegration programming to fit these options.[48] In current reintegration programs, ex-combatants are typically offered a list of options for training that do not necessarily fit the needs of the economy and for which there may be limited employment opportunities following training.[49] Ex-combatants rarely receive advice on selecting an appropriate program, nor are they tracked through training programs to enable an assessment of the outcome (i.e., whether they were able to find employment following the training). In many cases, ex-combatants have failed to find work following their training, sold their toolkits for cash, and faced limited prospects. By contrast, reinsertion programming does not promise sustained livelihoods, which cannot be achieved along the current DDR timeline, but instead short-term employment opportunities. These can aid in keeping ex-combatants off the streets, contribute to the reconstruction of vital infrastructure, and lay the groundwork for economic development. Reinsertion programming can fill the gap between immediate recovery needs and demands for stop-gap employment and longer term development strategies that produce viable sustainable employment options and incorporate communities as a whole rather than just ex-combatants.

Fifth, funding for reintegration is often difficult to obtain because it is based on voluntary contributions by member states. By contrast, disarmament and demobilization are funded through assessed contributions to peacekeeping operations, meaning that money for these two phases is usually available.[50] However, reinsertion of ex-combatants can be funded through the DD budget stream in peacekeeping contexts. This provides "transitional assistance for a period of up to one year,"[51] including many of the elements of "reintegration" as it is currently programmed. This offers a means of paying for reinsertion programming while planning and budgeting for longer term reintegration programs. If, instead, reinsertion benefits are considered part of the "reintegration" process, or they continue to be implemented as reintegration programs as is currently being done, then these activities cannot be funded under the DD budget stream.[52]

Sixth, the provision of reinsertion benefits to ex-combatants does not preclude other programs from offering benefits to the war-involved (e.g., child soldiers, porters, cooks), the war-affected (e.g., war wives, disabled), or to affected communities. Reinsertion helps ex-combatants to return to their communities, while other reinsertion-type programs apply to refugees and displaced persons. Reinsertion provides an important link between individual repatriation and community integration. A widely held view is that "reintegration should not be understood as an individual process, but rather as a community orientated process."[53] While reinsertion aims to return individuals to communities, reintegration aims to integrate these various groups (e.g., combatants, refugees, displaced persons) into the political, economic, and social fabric of the community. Reintegration is a process, not a program,[54] and determining how to link reinsertion (and the broader DDR program) to reintegration efforts and to long-term peace-building strategies is important to achieving stability, development, and sustainable peace.

Reintegration: Linking DDR to Postconflict Peace-building

While there is no single agreed-upon definition, *reintegration* has been defined as "a long-term, continuous social and economic process of development";[55] as a long-term process aimed at generating "sustainable livelihoods" and socially and economically embedding ex-combatants into their communities;[56] and as a "social and economic process with an open timeframe, primarily taking place in communities at the local level."[57] These definitions and others share several characteristics. They emphasize the multidimensional nature of reintegration to include the economic and social spheres and, in some cases, the political sphere. They emphasize the long-term, open-ended nature of the reintegration process. They also underscore the communal nature of the process, which entails individuals integrating into communities, but also communities accepting the return and inclusion of these individuals.

Reintegration is a long-term process that involves the political, economic, and social integration of a wide range of individuals into communities. In other words, the focus should not be on ex-combatants alone, but on the various "returnees" who enter communities after wars. These include ex-combatants, the internally displaced, and refugees, as well as new community members who have moved out of choice to join family members or to seek economic opportunities. In some cases, communities will already be socially cohesive, having been able to withstand the divisive forces of war, whereas in other cases there might be little "community" left. In the latter, efforts to rebuild social cohesion and a sense of community will be necessary, and "reintegration" will be the goal of all community members.

Reintegration is a truly complex process. It involves the integration of individuals into the social, economic, and political fabric of the community.[58] It takes place across these three domains.[59] At the political level, this involves community members accepting the formal (laws) and informal (customs) rules of behavior and having the opportunity (even if it is not taken) to actively participate in local governance and decisionmaking as well as governance at the national level through elections. At the economic level, this involves becoming a productive member of the community either through self-employment (e.g., farming, small trade), other legitimate employment options (e.g., wage laborer, government employee), or engaging in training or education. At the social level, integration involves acceptance by families and community.

Community based or focused reintegration has gained traction over the past several years. This approach recognizes that it is not only ex-combatants who need assistance, but that many communities have been adversely affected by war and require significant aid to function. Community-focused reintegration programs aim to bring together various members of the community, including the newly returned (e.g., ex-combatants, displaced persons, refugees), to work collaboratively on projects that benefit the entire community. In this way, these programs directly target the community at large rather than any subgroups. The intention is to aid in the recovery and development of the community as a whole, which in turn provides economic opportunities for individuals.

If reinsertion links to reintegration by returning former combatants to communities and initiating the process of reintegration, and reintegration is characterized as community-based programming to rebuild communities and integrating individuals socially, economically, and politically, then the next step is to identify how reintegration links to broader programs, including security sector reform (SSR), economic development, peace-building, political and judicial reforms, and transitional justice.[60] At present, there is little understanding of how these programs should interface. DDR moves the process forward to the reintegration phase, but current development programming falls short of moving beyond this starting point.

Many contend that DDR should be "conceptualized, designed, planned and implemented within a wider recovery and development framework."[61] While various academic and policy documents are full of rhetoric emphasizing the need to "link" DDR to broader programming, it is not clear how this is to be done, or what is meant by "linking." Authors have suggested "linking" DDR to security sector reform, arms control, economic recovery and development, peace-building, transitional justice, conflict prevention, and reconciliation.[62] The links between DDR and SSR and arms control programs are clearer. For example, some combatants who go through the DDR process will be provided an opportunity to join the national security forces (e.g., military, police). The availability of slots largely depends on the reform of the security forces. Similarly, the reform of a police force to the point that it provides security to citizens can encourage citizens to hand in weapons and perhaps convince some ex-combatants to enter a DDR process. Arms control measures, such as national legislation defining rules for civilian possession and the registration of arms, can reinforce gains made during disarmament. The links between DDR and peace-building, economic development, and governance reform are less clear cut. While a successful DDR process can support a stable and secure environment in which these activities can take place, direct links between DDR and these programs need to be investigated, identified, and elaborated on in order to promote such linkages and synergies.

Moving Forward: Next Steps

On the surface, it appears that reintegration is not being achieved in most postconflict contexts. Beneath this initial assessment, the reality is that there is no easy way of determining whether reintegration is happening because it has been poorly defined, programs have been designed to achieve short-term goals rather than true reintegration, and few programs have even been evaluated to measure their effectiveness. Yet the international community spends tens of millions on reintegration efforts each year without knowing whether, or how, it is making a difference.

Some experimentation with programming is taking place. Community-reintegration programs have replaced individual-focused efforts in some cases, but it is not clear that this is an improvement in practice. Debate continues over whether community reintegration should replace individual reintegration programming, or whether the two should be conducted alongside one another, addressing the different needs of their constituencies. In part, the inability to move forward is the result of ongoing competing views about what DDR should achieve and what kind of programming should be included. Without addressing this divide, it will be impossible to make structural improvements to DDR as a whole. This will require a fundamental reevaluation of DDR efforts.

Currently, a disjuncture exists between language and practice. While on the one hand there is the recognition that DDR programs are finite and limited in what they can achieve, on the other hand they continue to be implemented in the standard fashion. There remains a lack of clarity about what DDR is, what it should include, and what it should ultimately achieve. There is a pressing need to answer each of these questions and to delineate a set of indicators to measure achievement. This requires defining the goals of DDR more specifically and realistically.

Although practitioners have increasingly emphasized the need to develop measurement indicators and to monitor and evaluate programs accordingly, this agenda has not progressed very far. In large part this is the result of the failure to identify the goals of DDR, which makes developing indicators impossible. Defining indicators and evaluating programs will be critical to the future of DDR, not only to assess how programs have been implemented procedurally (some of that has been done), but to assess the substantive impact of these programs on the ground (very little of which has been done). This will require more than simply counting the number of combatants completing the program or the number of guns collected. Identifying and assessing what DDR can achieve will also contribute to a better understanding of where DDR fits within the broader peace-building and development agendas.

Finally, there is a need to do more than simply acknowledge the links between DDR programs and broader development strategies. Specific focused research on the linkages between DDR and other postconflict programs can contribute to identifying how these programs link conceptually and how to link them programmatically. It is insufficient to continue to say that the programs are related, that they need to be linked, that DDR needs to be embedded in peace-building, or that there needs to be close collaboration among agencies working these issues. There is little disagreement over these points. What is needed now is to identify how to do this conceptually and in practice.

Notes

[1] United Nations (UN), "The Role of United Nations Peacekeeping in Disarmament, Demobilization and Reintegration," Report of the Secretary-General, UN Document S/2000/101, February 11, 2000, 3.

[2] Sarah Meek and Mark Malan, eds., *Identifying Lessons from DDR Experiences in Africa: Workshop Report*, ISS Monograph No. 106, October 2004, Pretoria: Institute for Security Studies, 1.

[3] This paper focuses on DDR programs undertaken in post-civil war countries. It does not address demobilization programs (defined as downsizing of militaries) in postconflict and nonconflict contexts.

[4] There is no single agreed-upon figure for the number of DDR programs due to differences in definition and categorization. The Stockholm Initiative on Disarmament, Demobilisation and Reintegration, *SIDDR Final Report*, 2006, Regeringskansliet, available at <http://www.sweden.gov.se/siddr>, identifies 34 DDR programs between 1994 and 2006; Oxfam International, "Policy Compendium Note on Disarmament, Demobilisation and Reintegration (DDR)," May 15, 2007, available at <http://www.oxfam.org/files/oi_hum_policy_disarmament.pdf>, states that "several hundred thousand ex-combatants from more than 30 countries have taken part in DDR programs."

[5] See Guy Lamb, *Current Approaches to Disarmament, Demobilisation and Reintegration (DDR) Program Design and Implementation*, University of Bradford, July 2008, available at <http://www.ddrhumansecurity.org.uk/images/DDR%20Working%20Paper%201.pdf>; Small Arms Survey, "Managing 'Post-Conflict' Zones: DDR and Weapons Reduction," *Small Arms Survey: Weapons at War* (Oxford: Oxford University Press, 2005), 277–279.

[6] For a discussion of various lessons learned see Edward Bell and Charlotte Watson, *DDR: Supporting Security and Development: The EU's Added Value*, London: International Alert, September 2006, available at <http://www.conflictprevention.net/library/documents/thematic_issues/cpp_eu_ddr.pdf>; Meek and Malan; Leontine Specker, *The R-Phase of DDR Processes: An Overview of Key Lessons Learned and Practical Experiences* (The Hague: The Clingendael Institute, September 2008); United Nations, "Disarmament, Demobilization and Reintegration (DDR) and Stability in Africa," Conference Report from June 21 to 23, 2005, Freetown, United Nations Office of the Special Adviser on Africa and the Government of Sierra Leone (New York: UN, United Nations Development Program [UNDP], 2005), *Practice Note: Disarmament, demobilization and reintegration of Ex-combatants*, New York: UNDP.

[7] Additional research is needed on sequencing. Specker, *The R-Phase of DDR Processes*, v.

[8] UN (2005), 14.

[9] Mark Knight, "Expanding the DDR Model: Politics and Organisations," *Journal of Security Sector Management* 6, no. 1 (March 2008), 3–6.

[10] Meek and Malan, 2.

[11] Ibid., 9.

[12] Kees Kingma, *Demobilisation and Reintegration of Ex-combatants in Post-war and Transition Countries: Trends and Challenges of External Support* (Eschborn, Germany: GTZ, 2001), 14.

[13] See Tom Body, *Reintegration of Ex-Combatants through Micro-Enterprise: An Operational Framework*, Pearson Peacekeeping Centre, 2005, 2, for a description of typical process.

[14] For a discussion of this, see Joanna Spear, "From Political Economies of War to Political Economies of Peace: The Contribution of DDR after Wars of Predation," *Contemporary Security Policy* 27, no. 1 (April 2006), 168–189.

[15] UNDP, *Practice Note: Disarmament, Demobilization and Reintegration of Ex-combatants* (New York: UNDP, 2005), 34.

[16] Kingma, 14.

[17] Stockholm Initiative, 27.

[18] See Meek and Malan, 35; Spear, 171–172; Stina Torjesen, The political economy of Disarmament, Demobilization and Reintegration (DDR): Selective literature review and preliminary agenda for research, NUPI Paper No. 709, Oslo: Norwegian Institute of International Affairs, 2006, 7; UNDP, 34–35; U.S. Department of State (DOS), Office of the Coordinator for Reconstruction and Stabilization, *Lessons Learned: Disarmament, Demobilization and Reintegration (DDR) in Reconstruction and*

Stabilization Operations: A Guide for United States Government Planners (Washington: DOS, April 2006), 17.

[19] Lamb, 23.

[20] See UN (2005), 29; UN, *Integrated Disarmament, Demobilization and Reintegration Standards*, New York: UN (2006), available at <http://www.unddr.org/iddrs/>.

[21] Ibid.

[22] Lamb, 26–28.

[23] See UN (2000), 18–22; Knight, 3–6.

[24] For a good discussion of the challenges of integration in the UN postconflict interventions, see Susanna P. Campbell, "(Dis)integration, Incoherence and Complexity in UN Post-conflict Interventions," *International Peacekeeping* 15, no. 4 (August 2008), 556–569.

[25] UN (2006), 17.

[26] Anders Nilsson, *Reintegrating Ex-Combatants in Post-Conflict Societies* (Stockholm: Swedish International Development Cooperation Agency, 2005), 22.

[27] Ibid.

[28] Ibid., 27.

[29] Stockholm Initiative, 9–10.

[30] Leontine Specker, "Reintegration Phase of DDR Processes," expert meeting report, December 10, 2007, The Hague: The Clingendael Institute, January 2008, available at <http://www.clingendael.nl/publications/2008/20080128_cru_conf_ddr-r-phase.pdf>, 3.

[31] UN (2005), 27.

[32] Ibid., 6.

[33] Oxfam, 4; Specker, *The R-Phase of DDR Processes*, 3.

[34] Specker, "Reintegration Phase of DDR Processes," 9.

[35] UN (2005), 5.

[36] Ibid., 5.

[37] DOS, 5.

[38] UN (2005), 6.

[39] Mark Malan, Sarah Meek, Thokozani Thusi, Jeremy Ginifer, and Patrick Coker, *Sierra Leone: Building the Road to Recovery*, ISS Monograph 80, Pretoria, March 2003, 23.

[40] For a detailed discussion of reinsertion versus reintegration, and the various challenges of reintegration, see Body; Specker, *The R-Phase of DDR Processes.*

[41] UN Inter-Agency Working Group on Disarmament, Demobilization and Reintegration, *Briefing Note for Senior Managers on the Integrated Disarmament, Demobilization and Reintegration Standards*, UN DDR Resource Centre, 2006, available at <http://www.unddr.org/iddrs/SMN-FINAL.pdf>, 3.

[42] Stockholm Initiative, 24.

[43] Ibid.

[44] DOS, 23.

[45] Specker, *The R-Phase of DDR Processes*, 4.

[46] This distinction has been made by many authors. See, for example, Ball and van de Goor, 2–3; Mark Knight and Alpaslan Ozerdem, "Guns, Camps and Cash: Disarmament, Demobilization and Reinsertion of Former Combatants in Transitions from War to Peace," *Journal of Peace Research* 41, no. 4 (2004), 510–513; Specker, *The R-Phase of DDR Processes*, 3–7; Stockholm Initiative (2006), 25.

[47] See UNDP, 23, for a discussion of managing expectations.

[48] See ibid. for a discussion of economic assessments.

[49] UNDP, 54.

[50] See UN Inter-Agency Working Group, 9; DOS, 14.

[51] UN Inter-Agency Working Group, 10.

[52] See DOS, 10–11.

[53] Meek and Malan, 33.

[54] See Ball and van de Goor, 7.

[55] UN Inter-Agency Working Group, 3.

[56] Bell and Watson, 3; DOS, 23.

[57] UN (2006), 8.

[58] Nilsson, 26–27.

[59] Most discussion of reintegration to date has focused on the economic and social aspects of the process. See Nilsson, 27.

[60] See UNDP, 57–60, which highlights the issue areas that should be linked to DDR but does not provide any specific discussion of how these can be linked in practical terms.

[61] UNDP, 11.

[62] See, for example, Stockholm Initiative, 30; UN (2006a); DOS, 24.

Chapter 7

The Disarmament, Demobilization, and Reintegration of Former Child Soldiers

By Courtney R. Rowe, Eric Wiebelhaus-Brahm, and Anne-Tyler Morgan

The Nature of the Child Soldier Problem

The United Nations Children's Fund's (UNICEF's) 2009 *10-Year Strategic Review: Children and Conflict in a Changing World* estimated that just over 1 billion children under the age of 18 live in nations or territories that are affected by armed conflict, which is equal to nearly one-sixth of the world's total population.[1] Of these billion children, approximately 300 million are under the age of five. Increasingly, many of them have become involved in contemporary civil conflicts. Currently, the Optional Protocol of the Convention on the Rights of the Child, which strongly prohibits the use of child soldiers (CSs), has been ratified by more than 100 states, up from 77 in 2004.[2] Of these, two-thirds have committed themselves to the declaration that mandates the age for enforced and voluntary recruitment at 18.[3] On the surface, it appears that international support for keeping children out of combat is growing. Yet, many nations have either not ratified the protocol, have not complied with it, or have been powerless to prevent the recruitment of CSs by armed opposition groups. As a result, "tens of thousands of children remain in the ranks of non-state armed groups in at least 24 different countries or territories."[4] Over 18 million children were displaced by conflict as of 2006.[5]

Children's experiences during wartime have life-long physical, psychological, economic, social, and political consequences. However, Disarmament, Demobilization, and Reintegration (DDR) programs have historically ignored this reality of contemporary conflict. Only in the last decade have DDR programs focused on the particular needs of children. Peace agreements and transitional arrangements need to address the unique needs of CSs not only to make the postconflict peace more durable, but because it is ethically appropriate. Programmers have taken great strides in recent years to move in this direction, but there are still significant obstacles to effectively transitioning CSs to civilian life.

Particularly in sub-Saharan Africa, the importance of including CSs in DDR processes has attracted growing attention. In Sierra Leone, for example, the framework for DDR was based on a series of successive peace agreements and UN Security Council resolutions beginning in 1996. However, continued fighting delayed actual implementation until the signing of the Lomé Peace Accord in 1999. The agreement was especially significant because it was the first to contain special provisions for child DDR.[6] There is a lack of accurate statistics related to CSs in Sierra Leone, but their use in the conflict was notorious. The National Committee on Disarmament, Demobilization, and Reintegration (NCDDR) estimates that 6,845 children entered the DDR program, 513, or 8 percent, of which were girls.[7] In the Democratic Republic of the Congo (DRC), the World Bank began funding child DDR programs in 2002. In the absence of a national body to implement the program, it was initially carried out by UNICEF and supporting NGOs. In 2003, the National Commission for Disarmament, Demobilization, and Reintegration (CONADER) adopted a separate operational framework for child DDR. However, the national DDR initiative did not commence until 2005. By mid-2007, an estimated 30,000 children had been demobilized.[8] Finally, in Liberia, a preliminary DDR program was designed in 1997 but was delayed by continued hostilities until the August 2003 Comprehensive Peace Agreement.[9] It is estimated that more than 21,000 children were associated with government forces or armed groups during the conflict.[10] More than 10,000 children, including 2,300 girls, completed the disarmament and demobilization phases, and over 9,600 former CSs had been reunited with their families prior to the closing of Liberia's DDR program in 2004.[11] As one can see, the track record of including CSs in DDR is fairly mediocre.

Children are at risk of becoming recruited for armed service in Africa and elsewhere as a result of at least three major factors.[12] First, the contemporary proliferation of "total warfare" has blurred the line between civilians and combatants until it is virtually nonexistent. Second, the mass production of small and cheap weaponry has made it easier to arm poorly trained troops such as children. Finally, long-running conflicts often result in a dwindling number of adult fighters. Children are a suitable, inexpensive, and plentiful alternative.

Children who have been dragged into violent conflict lose the opportunity for a normal life. They are at a high risk of displacement, material deprivation, and loss of access to healthcare and education. Regardless of whether they voluntarily took up arms or were abducted by government forces or other armed groups, they are often removed from their family units and may be transported far from their homes. They are often frightened and isolated. In many cases, children suffer serious physical and mental harm as a result of their roles as CSs. They may have been wounded in combat, raped, or drugged to make them more compliant or aggressive. Moreover, they suffer the mental trauma of being victims, perpetrators, and witnesses to human rights abuses. Girls are often abducted into sexual slavery or taken as "bush wives" by adult male fighters. Child soldiers rarely have access to adequate healthcare, which could provide treatment for the physical and mental strain on their bodies. Finally, children who become associated with armed forces or armed groups also miss the opportunity to pursue a formal education and develop vocational skills that would allow them to succeed in noncombatant roles in society. This makes the disarmament, demobilization, and reintegration of former CSs particularly important in both the short and long term.

Clearly, DDR programs should be designed with children's needs in mind. Yet it is important to be cognizant of the fact that CSs are not a homogenous group. Differences among them affect their ability or willingness to participate in a DDR program.[13] Some former CSs are ex-combatants, while others are civilians. Some are children of adult combatants, while many were abducted or forced into combat. Some are anxious to get home, while others consider that impossible. Child soldiers are often willing to leave armed groups if they know they will not be in serious danger and will be supported for a sufficient period to ensure they can readjust to civilian life.[14] As a result, funding and program administration for CSs may need to extend for years beyond the expected timeframe outlined for a DDR process.

International Law and Child Soldiers

If the extent to which CSs continue to be used in contemporary conflict is any judge, an international norm against employing children in combat has not been fully realized. However, there is a growing body of international law on the subject. The principal rights at risk for former CSs include the right to life and bodily security, the right to a decent standard of living that allows for personal development, the right to be free from mistreatment, the right to self-expression and decisionmaking participation, the right to justice, and the right to play.[15] In addition to these child-specific rights, former CSs and their adult combatant counterparts share the right to healthcare, the right to education, the right to gender equality, and the right to work. Any DDR process geared toward former CSs must work to protect these fundamental rights.

On a basic level, constructing DDR programs tailored to CSs is hampered by a lack of consensus on definitions. States, international organizations, and international law have varying opinions on what constitutes a "child" versus a "youth" or an "adolescent."[16] The UN Convention on the Rights of the Child (CRC) identifies a *child* as "every human being below the age of 18 years."[17] By contrast, some international organizations define *youth* as persons between the ages of 15 and 24.[18] Other organizations have chosen not to establish a definition of "youth" due to the heterogeneous nature of the group. The World Health Organization (WHO) splits "youth" into three overlapping categories: children from ages 10 to 19 are labeled "adolescents," young people from ages 15 to 24 are called "youth," and all people from ages 10 to 24 are termed "young people."[19]

Of course, while a definition based on age provides clarity, children's maturation depends on a range of factors. As a result, one author defines adolescence as "a temporary stage in life between childhood and adulthood and subject to external circumstances."[20] Additionally, *childhood*, *adolescence*, and *adulthood* may need to be redefined based on the particular culture of a region or community.[21] Of course, such criteria are not easily applied quickly or uniformly by organizations implementing DDR programs. A final challenge related to setting age criteria for participation in child DDR programs is that it must be recognized that some individuals participated in a conflict as children but may be adults by the time a DDR program is in place. For children who came of age during the conflict, programmers must determine whether they should be treated as children or adults when it comes to DDR.

The leading international guidance for the DDR of CSs is found in the 2007 Paris Principles, which are based on the Cape Town Principles and Best Practices on the Recruitment of Children into the Armed Forces, and on Demobilization and Social Reintegration of Child Soldiers in Africa, adopted 10 years earlier. In agreement with the CRC, the Paris Principles identify a "child" as an individual under the age of 18.[22] They further define a "child associated with an armed force or armed group" as:

> anyone below 18 years of age who is or who has been recruited by an armed force or armed group in any capacity, including but not limited to children, boys and girls used as fighters, cooks, porters, messengers, spies or for sexual purposes. It does not only refer to a child who is taking or has taken a direct part in hostilities.[23]

In the past, some DDR processes have exclusively targeted former child combatants. However, in alignment with the Paris Principles and the Cape Town Principles, DDR processes should not discriminate between children who were active combatants during a conflict and those who were noncombatants.[24]

In addition to reinforcing international standards for the definition of a "child" and "child associated with an armed force or armed group," the Paris Principles take a rights-based approach in addressing the problem of child participation in armed forces or armed groups. Specifically, they reinforce the humanitarian commitment that calls for the "release of children from armed forces or armed groups at all times, even in the midst of conflict and for the duration of the conflict."[25] This initiative is further supported by United Nations (UN) Resolution 1882, which calls for compliance with the CRC and its Optional Protocol on the Involvement of Children in Armed Conflict, as well as the 1949 Geneva Conventions and their Additional Protocols of 1977. Furthermore, Resolution 1882 censures all violations of international law that involve the recruitment and use of children by any group that is party to an armed conflict. It also denounces the re-recruitment, killing, and other acts of physical violence, rape, and sexual assault, abductions, and denial of humanitarian assistance against children by all parties to armed conflict.

Designing Child-sensitive DDR Processes

Disarmament, Demobilization, and Reintegration (DDR) is the process of demilitarizing armed groups by reducing the number of arms in circulation during disarmament, disbanding the groups and reducing the number of combatants during demobilization, and assisting combatants' reincorporation into civilian life and rebuilding the social fabric of communities during reintegration.[26] Overall, DDR is an integrated process that seeks to rehabilitate soldiers and transform them into civilians.[27] This process is no less important for children than for adults. In fact, failure to reintegrate CSs into society may slow the peace-building process and deprive postconflict societies of a youth base that can act as a driving force for peace and development in the longer term.[28]

Kemper identifies three types of overarching approaches to the design and implementation of DDR programs among former CSs.[29] The approach most widely used by international organizations working toward the reintegration of children under the age of 18 is rights-based. The underlying belief of the rights-based approach is that children should have access to specific individual rights in adverse situations. This derives from the greater moral obligation to protect children because they suffer the most and are innocent; thus, ensuring their welfare is inherently in the interest of all. The second approach is economics-based and views former CSs as decisionmakers who rationally respond to the marketplace in their own self-interest. From this perspective, child combatants choose to take up arms out of the need for money and recognition. Moreover, CSs have become an integral part of contemporary warfare because of their abundant supply and pliability. As a result, DDR programs must provide CSs with skills, incentives, and opportunities to enter the civilian economy. A third approach outlined by Kemper is socio-political. While it remains largely conceptual, the socio-political perspective focuses on how youth perceive themselves and their roles in society. As opposed to assigning norms and values to youth, this approach argues that youth should act as agents of change; therefore, implementing organizations should actively listen to them and implement their ideas.[30] Notably, because the socio-political approach regards youth as actors, it has great potential for promoting their inclusion in postconflict peace-building processes. Kemper suggests synthesizing the three approaches into a holistic DDR process that emphasizes a rights-based outlook in the preventative stage, an economic approach in the disarmament and demobilization phases, and a socio-political view during the reintegration process. This would allow each approach's benefits to be maximized in the phase where it is most effective. However, avoiding program duplication would require greater coordination among the organizations implementing each phase than has often happened in DDR processes.

The remainder of the chapter considers a range of issues related to DDR program design. In order to ensure its effectiveness, it is important to design the DDR process to cater to the unique needs of former CSs. We highlight the ways in which the experiences and needs of children differ from adults in political transitions. We begin with a discussion of issues DDR planners should keep in mind in setting up programs for CSs. Then we turn to the problem of identifying program recipients. In particular, child DDR programs have historically neglected noncombatants and girls. From there, we proceed to examine each phase of the DDR process in turn. It is imperative that the best interest of the children be given priority during each phase in order to successfully disarm, demobilize, and reintegrate CSs.[31] We offer several examples of how recent DDR programs have attempted to address the particular needs of children. As we shall see, states, international donors, and nongovernmental organizations (NGOs) have used a variety of methods to implement child DDR.

Planning and Coordination

Actors implementing DDR must decide on the precise timing and sequencing of programs, determine who the beneficiaries will be, and delineate the benefits to be provided. The phases of disarmament, demobilization, and reintegration may occur sequentially or simultaneously in DDR processes. In some cases, former CSs do not receive reintegration benefits until they have been disarmed and demobilized, whereas in other instances they do. The sequencing of DDR is often driven by requirements set by the national and international organizations funding the DDR process. For example, many bilateral development organizations will not provide ex-combatants with financial assistance until they have been demobilized.[32] Furthermore, DDR may progress differently in each region of a country based on local circumstances. Fundamentally, each program should work toward the entire long-term goal of reintegration.

Ideally, DDR should be conducted under national ownership. While the terms prescribed for the administration of DDR programs are national in scale, the process must be implemented at lower levels. Among other things, this will help ensure that local customs and beliefs are taken into account when developing the programs. This appears beneficial in promoting the stability of former CSs.[33] Accordingly, it is imperative to consult the communities throughout all phases of the process.[34] Organizations implementing DDR should raise questions for community members to consider and advise according to the responses, as opposed to telling a community how to treat its children.[35] A community-based approach can generally support DDR processes better in the short term by helping to reduce hostility, thereby creating a more sustainable environment for long-term security.

As a means to encourage as much community involvement as possible throughout the DDR process, implementing organizations should provide the community with relevant materials and tools. Implementing organizations must also ensure that the community has the resources to rebuild society including regular access to child protection information, periodic training forums, and identity cards. Additionally, DDR administrators should facilitate exchange visits with other child protection groups, provide communities with opportunities to apply for funding, enable participants to initiate personal income-generating activities, and build links between the community and the organizations implementing DDR. A community is more likely to carry out DDR activities over an extended time if the process responds directly to local priorities rather than those of outside groups.[36]

While local control is important, the international community is usually essential to the success of child DDR programs. For DDR to succeed, key international actors must first support the process by mediating among parties and exerting political and economic pressure for its implementation.[37] International actors, often under the auspices of the UN, frequently help enforce the security provisions of peace agreements, without which the parties would likely be reluctant to implement DDR. It is also advisable that peacekeeping forces, members of the national armed forces, and law enforcement groups receive training on children's rights.[38] Once it comes to implementing DDR, most countries have limited resources and expertise. The role of the outside group should be to help a community identify common concerns with the larger DDR process and decide which resources the community has readily available to alleviate its concerns.[39] Of course, attracting national and international interest to the plight of CSs is not always easy given the competing demands of fragile transitions to peace.

Along with general political apathy, financing tends to be one of the largest constraints on DDR processes. For example, according to a U.S. Agency for International Development (USAID) report, the Displaced Children and Orphans Fund (DCOF) provided $6.3 million between 1994 and 2004 to support projects for children affected by war in Liberia.[40] A typical DCOF grant was between $1 million and $1.5 million over 3 years. USAID argues, however, that because of the overwhelming needs of children, this amount alone is not enough to make a sufficient impact on the education, skills training, and livelihood prospects offered to youth.[41] In particular, the lack of data regarding child combatants complicates the process of producing accurate and adequate funding requests for CS programs. There are never enough resources.

Based on the first DDR process in Liberia that lasted from 1994 to 1997, there is a significant need for adaptability and conditional strategizing among donors and partners in order to appropriately react to unforeseen circumstances and roadblocks.[42] In 1993, detailed plans had been developed for DDR programs, but the process was halted almost immediately as a result of ongoing fighting.[43] After the formal process stalled, child combatants in smaller groups demobilized spontaneously or without much notice and preparation. When it became clear to the national and international implementing partners that the DDR process would recommence following the August 1996 ceasefire, they were able to quickly reassess and redesign the organizational structure based on lessons learned from 1994 to 1996. DDR procedures should allow for on-the-ground decisionmaking as contingencies will naturally arise.[44]

Coordination is a final issue that virtually all DDR programs confront. A variety of national and international organizations are likely to be involved, particularly in the demobilization phase. In Sierra Leone's DDR process from 1998 to 2002, the NCDDR established the guidelines for demobilization while military observers, national and international child protection NGOs, and UNICEF were later responsible for the implementation of those guidelines.[45] The program's results were mixed. UNICEF and some smaller NGOs were successful in administering psychosocial and educational programs. However, the vocational skills training program, also guided by UNICEF, did not achieve the same results. This was largely a consequence of poor coordination between NCDDR and UNICEF in accurately assessing the economic realities of Sierra Leone, an issue that will be discussed later.

Identifying the Beneficiaries of Child Soldier Programs

Various groups have traditionally been left out of DDR processes. Some former combatants miss out because they are outside of the typical definition of a child. Most child DDR processes exclusively benefit those under 18. Former combatants over that age often ask to be considered for child DDR benefits because they were under that age when the conflict began. Unfortunately, there is rarely enough funding to include them in the target beneficiary group.[46] As a result, these individuals may be funneled to adult programs that do not cater to their needs or excluded from the DDR process entirely because they fall between the definition of "child" and "adult." In addition, children who escaped the fighting and demobilized themselves informally may be left out because they can no longer prove they were combatants. Child refugees are also often excluded. That is even more likely if they are foreigners who were kidnapped or forced to flee fighting across national borders.

Evidence shows that girls are consistently associated with armed forces or armed groups when conflict is present. Some research, for example, claims that 30 percent of the child soldiers in Sierra Leone and Liberia were girls.[47] However, former female CSs have historically been excluded from DDR processes for several reasons. First, some peacekeeping organizations use weapons tests to decide who will be eligible to receive DDR benefits. The tests force potential beneficiaries to present and demonstrate operational familiarity with weapons, which excludes many girls who may not have been armed during the conflict and therefore lack a weapon to surrender.[48] Second, programs that target ex-combatants are more likely to miss female CSs. Girls often perform domestic work or complete support tasks, such as carrying equipment for the armed forces or armed groups, but may not actually see combat. Finally, female CSs may be victims of abuses that make them reluctant to come forward. They are often held as sexual slaves or are abducted by combatants as "bush wives." For example, approximately 75 percent of demobilized girls in Liberia reported they were victims of some form of sexual abuse while they were associated with armed forces or armed groups.[49]

In many postconflict situations, these girls would be eligible for DDR benefits, but they do not participate. They may be intentionally kept from the process by commanders who want to continue exploiting them. While boys may be of little value to armed forces or armed groups during the postconflict period, girls can continue to be utilized for domestic and sexual purposes. Given the roles they typically play in combat, girl CSs are also more likely to be uninformed about how to participate.

Some organizations that implement DDR programs contend that fear and shame are more likely to keep girls from receiving DDR benefits than weapons tests.[50] In the DRC, for example, community-based initiatives were established in 2004 that were designed to respond to the needs of girls. However, due to a fear of stigmatization within their communities, it is estimated that thousands of former female CSs did not benefit from reintegration support.[51] Similarly, many in Sierra Leone received no assistance in the disarmament phase of DDR and encountered trouble returning home during the reintegration phase.[52] Sierra Leone's Truth and Reconciliation Commission (TRC) argued that failure to address the specific needs of girls was one of the biggest faults of the country's DDR process.[53] As a rule of best practice, girls should be included in child programs. However, if implementing nations and organizations do not allow females to participate, at minimum a parallel contingency plan should be established to deal with the special circumstances of former female CSs, including pregnancy and exposure to HIV/AIDS.[54]

It is not uncommon for the organizations that are implementing DDR to have diverse views regarding whether communities or individual former combatants should be the primary beneficiaries. Some argue that both former child soldiers and their communities should comprise the target group. Communities often suffer as a result of fighting, and they could become resentful if they receive little while former fighters benefit from DDR programs. Other organizations maintain that the perpetrators of violence should be the exclusive target group if the overall goal is to reduce hostility. Ultimately, however, the development of DDR eligibility criteria must be based on the nature of the political and institutional environment in which the process is to be implemented.[55]

Singling out ex-combatants as exclusively eligible for benefits could be viewed as a reward for their past violence. That could run counter to the long-range ambitions of DDR for reintegration by alienating them from the community. In order to decrease the marginalization of both ex-combatants and civilians, it is argued that an inclusive community-based approach best serves the needs of all parties in a postconflict environment. To help prevent continued stigmatization of former CSs by their communities, it is important that implementing organizations discuss the situation with local stakeholders, stressing the abduction and violence that many former CSs endured.[56] In general, offering services such as education and healthcare to the entire community rather than only former CSs provides communities with concrete benefits without depriving CSs of their needs.

Disarmament

As the initial stage of DDR, disarmament is critical to removing the tools for violence from a society. *Disarmament* involves the collection of small arms and other weaponry from combatants within a zone of conflict. The Clingendael Institute notes that, in addition to the collection of arms, actors in the disarmament process should develop responsible arms management programs and document control and disposal of small arms, ammunition, explosives, and light and heavy weapons.[57]

Historically, many DDR programs have required the surrender of a weapon for admittance into the DDR process. This practice has led to the exclusion of children, particularly girls. As mentioned earlier, girls often have not carried weapons and cannot surrender them. It is advised that future DDR programs grant children access to benefits without the surrender of a weapon.

In addition, disarmament programs are often elaborate formal programs established as part of a ceasefire or peace agreement that processes entire military units at once. The arrangements reached in the peace deals are designed to make combatants confident enough in their security to turn over their weapons. Yet CSs frequently do not operate with this mentality. They have typically been kidnapped and pressed into service. Thus, when they are able to escape life in the bush, they may take advantage of DDR programs. But the programs are not well suited to such spontaneous disarmament. Such complications raise questions about putting anything more than very limited criteria on DDR participation for children.

Demobilization

Demobilization is "the process by which parties to a conflict begin to disband their military structures and combatants begin the transformation into civilian life." Some demobilization programs have been designed as two-part processes. During the first phase, individual combatants may be processed in temporary centers or camps where troops are demobilized in large groups.[58] In the latter stage, identified as "reinsertion," demobilized persons are provided with a support package and are commonly transported to their civilian homes.[59] Reinsertion occurs in a shorter timeframe but ultimately supports the longer term process of reintegration.

Early DDR programs did not physically separate CSs from adults during demobilization. However, housing CSs together does not break the ties between children and their former commanders. In Sierra Leone, for example, former child combatants were immediately separated from adult combatants after they had been disarmed.[60] They were then divided by age. Children under 15 were sent to Interim Care Centers (ICCs) under the care of UNICEF and local child protection agencies. For many of these children, the move to the ICC was a way to separate them from their former commanders, protect them from additional abuse, disassociate them from being "fighters," and begin to rebuild their civilian identities.[61] Eligible CSs over 15 joined the NCDDR training and employment programs, for which they received a start-up kit with tools for their vocational training. Based on past DDR experiences, it is also advisable that boys and girls be demobilized in separate processing centers in order to best address the specific needs of girls.[62] Establishing special camps for children, including separation by gender, allows DDR programs to better focus their services.

Many child soldiers will have suffered some type of physical deprivation from spending extensive time in the "bush." This may be as a result of limited healthcare and malnutrition, which lead to a weak immune system and put youth at an increased risk for disease. The sustained physical well-being of former CSs is critical to their demobilization and rehabilitation. In Sierra Leone and Liberia, routine health services and medical treatment were incorporated into the DDR process. Physical health screenings in these nations revealed a high incidence of disease including malaria, worm infestation, respiratory tract infection, skin infection, diarrhea, and hepatitis B.[63] Some former CSs may also require treatment for issues related to mutilation, which can lead to stigmatization and psychological disorders. In Sierra Leone, for example, some insurgent groups carved their group's initials on child soldiers.[64] In 2001, USAID funded a UNICEF subgrant to the International Medical Corps for plastic surgery to remove such scars.

Demobilization should maintain a focus on a return to a normal life. Many children need to relearn culturally appropriate behavior and participate in rehabilitation activities. Moreover, regardless of whether they were civilians or former combatants, they suffer from mental trauma because of their wartime experiences. Evidence from Liberia indicates that many former child soldiers need a simple treatment plan to rehabilitate after their experiences during conflict.[65] Services offered at the ICCs in Sierra Leone included psychosocial counseling, healthcare services, and education. In addition, some commanders in Sierra Leone used drugs on CSs to diminish their inhibitions and more easily sway them to commit violent acts.[66] In the aftermath of the conflict, this led to a large number of former CSs who suffered from drug addiction and other mental health issues. Organizations and program administrators should approach mental health treatment understanding that the degree of trauma suffered will differ from child to child, which calls for individualized treatment plans.[67] They should also recognize that Western models of therapy may be neither necessary nor appropriate in treating psychological harm.[68]

Group exercises and play opportunities are also important for former CSs. For example, research has shown that basic recreational pursuits and self-help initiatives effectively supported rehabilitation from distress in both Sierra Leone and Liberia.[69] These activities included forms of expression and recreation that were used in conjunction with continued individual or family counseling, conflict resolution training, and peace education. Evidence from past DDR programs also shows that activities that encourage the revival of cultural heritage, including drama and dance, have supported the reestablishment of children's identities and should be utilized in future mental health rehabilitation processes.[70] In general, programs designed to promote the psychosocial rehabilitation of former CSs should incorporate local approaches and traditional healing mechanisms that address the sociocultural, religious, and political realities of the community.[71] Finally, group counseling among children has proven particularly effective in their rehabilitation and reintegration into civilian society.[72]

Generally, a return to the nurturing environment of the family is regarded as one of the best ways for former CSs to begin dealing with their traumas. As a result, family tracing and reunification initiatives are vital to their long-term psychosocial needs. Unfortunately, many CSs who were very young when they became combatants are unable to remember their families and cannot be reunited with them. Throughout the demobilization phase, organizations should conduct family tracing and mediation in preparation for reintegrating former CSs into civilian society.[73] For example, in the DRC, Save the Children–UK organized demobilization efforts using a community-based initiative conducted from temporary transit centers, where implementing parties traced a child's family, taught functional literacy, and provided basic health services, psychosocial counseling, and vocational training.[74] Most children arrived at the transit centers with some information regarding their families and where they were located. Many wished to be reunited as quickly as possible and were able to decide for themselves if it was safe to return. Some achieved reunification with relative ease because they had not been relocated far from home or else could maintain contact.

Demobilization programs also anticipate the problems children might encounter on returning. Part of this involves educating and sensitizing communities to the children and their experiences. In the DRC, Save the Children–UK focused on rebuilding safe environments for former CSs as a means to ensure their protection and to restore their self-confidence.[75] As family reunification and tracing processes continue in the longer term, it is important that additional agency personnel and transportation are provided to support tracing efforts, monitor former CSs who have been reunited with their families, and intervene where necessary.[76] An important element is the establishment of local child protection committees to provide continued support for this process.[77]

Addressing the economic needs of CSs is another important goal of DDR. Some economists see an excessive number of unemployed youth as a high risk factor for political violence because they are easily recruited into armed groups. A recent study, for example, found that youth often participate in violence because they feel that their concerns, especially those regarding education and employment, are neglected by the state.[78] There is a consensus that the prevalence of "youth bulges" in conflict-prone areas increases the risk of the reemergence of violence if the labor market cannot absorb demobilized youth.[79] In 1999, the Office of Transition Initiatives (OTI) in association with USAID developed the Youth Reintegration Training and Education for Peace (YRTEP) program in Sierra Leone. The program provided life and agricultural skills training, vocational counseling, and civic education.[80] Unfortunately, the organizations designing the DDR program in Sierra Leone had not accurately accounted for the economic realities of a postconflict society. Many former CSs were therefore not able to establish a sustainable business in the weak economic environment.[81] The OTI's training failed largely because it was unable to provide immediate results, and there was a lack of follow-up programs to help the beneficiaries utilize their newly acquired skills.[82] So programs need to be in sync with economic conditions in the community.

It is critical that the timeframe outlined for demobilization consider the needs of the region and the former CSs. What may be applicable to one area may not be effective in another. In Liberia, evidence shows that the rapid demobilization process failed to effectively break the ties between former CSs and armed forces or armed groups. Consequently, many frustrated former CSs eventually returned to their commanders, not necessarily to reestablish themselves as soldiers but to reconnect with the last person who supplied food, shelter, and protection.[83] In Sierra Leone, former CSs were not allowed to stay in the ICCs for longer than 6 weeks as a result of a USAID mandate, which said that extended stays could habituate former CSs to institutional life and impede future family and community reintegration.[84] After 6 weeks, former CSs who were unable to reunify with their families were placed in alternative living arrangements as family tracing continued, while some older children were allowed to cohabitate in small groups under supervision. In the DRC, over 30,000 children waited nearly 2 years for the demobilization process to begin due to a lack of political and military will, mismanagement of funds, and poor coordination.[85] Thousands more left their armed groups without completing the official demobilization process. Children should be in transition centers as briefly as possible. During that time, they must be given the tools to thrive in civilian life if long-term reintegration is to succeed.

Some past programs distributed cash among former combatants during demobilization. Such payments offer financial flexibility to ex-combatants but also pose the risk of abuse and mismanagement. Promising cash may heighten conflict among DDR recipients or between recipients and nonrecipients. In addition, some commanders may try to confiscate DDR payments from former CSs previously under their command. For example, the UN Mission in Liberia (UNMIL) and NCDDR distributed cash allowances of US $300 to former combatants, including children. Evidence has shown that this component of the child DDR process had a negative impact on the children it was meant to benefit by creating a situation in which they were exploited by their commanders and were unable to reintegrate into their communities.[86] In addition, there was a heightened fear of re-recruitment among former CSs near Monrovia, which contained a large number of active armed groups and few financial and social opportunities. Separating children from adults can go some of the way, but not all, in addressing this concern.

In some cases, cash benefits have been allocated to former adult combatants but not to former CSs. Children may be viewed as too irresponsible to be given money. They will likely be tempted by the opportunity to receive immediate cash benefits as opposed to skills training and education. Consequently, some former CSs have posed as adults to receive upfront financial support. It is essential that DDR program staff are trained to distinguish children from adults. Perhaps more importantly, programs must communicate the importance of the in-kind services provided to former CSs and design them so they actually do provide long-term benefits.

Reintegration

The Paris Principles define *child reintegration* as "the process through which children transition into civil society and enter meaningful roles and identities as civilians who are accepted by their families and communities."[87] Other organizations note that the time frame for reintegration is open and driven by local communities.[88] Additionally, adapting to their communities may be a complex and lengthy process for CSs whose experiences in combat have left them with psychologically damaging trauma.[89]

Planning and financing for programs that support reintegration should be set as soon as implementing nations and organizations are aware that children have been associated with armed forces or groups. CSs will require support even if a formal peacekeeping or DDR process has yet to be established. Due to the long-term needs of former CSs, funding should be made available as early as possible and continue after the termination of formal DDR processes.[90] Organizations should be prepared to appeal for supplemental funding for child reintegration programs to ensure their sustainability over the entire duration of child need.

The lack of funds allocated to programs that provide essential resources to former CSs is a major concern. Evidence shows that reintegration programs have only received marginal funding and analysis compared to disarmament and demobilization, which are the better-understood military aspects of DDR.[91] Research suggests that donors are hesitant to apply direct financing towards reintegration processes out of concern for the long-term commitment that may be necessary. Organizations and donors may also be reluctant to provide funds for reintegration because there is a lack of quantifiable results from previous reintegration programs, and many peacekeeping mandates regularly omit aspects related to reintegration processes.[92]

For the reintegration phase to be effective, and to prevent re-recruitment of former CSs, the situation must be carefully analyzed and the target group must be consulted.[93] With regard to curbing violence and promoting security, the Paris Principles urges including children and families in the design and implementation of prevention initiatives. Children who have previously taken up arms are best equipped to explain why they made that choice. Subsequently, including parents and other significant adult members of their communities has been integral in preventing children from joining or rejoining armed forces or groups.[94]

During the reintegration phase, former CSs should receive either formal education or adequate skills training, coupled with literacy and numeracy instruction.[95] Education offers young people a way to earn money and respect in ways not associated with combat, making it important throughout postconflict regions.[96] In addition, it exposes former CSs to the outside world, prepares some for future leadership roles, and provides an honor code through which they can build integrity and learn about their cultural heritage.[97] The lack of education among former CSs is not necessarily, or entirely, due to their roles as combatants. Previous experience shows that many had little to no formal education prior to their engagement with armed forces or armed groups. Education and training are generally well received by children. Many former CSs, especially the younger ones, view formal education as an appealing benefit of the DDR process.[98]

In Sierra Leone, most child soldiers had little to no education. In response, the Rapid Response Education Project (RREP) was administered for a 6-month period to prepare former CSs to return to school.[99] Even former CSs with some schooling were years behind and were ashamed to be placed in classes with younger children. As a means to encourage children to enroll without fear of stigmatization, a Community Rapid Education Program (CREP) was developed. It utilized a modified version of the national primary school curriculum to provide accelerated learning for children aged 10 to 14. This target group was able to complete 6 years of learning in 3 and quickly advanced towards the educational levels of their peers.[100] In addition, the CREP program was unique because it was also offered to noncombatant children who had been displaced by the war and had no prior opportunity to attend school.

During the later stages of DDR in Sierra Leone, a Community Education Investment Program (CEIP) funded by UNICEF was implemented by local NGOs with the intention of assisting the reintegration of children and reducing the stigmatization former CSs faced in their communities.[101] Participating schools received a standard package of material assistance that supported educational programs, as well as recreational equipment for each former CS admitted. This created an incentive for the schools and communities to accept children participating in the DDR process, and also allowed former CSs to make a positive contribution to their communities. Moreover, it provided tangible benefits to communities, and particularly to other children who would not have received DDR benefits otherwise.

During reintegration programs, DDR organizers should recognize that formal education might not meet the needs of all CSs. In Sierra Leone, those over 15 were given the option of participating in skills training or receiving an agricultural assistance package instead of attending school.[102] Apprenticeships were the primary method of skills training, under which each former CS was assigned to a master tradesperson. One failure on the part of UNICEF during the reintegration phase was the lack of an assessment linking the skills acquired by former CSs to the needs of the labor market in their communities.[103] In Sierra Leone, 70 percent of the population is dependent on semisubsistence agriculture. However, very few former CSs were provided with agriculture skills as an opportunity during reintegration.[104] Some did not want to pursue agricultural training because they associated it with a lower skill set, and instead chose a vocational training package.[105] As a result, there was an excess of youth trained in unneeded fields. Ideally, skills training initiatives should accurately evaluate the vocational needs of the communities into which former CSs will be reintegrating and extend over enough time to enable trainees to sufficiently learn their newly marketable skills.[106] Moreover, programs should also provide job search post-training to aid reintegration.

In addition to providing educational and skills training opportunities, it is important for DDR programs to support former CSs in developing healthy relationships with adults to support the greater goal of familial and community acceptance.[107] Former CSs often struggle with trusting adults as a result of their negative experience with having been kidnapped and exploited. Conversely, adults who were not part of the conflict may be concerned about the probability of former CSs becoming violent and may hesitate to befriend them.

Some regions have incorporated sensitization initiatives to encourage communities to openly accept the return of children into their families and support the development of a civilian identity in order to maintain peace.[108] In Liberia, child welfare committees were developed by the International

Rescue Committee (IRC) to cultivate relationships between former CSs and adults in the community.[109] These committees were typically comprised of ten individuals who were balanced in gender and age whose primary role was to raise awareness of child protection issues among community members and to help former CSs learn about their rights. The committees worked with the local police and the Ministry of Social Welfare to raise awareness about abuse and exploitation experienced by former CSs.[110] Additionally, in Sierra Leone the OTI managed to reconcile some former CSs with their communities by training them to better manage their tempers and understand cultural norms.[111] Future DDR-implementing organizations can learn from the OTI's process by rebuilding the same level of cooperation between former CSs and their communities and using a teamwork strategy to develop income-generating activities.

A notable and creative aspect of the reintegration process in Sierra Leone was the Search for Common Ground's (SFCG's) use of radio and other media to give marginalized youth a voice through child-centric news and entertainment broadcasts. The original idea came from a former Revolutionary United Front (RUF) child soldier, who was able to partner child protection agencies with young former ex-combatants to produce the radio program, which is now distributed over several mainstream stations.[112] Additionally, these media outlets have been used more recently to support the region's larger political process. The SFCG mobilized youth in Sierra Leone to assist with voter registration and monitor voting for the first postwar elections in 2002.[113] Initiatives are important in reconnecting communities and former CSs and have been increasingly used in DDR programs.

Finally, the Paris Principles argue that successful reintegration of children must be done in the context of local and national reconciliation efforts. The practice of transitional justice involves attempts to address past human rights violations. Transitional justice measures might include indigenous conflict resolution mechanisms. In Liberia and Sierra Leone, for example, traditional cleansing ceremonies, healing processes, and religious support have helped immensely with reintegration.[114] These practices incorporate traditional values, community belief systems, and spiritual rituals designed to liberate former CSs from evil.[115] Accordingly, they provide a culturally-embedded means for children to overcome their suffering and guilt while simultaneously promoting community healing and forgiveness.

National reconciliation initiatives can support peace-building and provide an incentive against the re-recruitment of former CSs. Truth commissions in particular have come to be seen as effective tools for educating society about past violence and forming recommendations to prevent their recurrence. In Sierra Leone, the TRC was established as a means of compiling an authoritative historical account of the civil war. Like many truth commissions, it interviewed thousands of victims, witnesses, and perpetrators to develop a broad picture of the nature of the conflict, its origins, and its consequences. The TRC also promoted public traditional forgiveness rituals at the end of its hearings in each province. The international community helped ensure the TRC's findings were widely distributed and accessible to children. UNICEF sponsored a children's version of the TRC's final report and the International Center for Transitional Justice produced a picture version. The German government financed the printing of 40,000 copies designed for secondary school use. Overall, some research claims that the national reconciliation process in Sierra Leone aided in promoting the concept of forgiveness for the crimes carried out by former CSs.[116]

The question of prosecuting CSs who committed human rights violations is more controversial. While there is no current international law regarding whether they should be charged for the atrocities they committed as combatants, international law does require that gross violations be prosecuted. To forego punishment for human rights violations committed by CSs is to potentially rob their victims of achieving justice. Yet most societies recognize that children cannot be held responsible for their acts in the same way as adults. Almost invariably, children are also victims, having become involved in the conflicts against their wills. Thus, transitional justice for them should be restorative rather than punitive.[117] In the absence of international consensus, it is essentially up to the national and international implementing partners to agree on a method of reconciliation.[118]

In the aftermath of the conflict in the DRC, children were arrested, detained, and tried in military courts for alleged crimes. At least 12 were sentenced to death.[119] In May 2005, military prosecutors in the DRC were advised that children who had been illegally recruited by armed forces or armed groups, and who had also been accused of committing crimes, were to be referred to a competent civilian court or to CONADER.[120] It is recommended that former CSs receive protection from retribution for acts committed during conflict to encourage their voluntary participation in the DDR process and to promote the ultimate goal of reintegration. In fact, UNICEF encourages the inclusion in peace accords of provisions that provide amnesty for former CSs regardless of their acts during hostilities.[121] If a former CS is to be prosecuted, he or she must be treated with regard to international standards of juvenile justice and in his or her best interest.[122]

Transitional justice architects should recognize that punishing children for acts they commit under duress or when their moral capacities are not fully developed seems destined to permanently alienate the child from society.

Conclusion

Children and youth under the age of 18 comprise a large portion of the global population, and many live in nations or regions that are conflict-prone. History has shown that when conflict is present, children will often become entangled in the fighting. In recent years, the international community has called for an end to the recruitment and participation of children in conflict through a series of international treaties and declarations. In addition, there is growing recognition that current and future DDR programs must include former CSs in order to bring a decisive end to hostilities, reduce the probability of recruitment of combatants, create a sustainable environment, and support long-term security initiatives.

Clearly, there should be no homogenous approach to DDR. Each situation will be unique and, consequently, will need to be addressed in its own specific context. Practitioners and organizations may utilize a variety of methods to approach DDR processes; given the world's relatively limited experience with child DDR, experimentation is welcome. However, examining previous cases such as Sierra Leone, DRC, and Liberia can shed light on past errors and suggest some child DDR best practices. For example, it seems clear that most programs would benefit from incorporating individuals, families, and organizations at the community level. Earlier experiences have shown that the postconflict environment is highly sensitive, and DDR processes must actively work to reduce stigmatization through education and community sensitization programs that rebuild relationships between former CSs and the members of their communities.

DDR can be useful for transitioning former CSs to civilian life in important ways. Its primary purposes are to assist disarmed and demobilized persons, promote sustainable peace, and restore civilian life.[123] Specifically, it can provide an arms reduction mechanism, dissolve militant command structures, and give militaries and rebels a face-saving way to lay down their weapons. In addition, DDR has the potential to build trust between former combatants and noncombatants, which increases the prospects for long-term peace. Through the provision of short- and long-term assistance to ex-combatants and their families, DDR can begin to break habits and transform the identities of CSs. DDR on its own cannot, however, prevent conflict from arising, act as a substitute for peace enforcement activities, or address the lack of economic and political development that was often the source of the original conflict.

It is also imperative that DDR programs design specific processes to ensure the inclusion of historically marginalized groups. Girls have been the most underserved group. They are routinely left out of DDR programs as a result of program design issues such as weapons tests or fear of the stigma that their families and communities will attach to their experiences. It is imperative that future DDR processes do more to encourage the participation of female CSs, regardless of their role with armed forces or armed groups. As girls become habitually included in DDR initiatives, nations and organizations also need to develop programs for their specific needs including prenatal and child care and the prevention and treatment of sexual abuse and sexually transmitted diseases. DDR processes have also excluded former combatants who were recruited as children but are over the age of 18 by the time demobilization occurs. Due to a lack of funding, these former CSs are often unable to participate in child DDR processes and consequently do not receive the youth-specific physical and psychosocial treatment that is critical to their long-term success in society. It is important for future DDR initiatives to design programs that specifically meet the needs of these groups in order to reduce their marginalization.

In general, the nations and organizations implementing DDR must be able to plan and coordinate their efforts effectively throughout the DDR process to ensure that former CSs receive the benefits they are entitled to and that are crucial to their reintegration. Many child DDR processes are designed by a national authority but require the financial and technical support of the international community. While some progress has been made in calling attention to the use of child soldiers and including them in DDR processes, the international community must learn from past experiences to create more effective child DDR processes that will lead to a decrease in re-recruitment and promote sustainable peace in post-conflict communities.

Notes

[1] United Nations Children Fund (UNICEF), *10-Year Strategic Review: Children and Conflict in a Changing World*, available at <http://www.unicef.org/publications/files/Machel_Study_10_Year_Strategic _Review_EN_030909.pdf> (accessed April 26, 2010).

[2] United Nations Children Fund (UNICEF), *Convention on the Rights of the Child*, available at <http://www. unicef.org/crc/index_30203.html> (accessed April 28, 2010).

[3] Coalition to Stop the Use of Child Soldiers, *Child Soldiers: Global Report 2008*, available at <http://www.childsoldiersglobalreport.org/files/country_pdfs/FINAL_2008_Global_Report.pdf> (accessed April 26, 2010).

[4] Coalition to Stop the Use of Child Soldiers.

[5] UNICEF, 19.

[6] Coalition to Stop the Use of Child Soldiers, 297; Kirsten Gislesen, *A Childhood Lost? The Challenges of Successful Disarmament, Demobilisation and Reintegration of Child Soldiers: The Case of West Africa* (Oslo: Norwegian Institute of International Affairs, 2006), 11.

[7] Coalition to Stop the Use of Child Soldiers, 298; National Committee for Disarmament, Demobilisation and Reintegration (NCDDR), *NCDDR Meeting March 2, 2004, Executive Secretary Report*, prepared by Dr. Francis Kai-Kai, Executive Secretary NCDDR, available at <http://www.daco-sl.org/encyclopedia/8_lib/8_3/NCDDR_ExecSecretary_report.pdf> (accessed May 6, 2010), 3.

[8] Coalition to Stop the Use of Child Soldiers, 107.

[9] Gislesen, 11.

[10] Ibid., 9.

[11] United Nations, *Report of the Secretary-General on Children and Armed Conflict*, UN Document A/59/695-S/2005/72, 9, 2005.

[12] Yvonne Kemper, *Youth in War-to-Peace Transitions: Approaches of International Organizations* (Berlin: Berghof Research Center for Constructive Conflict Management, 2005), 12.

[13] John Williamson, "The Disarmament, Demobilization and Reintegration of Child Soldiers: Social and Psychological Transformation in Sierra Leone," *The International Journal of Mental Health, Psychosocial Work and Counseling in Areas of Armed Conflict* 4, no. 3 (2006), 5.

[14] Canadian International Development Agency (CIDA), *Support to Former Child Soldiers: Programming and Proposal Guide*, available at <http://www.acdi-cida.gc.ca/INET/IMAGES.NSF/vLUImages/Childprotection/$file/ Child-Soldiers.pdf> (accessed April 10, 2009), 8.

[15] CIDA, 2.

[16] Gislesen, 5.

[17] United Nations General Assembly, *Conventions on the Rights of the Child* (New York: UN Security Council, 1989).

[18] Kemper, 3.

[19] Pan American Health Organization, World Health Organization (WHO), *Regional Strategy for Improving Adolescent and Youth Health* (Washington, DC, WHO, 2008), CE142/13, Rev., 2, 3.

[20] Kemper, 8.

[21] Ibid., 9.

[22] United Nations Children's Fund (UNICEF), *The Paris Principles: The Principles and Guidelines on Children Associated with Armed Forces or Armed Groups* (Paris: February 2007), available at <http:// www.un.org/ children/ conflict/_documents/parisprinciples/Paris Principles_EN.pdf> (accessed April 26, 2009).

[23] UNICEF, *The Paris Principles*, 7.

[24] Belinda Bernard et al., *Situation of Women and Children Combatants in Liberian Post-Conflict Period and Recommendations for Successful Integration* (Bethesda, MD: Development Alternatives, Inc., 2003), 60.

[25] UNICEF, *The Paris Principles*, 5.

[26] Nicole Ball, *Disarmament, Demobilization and Reintegration: Mapping Issues, Dilemmas and Guiding Principles* (The Hague: Luc van de Goor, Netherlands Institute of International Relations, "Clingendael" Conflict Research Unit, 2006), 16.

[27] Gislesen, 6.

[28] Ball, 5.

[29] Kemper.

[30] Jesse Newman, "Protection through Participation," background paper on the Conference on Voices Out of Conflict: Young People Affected by Forced Migration and Political Crisis, Cumberland Lounge, March 2004; Jo Boyden and Gillian Mann, "Children's Risk, Resilience and Coping in Extreme Situations," background paper to the Consultation on Children in Adversity, Oxford, September 2000, 10.

[31] CIDA, 6.

[32] Ball, 21.

[33] CIDA, 7.

[34] Guillaume Landry, *Child Soldiers and Disarmament, Demobilization, Rehabilitation and Reintegration in West Africa* (New York: Coalition to Stop the Use of Child Soldiers, 2006), 2.

[35] John Williamson, "The Disarmament, Demobilization and Reintegration of Child Soldiers: Social and Psychological Transformation in Sierra Leone," *The International Journal of Mental Health, Psychosocial Work and Counseling in Areas of Armed Conflict* 4, no. 3 (2006), 17.

[36] John Williamson and L. Randolph Carter, *Children's Reintegration in Liberia* (Washington: U.S. Agency for International Development, 2005), 10.

[37] Ball, 5.

[38] Landry, 2.

[39] Williamson and Carter, 10.

[40] Ibid., 2.

[41] Ibid., xv.

[42] Bernard et al., 4–5.

[43] Ibid., 5.

[44] Williamson, 17.

[45] Coalition to Stop the Use of Child Soldiers, 298–299.

[46] CIDA, 4.

[47] D. Mazurana, S. McKay, K. Carlson, and J. Kasper, "Girls in Fighting Forces and Groups: Their Recruitment, Participation, Demobilization and Reintegration," *Peace and Conflict: Journal of Peace Psychology* 8, no. 2 (June 2002), 107.

[48] Williamson, 4.

[49] United Nations, *Report of the Secretary-General.*

[50] Williamson, 7.

[51] Coalition to Stop the Use of Child Soldiers, 110.

[52] Williamson, 2.

[53] Sierra Leone Truth and Reconciliation Committee, *Report of the Sierra Leone Truth and Reconciliation Committee,* available at <http://www.sierra-leone.org/Other-Conflict/TRCVolume2.pdf> (accessed April 26, 2009).

[54] CIDA, 5.

[55] Ball, 14.

[56] Gislesen, 39.

[57] Ball, 2.

[58] UNICEF, *The Paris Principles*, 8.

[59] Bernard et al., 7.

[60] Williamson, 4.

[61] Gislesen, 19–20.

[62] Williamson and Carter, xiv.

[63] Gislesen, 23.

[64] Williamson, 6.

[65] Bernard et al., 87.

[66] Coalition to Stop the Use of Child Soldiers, 299.

[67] Bernard, 87.

[68] Williamson, 5.

[69] Gislesen, 30.

[70] Ibid., 31.

[71] Ibid.

[72] Bernard et al., 87.

[73] Williamson and Carter, xiv.

[74] Bernard et al., 20–21.

[75] Kemper, 18–20.

[76] Williamson, 11.

[77] Ibid., 12.

[78] Angela McIntyre and Taya Weiss, *Exploring Small Arms Demand, A Youth Perspective* (Pretoria: Institute for Security Studies, 2003), 3, 5.

[79] Kemper, 26.

[80] Ibid., 31.

[81] Coalition to Stop the Use of Child Soldiers, 298.

[82] Kemper, 32.

[83] Coalition to Stop the Use of Child Soldiers.

[84] Williamson, 5.

[85] Coalition to Stop the Use of Child Soldiers, 110.

[86] Ibid., 213.

[87] UNICEF, *The Paris Principles*, 8.

[88] Ball, 2.

[89] Kemper, 11.

[90] UNICEF, *The Paris Principles*, 24.

[91] Kemper, 11.

[92] International Peace Academy (IPA), *A Framework for Lasting Disarmament, Demobilization, and Reintegration of Former Combatants in Crisis Situation*, IPA–UNDP Workshop (New York: German House, 2002), 2.

[93] Williamson, 17.

[94] UNICEF, *The Paris Principles*, 22.

[95] Williamson, 3.

[96] Landry, 11.

[97] Williamson, 6.

[98] Gislesen, 44.

[99] Williamson, 13.

[100] Gislesen, 44.

[101] Ibid., 45.

[102] Williamson, 13.

[103] Kemper, 21; Gislesen, 47.

[104] Krijn Peters, "Footpaths to Reintegration: Armed Conflict, Youth and the Rural Crisis in Sierra Leone," thesis (Wageningen, Netherlands: Wageningen University, 2006), 128.

[105] Nicole Ball, Gebreselassie Tesfamichael, and Julie Nenon, *Peace in Sierra Leone: Evaluating the Disarmament, Demobilization and Reintegration Process* (Washington, DC: Creative Associates, 2004), 61.

[106] Williamson, 17.

[107] CIDA, 9.

[108] Gislesen, 38–39.

[109] Williamson and Carter, xii.

[110] Save the Children–United Kingdom, *What we do in Sierra Leone*, available at <http://www.savethechildren .org.uk/en/docs/Sierra_Leone_CB_2009.pdf> (accessed May 10, 2010).

[111] Kemper, 32.

[112] Search for Common Ground (SFCG), *Talking Drum Studio—Sierra Leone Radio Programs*, available at <http://www.sfcg.org/programmes/sierra/sierra_talking.html> (accessed May 12, 2010).

[113] Kemper, 43.

[114] Williamson and Carter, xiv; Williamson, 3.

[115] Gislesen, 40.

[116] Ibid., 40.

[117] Nienke Grossman, "Rehabilitation or Revenge: Prosecuting Child Soldiers for Human Rights Violations," *Georgetown Journal of International Law* 38, no. 2 (Winter 2007).

[118] CIDA, 3.

[119] MONUC Child Protection Section, Arrestations et Détentions Dans Les Prisons et Cachots de la RDC et la Détention des Enfants et la Justice pour Mineurs, Circular No. AG/0631/D8a, 2005.

[120] Coalition to Stop the Use of Child Soldiers, 110.

[121] UNICEF, *The Disarmament, Demobilization, and Reintegration of Children Associated with the Fighting Forces: Lessons Learned from Sierra Leone 1998–2002* (2005), 4.

[122] Vesselin Popovski and Karin Arts, *International Criminal Accountability and Children's Rights*, United Nations University Policy Brief No. 4, 2006.

[123] CIDA, 6.

Chapter 8

Consequences of the Forgotten (or Missing) *R*

By Judith Burdin Asuni

Introduction

Ateke Tom, a major militant leader in Nigeria's Niger Delta, was pictured on Al Jazeera television October 1, 2009, shaking hands with President Umaru Yar'Adua. He was not the first militant leader to accept the amnesty offered by Yar'Adua. Indeed General Boyloaf had been pictured shaking hands with the President more than a month before. What was remarkable about Ateke was that he had had a similar photo op 5 years earlier when he and his former enemy, militant leader Asari Dokubo, were photographed shaking hands with the previous Nigerian President, Olusegun Obasanjo. It was like déjà vu seeing Ateke posing with two Presidents at the October 1 Nigerian independence celebrations 5 years apart. One must ask, "How many times can the same person be disarmed?" And what went wrong the first time to require a repeat performance?

This chapter looks at the Disarmament, Demobilization, and Reintegration (DDR) processes in the Niger Delta from the viewpoint of a practitioner intimately involved in the first round and a close observer of the second round. It presents a sad case study of the consequences of the forgotten R of DDR, Reintegration. Finally it reflects my experience over the past 6 years suggesting that the reintegration element of DDR was not so much inadvertently forgotten as purposefully left out.

Militancy in the Niger Delta

To understand why DDR processes in the Niger Delta have not worked, it is necessary to look at the history and nature of militancy in the region. Armed youth groups have been prominent in various parts of Nigeria, but particularly the Niger Delta, for about 3 decades, during both civilian and military regimes. Several generations of young men have joined these groups for various reasons, including ideological protest about exploitation of the oil-rich region at the expense of environmental degradation, unemployment, and marginalization. Others have joined for protection of their communities, but more commonly for protection and promotion of their own confraternity or involvement in criminal activities. In the late 1980s, university confraternities began spilling out of the campuses in the form of street gangs, many of which became involved in the retail side of the drug trade and later in bunkering (the theft of crude oil). With the return of civilian democracy in 1999, large numbers of these new youth[1] from street gangs were hired and armed as political thugs to rig elections and intimidate members of the opposition parties.[2] Ballot boxes were stolen to prevent votes from being counted, and election officials were found to be announcing fictitious results based on their own vested interests. While the university confraternities still provide support networks (e.g., many politicians in the Niger Delta are members of the Vikings or Pyrates confraternities), the actual political thugs continue to be recruited from the street gangs.

The political violence of the 1999–2003 term centered on Rivers State, the eastern capital of the oil industry. By the 2003 and later 2007 elections, political thuggery had spread to all parts of Nigeria but was particularly common in the three core states of the Niger Delta, where high stakes from oil revenues make it literally a "do or die" business. The core states of Delta, Bayelsa, and Rivers account for most of the oil production, which is overwhelmingly the largest source of income for the country at approximately 95 percent. Of the federal revenue, the Niger Delta state governments directly receive 13 percent, depending on current production.[3] The monthly federal allocation is approximately N40 billion (U.S. $267 million) to Bayelsa State, N46 billion (U.S. $307 million) to Delta State, and N52 billion (U.S. $347 million) to Rivers State. Hence controlling this huge amount of money, over which there is little accountability, gives politicians the incentive to win elective offices by whatever means necessary.

Added to this mix of youth armed for the drug trade, oil theft, and political violence is the high level of armed intercommunal or interethnic conflict, often fought over control or "ownership" of oil and gas facilities. The result is a region of highly armed civilians and a large military presence, where socioeconomic development is low. There is little participation by the indigenes in the oil and gas industry, such as direct employment, ad hoc staff, award of contracts, etc. Thus the local people have little investment in the industry, which greatly impacts the environment and its people. The addition of poor governance, both in nondelivery of basic services and lack of fiscal transparency, makes the region a powder keg waiting to explode.

And explode it has done. There have been a number of fierce inter-ethnic wars, political riots, attacks on oil facilities, and kidnappings and occasional killings of foreign oil workers, which have evolved into kidnapping of Nigerian elites. The large ransoms paid to kidnappers have only exacerbated the problem as the stakes get higher and higher. While some groups began attacks and kidnappings for ideological reasons, the ransom payments brought in many pure criminals, who also specialized in piracy and bank robberies.

The economic violence that started with cults[4] who were used to rig the 1999 and 2003 elections in Rivers State came to a temporary halt in October 2004 with a peace agreement facilitated by President Obasanjo between the warring factions of Ateke Tom's Niger Delta Vigilantes and Asari Dokubo's Niger Delta Peoples Volunteer Force. Both groups were used by the Rivers State government for political thuggery during the 2003 elections, but soon thereafter the two groups began to compete for political relevance and oil bunkering wealth. This violent competition made it increasingly dangerous to live in Rivers State. President Obasanjo began to recognize the breakdown of law and order that threatened the stability of the entire region and began the discussions that culminated in an internationally covered peace agreement on October 1, 2004. As part of the agreement, a DDR process was initiated but broke down by mid-2005, by which time lack of political will nipped the budding reintegration process, and infighting within the former armed groups resulted in new formations and violence among them.

Tensions heightened in September 2005 with the arrest of Asari by federal security agents. The arrests of Asari and the former Bayelsa governor, Alamieyeseigha, became a rallying cry of the newly created Movement for the Emancipation of the Niger Delta (MEND), which took armed struggle to a new level. In January 2006, MEND kidnapped its first set of expatriate hostages, followed by massive attacks on Shell facilities in Delta State and more kidnappings. This led to a downward spiral of increasing attacks and kidnappings with ever higher ransom payments. Oil production was down to approximately half of its pre-2006 level, which resulted in declines in federal revenues.

Finally in 2009, President Yar'Adua, elected in 2007, announced an amnesty for all members of militant groups. The amnesty program was conducted in August–October 2009, and militants were theoretically disarmed and sent to demobilization camps. International standards deem that a documented census of militants, armed groups, and weapons is necessary for effective demobilization and disarmament. Reintegration should include medical services, livelihood packages, career and drug counseling, and job or education benefits. To date, no reintegration process in the Niger Delta has achieved all of these goals. The militants were taken to camps to be demobilized and theoretically registered, but there were no barracks to hold them, so many left the camps and came back only to collect their monthly stipends. The plans to create new camps by May 9, 2009, are now pushed back until June, a full 8 months after the disarmament process was completed.

We shall look at the 2004 and 2009 DDR processes in turn and consider the consequences of the lack of reintegration in each of them.

The 2004 Rivers State Peace Agreement and DDR Process

The 2004 peace agreement involved the two major groups that had been used, ironically by the same incumbent state government, to rig the 2003 election in Rivers State, i.e., the Niger Delta Vigilantes headed by Ateke Tom and the Niger Delta Peoples Volunteers Force headed by Alhaji Asari Dokubo. The power tussle between these two groups started in late 2003 and included fighting on the streets of the state capital, Port Harcourt, (including one group coming within half a mile of Government House), military attacks on several major towns, and threats by hundreds of Ijaw commanders (linked to Asari Dokubo) to attack oil and gas installations. This turmoil caught the attention of all Nigerians and indeed the world as oil prices skyrocketed in September 2004. Realizing the danger of such continuing violence, President Olusegun Obasanjo invited both leaders and their key followers to Abuja. After hours of discussion, the leaders signed a peace agreement, which was aired on CNN. Rivers State Governor Peter Odili was also invited to the meeting to explain his role in this conflict. Two subsequent meetings were held between the militants and the Presidency, at which two committees were set up: a Disarmament Committee headed by Governor Odili and a Community Governance Committee headed by Goodluck Jonathan, then Deputy Governor of Bayelsa State (now President of Nigeria). The Disarmament Committee consisted mainly of representatives from the various security agencies and was charged with collecting and destroying weapons. The Community Governance Committee had a broader membership of government and civil society representatives and was formed to find ways to rebuild the governments of the

Niger Delta. The disarmament process was indeed completed in that the 3,000 weapons the militants declared that they owned were turned in, so the Disarmament Committee's work was a success in that respect, but the process was not thoroughly documented by objective observers, which leaves its effectiveness open to question. The Community Governance Committee submitted its report to the President in 2005 but it was never really implemented. In sum, these two committees failed to foster effective and sustainable DDR.

Three of us from two civil society organizations—Academic Associates PeaceWorks, the nongovernmental organization (NGO) of which I am the Executive Director, and Our Niger Delta, an NGO started by several young men from Bayelsa and Rivers States—approached Governor Odili about working with the Rivers State Government on the peace process, and he willingly accepted. During October 2004, the Disarmament Committee collected weapons from all parties, which were kept at the military cantonment and publicly destroyed on November 15. Two disarmament observers from SaferAfrica in Pretoria (sponsored by the UK Department of International Development, or DFID) and a mobile policeman assigned to protect me documented and recorded serial numbers of all weapons received officially. Asari eventually handed in 3,000 weapons. Unfortunately, no clear record was kept of weapons handed in by Ateke's group before the official start of the disarmament. Also unfortunately, the committee chose to pay for weapons turned in, averaging N250,000 (U.S. $2,000) for a serviceable AK-47. As the United Nations Development Programme states, it is against international best practices to pay for weapons as an incentive to disarm.[5] A better alternative is to supply training, education, and employment opportunities to the ex-militants. By paying above market price for weapons handed in, as was done in the 2004 DDR process, the Disarmament Committee allowed the armed groups to buy more weapons with the money. It is also unclear what percentage of weapons was really turned in since little documentation was undertaken before the collection began.

At the time of the peace agreement on October 1, 2004, no one had a clear idea of exactly who had been involved in the intergroup fighting. The Security Services should have known who the genuine militants were and the makeup of their groups, but the 2004 peace agreement was a surprise, and no one had time to think ahead. It is important to have a deep analysis of each group with its structure, membership, leadership, and arms possessed in order to develop an effective DDR program. Therefore, the three civil society facilitators recruited a small number of young men from the region to go to each camp and write up a case study on each group. In this way, we were able to identify the real leaders, assess membership, and look for those who might cooperate with the DDR. I then met with the leaders of all of the groups and listened to their stories. Perhaps through the face-to-face interaction with hundreds of militants that began during this time, the militants came to trust me. I became known as "Mum" to the armed youth and "Mama Militant" to outsiders. This listening and mentoring was an important part of our rehabilitation process. While this rehabilitation was important and successful, it was not permanent. Many militants slipped back into their old habits. Without changing underlying structures, attitudes and behavior do not change permanently, as Christopher Mitchell theorized.[6]

On November 19, 2004, we organized a meeting between Governor Odili and 50 key group representatives. After hours of listening to the representatives, the governor hosted all of us to dinner in his official residence, and a peace agreement was signed at the end of the evening. Such an act was unheard of in Nigeria—an elite, a Governor, inviting 50 militants, many of whom had attempted to assassinate him, to his own home. This meeting showed acknowledgment by the Governor that the militants were serious actors in the Delta who needed to be taken into consideration. It also demonstrated some level of trust between the two parties. Thereafter began a series of activities that can be considered as partly demobilization and partly reintegration. The talking sessions between the militants and President Obasanjo, and later myself, exposed horrific acts, such as tying live people in sacks and throwing them into the sea or dropping them off high buildings. The October 2004 meetings between Obasanjo and the militant leaders were significant in that they showed that the President had realized the severity of the breakdown of law and order and decided to step in. The President also expressed surprise at the level of violence admitted to him by the militants, whose honesty only added to the drama of the meeting. One request from the militants themselves was a church service of confession and forgiveness. The process of the various groups jointly planning this service was the beginning of trust-building. It was extremely moving to see 2,000 young men, dressed in matching T-shirts and wrappers, praying and then dancing together. A number of people were in tears, including Governor Odili. Services were held for both the Christians and Muslims just before Christmas 2004.

Later, other militants requested a second service, which never happened due to lack of funding. They wanted to appear on television to show their families and communities that they had changed and could be accepted back home. One of the shortcomings of this DDR process was that there was virtually no attempt to foster reconciliation and reintegrate the militants back into their home communities. This meant that many militants could not return home for funerals without being attacked and were essentially socially exiled. Particularly in the Okrika local government that had been the scene of much fighting between Ateke and Asari, there were attacks on some former militants who tried to return home. This continued the circle of mistrust and fear. Thus, they stayed in Port Harcourt, where they were a captive audience for the next round of violence.

My two young Niger Delta male colleagues and I were co-opted onto the Rivers State Rehabilitation Committee, which was to plan the demobilization and reintegration of the ex-combatants. We organized a day-long meeting of potential contributors to the peace process, including the Social Services Department, the governor's wife's training program, Drug Enforcement Agency, Secret Service, Shell, European Union, etc. By December 1, 2004, the Rehabilitation Committee had a 34-Point Action Plan for DDR. While the government hosted these meetings formally, the civil society volunteers who organized it provided the technical input. Unfortunately, the government's involvement often served as an impediment to real DDR progress, and little of the 34-Point Action Plan was implemented.

One exciting innovation was an Outward Bound camp organized by Our Niger Delta and paid for by the state government, in which we took 700 ex-militants to a government leadership camp in Jos, in northern Nigeria. This was the first time the combatants from both sides were in close proximity, and it was a challenge to get them engaged in constructive, vigorous activity and to keep the peace. However, the camp was a turning point in the reorientation of many militants.

Immediately after the camp, a Central Coordinating Committee (CCC) was set up with representatives from the various groups. The committee worked well for about a month, planning out training and enlightenment activities for the Youth Office, which the Rivers State Governor had promised to establish. However, as this office was never set up and no other funds were available, the CCC meetings tapered off and disillusionment set in. That was unfortunate since the CCC did tap the leadership skills of the various members, and it provided an opportunity for people from both sides of the 2004 conflict to meet regularly in a safe environment.

Two training programs established by the state government did take off in early 2005. The first batch of 100 trainees was 100 percent ex-militants, and the former armed group leaders were at the training center to maintain peace among the former enemies. By the second batch of 100, the politicians were beginning to give the training slots to their friends and relatives, and over time the percentage of ex-combatants steadily declined until these programs became mainly a source of political patronage. Another center was established to train a further 700 "ex-militants." However, the quality of training left much to be desired. For example, many were trained in welding but had very little time to actually use a welding torch. The head of the Rehabilitation Committee and the Chief Security Officer are known to have inflated the number of registered militants to allow room for funds to be strategically given to nonmilitants. Again, this led to disillusionment, as did the tapering off of the promised scholarships to return to school. The promise to deploy some of the ex-militants to the army and police was also never kept. While the President pledged to integrate some ex-militants into the security services, no one below him took the effort to implement it. There was also resistance from the military in Abuja, who were upset by witnessing such close relations between the President and the militants.

Problems arose from the behavior of group leaders as well as the politicians. Money was paid for some hundreds of militants to participate in monthly sanitation exercises, where the group members were given low stipends to clean the streets. However, the money was paid through the militant group leaders and often didn't reach the militants themselves. In retrospect, this was probably purposeful to break up the group structure, although this too can be a risky process since breaking these natural bonds will dismantle the organization and perhaps even cohesion within the groups. This creates a vacuum where no one is in charge. In less than a year after the peace agreement, infighting had broken out within both Ateke's and Asari's groups, which the leaders could not control. Once again there was vicious fighting on the streets of Port Harcourt, this time among former allies.

A number of unkept promises helped to unravel the peace process. For example, President Obasanjo had given instructions for Governor Odili to establish Community Committees in the two most affected kingdoms, Okrika and Kalabari, with the goal of rebuilding the communities physically and socially. Although the committees were nominally established, they never were effective, largely due to lack of state government support. The Niger Delta Development Commission was also instructed to establish technical training centers in Okrika, Kalabari, and Ogbakiri. When NDDC finally did set up such centers, they were located in towns chosen by NDDC management for their own personal reasons. Our attempts to recruit funding from the foreign donor agencies, such as USAID, DFID, and the World Bank, met blank walls, as most agencies have multiyear programs of pre-committed funds that do not allow flexibility for quick responses to pressing situations. This was very frustrating as the donors missed a real opportunity to help prevent escalation of the Niger Delta crisis. These lapses reflect a lack of political will on the parts of government, development agencies, donor agencies, and ex-combatants, which allowed the DDR process to unravel within the first year. Donor political and financial will to adequately fund this peace and DDR process could have better consolidated the process and led to more effective implementation. Instead, the foreign governments often use cookie cutter models without creative adaptation to the current context. In addition, the oil companies remained silent and did not contribute to the positive reintegration of the ex-militants.

Lessons Learned from the Rivers State DDR Process

When we jumped into a sudden DDR process in early October 2004, most of us had not done anything like it before. We responded to immediate needs and planned things as we went along. Attempts by vested interests to abort or hijack the process for their own goals along with the consequent decline of interest and commitment by the state government presented great difficulties to our programming. It was only in June 2005, in preparing to write up our experiences, that I read the DDR literature and could analyze what we did well and poorly.[7] Some lessons learned from this experience will be elaborated on below.

Advance strategic planning with adequate investment is critical to a successful process. DDR should be part of an integrated recovery strategy that includes economic development, security sector reform, justice, and reconciliation. Regional strategies are also important, as neighboring states may benefit from the conflict, be involved in it, or be victimized by it. A neutral mediator with power to implement actions can sustain these initiatives most effectively. During the 2004 Rivers process, no one took the time to sit down and think through the consequences and needs of the DDR program. The atmosphere was very urgent and led us to jump into action to ensure we did not miss the window of opportunity. There was no central institution coordinating all of the processes, which led to duplication of programs, missing weapons or combatants, and overall confusion. That is why an information base with numbers of combatants and kinds and locations of people and weapons is necessary. This would have facilitated decisions on how to disarm combatants effectively as well as early registration of the combatants. Centralized information on the types of programs and donors active in the process would also be useful for effective DDR coordination across programs and regions. Comprehensive and periodic assessment of the various components of the DDR process and appropriate revisions should be conducted throughout the process to ensure consistent high quality and accountability.

Combatants are diverse and need different kinds of reintegration assistance. In the case of the Niger Delta, many combatants have committed or been victims of atrocities for which they need psychosocial counseling. There is also a need for work with the community that is expected to receive them back. Unfortunately, the lack of psychosocial counseling in the 2004 Rivers process was a major gap in combatant rehabilitation. Restorative justice should also be an important part of the psychological adjustment process in future programs. Reintegration should be community based, especially in those communities most affected by the conflict. In the 2004 process, Community Committees were not properly established, and the focus remained on individuals rather than communities, reinforcing the status and power of the warlords. The security of ex-combatants within these communities must be guaranteed. This was an issue in 2004 as the security agencies felt disempowered, both in the authority of rule of law and in the technical ability to uphold it.

Unfulfilled promises lead to frustration and disillusionment among the militants that can endanger the process. For example, the 4,600 jobs created during the 2004 Rivers process were not sustainable, adequately paid, or related to work needing to be done, thus virtually no real job creation occurred. The sanitation jobs were sporadic and of low prestige and thus did not give job satisfaction. No assessment was conducted of what job opportunities did or could exist. Only in 2006 did we do a technical needs assessment that showed that the oil and gas industry needed specific skills such as marine engineering, computerized vehicle repair, and heavy equipment operation. Thus no serious efforts were made to provide these skills in the 2004 DDR process. The Youth Office was never created, which led to unfulfilled promises about schooling, military integration, and job creation and placement. This issue was exacerbated because the NDDC training centers promised to the combatants were never established. These failures resulted in disillusionment and led many ex-combatants to return to violence, bunkering, and drugs. Viable alternatives to lives of violence should be provided for ex-combatants. These may include jobs paying reasonable salaries, loans for self-employment or small businesses, support for returning to school, and entry into the police or military.

Ex-combatants should be involved in building a new society that addresses some of the basic social justice issues and particularly governance issues. Inadequate public enlightenment about the end of amnesty and return of rule of law in 2004 led some former fighters to believe that they could still get away with anything. Ex-combatants should also be involved in designing and implementing their own reintegration programs, especially in building bridges with others. The Central Coordinating Committee was one such short-lived attempt.

There were several things we did well in the Rivers State 2004 DDR process, including:

- virtually immediate cessation of violence in that the peace agreement created a safe environment for the militants to leave the creeks, hand in at least some of their guns, return to the urban areas, and attempt to resume normal life
- reduction of tension and restoration of confidence in government
- intervention of top-level politicians who initially demonstrated the political will to make this happen
- willingness of political leaders to listen to all parties
- willingness of political leaders to initially invest financially in DDR
- involvement of many stakeholders in planning and implementing DDR
- an effort to change the mindset of members of the armed groups
- initial involvement of ex-combatants in the reintegration process
- training for hundreds of ex-combatants.

Breakdown of the 2004 Rivers State DDR Process

Within a few months of the peace agreement in October 2004, the political will to actually carry out a proper DDR process had dwindled. Unkept promises led to disillusionment. Technical training was planned but no jobs were available, training funds were often siphoned off through corruption, and scholarships ended after only two school terms. The arrest of Alhaji Asari Dokuo in September 2005—less than a year after the peace agreement—led to threats of renewed violence. Although we were able to keep the militants from fighting for some months, they were enticed into even greater violence by early 2006. It would appear that disgruntled politicians invested money in a semi-ideological struggle over the marginalization of the Niger Delta region. After the initial 2006 attacks on oil facilities and kidnapping of foreign oil workers, various government officials—

political and security agents—jacked up the ransoms to increase their own cuts of the payments. Eventually, some officials even sponsored such acts, especially kidnappings of political opponents.

In addition, as the 2007 elections approached, politicians rerecruited and armed youth to rig the elections in their favor, as documented in an AA PeaceWorks study of armed groups in Delta State, many of which had been created shortly before the 2007 election. Indeed, the level of rigging of the 2007 election was the highest ever. Some previously unarmed groups were armed for the event. All political parties participated in this rigging exercise. Unfortunately, the arms could not be collected back at the end of the election, so that led to an even higher level of arms in the Delta region.

The Current DDR Process, 2009–2010

President Yar'Adua promised the Niger Delta militants amnesty if they disarmed between August and October 2009. Although the process started slowly, by the beginning of October virtually all of the armed groups had theoretically disarmed. The payments of approximately $3 million to each major group leader, plus the threat of military attack if they did not participate, provided both the carrot and the stick. No one is sure what percentage of the weapons in the Niger Delta was handed in: based on conversations with observers close to the armed group leaders, I would estimate that 30–40 percent of those held by the militants were decommissioned. Some weapons were old and unserviceable, while others appeared brand new. The latter may be explained by the political competition that was taking place between two prominent politicians, Governor Timipre Sylva of Bayelsa State and Timi Alaibe, a likely gubernatorial aspirant also in Bayelsa, in which both wanted to be seen as producing more militants and guns. No one is sure how many militants disarmed. Media estimates have ranged from 5,000 to 20,000. Even official government figures are confusing. It has been stated that allowances are being paid to 18,193 "ex-militants," not including those from the camp of major warlord Tom Polo in Delta State, who refused to register. A recent proposal to retrain 2,000 of Tom Polo's militants was rejected, as he now claims to have 10,000 fighters in his group. However, the federal government reintegration plan released in January 2010 only includes training for 4,800, so one wonders what happens to the other 13,000–15,000. There has since been an announcement on March 3, 2010, that 20,192 ex-militants will be given training, a number more in line with the higher earlier estimate of participants in the amnesty program. In May 2010, Alaibe announced that 20,000 ex-militants will be rehabilitated, but no one is sure that the people who disarmed were really militants, as there was no accurate census taken before the exercise began. There were accounts of youth being bribed to participate in the amnesty by the government and of militants being excluded because they did not own their own weapons (many times the weapons were held by the group leaders). The inability to ensure that the right youth were getting the right benefits from the program led to many forsaking the amnesty and its doom of unemployment for life in the swamps.

In spite of offers of external technical assistance and the presence in Nigeria of at least two experts in DDR—one with DFID and the other with the United Nations Development Programme (UNDP)—the federal government refused all offers of assistance, saying that the amnesty would be done "the Nigerian way." That usually means that a fair amount of money changes hands and it appears that this also occurred in the 2009 amnesty. As far as I am aware, there was no neutral outsider observer of the disarmament process, especially since it seemed to take place in a number of places simultaneously with various people collecting weapons. As mentioned earlier, General Boyloaf was taken by the Bayelsa State Governor to meet with President Yar'Adua and theoretically disarm. Ateke Tom was later taken by Timi Alaibe for the same purpose. In some cases, members of the Federal Government Amnesty Committee went to the militants' camps to collect weapons, while a large show of disarmament was conducted at the town square in Yenagoa, the Bayelsa State capital.

It was only at the end of the amnesty that a Reintegration Committee was set up, and its proposed program was made public in January 2010, 3 months after the end of the amnesty. Reintegration should be planned and prepared for before Disarmament and Demobilization occur; and it should be implemented immediately upon the conclusion of the disarmament exercise. The Reintegration Committee not only had a late plan, but members of civil society were also largely disgruntled with it. A committee headed by Patterson Ogon, a human rights activist now working with the Bayelsa state government, studied the plan and pointed out a number of problems, including the fact that 80 percent of the budget was to go for consultants and services with only 20 percent benefiting the real beneficiaries. As of May 2010, this plan had still not been implemented 8 months after the end of the amnesty period. Other members of civil society have also attempted to fill the void by analyzing the DDR process and offering alternative lines of action. For example, the Open Society of West Africa (OSIWA) in May 2010 initiated a study of the DDR process with suggestions for improvement.

Fearing that the government reintegration plan might not be implemented effectively, the oil and gas industry set up its own committee to support the government efforts. In spite of promises of $30 million from the major companies, no actual activities have been started and only non-violence training has even been specifically identified by the group. Instead, the industry committee spent most of the next 8 months discussing the Special Purpose Vehicle through which this money will be spent rather than what it will be spent for.

In the meantime, the militants have been largely unengaged. As in any society where large numbers of unemployed youth have energy and initiative but no constructive outlet, trouble ensues. The militants were told to report to demobilization camps, but there were seldom the staff or facilities to handle them. For example, in Egbokodo near Warri, Delta State, bunks were moved into a would-be day training center, but there were no showers and only a few toilets for the proposed 400 residents. Therefore, the militants stayed a short time and only returned to collect their stipends. They were promised a monthly payment of about N65,000 ($433). However, when those staying at the demobilization camp at Aluu, near the University of Port Harcourt in Rivers State, were not paid, they went on a rampage to the nearby campus, attacking and raping many students. The students then marched to Government House to protest to the Governor. Yet payment has also created problems. Stipends are now paid through group leaders, who often take a cut, thus creating more distrust within the groups. At first, payments were to be made through banks. Even when payment was done through individual bank accounts, group leaders would often go to the banks with their men to collect their cut. These sightings of ex-militants at banks led to panic and riots by the civilians. In the future, cash should be given to the individuals in a safe, government-protected environment with an insider present to verify their identity and signatures to prove receipt.

The government reintegration plan included training in some of the more common skills such as carpentry and dressmaking. In 2006, the NGO that I headed was hired by UNDP to develop a skills training program. I changed the program from training community youth in basic skills such as tailoring and carpentry to a focus on the members of the armed groups and incorporating counseling on careers, psychosocial matters, drugs, life skills, business training, sports, English, math, and social studies. Our reorientation officers were themselves ex-militants who had dropped out of violence in 2004. We also studied all existing training centers in the three core Niger Delta states, current skills taught, and opportunity mapping to determine what training we would give. Representatives of armed groups were involved in all stages of the planning. We were told clearly by militant representatives that they did not want the usual training, such as basic welding, carpentry, hairdressing, and tailoring, but instead wanted to work in the oil and gas industry. In view of the few jobs available directly in the industry, consultations with the oil and gas industry showed that skilled workers in sophisticated welding, heavy equipment operation, local content contracting, and other specific areas were needed. This is where reintegration job training should have been focused.

The current government reintegration plan is not based on opportunity mapping of the current jobs needed in the oil and gas industry and is likely to result in the usual basic skills training, such as those mentioned above, which will not lead to sustainable jobs or self-employment opportunities. In addition, many second-rate training centers, without proper equipment or competent staff, have been identified for the reintegration program. Several government agencies, such as the National Directorate of Employment, have been identified to conduct technical training. However, such agencies do not consider the unique social and psychological background of these "trainees" and are poorly prepared to meet the challenges that will arise once training actually starts. One of the most important aspects has not been addressed, job creation. Even if ex-combatants do go through technical training, unless there are real jobs with desirable salaries or real opportunities for self-employment, the youth will return to violence. All of these factors bode badly for the success of the program. Out-of-the-box thinking will be necessary to come up with a creative plan for demobilizing and reintegrating the members of the armed groups and keeping them out of violence in the long term.

In addition to handing in their arms and being given new sources of livelihood, some members of armed groups insisted that the government address some of the fundamental issues in the Niger Delta region. President Yar'Adua began a series of meetings with various militant groups soon after the amnesty came to an end. He even met with the Aaron Team, made up of representatives chosen by the Movement for the Emancipation of the Niger Delta, to speak on their behalf in spite of early refusal of the government to recognize this team. Although nothing specific came out of these meetings, they at least were the start of a dialogue, as well as a safety valve for the frustrations of the youth. Unfortunately, President Yar'Adua was taken to Saudi Arabia on November 23, 2009, for medical treatment, and the discussions stopped. In effect, the whole federal government ground to a halt in the vacuum created by the President's departure without the proper handing over of presidential duties to the Vice President. On February 9, 2010, the National Assembly asked the Vice President, Goodluck Jonathan, to step in as Acting President; however, Yar'Adua returned secretively in the dead of night on February 24. The political uncertainty finally ended on May 5 with his death and the swearing in of Goodluck Jonathan as the substantive President. The Niger Delta reintegration program had been largely forgotten in the political vacuum until militants detonated two explosions at a public meeting in Warri, where several Governors and Ministers were discussing amnesty provisions. One bystander was killed and several were injured. This has given some impetus to the government to refocus on issues of the Niger Delta.

In the meantime, MEND and some other armed groups called off their ceasefire in late January when they saw that the reintegration had stalled due to the absence of President Yar'Adua. Generally, the youth of the Delta were happy when Goodluck Jonathan stepped in as Acting President in early February, as he is from the region and was governor of Bayelsa State. The return of President Yar'Adua later that month raised the youths' tensions once more, with fears that their native son could be sidelined. He was not, yet tension increased again. Threats resumed and indeed there were several attacks in March and in May 2010. The Niger Delta Governors met on the last weekend of February, warning the federal government that failure to implement the reintegration program could result in renewed violence.

With a Niger Deltan as President, it was hoped that there would be serious efforts at implementing the program. The reintegration camps, which were scheduled to start on May 9, were moved back to June. Timi Alaibe, the presidential adviser in charge of reintegration efforts, called major militant leaders to a meeting in Abuja in the third week of May, where most leaders vowed to support the program. However, some other leaders have disowned the process. Unless serious efforts are made promptly, the 2009 amnesty may well go the direction of the 2004 peace agreement due to lack of political will to complete the process, leaving the youth only partially disarmed, scarcely demobilized, and certainly not reintegrated.

The Conflict Economy

After conducting research on oil bunkering in the Niger Delta,[8] I now realize that the crisis there is perpetuated by some selfish individuals (many of them senior politicians and military, both serving and retired), who benefit from it even while the majority of people in the region suffer.

In the first 8 months of 2008 alone, $33.8 billion worth of oil was either stolen or shut in (i.e., not being pulled out of the ground); this is an enormous loss of funds to the Nigerian budget. However, some top politicians and security agents benefit from the bunkering business more than the militants in the creeks who blow up pipelines. If these militants were trained and given other jobs, the managers of the bunkering trade would have to recruit new operatives. In the same way, many politicians need to keep the armed youth at their disposal for the next election, with talented and brutal ones kept on standby to deal with political enemies. Even interethnic conflict is often a cover-up for lucrative businesses such as bunkering and the arms trade. Demonstrating a fair amount of initiative, some of the leaders of armed groups, such as Boy Loaf and Tom Polo, have used the money paid to them to participate in the amnesty process to buy new bunkering barges, thus perpetuating the criminal activity. As long as these criminal activities continue, there is little incentive to accept a small stipend to go for technical training.

Given the money at stake in these businesses, I believe that international intervention will be required to dry up the criminal activities—bunkering, drugs, arms importation, money laundering—that fuel the conflict economy in the region and prevent serious demobilization and reintegration. Intervention could involve many diplomatic or security efforts by the international community: action to dry up the market for stolen oil and the sources for small arms; coastal surveillance of the Gulf of Guinea waters; introduction of electronic bills of lading and methods to certify oil as "clean"; visa bans and prosecution of individuals and American companies, such as Halliburton, Chevron, and ExxonMobil, for corruption; and encouraging improved revenue transparency on the part of the government.

The lack of genuine political will on the part of the Nigerian government to combat this conflict economy and reintegrate the militants successfully, as well as the refusal to take measures to resolve the underlying sources of the conflict, explain the missing R in the DDR equation. Real demobilization and reintegration of militants are counter to the interests of the people benefitting from the conflict economy, such as the oil bunkerers, money launderers, and arms importers. However, it is in the greater interests of the majority of people in the Niger Delta and in Nigeria as a whole to close off this conflict economy and bring sustainable peace and development to the region.

Notes

[1] In Nigerian culture, as well as within many other African cultures, the concept of youth is a much boarder category than what is traditionally held in many Western countries. Many of the youth groups include men up to their late thirties.

[2] This summary is based on a working paper written for the Council on Foreign Relations: Judith Burdin Asuni, "Understanding the Armed Groups of the Niger Delta," Working Paper, Council on Foreign Relations (2009), available at <http://www.cfr.org/publication/20146/understanding_the_armed_groups_of_the_niger_delta.html>, accessed April 1, 2010.

[3] "Nigeria: Transparency Snapshot," Revenue Watch Institute, available at <http://caspianrevenuewatch.org/our-work/countries/nigeria-transparency.php>, accessed March 1, 2010. Revenue Watch Institute shows that the Nigerian government made US $24.5 billion from oil revenues between 2008 and 2009. According to the current Nigerian constitution, this would mean that $2.85 billion would be distributed to the Nigerian oil-producing states. No confirmation that the full amount has been received by the states has been found.

[4] While the members still referred to their groups as confraternities, outsiders preferred to use the word cults, intended to signify the secretive nature of these groups with their oaths, rituals, and behavior, which often strayed outside accepted social norms. Asuni, "Understanding the Armed Groups of the Niger Delta."

[5] United Nations, "Integrated Disarmament, Demobilization, and Reintegration Standards," (December 2006), available at <http://unddr.org/iddrs/>, accessed May 20, 2010.

[6] Christopher Mitchell, "Beyond Resolution: What Does Conflict Transformation Actually Transform?" available at <http://www.gmu.edu/programs/icar/pcs/CM83PCS.htm>, accessed May 23, 2010.

[7] Peace and Security Secretariat, "Niger Delta Peace and Security Strategy Background Papers," no. 43 (2006), unpublished paper.

[8] Judith Burdin Asuni, "Blood Oil in the Niger Delta," Special Report, United States Institute of Peace (2009), available at <http://www.usip.org/resources/blood-oil-in-the-niger-delta>, accessed April 1, 2010.

Part III
Managing DDR and SSR Programs

Chapter 9

Action Amid Chaos: The Ground Truth Imperatives of DDRR and Security

By Jacques Paul Klein and Melanne A. Civic

The conventional tendency is to think of Disarmament, Demobilization, Rehabilitation, and Reintegration (DDRR) as a linear process with separate, potentially sequential yet integrated components. The traditional stages are: negotiate the peace agreement, establish a United Nations (UN) Mandate, deploy peacekeepers and UN DDRR experts, remove the arms, and provide for rehabilitation, counseling, livelihood opportunities, and reintegration. Ideally, the rehabilitation and reintegration phases will overlap and even be integrated with disarmament and demobilization to capture momentum and lay the path for a new beginning.

So often, however, DDRR is executed under chaotic circumstances—from the chaos of the postconflict environment, to the chaos of the peacebuilding response, to the coordination challenges of the numerous entities involved. Negotiation of a peace agreement may proceed under a tenuous ceasefire that can revert back to armed conflict. Even where a peace agreement is successfully negotiated, rebel and faction groups may continue to perceive themselves as marginalized or as having no viable alternatives; accordingly they may remain poised for resurgence. And even where the postconflict environment is less than chaotic, the logistics of deploying DDRR personnel and peacekeepers and securing funding can itself be chaotic. These logistical responses start anew with each UN mission. Following each conflict that engages the international community, one needs to locate peacekeepers, equipment and other essentials, and crisis funding, and then coordinate resources and institutions.

The big picture is sustainable peace, yet one might consider the security imperative of removing arms and ammunition from circulation, breaking down the chains of command of rebel or faction groups, and beginning to resocialize former combatants. Disarmament and demobilization remove the method and means of armed conflict from disperse groups and thereby allow for the consolidation of force in the state. During the fragile period when hope and enthusiasm for security and stability are at their peak, peace can easily slip back into conflict, what are the actions of greatest priority? In the real-life circumstances immediately following conflict, does long-term strategic vision or short-term practical action take precedence? Where chaos and threats to security emanate from all points, where logistical delays in deploying peacekeepers and equipment complicates matters, and where financing is tied up in bureaucratic knots or otherwise unavailable, the ground truth is that disarmament and disbandment must proceed immediately and be the absolute focus of DDRR and peacekeeping to establish security for all else. Waiting to execute a plan of simultaneous and integrated DDRR may risk an immediate return to conflict before stability has a chance.

Liberia in 2003–2004 exemplified the multidimensional chaos of the host country environment, peacemaking and peacekeeping logistics, and coordination of DDRR efforts. It highlighted the ground-truth reality of the less-than-linear and not always integrated process. DDRR in Liberia proceeded within the context of a tenuous peace, amid the active threat of a return to war by various factions. Personnel, equipment, and funding resources had to be conjured up spontaneously. And numerous United Nations entities had to be coordinated, including the UN International Children's Emergency Fund (UNICEF), the World Food Program, the World Health Organization, and the UN Development Program, as well as donor nations and nongovernmental organizations (NGOs).

As the Comprehensive Peace Agreement (CPA) was being negotiated in Accra, Ghana, the ceasefire shattered. Nevertheless, negotiations continued and the CPA was signed by representatives of the Government of Liberia, Liberians United for Reconciliation and Democracy (LURD), and Movement for Democracy in Liberia (MODEL) faction groups on August 18, 2003. The CPA outlined arrangements for the cantonment, disarmament, demobilization, rehabilitation, and reintegration of combatants in considerable detail, and established a National Commission on DDRR (NCDDRR). The extra "R"—rehabilitation—aimed to redress the extreme circumstance of child soldiers, women, and other special groups, and assist a generation of Liberians who knew nothing other than the 14 years of war.

Obtaining UN Security Council consent was comparatively streamlined. Each of the permanent members had prominent national security interests for peace in Liberia. The French wanted to avoid cross-border conflict and aggravating the instability in the Cote d'Ivoire. The United Kingdom wanted to preserve the delicate stability it had achieved in Sierra Leone. And the United States had a lengthy history with Liberia dating back to the time of slavery in America, and wanted to promote peace. On September 19, 2003, a month after the CPA was signed, the UN Security Council passed one of its most expansive and comprehensive peacekeeping mandates, including DDRR. The UN Mission in Liberia (UNMIL) was established, and the international community pledged 15,000 peacekeeping troops, more than a thousand police, and several hundred civilian staff and military observers, representing the largest UN peacekeeping mission at the time.

Typically, once a UN Mandate is approved, the logistical challenges really begin. Where does one find the peacekeeping troops and the essential equipment? For Liberia, as elsewhere, the logistical arrangements were ad hoc. The UN Headquarters was tasked with acquiring the personnel and equipment, but the bureaucracy slowed down the process to the point of compromising the mission. The behind-the-scenes reality was that personal initiative was key—getting out the proverbial rolodex and calling donor nations directly. Sometimes the process was a bit like bartering, requiring give-and-take among donor nations. Then, to add to the balancing act of securing resources and keeping donors satisfied, when the European peacekeepers arrived, their quarters were so superior to those of the African peacekeepers that the disparity sparked resentment and undermined unity.

The necessary equipment came through the same type of ad hoc processes. Trucks were supplied by a U.S. contractor, while replacement tires were supplied from another country. Carburetors and other spare parts came from yet another country supplier. Some equipment was worn out or barely functional; some trucks were so old they would not reliably start, but still the contractor was paid. Some equipment was designed to run on petrol, while some ran on diesel. The equipment that could be salvaged or otherwise made functional needed fuel, although there was neither petrol nor diesel fuel in Liberia. Therefore, the acquisition and transport of fuel also had to be negotiated.

Once peacekeeping security forces began to be deployed and serviceable equipment was on the ground, priority could shift from logistics to strategy. Under the circumstances in Liberia, the top priority was to remove weapons from the field as soon as possible, and it was necessary to clean up the mess of the past postconflict mission as well. In 1993, the UN played an observer role exclusively, and few arms were removed from circulation since merely an estimated 10 percent of the insurgents were disarmed and disbanded.

Additionally, regional instability undermined local security. The instability emanated from Cote d'Ivoire and Sierra Leone in particular in the form of a virtually perpetual flow of mercenaries, arms, and financing back and forth across the porous borders. Later, as the weapons and ammunition collected in the DDRR program were documented and serial numbers recorded, much was identified as coming from all regional sources, as well as from Iran. Even ammunition from U.S. inventories was turned in by Liberian ex-combatants.

The first peacekeeping troops on the scene were from the Economic Community of West African States (ECOWAS). In November 2003, contingents from other countries began to arrive, and the mission was expected to reach its full strength by March 2004. The UN Mandate set a certain date for commencing the DDR program regardless of the troop force at the time.

Thus, the program in Liberia started before all of the "pieces" were in place—before sufficient numbers of troops were deployed or the DDRR infrastructure was ready. On December 3, 2003, the program commenced in Monrovia, where the peacekeepers had the best control. It was met with inflated expectations leading to frustration, violence, and rioting. The warring faction leaders spread the misinformation that $300 per person cash for arms was available only for the first to relinquish arms and ammunition voluntarily. Insurgent groups rushed the gates of the Monrovia containment camps and overwhelmed the resources. An informal agreement with the government allowed for 350 to 400 people a day to be processed and receive ablutions, tents, food, and healthcare. Instead, a thousand people showed up on the first day, but only a fraction could be processed. The number increased exponentially daily, and popular frustration and discontent led to violence. This first stage of the DDRR process shut down on December 17, 2003. Intelligence after the fact revealed that the riots were not spontaneous—they were orchestrated by rebel leaders to undermine the DDRR efforts, cast the United Nations as a failure, and destroy the peace.

There were also positive outcomes from this chaos. In just 14 days, more than 12,500 people were disarmed and nearly 8,700 weapons and 2 million rounds of ammunition were no longer circulating. Paradoxically, this apparent disaster also shifted the focus of grievances among the rebel groups from just insurgency to a common disgust with a benign "opponent"—the UN and the DDRR program's perceived inadequacies. But those rebels who participated in this initial DDRR program started to see that there could be an alternative to war through the cash support and educational and training programs.

Just a few weeks later, on January 15, 2004, UNMIL began to regroup. It organized a series of town hall meetings, consultations, and information campaigns. UNMIL representatives met with commanders of various factions to discuss restarting the DDRR program. Conditions included responsibility by all parties—the commanders to provide information on their troops and arms to UNMIL, and UNMIL to set up multiple cantonment and provide peacekeeping troops for security. Former combatant and arms numbers were not provided, but the DDRR program nevertheless was relaunched on April 15, 2004. By August, more than 100,000 ex-combatants and others in support roles, including 12,000 women and children, were estimated to have participated in the DDRR program.

The Liberian experience showed that the promise of money was the bottom-line, most compelling tool for inducing ex-combatants to participate in DDRR—money to encourage voluntary disarmament and money as a promise of future education and training in a livelihood other than pillaging in war. Disarmament was particularly effective in Liberia because persuasion and encouragement were coupled with the threat of force. The UN Mandate for Liberia permitted the threat of force to seize those arms not voluntarily relinquished, in which case the ex-combatant would be arrested and his or her family would get nothing for it. Thus, large numbers of ex-combatants chose to give up their weapons, receive the money, and have the opportunity to participate in training, schooling, counseling, and other rehabilitation and reintegration activities. This authority to use force was the critical counterpoint to the lure of money, and was key to the disarmament and demobilization successes. Money also enabled compensating informants, who would reveal where a stash of weapons was buried for $50 or less.

Despite the importance of money for ex-combatants, no discretionary fund existed for DDR, and the money-raising process was also ad hoc. Money for DDRR came from pledges by international donor nations. Some countries pledge from good will and the best intentions; others apparently pledge without any intention of ever paying. Nevertheless, at the time of the pledging conference, the headline read, "UN raises $520 million dollars for Liberia." As of the end of May 2004, not even 12 percent—$60 million of the $520 million—pledged at the donors' conference for Liberia 4 months earlier had been received.

Eligibility requirements are a much debated point of DDRR, with some arguing that overly expansive criteria may undermine ultimate success by excessively taxing the process and spreading resources too thin. Where the immediate goals are to remove arms and ammunition from circulation and to win the trust, eligibility standards seem unnecessarily restrictive and even trivial luxuries by comparison. In Liberia, the decision was made to accept any and all weapons and ammunition, regardless of condition or serviceability, and to include women, children, and other special groups simultaneously. Estimates vary widely, but upwards of 38 to 50 percent of ex-combatants and those in combat support roles were women and children. They participated involuntarily and voluntarily—as a result of force, dire economic circumstances, or belief in the cause. The expansive disarmament collection process presented an opportunity to encourage a wide range and large numbers of individuals directly impacted by the conflict to pursue schooling, training, and alternative livelihood opportunities. The initial cash stipends provided the added benefit of injecting money into the system and jumpstarting the economy, even if in an incremental way.

Lessons learned in the aftermath of the chaos included the need for better intelligence, either through the development of a UN intelligence capability or in collaboration with intelligence gathering and analysis by the international community. Practice also confirmed the earlier recommendations of the Brahimi Report of the critical importance of establishing a pre-mandate financing mechanism with a pool of discretionary funding separate and apart from country-specific donor's pledges; and a system of readily available and reliable equipment and personnel. Although it may be debated elsewhere, in the Liberian case, loose and flexible weapons criteria and expansive eligibility standards that included women, children, and other special groups in the DDRR program should be considered good practices.

Reliable intelligence reporting would inform decisionmaking and supply information on who the combatants trust, what they perceive as a threat, where their allegiances and force strength resides, and other critical information. Appropriate intelligence may have prevented the violence and rioting in December 2003. Yet the UN has no formal intelligence capacity and depends on others to supply its intelligence gathering and analysis.

The assessed budget should include discretionary funds for disarmament and demobilization rather than depending on donor pledges. Although postconflict needs are uncertain, they are not unforeseeable. In any given budget cycle, postconflict, peace-building, and disarmament and demobilization needs can be anticipated for somewhere in the world. The alternative of depending on donor pledges once the crisis is at hand compounds uncertainty, politicizes the process, adds to the administrative complexities and delays, and deepens frustration within the local populations. Furthermore, progressing from disarmament and disbandment to rehabilitation and reintegration is where donors typically lose interest in peacekeeping and shift the responsibility to longer term development agencies. In Liberia, with upwards of 70 to 80 percent unemployment following the conflict, and an illiteracy rate of 80 percent, ex-combatants found limited reintegration opportunities. USAID committed $880 million in 2004–2005 and $94 million in 2006 including high-impact programs on literacy, education, and training, among other transition initiatives. Economic opportunities, however "quick impact," typically are needed faster than they can be implemented.

New Integrated DDR Standards (IDDRS) policy guidance on the relationship between DDR and SSR developed by the United Nations Interagency Group on DDR seeks to break down some of the "stovepiping" that undermines coordination of the process. Nevertheless, without discretionary funds, intelligence support, and readily available trained personnel and equipment, the chaos of the postconflict environment will continue to be matched by a chaotic, ad hoc, and insufficiently coordinated response.

Chapter 10

Managing DDR and SSR Programs in the Philippines

By G. Eugene Martin

The Republic of the Philippines (RP) has confronted insurgencies since its independence in 1946. The government offered amnesty, resettlement, and integration into the security services to diverse groups, beginning with the leftist Hukbalahap rebellion after World War II. Counterinsurgency (COIN) tactics and strategies implemented by President Ramon Maysaysay and his American advisor, Lieutenant Colonel Edward Lansdale, persuaded many Huks to surrender to government forces during that period. In return, the government offered land and resettlement in Mindanao, in effect demobilizing, disarming, and reintegrating many Huks into civilian society.

The government's most recent attempt to incorporate Disarmament, Demobilization, and Reintegration (DDR) principles into a peace process was in the 1996 peace agreement with the Moro National Liberation Front (MNLF), representing the Muslim minority in the southern Philippines. Its efforts to reform the security sector to better address external and internal challenges have enjoyed mixed success over the years.

As the administration of President Benigno Aquino III prepares to resume peace negotiations with the Moro Islamic Liberation Front (MILF), the government's experiences with MNLF could provide valuable guidelines for future DDR programs. The MILF is expected to insist on a different formulation for the integration of DDR and Comprehensive Approach to Security Sector Reform (SSR) principles. The feasibility of any peace agreement could well rest on whether the two sides can find a viable formula to resolve heretofore unworkable security problems.

DDR of the MNLF

The status of combatants was a critical issue during negotiations between the government of the Republic of the Philippines (GPH) and the MNLF to resolve the Moro rebellion in the southern Philippines. Twenty years of negotiations concluded with the signing of the GPH–MNLF "Final Peace Agreement" (FPA) on September 2, 1996. The FPA called for the devolution of political authority in the Autonomous Region of Muslim Mindanao (ARMM) to the MNLF, the establishment of the Special Zone of Peace and Development (SZOPAD) in conflict areas with majority Moro communities, and the integration of MNLF combatants into the Armed Forces of the Philippines (AFP) and the Philippine National Police (PNP). These three components of DDR—demobilization by granting political authority, disarmament through integration into the security services, and economic livelihood programs to reintegrate combatants into civilian society—were seen as means to end a long conflict. The U.S. Government (USG) actively welcomed the peace agreement and signed a number of U.S. Agency for International Development (USAID)–MNLF livelihood development agreements with MNLF Chairman Nur Misuari. There was optimism that the long conflict in Mindanao might at last be on its way to resolution.

Regrettably, the FPA has not been well implemented, in part because of weaknesses in the form of DDR adopted. As General James Mattis, USMC, pointed out during the National Defense University/Chief Operations Officer seminar, DDR is difficult to accomplish unless the enemy is defeated and acknowledges it, opening the door for a political settlement. In the case of the GPH–MNLF agreement, the three aspects of DDR were undercut by the MNLF's view that it had gained power in the ARMM through devolution of political and economic authority. The MNLF therefore sought to preserve its military capabilities to ensure its new autonomous authority in the face of mistrust of the government.

Demobilization

Given control of the ARMM, the MNLF refused to dismantle its revolutionary organization or command structure and become a political movement. Allowing the MNLF to remain a revolutionary organization and retain its military command structure and weapons complicated rather than ameliorated the political situation in the southern Philippines. The FPA called for 1,500 MNLF fighters to be incorporated into the PNP with another 5,750 to be integrated into the AFP. The MNLF anticipated that its combatants would be integrated as units rather than as individuals (at least initially) and would become a Special Regional Security Force

(SRSF) in the ARMM. It soon became clear, however, that the GPH and AFP/PNP did not interpret the FPA as obligating them to the integration of complete MNLF units and their subsequent exclusive assignment to the ARMM. Rather, the GPH insisted Moro integrees would be inserted individually into AFP units and could be stationed anywhere in the country. While this continues to be an irritant, the AFP and PNP have generally succeeded in their efforts to integrate MNLF integrees into their organizational structures. Sensitive handling of religious and cultural issues have eased the transition, while remedial education and training have helped to better level the contrasts between the different cultures.

The MNLF had another stratagem to sustain its combat capabilities. Many, if not most, of the MNLF individuals integrating into the security services were either older combatants or relatives of fighters who bought their way into the AFP or PNP. The older integrees were veterans of over 2 decades of conflict who were tired and ready to settle for a comfortable military position that offered pay and benefits, unlike the MNLF. Because of either MNLF leaders' orders or personal preferences, most active combatants did not apply for integration, preferring to wait and see how the FPA was implemented. Instead, since the FPA permitted undefined "MNLF elements" to integrate into the AFP and PNP, many combatants substituted their relatives. This negated the objective of the integration—to demobilize and disarm the MNLF.

Reintegration

The Philippine congress took 5 years after the signing of the GPH–MNLF peace agreement to pass legislation enabling the FPA. Even then, the implementing legislation did not give the ARMM government the financial resources or budgetary authority to provide livelihood skills training or material needs for ex-combatants. Most programs were based on contributions from international donors. While USAID devotes a majority of its Philippine program funding to Muslim communities in Mindanao, the Moro provinces remain the poorest in the country. Non-Moro interests continue to control many of the economic levers of power and influence in Moro-majority areas, leading to limited educational and employment opportunities, especially for young Moros. Continued security concerns and poor infrastructure discourage investment and business creation. Livelihood projects for former MNLF combatants focus on providing agricultural support for small family plots or fishing equipment. Many MNLF members became fighters at a young age and have little education, experience, or interest in farming or fishing, complicating efforts to transition them into civilian economic pursuits. The ARMM's inability to develop and control its own economic and budgetary resources without Manila's direction leaves it few opportunities to formulate policies and programs to address these problems. In areas where it does have control, wasteful and ineffectual expenditures and corrupt officials further prolong poverty and dissatisfaction. As a result, young Moros are susceptible to the blandishments of drug traffickers and criminal gangs that are often sponsored or facilitated by politicians. Furthermore, as most MNLF fighters are Tausugs, they frequently have familial relationships with members of the Abu Sayyaf Gang (ASG), who employ terrorists' methods in pursuit of their essentially criminal goals.

Disarmament

Since the MNLF remained a revolutionary organization, it was able to refuse to relinquish the front's major weapons when its fighters were integrated into the AFP or PNP. Unlike other disarmament programs, which call for the surrender or at least cantonment of an organization's arms, the FPA only required integrees to turn in a weapon when joining the security services. As a result, individuals planning to integrate had to find other guns to turn in. Since a lack of a reliable justice system and the Tausug culture call for males to retain weapons for personal or family safety (as well as image), few were willing to turn in their personal weapons. Rather, they often took loans against future earnings to purchase inexpensive, low-caliber firearms to submit. The result was more guns in Moro areas and the retention of the MNLF's more modern, high-powered weapons.

DDR is normally a step in a lengthy implementation scenario. Once the bona fides of a peace agreement are tested and confirmed through joint action, trust can be established between parties and a successful political settlement is more likely. Given the lack of trust between the Moros and the Philippine government, based on a long history of broken promises and unfulfilled agreements, the MNLF decided to "keep its powder dry" by withholding its real combatants and good weapons until it saw if the FPA would be successful. Initial levels of confidence and trust had dissipated by the time congress passed legislation in 2001 to implement the FPA—the amended ARMM Organic Act (RA-9054), passed 5 years after the FPA was signed.

The FPA implementation failure can be attributed to both parties. The MNLF leadership's inability to transition from rebellion to governance led to internal divisions and rent seeking. While individual commanders were given "government" positions in the ARMM, their loyalty remained with Chairman Misuari and the MNLF. It soon became apparent that the transition was not going well, particularly as the central government continued to meddle in the reputedly "autonomous" region. Congress refused to authorize the Front's expectation that ex-MNLF forces could join the AFP and PNP as autonomous units and be assigned to an SRSF during the initial transition phase, pending gradual integration into regular AFP/PNP units. This left few opportunities for most MNLF combatants. With little indication of future improvements of the security situation or of economic development, Moro grievances and frustrations festered. The failed implementation of the MNLF FPA led the MILF to insist on GPH guarantees that the congress or successive governments would not unilaterally alter a negotiated peace agreement with them. As has been seen, the Philippine supreme court aborted the August 2008 draft GPH–MILF Memorandum of Agreement on Ancestral Domain on constitutional grounds. The congress likely would have rejected it in any case.

The government's shortcomings on devolving genuine political and economic authority to the ARMM government were matched by its continued subversion of what little autonomy the ARMM had. Parsimonious allocation of resources did not improve Moro economic or employment opportunities. Presidential power brokers succeeded in subverting the MNLF Central Committee by undercutting the generally ineffectual chairman and establishing the "Council of 15" beholden to the Philippine Presidential Malacanang Palace. Growing factionalization among the 15 councilors and continued ethno-linguistic differences between the MNLF's core Tausug elements and other tribal representatives further weakened MNLF capabilities, leaving the MNLF an acephalous body. Some of its members joined the MILF, which had split from the MNLF in 1983, while others cooperated with more extremist groups such as the ASG.

The U.S. Government's efforts to help the AFP to counter terrorist groups and meet threats in the southern Philippines through the Joint Special Operations Task Force–Philippines have complicated DDR efforts with the MNLF. Operations against the ASG on the islands of Basilan and Jolo, the ASG's main base of operations, encounter familial ties between the ASG and the MNLF, both of which are composed primarily of Tausugs. Pursuit of and combat with the ASG often encounter communities with former MNLF combatant or integree families and relatives, as most ASG members come from the same clans. Such AFP operations trigger clan loyalties, retarding efforts to eliminate the ASG fish in the Tausug pond.

The question now is what DDR issues will arise in prospective peace negotiations with the MILF. The unsatisfactory experience with the MNLF is likely to prompt the GPH to seek comprehensive disarmament and demobilization of MILF combatants. The MILF, in turn, will insist that its Bangsamoro Islamic Armed Forces (BIAF) units become the primary security force in the hoped-for autonomous governance structure, the Bangsamoro Juridical Entity (BJE). DDR has not been thoroughly discussed in negotiations, which have focused on the geographical extent of the BJE and the powers devolved to it. In view of GPH fears that granting self-determination to the Moros will lead to future separation and independence for Muslim-majority areas, resolution of the BIAF's future and who will be responsible for security is sure to be a difficult issue.

Security Sector Reform

The Philippine government's efforts to enhance domestic security are obstructed by incomplete SSR. Philippine security services have been reformed and reorganized to meet changing challenges several times over the past century. When the United States succeeded Spain as the islands' colonial authority, the U.S. Army was responsible for establishing and maintaining security through the end of the Philippine-American War (1899–1902). As stability returned, the Philippine Scouts and the Philippine Constabulary (PC), modeled on the former Spanish Guardia Civil, were established in 1901. Following the founding of the Commonwealth in the 1930s, Filipino military personnel were formed into the AFP. They were incorporated into the U.S. Armed Forces Far East at the outbreak of the Pacific War in 1941, becoming the core of the postindependence AFP upon independence in 1946.

Since independence, the AFP has had an ambivalent mission—a mixture of external and internal security responsibilities. With sizeable U.S. forces remaining in the country after independence under the U.S.–RP Mutual Defense Treaty, the AFP did not give much attention to external defense. The PC, while a branch of the AFP, was responsible for internal security. This changed under President Ferdinand Marcos when he declared martial law in 1972. The AFP became a politicized tool for the suppression of dissent and opposition to the regime, sundering the previous societal identification and bond between the force and society. Relations remain largely antagonistic to this day, exacerbating the appeal of the communist New Peoples Army (NPA).

After Marcos, the Corazon "Cory" Aquino administration efforts to depoliticize the AFP met with marginal success. Seven attempted coup d'etats during "Cory's" 6-year term were caused by elements within the AFP unwilling to relinquish the heady political role they attained in the overthrow of President Marcos. President Fidel Ramos, based on his PC and military career, instituted military discipline and reform, including the transformation of the PC into the PNP, responsible for internal security and police functions. The PNP was weakened, however, when local government units (i.e., mayors and governors) were given authority over local police forces, with the Department of Interior having only oversight and logistic control. The PNP continues to see itself as the successor to the PC and thus as a national paramilitary force rather than a police force, but without responsibility to the national command authority.

A legacy of the Marcos era continued by his successors is the use of irregular local militias and volunteers to extend the reach of security services. The Civilian Armed Force Geographical Units (CAFGUs) and various Civilian Volunteer Organizations (CVOs) were established to counter local communist NPA and Moro threats. The CAFGU units were to be armed and led by AFP noncoms while the CVOs were to be unarmed "neighborhood watch" groups reporting to local officials. In practice, they often became the officials' private armies, used to keep dynastic families in power by threatening political opponents, intimidating critical media and civil society, and ensuring "adequate" voter turnouts during elections. The November 2009 massacre of opponents by the Ampatuan clan in Maguindanao was the inevitable result.

The withdrawal of U.S. forces from Clark Air Base and Subic Naval Base in the early 1990s and reduction of U.S. military aid, training, and liaison with the AFP weakened Philippine security capabilities and mission focus. The end of the Cold War, along with China's growing economic integration into the world and soft power influence in Southeast Asia, reduced potential external threats to the Philippines. The 1996 peace agreement with the MNLF and diminishment of NPA activities suggested a lessening need for a robust security sector. The prevalent traditional political structure was based on politically powerful provincial family dynasties who did not want central government control of their security, preferring to manage their own issues albeit with central logistic and financial support.

The AFP was repoliticized in the late 1990s under Presidents Joseph Estrada and Gloria Arroyo. Estrada used the force to destroy the MILF base, Camp Abubakkar, in 2000 to boost his slipping popularity. The following year, then–Vice President Arroyo persuaded the AFP to "withdraw support" from Estrada in her push to remove him from office so she could become president. She subsequently drew on AFP support in her 2004 election to a full second term. In return, she appointed supportive military officers to higher military and civilian positions. More importantly, she encouraged the AFP to eliminate the NPA insurgency during her term of office with few restraints on the means to be used. The resultant wave of extrajudicial killings of suspected leftists finally prompted U.S. congressional and UN Human Rights Commission investigations and criticisms.

By the mid-1990s, AFP capabilities had so deteriorated that Presidents Ramos and subsequently Estrada responded positively to U.S. proposals to negotiate a quasi-Status of Forces Agreement to permit a resumption of Philippine-American military relations. The Visiting Forces Agreement (VFA) was carefully couched to address Filipino nationalist sentiments against renewed U.S. bases and permanent presence. Estrada's forceful personal interventions succeeded in persuading a majority of senators to approve the VFA. It permits temporary visits of U.S. military personnel to conduct joint training exercises and civic action programs to foster closer bilateral cooperation and understanding.

The VFA was critical after 9/11 as Washington anticipated that Southeast Asia, and the southern Philippines specifically, would become a "second front" in the Global War on Terror. The U.S.–RP military relationship became a high priority for both governments. The United States saw a need to counter al Qaeda and Indonesian Jemaah Islamiyah inroads into Islamic communities in the southern Philippines. The RP, in turn, saw a potential revival of U.S. assistance (both military and developmental) and military training and materiel. The AFP needed help in redefining its mission and believed cooperation with the United States would augment its internal *and* external security capabilities. Washington was willing to work with the AFP to develop the RP Defense Reform Program to help the AFP become a full partner in the perceived priorities of the new century.

The internal security situation, however, has not improved since the mid-1990s. As noted above, the failure of the GPH and MNLF to implement their 1996 peace agreement undermines the security and stability of the south. The criminal ASG on Jolo and Basilian remains an active threat despite massive AFP presence and U.S. fusion support. The MILF, while continuing to engage in peace negotiations with the government, continues to regard the AFP as an alien occupying force pursuing policies similar to Spanish and American colonial armies. The AFP's inability to eliminate the ASG or develop positive relations with the Moro minority raises questions about its ability to address internal weaknesses even with U.S. assistance.

The most pressing security sector reform need is dramatized by the November 23, 2009, massacre in Maguindanao Province of Mindanao. Fifty-seven people were murdered by militia under the control and command of the Ampatuan clan, the de facto warlord of the Maguindanao portion of the ARMM. The targets were the wife and relatives of a political opponent, but accompanying journalists and innocent travelers were shot and mutilated.

The Ampatuan clan had allied itself with President Arroyo. She gave them nearly free license to rule their area of the ARMM in return for their political assistance and overwhelming electoral support of nearly 100 percent of the votes in the 2004 election. With the administration's concurrence, the clan was allowed to amass a private militia that was better armed than the AFP. The clan, headed by the provincial governor, arranged for his relatives to become the ARMM governor and most mayors, running their territory as a private fiefdom. Their CAFGU militia and illegally armed CVOs ensured there was no opposition to their wishes, policies, or continuance in office. The police were under their control and the military commanders were either beholden to the clan or afraid to cross such a well-known ally of the president. No one who had followed the steady expansion of private armies and militias throughout the country was surprised by this denouement.

The political uproar the massacre caused opened an opportunity to institute local security sector reform in the Philippines. Demobilizing and disarming CAFGUs and CVOs and returning police control to higher level authorities was a necessary but difficult first step. Even the institution of temporary martial law in Maguindanao Province after the massacre did not prevent militia members from refusing to surrender or to turn in their sophisticated weapons. Persuading provincial politicians and elite families to give up their armed security forces, several numbering in the hundreds, will be a test of the government's willingness and ability to ensure the safety and security of its citizens. Unfortunately, the effort must extend beyond police and military reform as it needs to include the nation's justice system and the institution of the rule of law over all citizens, even the politically powerful. It may take more than one massacre to make a difference. And it would have to take place in a non-Moro, Christian area rather than being a contest between Moro politicians, since the Ampatuan-Mangadadatu rivalry is seen by most of the population as just another example of *rido* (clan warfare) between two uncivilized Moslem warlords.

Regrettably, President Arroyo was unable or unwilling to seize the opportunity to reform the security sector by curtailing and eventually eliminating the CAFGU and CVO militias during the last 7 months of her administration. She may not have been prepared to risk exposure of her reliance on warlord support for her reelection in 2004, when the Ampatuans (and perhaps other powerful local families) delivered enough votes for her victory.

The election of Cory Aquino's son, Benigno "Noy-Noy" Aquino, as President in May 2010 provides another opening for security sector reform. His father's assassination by security forces under the Marcos martial-law regime gives him a personal interest in such reform. Unfortunately, his selection of a personal friend rather than a competent professional with security experience as Under Secretary of the Department of Interior, responsible for supervision of the PNP, is not encouraging. Until the PNP is professionalized and quarantined from local political interference, security and justice will be impaired.

Conclusion

The failure to implement effective DDR under the GPH–MNLF peace agreement and the unsuccessful reform of the Philippine security sector vividly demonstrate the cause of continued instability, particularly in the south. Despite incorporation of DDR concepts in the 1996 Final Peace Agreement, contradictory interpretations of imprecise provisions, political backsliding, sabotage, and a paucity of political will by members of both parties result in prolongation of the conflict and a risk of renewed violence. The DDR record over the past 14 years is a poor basis upon which to plan for negotiations with the Moro Islamic Liberation Front, which will look for a more effective means of maintaining its influence over security in its area. The inability of the government to establish a competent police force and disband irregular militias perpetuates political power centers focused on protecting their positions and privileges. Until the national leadership and key subnational groups are able to resolve differences and reach a political and economic accommodation, the Philippines will continue to present an image of weak and ineffective government with serious internal security problems.

Chapter 11

Managing DDR Risks in Sudan: A Field Perspective

By Adriaan Verheul

DDR in Sudan

The Disarmament, Demobilization, and Reintegration (DDR) program in Sudan as envisaged in the Comprehensive Peace Agreement (CPA) of January 9, 2005, was characterized by a number of key features that make it unique.

First of all, there was the scale of the program. The caseload indicated by the government covered some 180,000 ex-combatants of various categories who were to be demobilized and reintegrated into civilian life over a territory the size of Western Europe, which posed serious challenges of design and management.

Second, the DDR program was part of a fragile and complex peace process on which it depended for success. The process aimed to deal with a very complex conflict with multiple nested layers: ethnic, political, regional, economic (including natural resources), and social.

Third, the program under the CPA only covered the north-south dimensions of conflict in Sudan and did not include DDR efforts in East Sudan or Darfur or the potential for DDR of Lord's Resistance Army (LRA) rebels crossing into Sudan.

Fourth, the United Nations (UN) approach in Sudan included two innovative features: an integrated approach that put members of the UN Peacekeeping Operation in Sudan (UNMIS) and of the UN Development Programme (UNDP) in a single integrated unit, and the use of peacekeeping budget funds (also known as assessed contributions) instead of voluntary donor money to meet demobilization expenditures.

Fifth, the negotiation, design, and early implementation required a delicate balancing act between creating momentum politically and ensuring the integrity of the program from a fiduciary angle.

Finally, "DDR" was a misnomer: there was no disarmament of ex-combatants stricto sensu, nor did it include the disarmament of civilians.

This chapter is written from a field perspective and covers the political and program aspects of the adult DDR program under the CPA only and includes a few observations on DDR in general, in particular on the need to develop a market-based reintegration approach. The period under review stretches from the end of 2007 to the end of 2009.

Objectives and Logic

The DDR program in Sudan has multiple objectives, according to the CPA. In the long run, the overarching objective is to contribute to creating an enabling environment to human security and to support post–peace-agreement social stabilization across the Sudan, particularly in war-affected areas. Also, "the DDR program shall take place within a comprehensive process of national reconciliation and healing throughout the country as part of the peace and confidence building measures."

The overarching logic of the DDR program was embodied in a two-stage approach. During the first stage, corresponding to the initial phases of the peace process, both parties would first allow voluntary demobilization of nonessentials (child soldiers and elderly, disabled, and (noncombatant) women associated with the armed forces). The second phase caseload would then absorb those soldiers who would be laid off as a result of what the CPA called "proportional downsizing," a confidence-building measure between the North and South that would also potentially lead to a smaller Sudanese national army in case the peace process brought unity. After the completion of redeployment of northern Sudanese forces to the north of the 1956 border, the parties were expected to begin the negotiations on proportionate downsizing. According to the CPA timetable, they were supposed to start in autumn 2008, but no progress has been reported to date.

A Slow Start

The DDR program was supposed to begin in 2005, but it did not commence in earnest until early 2009. The reasons not only were linked to the complexities of the program, but also to the difficulties of building trust between the parties themselves (which was subject to the overall peace process) as well as between the parties and the United Nations as their principal partner. In 2007, the Sudan People's Liberation Movement (SPLM) had withdrawn from the Government of National Unity and would not return to the table until early 2008. In 2007, UN relations with Sudanese authorities in both North and South were in bad shape, largely because of unmet and/or unrealistic promises made by the United Nations as well as erroneous assumptions about what the UN could deliver and within which time frames. Both northern and southern Sudanese officials were either suspicious or pessimistic, if not cynical, about UN support, indicating that they were ready to go it alone if the United Nations failed to deliver.

Moreover, the United Nations was blamed for all delay related to the program because it had "failed to provide the funds," which was manifestly untrue. There were monies available in the UNMIS budget but no plan of any detail on which of these funds could be spent. Donors' confidence was low in view of the lack of progress on the ground by the government and the United Nations. Processes for planning and strategic-level coordination with partners were lacking. While there was some demobilization of child soldiers, the process of adult DDR of the "nonessentials" had yet to begin.

At the level of program design, little progress had been made beyond the Interim DDR Programme (IDDRP, started in 2005), whose main objectives were to set up and build the capacity of DDR institutions and civil society, while initiating basic DDR processes for selected priority target groups (women, children, disabled, etc.). The understanding was that its successful development and implementation would lay the groundwork for the development and implementation of a multiyear DDR program. While some valuable experience had been gained and some useful activities had been launched (child demobilization, awareness-raising among women), the latter assumption did not pan out.

Going Forward

An important milestone was the adoption in November 2007 by the National DDR Coordinating Council (NDDRCC) of a National DDR Strategic Plan in November. This document was based on a draft that the United Nations had been working on with the government. This plan was by no means a perfect policy from a program perspective. What was lacking in particular were the precise role of the United Nations, how reintegration would work, and what benefits would be involved. Subsequent negotiations on this proved difficult. The government had removed a reference to a UN role in the verification of eligibility and disarmament from the earlier drafts. More seriously perhaps, there was no linkage to security sector transformation to give the international community some comfort that it was funding a serious effort towards confidence-building and lower defense expenditures, rather than buying off old fighters' loyalty. Nevertheless, the document provided a useful legal and political basis on which to conduct planning and preparations.

However, the plan left open how the parties would manage DDR in the Three Areas (Blue Nile State, Southern Kordofan, and Abyei). This effectively prevented the United Nations from assisting the parties in a balanced manner because the majority of the caseload in the North was located in these areas, but the UN could not help until both sides agreed on an arrangement for the governance of DDR. This issue was solved in July 2008 after the opposing parties adopted a solution whereby DDR in the Three Areas would be managed through Joint DDR Commissions.

At the same time, there were serious misunderstandings about the kind of support the United Nations would be able to provide. These misreadings had led to disappointment if not disillusionment with the United Nations. The UN team tried to create clarity by adopting a "UN framework for assistance," which was negotiated inside the UN system and communicated to the parties. However, some key interlocutors still did not grasp how UN support for DDR is structured. Admittedly, this is quite complex. In essence, there were two lines of funding by the international community, one through the assessed contributions to the UNMIS peacekeeping budget (a guaranteed source of funding) for demobilization and the other through voluntary donor contributions to be channeled through a UNDP-managed trust fund. Both funding streams have their own modalities for disbursement, management, and accounting.

Planning for this program was further complicated by the absence of clear timelines. A chicken and egg situation presented itself. A decision on timelines required planning, but planners needed a horizon in order to plan. In this regard, it was helpful to have a deadline imposed from the outside. An important factor in pushing through decisions was the May 2008 Sudan Consortium in Norway, which gave a deadline for presenting a reasonable and likely acceptable DDR program outline to donors, which helped in getting basic agreement on key outstanding issues including the level of benefits. Initial negotiations started with nearly unbridgeable differences in expectations between Sudanese and international partners related to the caseload size, benefits, and reintegration program management, but these were by and large resolved on the eve of the last day of the Oslo meeting. Subsequently, there was some backtracking on the part of Southern Sudan related to the management modalities of the program, but that did not stop the elaboration and later adoption of a reintegration program document. Planning for demobilization was given a boost by persuading the parties to agree to a potential starting date for demobilization (August 2008). This date was artificial to some extent, but its mention in a Secretary General's report to the Security Council gave UNMIS and the parties a clear focus. Of course, the date shifted many times, but the key was that the process had been set in motion.

DDR Program Outline

In short, names of members of the armed forces on both sides, as well as of other armed groups which have been absorbed into these forces, are put forward by their commands on a list, which is submitted to the Southern and Northern Sudan Commissions, respectively. DDR candidates are first discharged from service and disarmed at their units, with weapons remaining with their respective armies. Next they report to the nearest demobilization site, set up on a semimobile basis, where their eligibility is verified and they receive a briefing on the overall process and a DDR ID card, as well as a reinsertion package that consists of food rations for 3 months, a cash benefit equivalent to U.S. $400, and a bag with a score of nonfood items. At a later date (usually a few months), they receive individual counseling on their reintegration options (agriculture, education, small business start-up, etc.), which option then will be provided as a package by a local contractor or NGO. The cost of these reintegration packages is approximately U.S. $1,500.

Ownership

The Government of National Unity (GoNU) and the Government of Southern Sudan (GOSS) were extremely keen on the national ownership of the program at all levels: strategic, management, and implementation. However, this was constrained by limited capacity and also—to some extent—a lack of understanding of the enormity of the planning, logistical, and operational challenges. Moreover, from the outset there were erroneous and persistent perceptions about financial management modalities, both with regard to assessed and voluntary funding. Reaching a good understanding sometimes meant waiting until implementation was well underway and the requirement to adopt clear procedures became unavoidable. Signing off on joint procedures for both Disarmament and Reintegration often had to await the confrontation with reality. This implies that momentum could be built, but at the expense of the quality of procedures and the integrity of the program. This is a risk that was taken consciously and which will continue to require careful management.

Getting the parties moving forward required a delicate balancing act. On the one hand, the United Nations needed to provide vital technical assistance and input at all levels, and on the other hand such assistance and input had to be prepared and presented in such a way as not to create the impression that the United Nations was imposing its view or was prejudging the outcome of national decisionmaking processes, which was never the intention. Once the DD process had started, it was important to bring the parties on board to tighten up and enhance procedures, especially with regard to the eligibility of participants, which was open to abuse and manipulation. For that reason, the idea of an independent assessment of the first phase caseload was presented in late spring 2009. The results of this assessment, issued in December 2009, confirmed the findings of the United Nations itself, which have been communicated to the parties in various instances. The assessment identified concerns, chief among them being that the process by which the Sudan Armed Forces, Popular Defense Force (PDF), and Sudan People's Liberation Army (SPLA) identify their participants was not known; the National DDR Strategic Plan does not articulate key policy issues clearly enough; master lists generated in the 2007/2008 preregistration have been abandoned in favor of new lists; criteria for entry for women associated with armed forces (WAAF) and PDF candidates are not sufficiently clear; a mechanism for the collection and management of weapons has not been agreed on; and receiving communities have not gotten sufficient sensitization on the process. At the time of writing, the results of the assessment are followed up on in a constructive spirit and with the government in the lead. A new set of procedures has been agreed to by both North and South DDR Commissions, and the overall coordination structures have become more inclusive and effective.

At the same time, it was very difficult to establish benchmarks that would tie international funding to the parties meeting certain criteria related to program quality. First, after losing credibility with the parties early on, the UN was in no position to impose conditions on DDR planning. The parties would have taken a greater political distance from the United Nations, making it more difficult to engage them on programming and leading to further delay. Plus the parties were quick to point out that their strategic plan was based on a UN draft and that UN concurrence was therefore implied. Second, it was politically important that some progress be made soon in CPA implementation. On balance, the risks of starting the program without fully developed checks and balances were offset by the benefits of gaining momentum in an otherwise stalling peace process.

At the strategic level, the United Nations had no seat on the National DDR Strategic Council. In fact, a standing recommendation from UN headquarters was to persuade the Presidency to accept a UN role in this body. After the adoption of the strategic plan, it was clear that this was an unrealistic expectation, especially given that the United Nations was initially held in low esteem as far as DDR was concerned. In addition, there was no process or forum at which the Sudanese authorities, donor representatives, and the United Nations could exchange views on the program. In particular, donors expected the UN to act as proxies for them (and still do). To remedy this, the United Nations proposed holding a DDR roundtable, inviting donors, UN agencies, and government entities. The government agreed. The experience with this forum (three have been held) has been by and large positive, which may well continue provided each meeting is prepared for well in advance, and the NDDRCC has had time to reflect and decide on key outstanding issues.

Disarmament, Demobilization, and Reintegration have now been underway since early 2009, with over 20,000 ex-combatants (or over 10 percent of the declared caseload) having entered the program and significant momentum being built. However, to date only 250 have received reintegration packages. Beyond the numbers and logistics, UN support to DDR in Sudan contributed to progress in a key area of CPA implementation (which was lagging in other areas), established excellent and pragmatic cooperation with and between North and South (quoted often as an example for other areas), and provided a tangible peace dividend to various groups in the Three Areas and South. It has also contributed to the management of a looming fiscal and social crisis in the South. The big question remains whether DDR will make a difference in long-term peace and stability as part of a multitrack peace process.

"Not Meaningful"

The mobilization of the first phase caseload of the old, disabled, women, and children had a mix of motives: fiscal, moral, and political (maintaining loyalty and preparing the ground for elections). This aspect has been criticized by donors and others. Not being "militarily relevant or meaningful," it was not quite understood why the DDR of this caseload—except of course for the children—should deserve international funding. It was thought that DDR should lead to an immediate reduction in military capacity (perhaps naively so early after a long war with mistrust running high).

However, this point of view failed to take account of what in my view constituted the most important "D" in any DDR program, "Dignity." One cannot simply dismiss those elderly and disabled who in some cases have fought for 20 years for their cause. If not treated with a minimum of respect, such groups could develop grievances that constitute both a security risk and a political liability to their leaders. At the end of 2008, this first stage caseload became a real issue for the Government of Southern Sudan. Following the drop in oil prices, the GOSS was under tremendous pressure to reduce expenditures including the payroll of the (southern) SPLA, which included some 35,000 elderly, female, and disabled ex-combatants. In addition, the SPLA was keen to turn itself from a rebel movement into a professional organization in which there was no place for old or disabled veterans. The DDR program, which was largely financed by the international community, offered a social safety net as well as a fiscal escape route, and donors—conscious of the risks of a fiscal and social collapse in southern Sudan—were quick to support the DDR of that first phase caseload.

Proportional Downsizing

The next phase caseload was expected to flow from the "proportional downsizing" as envisaged in the CPA. However, this is not very likely to materialize. Each side may engage in unilateral downsizing for its own reasons involving fiscal considerations while seeking to advance professionalism (including the police in the South), but not as a result of mutually agreed steps between North and South. Donors continue to raise the issue of more transparency with regard to defense policy and budgets. However, to push these issues articulated in this way may have caused an adverse reaction on the part of those Sudanese who were either still actively engaged in conflict in Darfur or preparing for a worst-case scenario between North and South. Instead of asking for transparency, donors and the United Nations followed the terminology of the CPA, according to which negotiations on proportional downsizing were supposed to have started around November 2008. This did not happen then and it looks increasingly likely that it will remain a dead letter of the CPA. Nevertheless, if the two sides are serious about DDR in Sudan beyond the "nonessentials" and other armed groups, they need to engage with the United Nations and donors on this matter at an early stage and work out a mutually acceptable compromise. If they do not, the program will effectively end after the "nonessentials" caseload is done.

Disarmament Aspects

The use of the "DDR" acronym caused some unrealistic expectations. Donors, in particular, wished to ensure that demobilized ex-combatants verifiably surrendered their weapons. Many of our interlocutors still look at Sudan according to the Liberian model, where DDR would demobilize armed groups who operate outside the law. The first "D"—in spite of being in the CPA—is really a misnomer. Instead the program deals with two statutory armed forces that have the right to acquire and manage weapons as a matter of sovereignty. Any access to weapons by the United Nations or other third parties will have to be on a voluntary basis, and both SAF and PDF will have the right to refuse for security reasons. Even if access is given, there is considerable doubt that one can adequately establish a paper trail that links weapons to demobilized personnel.

Moreover, "Disarmament" was more commonly understood, especially in the South, as efforts to remove small arms from the population commenced. This was not found in the formal DDR program and was conducted by GOSS as part of a law enforcement program that was not without its difficulties. The DDR of statutory armies aside, the key issue threatening stability in Sudan and the region is the availability of weapons and the possibility that ethnic or tribal conflicts might spur the formation of armed groups outside the law. There is a real need for a coherent approach that includes civilian disarmament, community security efforts, (real) DDR of armed tribal and ethnic groups, and the downsizing and professionalization of the security sector, including the police. The most urgent of these is the DDR of nonstatutory armed groups, which should only be undertaken as part of a wider reconciliation effort. At the end of the day, it is not about the weapons but about the removal of reasons to acquire, keep, and use them. The complexity of this effort is easily underestimated, but the international community should take this issue up soon with the parties concerned, especially in the South. The efforts by GOSS in the period under review were focused on forcible disarmament alone without addressing the underlying causes of weapon ownership (insecurity, lack of police, interethnic strife, etc.). In this context, such efforts only lead to an increase of the local market price of weapons and a new supply and demand cycle that leads to rearmament after disarmament.

The Right DDR Logic

The logic of the CPA was highly dependent on developing trust between the parties and to some extent was flawed. While the DDR of "nonessentials" posed no threat to either side, and even had fiscal and social benefits, the proportional downsizing of armed forces was not going to happen until sufficient trust had been built, something that the DDR of nonessentials by itself cannot do. To apply a DDR solution to both types of caseload in Sudan was perhaps not the best solution. The inclusion of DDR references in peace agreements, especially in Africa, may well have become a negotiators' reflex. In addition, the abbreviation "DDR" itself has led to assumptions about program design and parties' behavior that are not supported by political realities on the ground.

Some additional reflection and research might have led to alternative solutions that were more suited to what is essentially a reform and downsizing process of two statutory armed forces in Sudan, rather than the peaceful dissolution of armed groups that have operated outside the law, which is what DDR is usually associated with. For example, for both North and South Sudan it may have been cheaper and more effective to set up, for example, a hybrid reintegration—a pension/veterans benefits plan based on a small stipend per month for a minimum of 5 years, combined with a flexible reintegration component for those who are truly unable to cope after demobilization. Offering individuals the freedom to (continue to) fend for themselves, rather than a high-cost,[1] overhead-heavy, and somewhat paternalistic demobilization and reintegration approach that creates dependencies and unrealistic expectations, would—with the benefit of hindsight—perhaps be a more sustainable solution. In this regard, it is advisable for negotiators to look at DDR modalities and alternatives at an early stage.

In fact, a key point of criticism of the UN Integrated DDR Standards (IDDRS) is that it fails to present alternatives to traditional DDR. Current and soon-to-be-published work by the UN on what is called "Second Generation" DDR will address this. The term describes a set of evolving practices and ideas expanding on "traditional" DDR as part of a broader and more sophisticated agenda of promoting stability and security in a peacekeeping context, in response to a trend where the UN is increasingly asked to do DDR where the basic political, security, and economic conditions for DDR are lacking. Sudan, but also Haiti, Côte d'Ivoire, and the DRC are examples. The "Second Generation" DDR practices indicate a shift away from targeting ex-combatants to the benefit of larger communities that have been affected by violence. They also provide guidance for what can be done if the preconditions for DDR do not exist in order to build trust and contribute to a conducive environment for peacebuilding instead of or in parallel to "traditional" DDR.

There are three broad categories of "Second Generation" DDR activities: first, postconflict or postdisaster stabilization measures that include emergency employment or reinsertion programs as well as subnational and community oriented programs that aim to curb the effects of violence perpetrated by various actors with multiple motivations (crime, interethnic tensions, etc.) in the absence of effective state actors; second, programs that target specific groups that may or may not be part of the peace process, such as militias, at-risk youth and gangs, and members of the armed forces; and third, alternative approaches to disarmament and unlawful weapon possession, including through flexible sequencing (e.g., reintegration before disarmament), weapons registration and management programs, and "weapons for development" or lottery initiatives.

Thoughts on Using Assessed Contributions for DDR

Sudan was also the first instance where demobilization and reinsertion payments were specifically included in the mission budget from assessed contributions as authorized by the General Assembly. Without it, there would be no DD. While some experience with cash payments to ex-combatants was gained in Liberia, the Organization did not have a clear policy. It took considerable time to get a system off the ground that would satisfy both operational/political needs and UN rules and regulations. UNMIS is now using private banks for the distribution of cash, which offers good value and low risk compared to some alternatives. A lesson learned is that such a system needs to be agreed on at the earliest possible stage, preferably during the planning and deployment phase of the mission. Overall, if peacekeeping operations are to become more involved in program delivery, such as rule of law, community violence reduction, and DDR, they will need programming rules similar to those of UN agencies to be more effective.

In spite of the complexities imposed by UN financial, procurement, and recruitment rules and regulations, the use of assessed contributions in the peacekeeping operations' budgets for demobilization and reinsertion has been a successful first in Sudan. Among its key benefits was the ability to start the program and maintain momentum, independent of government and/or donor funding. De facto, UNMIS became the first and largest donor to the overall program, providing it with certain leverage as well with the fiduciary responsibilities vis-à-vis Member States. In managing these aspects, the challenge was to strike the right balance between political pressure to start the program, its relevance to the overall peace process, the extent of leverage exercised on the parties, and the need for procedures that are tight enough to meet fiduciary standards. The political nature of the UNMIS mandate and the source of its funding give it more flexibility in finding that balance than the UNDP or World Bank enjoyed. In exercising that leverage, the mission at one point temporarily suspended operations to allow the parties to make necessary adjustments. A full stop of the program should only be contemplated in case of widespread and systematic abuse and/or a total breakdown of political support.

There are opportunities to extend the use of assessed contributions to reintegration as well. In particular, it is important for a host of reasons to start reintegration planning at an early phase and put it on a solid footing. Valuable time may be lost if the recruitment of reintegration planners needs to await donor funding. The use of assessed contributions could enable the early recruitment of a core of reintegration planners who may be seconded from UNDP or other agencies, which would allow for a more timely analysis of job markets, reintegration opportunities, capacity of implementing partners, etc. There are other ways of covering this, but the advantages of assessed contributions are clear enough to warrant further study.

Assessed contribution funding of the reintegration component is more problematic. Unless the United Nations establishes more flexible rules of program management on the ground, peacekeeping operations will be unable to handle the complexities of reintegration. Nevertheless, the assured funding through the assessed budget offers considerable advantages. On the other hand, such an arrangement would leave donors without either a role or the political leverage that could be useful in a partnership setting. Therefore, as an intermediate stage, assessed contributions could cover key start-up costs for reintegration (infrastructure, planning, staffing, etc.), with donors covering the actual costs of the individual reintegration of former combatants. There is a political angle to this financial issue as well. As peacekeeping operations will bear more of the costs of DDR, it will become more important for peacekeepers to be involved farther upstream in negotiations and setting benchmarks.

Integrated Approach

Another unique feature of the DDR program in Sudan was the support provided through a UN Integrated DDR unit that included staff members from the peacekeeping operation (UNMIS) as well as the United Nations Development Programme (UNDP). Integration is the guiding principle for the design and implementation of complex UN operations in postconflict situations and for linking the different dimensions of peacebuilding (political, development, humanitarian, human rights, rule of law, social, and security aspects) into a coherent support strategy. An integrated mission is based on a common strategic plan and a shared understanding of the priorities and types of program interventions that need to be undertaken at various stages of the recovery process.

According to the IDDRS, the aim of establishing an integrated DDR unit is "to ensure joint planning and coordination to bring about effective and efficient implementation. The integrated DDR unit also employs the particular skills and expertise of the different UN agencies, funds and programs to ensure flexibility and responsiveness within the DDR program, which gives it a greater chance of success." The IDDRS includes more detailed provisions on the structure of an integrated unit, which envisages joint planning, monitoring and evaluation, and other joint units. Theoretically, the potential benefits of an integrated approach are many: speaking with one voice, greater efficiency and coherence, enhanced leverage vis-à-vis government, cost savings, improved monitoring, etc. It was decided to run pilots in Haiti and Sudan. Neither environment was ideally suited for such an experience. Haiti did not present a clear DDR scenario and in Sudan the situation was complicated by vast logistical challenges, two parties, and parallel DDR efforts in Darfur and East Sudan for which UNDP also had responsibilities outside the context of the integrated unit.

Aside from the IDDRS, there was no written direction or guidance to the field pertaining to the process of integration, division of labor, staffing procedures, and financial mechanism, pointing to a shortcoming in the translation of policy into operational concepts that need to work on the ground. Nevertheless, progress was made. There was a broad understanding of the division of labor between UNMIS and UNDP. The former would focus on overall political aspects and demobilization, while the latter would handle donor relations and reintegration. The signature of a Memorandum of Understanding between UNDP and UNMIS in early 2007 made possible what would become the most successful feature of the integrated approach: collocation. The Memorandum of Understanding gave the UNDP staff in the unit access to UNMIS resources (office space, computers, transport, etc.) at par with the UNMIS staff. Collocation made it possible to have direct access to colleagues for consultation and to build a team approach and mutual understanding of challenges in spite of different corporate cultures, conditions of service, recruitment cycles, and career perspectives. By and large, the integrated approach worked well, even though there remains (as always) room for improvement.

In particular, the management of the relationship between DD and R implies that we must be able to forecast. Included in such forecasting should be how many clients will be demobilized and by which date, so planners know the numbers who will require reintegration packages and when. We also need to know the "back cast": for example, what is the cash flow and the absorptive capacity of implementing agencies over time so we know how many clients can responsibly be demobilized at which stage? This requires the joint analysis and management of complex and dynamic information through a single integrated planning and risk management tool, which has yet to be established. The latest figures illustrate the need for such an instrument. Against 20,000 demobilized, only 250 had received their reintegration packages (1 in 80) a year after demobilization started, which may present a real risk to stability when disenchanted ex-combatants take to the street or resume armed activities.

A Proposal for Market-based Reintegration Approach: Private Sector First

The "classical" reintegration model assumes that the job markets will have the capacity to absorb ex-combatants who, when sustainably employed, no longer pose a threat to stability. In a more political view, the DDR process helps to buy time by keeping the ex-combatants busy through the reinsertion and reintegration program for as long as necessary for the other elements of the peace process to take root, in which case the risk of their being employed or not is more easily managed and the chances of economic growth are higher anyway. But what of the conceivable scenario that the peace process fails and the economy does not grow? Then DDR will have created an army of unemployed but skilled ex-combatants with grievances.

DDR creates a supply of labor, and it is assumed that parallel processes will help to create the demand. I believe that this is a dangerous approach and that more should be done to stimulate demand through the promotion of the private sector. In particular, the engine of economic growth lies with agriculture and indigenous small and medium size businesses. What we are looking for is the capacity to scale up. Give a man a hammer and make him a carpenter, providing him with income for him and his family (if there is a market). Give a woman with a good business plan the necessary capital and she will start a construction business that may employ dozens. Therefore, in the reintegration component there should be room for a window that rewards entrepreneurship through funding at a larger scale on the basis of a good business plan, preferably employing ex-combatants (sponsored by the DDR program). In this regard, the reintegration program should look beyond individual ex-combatants and communities and consider where the business opportunities are regardless of who is involved. Rather than individual or community-based DDR, we should look at market-based DDR and promote the demand for labor through the private sector.

In civil war, the private sector is usually punished twice: first, during the war through the destruction of assets, markets, and infrastructure, and second, after the war through the lack of capital to rebuild or start businesses. Where banks exist, they demand high collaterals or charge exorbitant rates. Investors shy away from the risk of renewed fighting and ongoing corruption in spite of the obvious needs as well as the opportunities that exist after wars. Government donors prefer to invest in schools, hospitals, and democracy.

Short-term donor funding and political attention often focus on the social sector (health and education) and the building of viable security frameworks and democratic processes, and these are legitimate priorities. But the promotion of investment and a good climate for business is often neglected in peace-building strategies. Experience also shows that it is exactly during the first 3 years that peace is most vulnerable. Historical analyses indicate that half of the countries that make peace fall back into conflict within a decade. During those early years, making peace stick is a high-risk and high-reward challenge that involves creating an environment where market forces can do their work earlier and better.

Of course, investments are made during and after war, but these will not necessarily help stability or create peace. In the Democratic Republic of the Congo, shadowy operators link up with human rights–abusing rebels to dig out the country's minerals, exacerbating the conflict. Official Development Assistance (ODA) by donor countries has little to show for its effort to date, according to some analyses. It can create dependencies and even encourage corruption. The micro-credit industry has also made significant contributions to fighting poverty at the individual level, but it does not bring the kind of rapid growth that is required after wars. Investments need to have multiplier effects and create scalable businesses for genuine growth. There are also investment funds that target former war-torn countries such as Angola, Mozambique, and Rwanda. But this occurs after stability is established. These for-profit investments serve to consolidate stability, not create it when it is most needed. Finally, emergency job creation schemes usually buy time but not growth.

Paradoxically, countries that have the worst climate for business are those that need economic growth the most; they are at the bottom of the rankings, either suffering from or prone to conflict. (Compare the 2010 *Doing Business* report by the World Bank with the Failed States Index by the Fund for Peace, as published by *Foreign Policy*.) Of course, the correlation between unemployment and conflict is generally valid, but it needs to be seen in a wider context of political and socioeconomic grievances as well as cultural dimensions.

How to solve this paradox? Obviously, investing in the postconflict private sector would help in the same way as reconstructing roads, hospitals, and schools and demobilizing soldiers. But this may not be enough. Economies that need to recover from conflict suffer from failing government institutions, weak and single-interest or ethnic-based business associations, high levels of corruption, and lack of transport and financial infrastructure. Therefore, in addition to putting money into business, one would need to work with public and private partners to advocate for regulatory reform and strengthen local institutions, such as chambers of commerce and business federations. Then business would more readily be a vehicle for peace and growth. Advice on "how to start and run a good business" would need to accompany any assistance.

Support for business should start as soon as there are viable prospects for peace. In addition to the economic benefits of early investments, there are also enormous psychological benefits to the population. People who suffered from war will embrace even the smallest signs of hope and feed off it as they begin to look forward.

In Closing

Looking forward, a number of risks remain with regard to the DDR program under the CPA. These dangers could cause the program to fail and become as much a liability as an asset. First, there is the widening gap between DD and R. More candidates are processed through the "D" process than can be absorbed down the line in the "R." Enhanced coordination and integrated planning will need to be firmly entrenched in the management of the program in order to match DD output to R absorption capacity. This requires full transparency to the parties who are keen on putting as many people through the process as possible as soon as possible. If necessary, the United Nations and the parties can and should suspend or slow the DD intake. As explained above, this requires joint analysis and management of complex and dynamic information through a single integrated planning tool. Even if this produces more uncertainty than clarity, at least the uncertainties become known and risks can be managed accordingly. Second, there is the matter of balancing momentum and quality. Having achieved the goal of momentum, procedures need to be put in place and monitored to enhance international and domestic confidence in the program in a way that does not negate its political gains. Third, and as explained above, DDR alone cannot make peace or create employment. Without parallel progress in the overall peace process (which is now entering a delicate and potentially dangerous phase in Sudan) as well as in economic growth and domestic job creation, the program may create a group of unemployed people with grievances. The management of these risks will require a strong consensus among the parties, donors, and UN agencies involved.

Note

[1] When all expenses are added up, the total cost of DDR in the CPA areas to the international community will approach US $4,000 per capita.

Part IV
The Monopoly of Force

Chapter 12

There's a New Sheriff in Town: DDR–SSR and the Monopoly of Force

By Sean McFate

The only stable state is the one in which all men are equal before the law.
—Aristotle

The sine qua non of nation-building, stabilization operations, and similar efforts, is establishing the rule of law. However, before this can happen a state must first have the monopoly of force to uphold the rule of law. The concept of "monopoly of force" is derived from German sociologist Max Weber's classic definition of the state as "a human community that claims the monopoly of the legitimate use of physical force within a given territory."[1] Without the monopoly of force, the state has few ways to enforce rule of law and protect citizens from threats.

By definition, conflict-affected states have lost their monopoly of force since they cannot contain armed nonstate actors such as insurgencies, organized crime, and militias that threaten innocent people and challenge the state's legitimacy to rule. Worse, such armed nonstate actors can cast a region into war. Only by gaining the monopoly of force can states manage these groups to safeguard public order and governmental legitimacy as well as provide the necessary security that fosters long-term development—social, political, and economic. Additionally, a state's capacity to secure itself is a key component to the exit strategy of costly peacekeeping and counterinsurgency operations. Helping a weak state regain the monopoly of force is vital to its recovery, and failure makes rule of law difficult to achieve.

The primary tools to assist a fragile or failed state in gaining the monopoly of force are Disarmament, Demobilization, and Reintegration (DDR) and Security Sector Reform (SSR). DDR serves to consolidate the monopoly of force by disbanding armed nonstate actors who compete with statutory forces and threaten the country's ability to impose its governance. SSR acts to professionalize and grow the state's armed actors so they can responsibly enforce the law of the land.

Conventional wisdom holds that DDR and SSR are separate and distinct programs because they involve different actors, priorities, time lines, and functions. DDR is often viewed as a relatively quick process, while SSR starts when DDR finishes and plays out over time.[2] For example, most academic literature treats one or the other but not both, creating essentially two distinct fields which both work—in disjointed ways—to help the state monopolize force.[3] Practioners' guides for the field are no better. They generally specialize in one or the other but not both. For example, the United Nations (UN), a leader in conducting DDR, issues DDR standards with little consideration for SSR concerns. Similarly, the Organization for Economic Cooperation and Development–Development Assistance Committee (OECD–DAC) issues a *Handbook on Security System Reform* that does not substantially address DDR.[4] Both the literature of theory and practice tend to treat DDR and SSR in isolation from one another, which has produced incongruent, disjointed, and deleterious effects in the field.

The perception that DDR and SSR are separate processes is wrong. They work together like two sides of the same coin to establish the state's monopoly of force to uphold the rule of law. As such, they rise and fall together and should be planned, resourced, implemented, and evaluated in a coordinated manner. Regrettably, despite their importance in stabilizing fragile states, they remain an underdeveloped concept and capability of the U.S. Government. This chapter outlines what DDR and SSR are, examines their political nature, and concludes with recommendations for designing and managing DDR and SSR programs in the field.

DDR: Consolidating the State's Monopoly of Force

The first step in establishing a state's monopoly of force is disbanding the competition. This means disarming, demobilizing, and reintegrating nonstate combatants safely into civil society and enabling them to earn livelihoods through peaceful means instead of violence. DDR is essential in conflict-affected countries. In the short term, ex-combatants who do not find peaceful ways of making a living are likely to return to conflict. In the longer term, disaffected veterans can challenge public order and polarize political debate since they are easy targets of populist, reactionary, and extremist movements. To date, the United Nations is a leading actor in the development and implementation of DDR, with programs in Burundi, Cote d'Ivoire, Democratic Republic of the Congo, Liberia, Sierra Leone, Sudan, Uganda, Afghanistan, Nepal, Solomon Islands, and Haiti. According to the UN, a DDR process "deals with the postconflict security problem that arises when combatants are left without livelihoods and support networks during the vital period stretching from conflict to peace, recovery and development."[5]

As the term implies, DDR is a three-stage process. The first stage involves disarming combatants, who report to a safe and secure DDR site within the conflict zone to turn in their small arms, munitions, and light and heavy weapons. Ideally, this portion of DDR is also linked to a broader small arms and light weapons counterproliferation program that documents and destroys the weapons and munitions. The second stage demobilizes and disbands the armed nonstate groups, formally breaking up command structures and marking their official entry into "civilian life." Lastly, ex-combatants are reintegrated into civil society to prevent a new escalation of the conflict. This typically is divided into two parts: initial reinsertion and long-term reintegration. Initial reinsertion entails giving ex-combatants a short-term support package and transporting them back to their home to begin their new life. Reintegration is also the long-term process of job training and placement programs, working with communities to accept ex-combatants, and monitoring progress in the difficult transition to civilian life. Sometimes the international community will add a fourth "R" for "rehabilitation," which attends to the physiological needs and mental health of ex-combatants. However, nearly every DDR or DDRR program addresses this challenge in some capacity. The overall goal of DDR is ensuring permanent disarmament and sustainable peace.

DDR has a better chance of success if the following preconditions are met. First, fighting in the theatre of interest must be completely or at least nearly ended, preferably negotiated through a political agreement that includes all warring parties. Generally, combatant groups will only disarm if *all* disarm in an "all or nothing" proposal; otherwise, the disarmed will be completely vulnerable to the armed. Also, if the political agreement provides a clear framework for the progression of a DDR process, it is more likely that the process will succeed. For example, it should include, at a minimum: eligibility criteria for participation in the program; international or national actors assigned responsibility to manage the program; creation of credible responsible institutions; definition of realistic goals;

and a timetable for implementation. Who is eligible to receive benefits is one of the most frequently contested—and exploited—aspects of DDR, and therefore it should be stated directly in the peace agreement to minimize abuse. Leaders must personally commit to the peace process and direct their followers to lay down their arms. Often former combatant groups hold back their best fighters and most modern weapons to gain advantage or as a hedge against manipulation of the political process.

Second, a competent peacekeeping force must be in place to manage the DDR process. It must be large enough to monopolize force, guarantee security for all, and deter defections by armed actors. It must also be credibly neutral. Combatants will not relinquish their weapons if they do not believe the peacekeeping force will ensure their safety. Lastly, it must be capable of disarming all combatant groups simultaneously, a significant operational challenge for peacekeepers already working in a highly chaotic and dangerous environment. However, failure to disarm all the groups at once will result in some groups becoming defenseless against armed enemies seeking reprisals or advantage.

Third is the challenge of ensuring that sufficient funds are in place. A DDR program that runs out of money halfway through risks disaster, as it may provoke an attack by the armed on the unarmed, cause reprisals against the DDR staff, or encourage ex-combatants to take up their guns again to make a living. Owing to this, many DDR programs prioritize the DD but leave the R to wither. That creates a new problem that some call "the forgotten R." Not fully reintegrating ex-combatants into society risks them turning rogue again and perpetuating the cycle of violence as they return to violent crime. This manifests itself most visibly in criminal gangs, which often form from demobilized groups and can terrorize the population, hinder reconstruction, and challenge the new security sector's legitimacy. Worse, unlike combatant groups, gangs cannot undergo DDR because they are a law enforcement problem and must be arrested, tried, and incarcerated within the criminal justice system. This presents an additional layer of complexity to the already complex situation.

Lastly, because every conflict is unique, DDR programs must recognize that not all ex-combatants have the same needs. Effective programs must be adaptable to the specific requirements of different target groups, especially vulnerable groups such as the disabled, child soldiers, women, and widows. These groups often receive no benefits from reintegration programs that do not specifically take their needs into account. This is especially troubling for child soldiers who grew up in armed group camps and were exposed to human atrocities and exploitation. Many women associated with fighting groups were abducted for sexual services and do not qualify as ex-combatants. Similarly, families of combatants, which live in armed camps and provide the logistical support to the organization, typically do not qualify for benefits. Because women and children often have no "official" rank or status within the combatant group, they are dependent on male counterparts to vouch for them in a DDR process, which they may or may not do. Yet arguably these groups have the greatest needs.

SSR: Developing the State's Monopoly of Force

SSR is the essential tool to help a fragile state establish or reestablish its monopoly of force within its sovereign territory so it can uphold the rule of law. Security in this context means the protection of citizens and the state from threats that endanger normal life, public safety, and survival.[6] The "security sector" is generally composed of public organizations and government agencies whose primary mission is providing security. SSR is the complex task of transforming these organizations and institutions into professional, effective, legitimate, apolitical, and accountable actors that support the rule of law. SSR is more than a "train and equip" program, which is necessary but insufficient for comprehensive transformation of the security sector. For example, SSR in countries like Afghanistan, Iraq, and Liberia involved the creation of new institutions, significant force structure decisions, the formulation of a new national security strategy and doctrine, human rights vetting of recruits, building military and police bases and road infrastructure to support them, the selection of leadership, and many other complex tasks that go well beyond simple "train and equip" programs. In short, SSR transforms a soldier or policeman into someone a child would run towards for protection rather than away from in fear.

Typically, the security sector encompasses three types of actors. *Operational* actors interact directly with the public on security matters and may include law enforcement, the military, paramilitary and police units, border control, customs, immigration, coast guard, intelligence services, etc. *Institutional* actors manage the policy, programs, resources, and general administration of operational actors and may include the Ministries of Defense, Interior, Justice, and the like. *Oversight* bodies monitor and supervise the security sector. Ideally, they are civilian led, democratically accountable to the citizens, and ensure the security sector serves the people and not vice versa. Oversight bodies may include the executive, legislature or parliament, judiciary, and municipal and district governments/councils. The security sector may be conceptualized as a pyramid of actors (see figure). Not included in the security sector are nonstatutory security forces.

Conflict will often produce nonstatutory forces such as liberation armies, guerrilla armies, private security companies, and political party militias. After the conflict, all such forces should be disarmed, demobilized, and reintegrated into civil society. Following this, SSR will reconstitute the security sector, drawing from all segments of society, and rebuild a legitimate security force under the statutory control of the government, thus protecting the state's legitimate monopoly of force.

Figure

Oversight Bodies	Executive, congress or parliament
Institutions that manage operational actors	Ministry of Interior Ministry of Defense Ministry of Justice
Operational actors in direct contact with the population	Armed forces, law enforcement, border control, immigration, prisons, etc.

In addition to a variety of security actors, the security sector is also composed of subsectors. States typically achieve overall security through a variety of channels best conceived of as "security subsectors." They may include, but are not limited to, military, law enforcement, border management, foreign relations, and intelligence players. Each subsector is distinguished by unique objectives, technical knowledge, capabilities, best practices, institutional culture, and professional ethos. There may be overlap between subsectors, and they can vary widely between countries. However, the idea of security subsectors serves as a useful conceptual tool to help whole-of-government planners understand and diagnose the security sector, and then develop an appropriate SSR program.

Taken together, the hierarchy of actors and security subsectors form a matrix of the security sector, as seen in the accompanying table. Building subsector capacity and professionalizing actors can span myriad areas of expertise, making SSR a fundamentally interagency effort requiring a "whole-of-government" approach. Arguably, for each box in this framework there is a commensurate U.S. agency or department that could contribute substantial subject matter expertise and mentorship. For example, the Department of Homeland Security may be best suited to train customs and immigration actors, while the Department of Defense is best suited to transform the military subsector. Other Departments such as Treasury can offer cross-cutting reform in the area of fiscal best practices and resource management, which apply to every actor of the security sector. A common framework for understanding the security sector would also help show capability gaps within the U.S. Government, such as the capacity to create law enforcement at the operational level (e.g., police). An SSR Center could help lead this effort by identifying synergies of expertise within the interagency for SSR, helping agencies develop doctrine and training programs that are consistent with the interagency at large, and fostering "communities of capability" between agencies. Deconflicting roles will help erode wasteful redundancy, identify gaps in implementation, and enable a "whole-of-government" approach to SSR.

Table. Conceptual Framework of the Security Sector

Security actor/ security subsector	**Operational actors**	**Institutional actors**	**Oversight actors**
Military	Military, civil defense forces, national guards, militias, paramilitary	Ministry of Defense	Executive, legislative
Law enforcement	Police, gendarmerie, prison, criminal justice, presidential guard	Ministry of Interior, Ministry of Justice	Executive, legislative, judiciary, municipal and district governments/ councils
Border management	Border control, immigration, coast guard, customs authorities	Ministry of Interior, Ministry of Defense	
Foreign relations	Embassies, attachés and security liaison officers	Ministry of Foreign Affairs, Ministry of Defense	Executive, legislative
Intelligence	Collection assets	Intelligence agencies	Executive, legislative

Although SSR serves to uphold the rule of law, it should not be confused with Justice Sector Reform (JSR). Both programs serve the same purpose and are interdependent, but they entail some distinctly separate tasks. An SSR program should not attempt to rewrite a country's constitution or laws, address past human rights abuses and crimes against humanity, or integrate indigenous systems of justice with international norms. Nor should a JSR program try to recruit military and police forces, determine weaponry and organizational structure of security forces, or draft the national security strategy. Such attempts would likely fail, owing to a mismatch of expertise and functions.

Where SSR and JSR intersect is the development of criminal justice institutions and personnel. An SSR program operating without a corresponding JSR program will likely be unsuccessful. For example, police need legitimate laws to enforce; otherwise their own legitimacy will suffer, or, worse, they can end up being stooges for a corrupt legal system. Similarly, a JSR program operating without a commensurate SSR effort will probably fail because criminal justice systems require professional police, prisons, customs, and other instruments of law enforcement. Where SSR and JSR primarily intersect is law enforcement, but each has a distinctly different role in establishing the rule of law.

Despite the significance of consolidating a fragile state's monopoly of force, SSR remains a major unmet challenge for the international community, notwithstanding the growing prevalence of peacekeeping missions around the world. Consequently, few practical models for SSR have been developed, and recent efforts to reestablish the security sector in Iraq and elsewhere have been ad hoc and disappointing. This has perpetuated the cycle of violence in fragile states and prolonged costly peacekeeping missions. For example, there is no comprehensive approach to SSR in the United States. There is no practicable doctrine, best practices, or even common terminology. In fact, even the idea of "security sector reform" defies common definition and has many labels: security and justice reform, security governance reform, foreign internal defense, security force assistance, security system transformation, and so forth.[7] This is primarily due to SSR's recent development as a post–Cold War concept, difficulty in safely implementing SSR programs, and interagency challenges since SSR straddles the security-development nexus. However, recent efforts at the Center for Complex Operations and the U.S. Institute of Peace are working to address these challenges.

All Politics Is Local

DDR and SSR are deeply political processes, as they dismantle the de facto institutions of power in conflict-affected countries. This makes them both difficult and dangerous to operationalize in the field. Convincing a general or warlord to put down his gun and become a farmer may not be welcomed and could even provoke violence, as occurred in Cote d'Ivoire. In 2002, the government attempted to demobilize 750 soldiers, who then staged a coup requiring a French and UN armed intervention. However, this intervention did not prevent a civil war, which lasted for several years and still simmers today. DDR and SSR are inherently dangerous efforts, and purely technical approaches will fail.

Also, there is sometimes a natural tension between transitional justice programs and efforts to restructure security institutions. Transitional justice generally refers to a range of judicial and nonjudicial mechanisms to redress past human rights violations committed in countries transitioning from conflict to peace. Examples of judicial mechanisms include special courts, either domestically or internationally, such as Sierra Leone's Special Court, the International Tribunal for Rwanda and Yugoslavia, and the International Criminal Court, which claims universal jurisdiction. Nonjudicial mechanisms include Truth and Reconciliation Commissions (TRCs) at the national level (e.g., Argentina in 1983, Chile in 1990, South Africa in 1995, and Ghana in 2002) or international level (e.g., El Salvador in 1992, Guatemala in 1997, East Timor in 2001, and Sierra Leone in 2002). The efficacy of transitional justice is not without debate, but in general the primary purpose is to end cultures of impunity and reaffirm the rule of law within a context of democratic governance.

In theory, it is assumed that justice and security buttress one another in conflict-affected countries, but in practice such a supposition is less clear. Take, for example, the notion of amnesty. Granting amnesty to those who committed atrocities during a civil war is anathema to transitional justice, which seeks to redress past crimes through special courts or truth commissions. However, programs like DDR and SSR depend on amnesty to succeed. For example, ex-combatants seldom show up to a DDR site if they are not granted some form of amnesty. If they have the perception that they might be arrested, detained, or investigated for the purposes of a special court or truth commission, the DDR process would be discredited and combatants would not participate. In fact, it may encourage ex-combatants to bury their weapons and clandestinely regroup their command structures, which can threaten the ceasefire. Amnesty is a vital component of DDR, yet it can also work at cross-purposes to transitional justice.

Similarly for SSR, potential recruits will be discouraged from volunteering for the new security forces if they believe that results from background checks will be used against them in a special court or truth commission. Human rights vetting of candidates for security forces is a mandatory component of SSR, yet vetting in postconflict societies is difficult owing to the lack of credible public records. A technique used in postconflict Liberia involved interviewing witnesses who provide character references for recruits, and their cooperation depended in large part on guaranteeing anonymity. Should a special court or truth commission obtain these records, the guarantee of anonymity could not be assured since SSR programs do not control transitional justice programs. If this happened, vetting sources and methods could be compromised, possibly resulting in reprisal killings against witnesses who spoke against candidates on condition of anonymity. Also, the SSR program's credibility would be irreparably damaged, since it would be viewed as a shill for transitional justice mechanisms. It is important to note that sometimes transitional justice programs are not wholly embraced or trusted. Some may perceive them as "witch trials." Consequently, even "innocent" candidates will refrain from volunteering to serve in the new security sector if they believe that a failed background check could lead to a trial and false conviction in a special court or commission. This would devastate SSR efforts. Accordingly, SSR should be partially or completely isolated from transitional justice programs.

Another political aspect of DDR and SSR is the challenge of gaining "local ownership" for the programs. For example, while most conflict-affected populations see the necessity in disarming and demobilizing combatants who may have terrorized the population in the past, some noncombatants may take umbrage with rewarding combatants with money and job opportunities, especially when innocent civilians receive fewer benefits. Additionally, not all communities will welcome ex-combatants, particularly if they are linked to atrocities and war crimes. Similarly for SSR, populations traumatized by abusive security forces may not embrace the idea of rearming and training new security forces. DDR and SSR programs may require sophisticated public outreach programs to clearly explain why and how they are conducting DDR and SSR.

There is a growing consensus that early local ownership is a critical component of DDR and SSR sustainability, yet how to translate this principle into concrete reality remains a challenge.[8] In fact, even the definition of *local ownership* remains contested. For instance, who gets to decide who the "key stakeholders" are when determining local ownership? Deciding which local leaders and political groups truly represent local aspirations is fraught with uncertainty and has political ramifications both within indigenous and international politics. Also, local actors will often have competing visions and priorities, and choosing local partners can be perilous in conflict-affected countries where there is often imperfect knowledge of parochial agendas. For example, it may prove difficult to keep insurgents and spoilers out of the process, and if they are deemed "key stakeholders," it provides them a platform of legitimacy and the ability to obstruct progress from within while making it difficult to expel them. Finally, measuring "ownership" is difficult. For example, should metrics privilege local or international values and priorities? Local ownership is sound in theory but can be ambiguous in practice.

Principles for Practioners

DDR and SSR are essential to stabilizing fragile states since they consolidate the state's monopoly of force to uphold the rule of law. As such, they must be planned, resourced, implemented, and evaluated together. The following principles can help U.S. planners frame objectives and program architecture in the planning phase. Key to success is the principle of partnership with the host nation and genuine "ownership" of the reforms by the local population. Reforms enforced by outsiders to an unreceptive population will not last beyond the stay of the international community.

At the Oversight Level

DDR and SSR are deeply political processes. DDR and SSR are political because they dismantle the de facto institutions of power in conflict-affected countries. This makes them both difficult and dangerous to operationalize in the field.

Political will. It is important that all parties develop ownership of DDR and SSR and its outcomes and not feel discriminated against. Parties must believe they are being treated equitably and given the same opportunities in the development of the security sector. Ownership should be built by involving stakeholders early and incorporating their indigenous perspective into the DDR and SSR plan. They will then be more likely to generate domestic support for the program within their constituencies.

Unambiguous lines of authority. The country's constitution must establish oversight mechanisms for the security sector. It must clearly delineate lines of authority in terms of command and control, checks and balances, budgetary authorization and appropriation, and other fundaments of oversight.

Security versus justice? In postconflict settings, the utilization of amnesty is an important and necessary tool to help a country reemerge from conflict. However, balancing the amount of amnesty for the security sector is tricky. Too much amnesty for ex-combatants and new recruits will lead to public mistrust and fear of the new force, compromising its legitimacy. However, allowing a Truth and Reconciliation Committee to vet each candidate may prevent people from wanting to serve regardless of their background.

Public sensitization. Often in postconflict situations, the security sector was complicit in atrocities against the populace, and the formation of new security forces among an already traumatized public may be unwelcome. This is also true in conflict prevention programs, where authoritarian regimes have a history of misusing the security sector to quash domestic dissent. Owing to this, enhancing the security sector may not be a welcome activity. Consequently, DDR and SSR are extremely sensitive and political and must be preceded by a wide-ranging sensitization program informed by indigenous expertise.

At the Institutional Level

Build the institutions first. Begin with institutions and not operational actors. This may prove challenging in some political settings, especially in transitional governments, owing to policy and political considerations. However, the institutional actors will steer many of the "downstream" decisions driving DDR and SSR at the operational level.

All institutions must rise together. Institutional development must be synchronized, as all institutions are interdependent. Failure will at best delay national recovery and consume precious resources; at worst it may compromise the entire recovery process, potentially resulting in a relapse to conflict. For example, programs to develop the police, courts, and prisons must go forward simultaneously to ensure the creation of a functioning judicial system. A court system without prisons is a dysfunctional justice system; similarly, unpaid soldiers are a recipe for a coup d'etat, which is why the Ministry of Finance must develop a capacity commensurate with the defense sector. Synchronization will dictate the rate at which DDR and SSR can proceed, and delays are expensive.

Civilian control of the military. The new security sector should be accountable to the civil authority of a democratically elected government. For example, the Minister of Defense should be a civilian, as should much of the Ministry of Defense's bureaucracy.

Resist bloated bureaucracies. Excessive personnel tend to make organizations less efficient. Also, a personnel audit of large ministries may be required, as some may have "ghost" employees or individuals on the payroll without specific functions.

Maximum practicable transparency. Where it does not compromise security, transparency of security force planning, programming, personnel management, procurement, budgeting, and resource management earns public confidence and legitimacy. In the case of the armed forces, it also fosters a balanced civil-military relationship.

Eschew ill-fitting templates. The temptation to adopt U.S., European, or other developed nations' doctrines and practices wholesale is a starting point at best and catastrophic at worst. Tailor-make a security sector for the country's needs and institutionalize a lessons learned capability within the security sector so its doctrine can evolve with the needs of the nation.

Leadership by example. If the institutions that manage the security sector are corrupt, then the operational actors will follow suit.

At the Operational Level

DDR-specific recommendations:

Disarmament. Disarmament criteria may focus on specific weapons, individuals, or groups. Of these, identifying a specific group for disarmament may be the most effective strategy since it employs the cooperation of commanders. However, it may also have undesirable consequences such as strengthening the commanders' control over the combatants or enabling abuses by commanders who "sell" access to the DDR program.

Demobilization. Demobilization involves three steps: assembly of ex-combatants, orientation programs, and transportation to the communities of destination. First, combatants assemble, are registered with biometric capture, and should receive an official and durable civilian picture identification card. Encampments are not designed to house people for long periods and should provide life essentials such as food, water, shelter, and medical treatment. They should also be prepared to house dependents. Second, orientation is important to reinforce ex-combatants' beliefs that the DDR program offers viable alternatives to conflict as a livelihood. It also provides ex-combatants and their families with basic information about the benefits. If possible, transportation of large groups should be timed to coincide with phases of civilian life that facilitate reintegration, such as crop and school cycles.

Reintegration. Immediate reinsertion assistance consists of short-term relief such as housing, medical care, food, and elementary education for children. DDR programs should work in partnership with local social networks to ensure longer term reintegration and provide psychological support and counseling to individuals and initiatives regarding the reunification of families.

Child soldiers. Children should be separated from other ex-combatants in order to tend to their unique needs. They should be quickly discharged and reinserted into long-term reintegration programs that give priority to family reunification. They may also require long-term mental healthcare to recovery from traumatic experiences during the war and limit asocial attitudes and aggressive behaviors. Also, in order for them to earn a sustainable livelihood, they require formal education and professional training.

Women. DDR programs should recruit female staff and gender specialists, and encampment facilities should be adapted to accommodate women and girls. Abducted girls should be allowed to register separately from their "partners," and young girls may need special psychological support. Also, special medical care should be offered for female healthcare needs. Lastly, resettlement logistics plans should seek to reunify ex-combatants' families.

SSR-specific recommendations:

It may be necessary to start over. If the public does not trust the legacy security forces, it may be necessary to fully demobilize the standing force and reconstitute it from scratch. This is especially true in postconflict situations, where security forces may have been complicit in atrocities. For example, this was done with the Liberian military after the departure of Charles Taylor. Although this might seem an excessive measure, it is more efficient than the alternative of permitting corrupt or terrorist practices in the ranks, which deepens the distrust of the people and the illegitimacy of the state. It is unwise to inherit a rotten legacy, as trust is the currency of legitimacy.

Vigorously vet all candidates. To help ensure a corruption-resistant force and prevent a relapse into violence, it is important to enlist honorable people. Vetting indigenous security forces in fragile or failed states is typically deficient, owing to the lack of credible records and other instruments of background checks. However, failure to vet candidates may lead to undesirables infiltrating or corrupting the security sector, a problem not easily undone (e.g., the Iraqi police forces). Currently, neither the United States nor the United Nations employs a systematic methodology for vetting in postconflict settings; however, models may exist.[9]

Decouple vetting from transitional justice. The vetting process must remain absolutely disconnected from instruments of postconflict justice. It is tempting to hand over vetting records to Truth and Reconciliation Commissions (TRC) or the like. However, this may compromise DDR and SSR for several reasons. First, the TRC might reveal vetting sources and methods, discrediting the entire program in the public eye. For example, a TRC might intentionally or unintentionally expose witnesses who gave testimony to the vetting team on condition of anonymity, tempting reprisals from those who allegedly committed the witnessed war crimes. Second, it will discourage people from volunteering for the security sector if they believe the process is a front for a TRC, which may not be fully trusted by the traumatized populace. Questions of amnesty in postconflict settings remain challenging, and security and justice are often at odds.

Respect for the rule of law, human rights norms, and international humanitarian law. The new security force must understand that it serves the people of the country and government, not vice versa. Human rights courses should be integrated into all professional training.

Allegiance to the constitution rather than an individual leader or faction. Professional security forces are apolitical and sworn to defend the legitimate government. Often in postconflict countries, a constitution may not exist, or it exists in many versions. In such cases, SSR and other development programs cannot wait on the redrafting of the constitution, which may take years. Putting a country's development on hold for the sake of the constitution risks stymieing the country's recovery. Owing to this, it may be necessary to creatively integrate basic civics classes into training to foster a professional ethos.

Force structure must reflect the country's needs. Most nations require a small, basic, and well-trained security force able to accomplish its mission. This should be reflected in its size, organization, equipment, and training (e.g., the Liberian military does not require F–16 fighter jets).

Small arms and light weapons (SALW) accountability. DDR should be linked to a larger SALW counterproliferation program and institute a strict accounting system and culture of responsibility for SALW in SSR. This is especially true for handguns, the scourge of many oppressed populations. The reutilization of weapons is a serious concern in conflict-affected countries, and therefore all returned SALW should be cataloged and destroyed, with a credible, neutral third party onsite to verify destruction. This information should be integrated into a regional information fusion cell that tracks overall SALW trends and patterns in the region. Knowing the number of SALW present may help estimate future outbreaks of armed violence.

Defense-oriented force posture with limited force-projection capability. It is important to strike a balance between a force posture that is strong enough to defend the integrity of the nation's borders, yet not so strong that it threatens neighbors with its force-projection capability.

Size constrained by government's ability to pay salaries. Perhaps most critically, the security force must not be so large that the government cannot afford its salaries. Nonpayment is a precipitant to corruption, political violence, or perpetual reliance on funding by donor nations. In some threat environments, it may be less risky to have a paid force that is too small rather than a large force that is unpaid.

Limited special operations units, clandestine services, and heavy weapons units (e.g., tanks, artillery, armed helicopters). Large numbers of such units are not necessary to accomplish most security force missions and have been misused against civilians in the past.

Volunteer force preferable. For militaries in particular, smaller, all-volunteer forces are generally easier to discipline, train, and maintain than large, unwieldy conscript forces.

Professional culture based on merit. Promotion and assignment selection must be free of cronyism and nepotism for the security forces to be credible and effective. Avoid this by making the personnel system as transparent as possible. This is feasible in institutional transformation programs, when human resources, resource management, operations, and other organizational "systems" are essentially reprogrammed. Creating built-in checks and balances to guarantee transparency as well as meaningful punishments for those who violate the rules encourages a merit-based system.

Foster a national identity. Political identity and allegiance may not be first and foremost to the state, which instead may be organized around religion, ethnicity, or other categories. Help instill a new national identity through civics classes at every level of training and leadership development. Such instruction should be indigenously conceived and delivered to maximize local ownership.

Balanced ethnic mix in the ranks. Strive for a balanced mix of ethnicity, religion, gender, tribe, and other political categories so one group does not dominate the security forces. Imbalance is a source of instability.

Literacy is important. A functional level of literacy is required for a professional force. However, this may prove challenging in postconflict societies where war may have disrupted education for years, or access to education was limited to privileged ethnic or religious groups. Literacy requirements may have to be waived to achieve ethnic balance in the ranks.

One solution to this conundrum is to incorporate literacy classes in training, which can also be a draw for the recruitment campaign.

Conclusion

For a weak state to become strong, it must have a monopoly of force. Without it, the state has few ways to enforce rule of law and protect citizens from threats. However, assisting a country in accomplishing this is fraught with difficulty and danger since altering the balance of power in conflict-affected countries, where power often comes at the end of a gun barrel, is deeply political. Technical approaches alone will likely fail and cast a country back into conflict.

Two linked programs help a government to regain its monopoly of force: Disarmament, Demobilization, and Reintegration and Security Sector Reform. DDR consolidates the state's monopoly by disbanding competitors, such as militias and insurgents. SSR develops and expands that monopoly by professionalizing the security sector to uphold the rule of law. Conventional wisdom holds that DDR and SSR are separate and distinct programs because they involve different actors, priorities, time lines, and functions. DDR is often viewed as a relatively quick process, while SSR starts when DDR finishes and plays out over time.[10] However, this perception is wrong.

DDR and SSR are fundamentally linked and interdependent since failure of one risks failure of the other. If ex-combatants are not properly reintegrated into civil society through DDR, they will complicate and potentially compromise SSR. Ex-combatants who do not successfully transition to civilian life may take up arms again, or they may form criminal gangs. This would challenge newly created security institutions and forces, which may lack sufficient capacity to control such threats. Consequently, the population would be vulnerable to violence, and the inability of the state to protect its citizens would challenge its legitimacy.

Inversely, if DDR succeeds but SSR falters, people will turn to nonstate actors such as ethnic- or religious-based militias or village self-defense forces for security. For example, in some parts of Afghanistan where the reach of national law enforcement is limited, Afghans may turn to tribal authorities or the Taliban to provide security and justice. This can erode the state's legitimacy. Worse, such states can offer safe havens for armed opposition groups, insurgents, organized crime, and other armed nonstate actors that instigate conflict and destabilization. Accordingly, DDR and SSR rise and fall together and should be planned, resourced, implemented, and evaluated in a coordinated manner.

Despite the criticality of DDR and SSR, they remain surprisingly undeveloped instruments in the U.S. toolbox. There is no doctrine, best practices, or even common terminology concerning DDR and SSR. A comprehensive approach to these programs is needed if the United States plans to effectively support good governance programs in states emerging from hostilities. Washington also needs a formal interagency structure for managing DDR and SSR programs. Without this capability, stabilizing fragile states such as Iraq and Afghanistan will remain a significant challenge.

Notes

[1] Max Weber, "Politics as a Vocation," *From Max Weber: Essays in Sociology*, ed. and trans. Hans Heinrich Gerth and C. Wright Mills (New York: Oxford University Press, 1958), 77.

[2] This view is confirmed in recent academic literature and even in practioner-focused manuals, which have developed in relative isolation of one another. See, for example: UN Integrated DDR Standards (IDDRS), available at <http://www.unddr.org/iddrs/iddrs_guide.php>; Organization for Economic Cooperation and Development–Development Assistance Committee (OECD–DAC), *Handbook on Security System Reform*, available at <www.oecd.org/dac/conflict/if-ssr>.

[3] Notable exceptions include Atsushi Yasutomi, "Linking DDR and SSR in Postconflict States: Agendas for Effective Security Sector Reintegration," *Central European Journal of International and Security Studies* 3, no. 2 (May 2008); Owen Greene and Simon Rynn, "Linking and Coordinating DDR and SSR for Human Security after Conflict: Issues, Experience and Priorities," *Working Paper 2* for Center for International Cooperation and Security, July 2008; Michael Brzoska, "Embedding DDR Programme in Security Sector Reconstruction," in *Security Governance in Post-Conflict Peacebuilding*, ed. Alan Bryden and Heiner Hanggi (London: Geneva Centre for the Democratic Control of Armed Forces (DCAF)/Transaction Publishers, 2005), 104; Alan Bryden, "Understanding the DDR–SSR Nexus: Building Sustainable Peace in Africa," Second International Conference on DDR and Stability in Africa, Kinshasa, Democratic Republic of the Congo, June 12–14, 2007, (OSAA/DRC) Issue Paper (June 2007); Jeremy Ginifer, "Support for DDR and SSR after Conflicts in Africa: Lessons Learnt; and New Agendas in Africa, Conflict Prevention, Management and Reduction in Africa," Paper 3, a joint project of the Finnish Institute of International Affairs and the Centre for International Cooperation and Security (Helsinki: Ministry for Foreign Affairs of Finland, 2007); Multi-Country Demobilization and Reintegration Program (MDRP) Secretariat, "Linkages between Disarmament, Demobilization and Reintegration of Ex-Combatants and Security Sector Reform," MDRP, October 2003.

[4] See, e.g., United Nations Disarmament, Demobilization, and Reintegration Resource Centre (UNDDR), *UN Integrated DDR Standards* (IDDRS), available at <http://www.unddr.org/iddrs/iddrs_guide.php> (accessed April 14, 2010); Organization for Economic Cooperation and Development–Development Assistance Committee (OECD–DAC), *OECD DAC Handbook on Security System Reform* (Paris: OECD, 2007), available at <www.oecd.org/dac/conflict/if-ssr>, (accessed April 12, 2010).

[5] *UN Integrated DDR Standards* (IDDRS), 24, available at <http://www.unddr.org/iddrs/iddrs_guide.php>.

[6] There are multiple models of security, including "Human Security." However, a detailed analysis of how these different security models influence the state's monopoly of force is beyond the scope of this chapter.

[7] While recognizing that these terms may connote subtle differences in conceptualization, this article will assume the term *security sector reform* is generic and all-encompassing.

[8] For more information on this topic see: Liz Panarelli, "Local Ownership of Security Sector Reform," *USIP Peace Report* (Washington, DC: USIP, 2009); Marc J. Cohen and Tara R. Gingerich,

"Protect and Serve or Train and Equip? U.S. Security Assistance and Protection of Civilians" (Washington, DC: Oxfam America, 2009).

[9] See Sean McFate, "The art and aggravation of vetting in post-conflict environments," *Military Review* (July–August 2007), 79–97.

[10] This view is confirmed in recent academic literature and even in practioner-focused manuals, which have developed in relative isolation of one another. See, for example, *UN Integrated DDR Standards* (IDDRS), available at <http://www.unddr.org/iddrs/iddrs_guide.php>; Organization for Economic Cooperation and Development–Development Assistance Committee (OECD–DAC), *Handbook on Security System Reform*, available at <www.oecd.org/dac/conflict/if-ssr>.

Chapter 13

The DDR–SSR Nexus

By Alan Bryden

Introduction

In the early 1990s, peacebuilding activities placed relatively little emphasis on the sensitive work of facilitating the building of domestic capacities to provide security. This has now changed. Issues such as Disarmament, Demobilization, and Reintegration (DDR) and Security Sector Reform (SSR) are increasingly recognized as priority peacebuilding tasks. The importance of a holistic approach to postconflict peacebuilding was highlighted by the Presidential Statement emerging from the February 20, 2007, Open Debate in the UN Security Council which "recognises the interlinkages between security sector reform and other important factors of stabilisation and reconstruction, such as transitional justice, disarmament, demobilisation, repatriation, reintegration and rehabilitation of former combatants, small arms and light weapons control, as well as gender equality, children and armed conflict and human rights issues."[1] This points to the need for policymakers, analysts, and practitioners to understand the interrelationships among different elements of postconflict peacebuilding, avoid "stovepiping" in planning and operations, and use the resulting synergies to promote coherent, effective, and sustainable peacebuilding.

International engagement in these areas reflects an inherent tension between intervention and ownership in the most delicate area of public policy. Achieving such a balance is essential if there is to be a shift from short-term security to longer term development involving the timely handover of responsibilities to national actors. It is thus fundamentally important to recognize that DDR and SSR are not only "technical" activities but form part of a wider national security discourse during highly sensitive political transitions. This chapter argues that considering both DDR and SSR as integral parts of efforts to enhance security sector governance can help to mitigate such tensions and move this agenda forward. On the one hand, reinforcing the capacities of security sector governance institutions—management functions as well as statutory and nonstatutory oversight bodies—will contribute to more meaningful national ownership of and commitment to DDR and SSR processes. On the other, a governance-driven perspective points to the wide array of public and private actors at local, national, regional, and international levels that need to be engaged to ensure the legitimacy and sustainability of DDR and SSR.

While there is an emerging policy literature on the linkages between DDR and SSR, their programming implications should be carefully unpacked. In particular, there is a need for caution since, although on one level there is a clear relationship between the two, the objectives, activities, and actors involved in DDR and SSR may be very different. The imperative to "do no harm" argues for the need to avoid prescription and instead acknowledge the importance of context and flexibility if we are to bridge the sometimes wide gaps between "ideal" policy statements and the realities of DDR and SSR programming in postconflict environments that have their own political, security, and cultural dynamics.

There are no miracle solutions for these complex, sensitive, and highly context-specific postconflict peacebuilding challenges. The purpose of this chapter is therefore modest and practical. It begins by identifying some of the key linkages between DDR and SSR. It then considers different elements of a security sector governance approach to DDR and SSR before signposting a number of related programming issues and questions. It concludes by highlighting considerations that should be taken into account in developing policy frameworks and approaches that seek mutually reinforcing synergies between DDR and SSR.

The DDR–SSR Nexus

The relationship between DDR and SSR can be considered in both supply and demand terms. On the supply side, DDR provides the basis for SSR by shaping the size and nature of the postconflict security sector. On the demand side, how DDR is conducted influences the security situation on the ground and therefore the prospects for SSR. These linkages can play out in different ways:[2]

- DDR shapes the terrain for SSR by influencing the size and nature of the security sector.
- Successful DDR can free up resources for SSR activities that in turn may support the development of efficient, affordable security structures.

- A national vision of the security sector should provide the basis for decisions on demobilization.
- SSR considerations (required skill sets as well as past conduct) should inform criteria for the integration of ex-combatants in different parts of the security sector.
- DDR and SSR offer complementary approaches that can link reintegration of ex-combatants to enhancing community security.
- Capacity-building for security management and oversight bodies provides a common means to enhance the sustainability and legitimacy of DDR and SSR.

As well as pointing to important synergies, there are also potential costs to not addressing linkages between DDR and SSR. DDR dynamics can contribute to but also upset efforts to develop effective armed and security forces committed to the state and its citizens. Conversely, the absence of demonstrable advances on SSR may block progress in DDR. Additional strain can also be placed on the security sector if badly implemented DDR results in increased pressure on the police, courts, and prisons.

The rest of this section considers the DDR–SSR nexus in two dimensions: early entry points and security sector integration.

Early Entry Points

There is no fixed model for linking DDR and SSR; the potential for synergies is dependent on context. Processes may be parallel, with little direct relationship between the two. In some cases, DDR provides an entry point for SSR or vice versa. In others, it can be considered an integral part of a broader SSR program. The bottom line is to avoid situations—like the stage in Liberia when disarmament measures in Monrovia led to riots that raised wider security concerns[3]—where efforts in one area cause ripple effects that adversely affect the broader peacebuilding picture.

The immediate pressures of postconflict stabilization mean that governance-focused SSR is often considered as a later priority that comes after DDR. This is confirmed by a 2-year review of the roll out and implementation of the *Handbook on Security System Reform* developed by the Organisation for Economic Co-operation and Development's Development Assistance Committee (OECD DAC). The review shows that activities to support security sector oversight and accountability frequently fall behind efforts to improve security sector effectiveness.[4] Indeed, both DDR and SSR are lengthy and unpredictable processes. For this reason, the *UNDP Practice Note on DDR* emphasizes that the specific sequencing of activities depends on the particular circumstances of each country and that careful timing is essential in order to achieve complementarity.[5] A rigid approach to sequencing may therefore result in lost opportunities. Timely efforts to build capacities in areas such as human resource and financial management or to support the oversight roles of parliament and civil society may not only realize common DDR–SSR goals but also contribute to wider confidence-building at national and international levels.

Early entry points that can build synergies between DDR and SSR may be offered in the context of peace negotiations. It is self-evident that decisions as to the size and nature of postconflict security forces are inherently interest-driven and if left to former warring parties will reflect the need to maintain a power base and reward allies. But agreements that may be beneficial in terms of brokering a peace deal on the numbers and type of soldiers retained or demobilized can actually be counterproductive for longer term SSR prospects. This argues for flexibility to ensure that agreements do not bind parties too tightly to unrealistic figures that will later have to be adjusted. This was the case in Burundi, where a two-step process saw ex-combatants integrated into the armed forces before being demobilized at a later stage. The lack of transparency and the criteria used in this process led to uncertainty and frustration. Moreover, the skills developed by integrated ex-combatants were then lost.[6] Reflecting the DDR–SSR link in peace agreements can provide a valuable opportunity to shape the framework for SSR[7] (as opposed to simply enduring the consequences of a laissez-faire approach). Wider perspectives can be encouraged through the provision of impartial security advisers, possibly drawn from regional organizations. Such support from, for example, the African Union and the Economic Community of West African States (ECOWAS) has added the benefits of contextual knowledge and legitimacy in the eyes of negotiating parties.[8]

Security Sector Integration

Reintegrating ex-combatants into different parts of the security sector may meet the needs of both DDR and SSR while building on the existing skill sets of those concerned. However, using former soldiers in policing roles has seen negative results in cases where candidates have not been properly screened or adequately trained. Problems have included applying military approaches to policing tasks that require sensitivity and communication rather than direct force, or engaging ex-combatants with a prior history of war crimes. This is not only unfortunate on an individual level but undermines trust in "reformed" security forces as well as the institutions responsible for their management and oversight. Vetting can therefore contribute to the effective integration of former combatants into state military and security forces. On a related point, having former combatants who have committed war crimes and/or sexual violence against women and children released back into their communities for "reintegration" seriously affects community perceptions of safety and undermines the legitimacy of the justice system. Although there may be a careful balance to be struck between concerns of peace and justice, DDR programs need to be linked with justice mechanisms that ensure accountability for war crimes and human rights violations.

The private security sector also offers a reintegration avenue for former soldiers. This reflects the reality that in some contexts commercial or community-based security actors have a much more significant role than the state in providing security to communities and individuals. However, private security providers tend to be subject to even less oversight than state actors, so the risks of their playing a negative role may be significant. A telling example of privatization and its impact on DDR and SSR is found in South Africa. Although there are many positives to be drawn from the transformation of South Africa's security sector, the consequences of post-Apartheid downsizing and reform still play out today. In defiance of national legal constraints, the same resource pool of ex-South African Defence Force (SADF) personnel fuels both private military and security companies and mercenary activities in Third World countries.[9]

The blurring of roles of different security actors is perhaps best exemplified by the "sobel" (soldier and rebel) phenomenon—combining a role in the state security sector with engagement in criminal activities for profit.[10] Thus, "an important part of the link between DDR and SSR programs is to clearly distinguish these roles, codify the distinction in legislation, and raise awareness on this issue."[11] SSR considerations—in the shape of clear criteria for entry into the security sector—should therefore come first in such arrangements. If the requirements of reintegration can be met, that is a bonus; but they should not be a driver of policy. Consequently, if it is a stated DDR goal to place former soldiers in other parts of the security sector, it needs to contribute to the integrity of security institutions and match the capacity of the security sector to absorb them.[12]

A Security Sector Governance Framework for DDR and SSR

The evolution of the SSR discourse has been marked by different understandings of what constitutes SSR. However, there is a strong international consensus emerging around a definition and approach that emphasizes the goal of developing effective *and* accountable security forces in order to improve state and human security.[13] By contrast, the purpose of DDR can reflect anything from a desire to downsize as a cost reduction exercise to forming a central pillar of a peacebuilding strategy. These conceptual distinctions are reversed in practice. The activities comprising DDR, although varying according to context, are relatively standardized, whereas the SSR agenda is exceptionally broad, spanning political dialogue, policy and legal advice, training, and technical assistance in order to reform security actors and their management along with oversight bodies.[14]

The scope of DDR and SSR activities is reflected by the key actors that participate in them. For DDR, once the political decisionmaking process has been conducted, a distinction can be made in practice between the predominantly technical defense- and security related expertise involved in the "two Ds" and the development-related experience directed toward reintegration-focused activities. As shown in the accompanying sidebar,[15] actors involved in SSR come from a much broader pool of both domestic and international political actors and specialists.

Core security actors, including law enforcement institutions: armed forces, police, gendarmeries, paramilitary forces, presidential guards, intelligence and security services, coast guards, border guards, customs authorities, and reserve and local security units.

Security management and oversight bodies: parliament/legislature and relevant committees; government/executive, including ministries of defense, internal affairs, and foreign affairs; national security advisory bodies; customary and traditional authorities; financial management bodies; civil society actors, including the media, academia, and nongovernmental organizations.

Justice institutions: justice ministries, prisons, criminal investigation and prosecution services, the judiciary (courts and tribunals), implementation justice services (bailiffs and ushers), other customary and traditional justice systems, human rights commissions and ombudsmen.

Nonstatutory security forces: liberation armies, guerrilla armies, private bodyguard units, private security companies, political party militias.

Considering DDR and SSR within a security sector governance framework provides a means to identify relevant actors and integrate activities that have in the past been conducted as separate efforts. At the heart of this approach is the need to pay due attention not just to enhancing the performance of security providers but to national capacities to manage reform processes while ensuring democratic control and oversight of the security sector by parliaments as well as civil society. From this perspective, component DDR activities can be linked to broader security sector governance concerns:

Disarmament is understood not just as a short-term security measure but part of a broader process of state regulation and control of weapons (hence, for example, it is directly linked to police reform, stockpile management, and civilian disarmament).

Demobilization is often narrowly treated as an aspect of DDR but needs to reflect a rational assessment of security sector needs as well as SSR measures to address potential consequences (e.g., security vacuums).

Reintegration decisions need to reflect the longer term opportunities and costs as well as resulting strains on the security sector. Equally, integration of ex-combatants into reformed security sector bodies needs to take proper account of both required skills and past conduct.

Promoting democratic governance of the security sector can help to situate DDR policymaking and programming within the framework of a broader political transition process. Security sector governance institutions should be a key focus of efforts to link these activities since they contain stakeholders common to both DDR and SSR. These institutions are well placed, as part of efforts to promote a transparent and participative decisionmaking process, to address the question of who should be demobilized, how reintegration should be conducted, and what should be the shape and size of the reformed security sector. Assisting national authorities in building effective, legitimate, and sustainable security institutions can also provide a bridge between immediate postconflict stabilization and longer term recovery and development.

A central goal of postconflict peacebuilding is to address cleavages among national authorities, the security sector, and cititzens that have been exacerbated by conflict. Encouraging transparency and accountability in decisionmaking enables actors at different levels of society to contribute to defining their own security needs—an essential component of legitimate, sustainable peacebuilding. This helps shape programs that truly reflect national needs, requirements, and capacities while also ensuring that DDR and SSR processes take root at local levels.

The diversity of security sector governance stakeholders should not be underestimated. In particular, influential roles played by a range of non-state actors demonstrate the reality that in many contexts the state is either unable or unwilling to provide security (or justice) to its citizens. This reflects the existence of informal or community-based security sector governance arrangements that may have long historical roots. Consequently, an important conclusion from a security sector governance perspective is that basing DDR or SSR solely on the rebuilding of a state monopoly on the use of force may be both inappropriate and ineffective.

Programming Implications

DDR programs have been conducted over a number of years in numerous countries while SSR, understood as such, is relatively new and policy guidelines heavily outweigh lessons learned from concrete SSR programming.[16] Moreover, while much DDR support has been provided by the UN, SSR has until recently been predominantly the focus of bilateral efforts. While these differences in emphasis are significant, situating DDR and SSR within a security sector governance framework points to important areas where agendas and interests converge. This section signposts a number of programming issues and related questions for DDR and SSR under four headings: *Working from a Common Vision, Shaping the Programming Cycle, Operationalizing Local Ownership*, and *Targeting Resources.*

Working from a Common Vision

Ideally, decisions on DDR should follow a broad-based SSR assessment process that would analyse political, security, and socioeconomic framing conditions. National stakeholders, supported by the international community, would define their own security needs to determine the size and nature of the security sector. The development of Sierra Leone's Defence White Paper provides a positive example of such a process. Specific reforms were framed by a strategic-level appreciation of the country's security context including threats, priorities, and, in particular, the values that should underpin the security sector.[17] Moreover, a 10-year resource commitment by the United Kingdom to support SSR in Sierra Leone has provided confidence in the long-term nature of the process.

Of course, the reality is that key decisions shaping DDR and SSR programs will often be made well before there is the means or political will to engage in such a visioning process. However, within peace negotiations or in early postconflict phases, establishing broad-based consultation mechanisms provides a process-based approach to decisionmaking that is deliberative and may contribute to taking some heat out of sensitive political issues. Supporting the convening of national seminars can help foster common understandings of DDR and SSR challenges. Broad participation, including transitional or elected authorities as well as representatives of the security sector, oversight bodies, and civil society is important. Including influential community figures and underrepresented groups is also crucial. For example, as part of a national dialogue process, a national seminar held in the Central African Republic April 14–17, 2008, considered DDR and SSR together. It contributed to providing locally generated understandings of security needs and laid out a roadmap to inform longer term reform processes.[18]

National policy development processes should provide a unifying framework for international support. This is consistent with obligations under the *Paris Declaration on Aid Effectiveness* and the *Accra Agenda for Action*,[19] which underline the importance of coherent donor approaches to security and development assistance in a given context. Increasing emphasis on "whole-of-government" or "whole-of-system" approaches by bilateral donors and international organizations offers opportunities to pool knowledge and build coherence within and across different agencies. The development of donor coordination matrices at country level to map all donors working in SSR-related areas also provides for increased transparency. However, implementing a common vision in practice demands both political will and shared programming procedures. It also requires determined and ongoing efforts to link programs to national planning processes. There is thus a need for strategic level commitment to facilitate coherence on the ground. Key questions are:

- Is there a strategic policy framework or a process in place to develop a national security strategy that can be used to inform DDR–SSR decision-making? How can national dialogue be facilitated?
- Is there broad national participation and consultation in processes that shape DDR–SSR programs? Are community figures and underrepresented groups brought within this process?
- Are mechanisms in place to coordinate support by bilateral donors and multilateral organizations?
- By what means is international support aligned with national decision-making structures?

Shaping the Programming Cycle

Mutually supportive efforts can only be realized if DDR and SSR are linked in assessments, program design, monitoring, and evaluation. In order to identify appropriate programming options prior to program development, needs assessments should benefit from both DDR and SSR expertise that includes regional knowledge and local language skills. For more general assessments, knowledge of the political and integrated nature of an SSR process may be more valuable than sector-specific expertise. Monitoring and evaluation provides an important entry point to review programs and ensure DDR–SSR are being implemented in a mutually supportive manner. Midterm reviews are increasingly recognized as significant mechanisms to assess program impact, identify unintended consequences, and undertake course corrections.

Common to all phases of the program cycle is the need for relevant, timely, and accurate knowledge capture. Mapping relevant (state and non-state) security actors and management and oversight bodies provides an important point of departure for grounding programs within a given context. Important DDR–SSR issues that require ongoing monitoring may include flows of ex-combatants, the impact of reintegration at the local level, or community perceptions of security provision and vulnerabilities. In order that interventions meet the "do no harm" ideal, context-specific analysis is essential to define options but also to identify where doing nothing may be the best course of action.

Inadequate institutional memory through reliance on key individuals rather than knowledge management strategies constrains the ability to learn from past experience. Moreover, information gained in disarmament or demobilization processes that may be highly relevant for SSR purposes often remains stovepiped. Standardizing knowledge-based approaches and ensuring access to key data and analysis will facilitate lesson learning processes. Key questions are:

- What is the level of integration of DDR–SSR issues and expertise in assessments? Are efforts made to link these issues to broader national and international planning processes?
- Are information-gathering mechanisms in place to identify key factors that should determine SSR priorities and sequencing or potential unintended consequences?
- How is knowledge captured and assessed? Is there a specific body responsible for identifying and disseminating lessons learned?

Operationalizing Local Ownership

Embracing local ownership requires that external actors accept and internalize the premise that they are only facilitators for a peacebuilding process designed, implemented, and managed at the national level. This principle is firmly enshrined in the *Integrated Disarmament, Demobilization, and Reintegration Standards* (IDDRS), which states that "the primary responsibility for DDR programs rests with national actors. . . . (G)enuine national ownership requires the participation of a wide range of state and nonstate actors at the national, regional and local levels."[20] Although also a fundamental principle of SSR good practice, a case can be made that "local ownership is much more a rhetorical device than an actual guide to implementation."[21] In part, this reflects the difficulty (particularly if underestimated) of applying this principle at a time when national capacities are at their weakest and local actors lack both expertise and legitimacy. The conflicting interests of different domestic constituencies and the presence of spoilers are particularly problematic. Yet, as with any other part of the peacebuilding agenda, the challenging framing conditions that shape any postconflict intervention should not mask shortcomings in policy and practice that ignore local actors or demonstrate a lack of flexibility in programs and their financing, or in political agendas and timeframes which may be inimical to local realities, interests, and priorities.

While the buy-in of national elites is necessary, ultimately it is at the community level that DDR and SSR processes succeed or fail. Without underestimating the difficulties, involving local authorities and communities in program planning, implementation, and monitoring is the only way to ensure responsiveness to local needs. Encouraging community dialogue is one way to address local security concerns and inform decisionmaking on the timing of disarmament and of reintegration measures. This can help counter perceptions that DDR processes "reward" former combatants at the expense of civilian populations. The Final Report of the Stockholm Initiative on DDR (SIDDR) recommends parallel DDR programs that mirror measures in favor of ex-combatants with support for the communities that receive them.[22] Dialogue is also essential if reformed security forces are to gain acceptance and trust. This calls for public consultation and information programs to build support for DDR and SSR processes through openly addressing concerns. Key questions are:

- How can international support be demonstrably linked to national leadership? Is an advisory or mentoring (rather than "doing") approach apparent?

- Does ownership extend beyond state authorities to engage with diverse national stakeholders?
- Are community security needs a focus of DDR–SSR policy and programming?

Targeting Resources

The UN Secretary-General's 2006 report on DDR recognizes the problems posed by the absence of adequate, timely, and sustained funding. This has frequently resulted in a gap between the "two Ds" and reintegration-focused activities. The former may be relatively easy to fund, plan, and implement, while reintegration is dependant on expertise and conditions that are not always present in a timely manner in a postconflict environment.[23] Relatedly, financial resources provided for DDR and SSR processes have not in the past been tailored to the budget limitations of national authorities. The IDDRS reinforces this point by stressing that while taking ex-combatants into public service may be an important part of overall reconciliation and political integration strategies, especially as part of SSR, it can be sustainable only when economic circumstances allow for the expansion of public services.[24] The *OECD DAC Handbook* stresses the importance of tailored financial support if reforms are to be sustainable and that "great care should be taken to ensure that such assistance is eventually assimilated into government budgets and revenue streams so as to minimize the risk of creating fiscally unsustainable services."[25]

An onus on strengthening available human resources is a common DDR–SSR requirement. This is a two-way street. Supporting the development of cross-cutting skills at the national level such as human resources, line management, budgets, and financial management will enhance the effectiveness of DDR and SSR at the national level while also creating capacities with wider application beyond these specific processes. It also emphasises the skills-transfer–based approach necessary for effective international support to national capacity building. Given that the international community utilizes a wide range of service providers in these fields, robust contracting and oversight procedures are essential. Promisingly, innovative service delivery mechanisms such as DCAF's International Security Sector Advisory Team (ISSAT)[26] are emerging to help fill this gap. Key questions are:

- Is funding for DDR–SSR programs designed to become sustainable through national budgets?
- Is financial support accompanied by capacity building in the national institutions that must manage and oversee DDR–SSR programs?

- Does international support focus on the development of cross-cutting skills that will contribute to long-term institutional integrity?
- Are mechanisms in place to oversee and monitor service delivery and thus ensure appropriate support to nationally driven processes?

Conclusion

The need to understand and operationalize the linkages between DDR and SSR is increasingly recognized. It forms part of a growing awareness of the imperative to provide more coherent and coordinated support from the international community across the postconflict peacebuilding agenda. In order to operationalize such a linkage, there is a need to marry findings drawn from the policy literature with a clear picture of how engagements have been planned and implemented at headquarters and in the field. These are highly nuanced, politically sensitive issues. The size, shape, and orientation of the security sector reflect the interests of national political actors and other interest groups. This chapter argues that focusing on the security sector governance dimensions of DDR and SSR can remove the heat from some of these sensitivities through supporting processes that seek to foster participation, enhance oversight, and build trust.

A security sector governance focus enables international efforts to more closely engage with context-specific political and security dynamics. It also recalls the underpinning goal of both DDR and SSR—to enhance the long-term security of the state and its citizens. In this regard, providing a people-centered focus is critical to durable peacebuilding yet remains underemphasised. Reinforcing state institutions may be important to these processes, but this work should be properly understood as a means rather than an end of building sustainable peace. Considering the security concerns of individuals and communities highlights the range of nonstate actors that may be at least as significant as the state in influencing how men, women, girls, and boys experience security. Thus, a security sector governance lens allows us to prioritize, sequence, and link DDR and SSR in ways that highlight sensitivities but also take into account the differentiated security needs of societies in different parts of the world.

Finally, it is important to emphasise that promoting greater coherence on the levels of actors and issues is not about blurring lines between distinct activities or simplifying complex relationships between stakeholders with different approaches and objectives. Rather, it recognizes that we are all working towards achieving certain common outcomes. And while many technical activities may be involved, this process is inherently political in nature. An integrated, long-term approach that takes these factors into account should thus have major consequences for how we conceive, implement, and evaluate DDR and SSR policy and programs.

Notes

[1] Statement by the President of the Security Council at the 5632[d] meeting of the Security Council, held February 20, 2007.

[2] *Integrated Disarmament, Demobilisation and Reintegration Standards* (IDDRS), Module 6.10, 3.

[3] Organisation for Economic Co-operation and Development (OECD), *OECD DAC Handbook on Security System Reform: Supporting Security and Justice*, OECD DAC (2007), 108.

[4] A. Bryden and R. Keane, "Security System Reform: What Have We Learned? Results and Trends from the Publication and Dissemination of the OECD DAC Handbook on Security System Reform," OECD DAC (2009), available at <http://www.dcaf.ch/publications>.

[5] UNDP Practice Note: DDR of Ex-combatants, available at <www.undorg/bcpr/whats_new/ddr_practice_note.pdf>.

[6] S. Rumin, "Burundi," in Bryden and Scherrer.

[7] OECD DAC (2007), 101.

[8] Ibid., 102.

[9] R. Taljaard, "Implementing South Africa's Regulation of Foreign Military Assistance Act," in A. Bryden and M. Caparini, eds., *Private Actors and Security Governance* (Berlin: Lit Verlag, 2006), 167–186.

[10] U. Schneckener, "Fragile Statehood, Armed Non-State Actors and Security Governance," in Bryden and Caparini, 27.

[11] OECD DAC (2007), 105.

[12] J. Ginifer, "Support for DDR and SSR after Conflicts in Africa: Lessons-Learnt and New Agendas in Africa" (2004), 17, available at <www.upi-fiia.fi/document.php?DOC_ID=166>.

[13] Organisation for Economic Co-operation and Development, "Security System Reform and Governance; A DAC Reference Document," (2005); Council of the European Union, "EU Concept for ESDP support to Security Sector Reform (SSR)," Council document 12566/4/05, October 13, 2005; Commission of the European Communities, "A Concept for European Community Support for Security Sector Reform," SEC (2006) 658, May 24, 2006; Economic Community of West African States (ECOWAS), "ECOWAS Conflict Prevention Framework (ECPF)," enacted by Regulation MSC/REG.1/01/08 of the Mediation and Security Council of ECOWAS, January 16, 2008; and United Nations Security Council, "Annex to the letter dated November 20, 2007, from the Permanent Representatives of Slovakia and South Africa to the United Nations addressed to the Secretary-General; Statement of the Co-Chairs of the International Workshop on Enhancing United Nations Support for Security Sector Reform in Africa: Towards an African Perspective," S/2007/687, November 29, 2007.

[14] M. Brzoska, "Embedding DDR Programs in Security Sector Reconstruction," in A. Bryden and H. Hänggi, *Security Governance in Post Conflict Peacebuilding* (Berlin: Lit Verlag, 2005), 96.

[15] OECD DAC (2005), 20–21.

[16] *The OECD DAC Handbook on Security System Reform—Supporting Security and Justice* is the most elaborated guidance for SSR policymakers and practitioners. It provides extensive guidance on both political and technical aspects of SSR through the different phases of the program cycle; available at <http://www.oecd.org/dataoecd/43/25/38406485.pdf>.

[17] Available at <www.statehouse-sl.org/policies/defence-white-paper.html>.

[18] See Boubacar N'Diaye, "The Central African Republic," in Bryden and Scherrer.

[19] *The Paris Declaration on Aid Effectiveness* was endorsed on March 2, 2005 by more than 100 ministers, heads of agency, and other senior officials. *The Accra Agenda for Action* was drawn up in 2008 and builds on the commitments contained in the Paris Declaration; available at <www.oecd.org/document/18/0,3343,en_2649_3236398_35401554_1_1_1_1,00.html>.

[20] United Nations, *Operational Guide to the Integrated Disarmament, Demobilisation and Reintegration Standards* (United Nations, 2006), 29.

[21] E. Scheye and G. Peake, "Unknotting Local Ownership," in A. Ebnöther and P. Fluri, eds., *After Intervention: Public Sector Management in Post-Conflict Societies—From Intervention to Sustainable Local Ownership*, Partnership for Peace Consortium Working Group on SSR (2005), 240.

[22] Stockholm Initiative on DDR Final Report (2006), 27–28.

[23] United Nations, United Nations Secretary General Report on DDR (2006).

[24] IDDRS, chapter 4, 30.

[25] OECD DAC (2007), 105.

[26] ISSAT is a multidonor initiative established within the DCAF, whose current membership consists of 14 countries (Austria, Belgium, Canada, Estonia, Finland, France, Germany, Ireland, the Netherlands, Norway, Slovakia, Switzerland, Sweden, and the United Kingdom) and 6 multilateral actors (the Council of the European Union, the European Commission, OECD, UNDP, UN Department of Political Affairs, and UN DPKO). ISSAT was created to support SSR programming in line with international good practice through four core services: advisory field support, operational guidance tools, knowledge services, and training support. See <http://issat.dcaf.ch>.

Chapter 14

Afghanistan and the DDR–SSR Nexus

By Mark Sedra

Introduction

A notable lesson of the postconflict reconstruction experience over the past decade is that the process of Security Sector Reform (SSR) and the Disarmament, Demobilization, and Reintegration (DDR) of former combatants are intricately connected and mutually reinforcing. The failure to recognize the symbiotic relationship between the processes in a specific context could do harm to the wider goals of reconstruction and stabilization. Investing the state with a monopoly over the use of force in a manner consistent with democratic norms—the primary goal of SSR—is dependent to a certain degree on the removal or breakdown of nonstate armed groups that contest that power and authority—one of the key objectives of DDR. Inversely, nonstate armed actors will invariably resist demilitarization unless they feel the state is capable of providing a base level of security and justice in an effective and equitable manner—one of the purposes of SSR. As such, SSR and DDR are interdependent and will be hard-pressed to succeed individually unless appropriately coordinated.

In the Afghan case, the design of the SSR and DDR programs reflected the imperative of coordination. In fact DDR was recognized as a pillar of the SSR process under the G8 donor framework established to oversee it.[1] However, in practice Afghanistan's DDR process was advanced independently of the SSR process, with few linkages between them. The failure to build on the natural synergies between SSR and DDR programming not only represented a missed opportunity but set back both processes.

This chapter will begin by outlining the DDR–SSR nexus in the Afghan context. It will proceed to identify lessons learned from 8 years of DDR and SSR implementation, dividing them into 3 categories: context, process design, and program implementation. From this analysis, some conclusions on the challenges of operationalizing the DDR–SSR nexus will be presented. Deriving general conclusions from a single case study, particularly one that is so challenging and complex, is a fraught exercise; nonetheless the Afghan case does yield some important insights. If nothing else, it informs future DDR and SSR initiatives within Afghanistan.

The DDR–SSR Nexus

After the fall of the Taliban regime in the autumn of 2001, two of the top priorities identified by the international community and the nascent Afghan administration were the Disarmament, Demobilization, and Reintegration of ex-combatants and Security Sector Reform. But it soon became apparent that few environments are more difficult for the implementation of DDR and SSR than Afghanistan. The most imposing obstacle has been the adverse security environment, driven by a growing Taliban-led insurgency, the resurgence of warlordism, the burgeoning narcotics trade, and a rise in general criminality. A strong case can be made that Afghanistan has yet to enter a postconflict phase and is actually fixed in another stage of its 3-decade civil war. Due to the present security crisis facing Afghanistan, the DDR and SSR projects tend to be viewed by the international community and segments of the Afghan government not as elements of a broader peace-building and state-building process—as they are designed to be—but rather as instruments to address immediate security threats. This has had the effect of distorting those processes, giving them an overtly short-term focus in the best-case scenario, and undermining them altogether in the worst-case scenario.

Due to the perceived geostrategic importance of Afghanistan, donor resources have not been the primary obstacle to DDR and SSR. The United States has earmarked over $13 billion to the Afghan National Security Forces (ANSF) in 2009 and 2010 alone, and the DDR program, which cost almost $150 million—primarily funded by Japan—stands as one of the most expensive such programs in history. However, despite these ample resources, a common vision for the future of the Afghan security apparatus has proven elusive. Coordination has been a problem at every level of the DDR and SSR processes, and by early 2010 an overarching long-term strategy for the security sector still did not exist. Afghan political will for reform has not kept pace with the growth of international engagement in the DDR and SSR processes. The deep ethnic and political divisions that characterize the Afghan administration are also omnipresent in the security sector. There is no consensus among the Afghan political elite concerning key issues such as demilitarization; as insecurity has grown, many Afghan actors have begun to resist demilitarization activities and, more worryingly, view them as a threat. Rampant corruption and clientelism at the highest levels of government have impeded and even paralyzed reforms, particularly in the judicial system. Even where political will is robust, chronic shortages of human and institutional capacity in the Afghan administration has made change grindingly slow and has undercut genuine local ownership.

In Afghanistan, DDR must be understood within a broader framework of demilitarization. Several interlinked initiatives have been undertaken under the auspices of a broader demilitarization process. They include a DDR program focusing on the assemblage of militias that constituted the Northern Alliance, dubbed the Afghan Military Force (AMF); a Disbandment of Illegal Armed Groups (DIAG) program targeting all armed groups in the country outside the AMF, which are deemed illegal; a Heavy Weapons Cantonment (HWC) program that sought to collect, deactivate, and canton heavy weapons in the hands of nonstate actors; and an Ammunition and Mine Action program mandated to collect, stockpile, and destroy the estimated 100,000 metric tons of uncontrolled ammunition and explosive material littering the country.[2] Accordingly, the chapter will at times use the term *demilitarization* when referring to DDR and its associated processes.

The key implementing body for demilitarization programming is the Afghanistan New Beginnings Programme (ANBP), which was established through a partnership between the United Nations Development Programme (UNDP) and the United Nations Assistance Mission in Afghanistan (UNAMA). Although Japan was the lead donor for the process under the G8 lead donor scheme, and the Afghan government was intended to be the key policymaking actor through the Demobilization and Reintegration Commission, the United Nations (UN) has in reality driven the process from its inception.

While the UN has played a key role in the elaboration of the DDR process, its involvement in SSR has been limited. UNDP has had some involvement in the police reform process via the Law and Order Trust Fund for Afghanistan and is implementing some justice reform initiatives, largely funded by Italy and the European Commission. However, a lack of intensive involvement in the SSR agenda has contributed to a disconnect between the DDR and SSR processes. One of the principal obstacles encumbering the SSR agenda is the absence of clear leadership and a unified strategic vision. There are various conflicting interests at play among the external actors engaged in the security sector. No overarching strategy or coordination body has emerged to provide the needed leadership in SSR implementation. It was widely hoped that Afghan bodies such as the Office of the National Security Council (ONSC) could assert an oversight and coordination role, but it has not demonstrated either the capacity or willingness.

The Afghan DDR process, which ran from 2003 to 2006, was one of the largest in history. Its numerical achievements—the demobilization of 63,000 combatants and the collection of over 58,000 weapons—seem impressive, but as with any statistics it is important not just to ask what they say, but what they don't say. What the numbers of Afghanistan's DDR program don't say is whether the program effectively broke down militia structures, improved security in the areas where it was implemented, or buoyed public confidence in the state. A close look at the situation in Afghanistan in early 2010 would prompt a negative response to all three questions. The patronage-based networks that have sustained Afghanistan's local militias survived the DDR program intact in most areas; security conditions have steadily deteriorated since the conclusion of the DDR program in 2006; and public faith in the state, particularly in its ability to provide security, has deteriorated with each passing year.

Progress in SSR has been uneven across its various pillars and individual projects. The significant gains made in training and equipping the Afghan National Army (ANA) belie the paralysis in police, judicial, and corrections reforms. Moreover, key areas of the SSR agenda such as the development of executive and legislative oversight mechanisms, the application of sound public finance management procedures, and the empowerment of civil society have received scant attention. This, in a sense, can be understood as a natural feature of an SSR process "under fire," a process being implemented during a conflict rather than in a postconflict environment, a situation where nonstate armed groups are increasing in strength rather than being disbanded and disarmed. It raises the question of whether the SSR agenda, as it is understood in documents such as the *OECD–DAC Handbook on SSR* and the *Report of the United Nations Secretary General on SSR*, is even feasible under the conditions prevalent in Afghanistan and Iraq. A reconceptualization of the model may be needed for such contexts.

As already stated, the Afghan demilitarization and SSR processes have largely been advanced in two parallel tracks. Although DDR has been framed as a pillar of the SSR process, it was designed and implemented as a standalone program. As one senior ANBP official stated, "DDR was in isolation . . . [and] lacked official connectivity with the other four SSR pillars."[3] Surprisingly little thinking was dedicated to the integration of DDR and SSR programming. One reason was the decision of the U.S. military to turn down proposals to absorb former militiamen and jihadi fighters into the new ANA. This removed a natural link between the military reform process and DDR program. Former combatants were not formally barred from enlisting in the ANA, but the age restriction of 18–28 naturally disqualified many. In building a new army from the ground up, the United States sought to construct a new culture for the military establishment, distancing it from the tainted legacy of the communist, jihadi, and Taliban regimes. The effort has been largely successful, with the army widely perceived by the population as a one of the few symbols of pride and professionalism in the post-Taliban era. In this case, the disconnect between the DDR and SSR programs had a beneficial effect, demonstrating that context should always be the driving factor in operationalizing the DDR–SSR nexus.

The Afghan government's 2005 *Millennium Development Goals Report* explicitly recognizes the inextricable link between demilitarization and SSR and the importance of both enterprises in advancing security and stability. However, it treats demilitarization as a distant or ancillary goal to be achieved only after meaningful reforms have been enacted in the security sector. The report argues: "large scale civilian disarmament, without the strengthening and reform of the police and justice systems, is likely to be both difficult and may also increase peoples' vulnerability and perception of mistrust of the state." It goes on to state that "the registration and regulation of small arms may be a more viable option" when reforms in the security sector have reached a more advanced stage.[4] While these conclusions are not unreasonable in light of Afghanistan's security crisis, they ignore the reciprocal importance of demilitarization in providing an enabling environment for SSR.

Some concrete links were established between the DDR and SSR processes around the issue of small arms and light weapons. Technical initiatives to transfer collected weapons from the DDR program to the nascent national security forces involved direct cooperation between the DDR and SSR programs.

The level of connectivity between the SSR process and demilitarization programming has increased under the auspices of the DIAG program, the successor initiative to DDR. In 2008, the government authorized the creation of a central DIAG unit in the Ministry of Interior. The unit comprises three sections: operations, private security company registration, and individual weapons registration. The ANBP completed the set-up of the unit in April 2009 and was in the process of building the capacity of its regional offices as of early 2010.[5] The establishment of the unit should permit greater integration of police development and demilitarization activities.

In 2009, ANBP considered other strategies to better link with the police reform process. One approach discussed was to tie the DIAG program to the Focused District Development (FDD) initiative for the Afghan National Police (ANP). Under the FDD program, Afghan Uniformed Police are removed from their home districts and transferred to one of the country's five Regional Training Centers to undergo 8 weeks of training, after which they are equipped and returned to their districts under the guidance of police mentor teams. ANBP officials have considered adjusting the DIAG rollout schedule to match that of FDD. This would allow the DIAG program to build on the momentum of FDD in targeted districts, to benefit from the level of security provided for it to take place, and to sensitize the police involved on the intricacies of demilitarization. As of mid-2009, this was only a proposal and there was little to indicate that it would materialize.

These nascent initiatives to align the DIAG program with police reform activities, while slow to emerge, could set a precedent for the construction of further bridges between the demilitarization and SSR spheres. Other areas where joint programming could yield positive results for the wider stabilization and reconstruction agenda include:

Veteran's administration. There is a clear need in the Afghan state for a body capable of providing assistance and support to both DDR beneficiaries and retired military personnel, whether disabled or able-bodied. There were, in the initial phases of the ANBP, plans to gradually transition the ANBP into such a structure, but such notions have largely faded from consideration. The Ministry of Defence, ANA, Demobilization and Reintegration Commission, and ANBP should come together to develop such an institution, which would be vital to ensuring that former fighters do not fall back into patterns of violence and that they receive the appropriate care.

Demobilization of police. It has become clear over the past 7 years that a large cross section of the ANP, many of whom emanated from militia groups, are unsuitable for policing and should be phased out of the force. Some observers of the process have called for a specialized program to purge unqualified police, providing incentives to facilitate their retirement and reintegration into civilian society. Rather than following this route, international and national stakeholders have sought to strengthen the training regimen as a means to overcome existing gaps in professionalism, to marginal effect.

Vetting and management of informal security structures. As the security situation has deteriorated over the past 7 years, there have been increasing calls for the mobilization of informal security structures akin to militias or community watch groups, to supplement and complement the formal security architecture. Recent iterations of such thinking are the Afghan Public Protection Program (APPP)—district-level militia units chosen by specialized district *shuras* and overseen by the Ministry of Interior—and the Afghan Guard Force (AGF)—a centrally directed force of local security personnel responsible for static guarding and facility protection. One of the major problems encountered in establishing such structures is the vetting of personnel to militate against infiltration by spoiler groups and criminal entities. The ANBP with its database of armed groups could assist with or even manage this process. It could also be involved in the registration of all weapons used by these informal personnel, providing another layer of accountability and oversight. To step into this role, the ANBP has sought to update its existing database on armed groupings, which was assembled with questionable methodology and has not been appropriately updated. A remapping process, based largely on questionnaires filled in by provincial governors, was completed in April 2009; however, since the results of the study have not been released, there is little evidence that the updated database is any more sophisticated than previous iterations. Given that the remapping process relied on crude questionnaires to actors, many with a vested interest in providing false information due to their own connections to illegal armed groups, as well as updated information from state security agencies that have shown only a tepid interest in supporting the process, it is difficult to be optimistic about the results of the study.

Weapons management. According to a report of the U.S. Government Accountability Office (GAO), "roughly 17 percent of small arms, mortars, and grenade launchers supplied to the Afghan security services since 2002 are unaccounted for."[6] There are numerous reports of weapons provided to the Afghan security forces leaking to the black market and even to spoiler groups.[7] To address this urgent problem, the United States is working to develop more stringent asset management procedures for both the ANA and ANP. Nonetheless, as of early 2009 a senior ANBP official reported that there is still no way of fully verifying where weapons transferred by the demilitarization program to the ANA go after they reach their main weapons depot. The development of a weapons control and stockpile management regime within the security sector represents a natural area of overlap between demilitarization and SSR and an obvious entry point to facilitate joint planning and implementation.

Lessons Identified

Three types of lessons can be identified from the experience with DDR and SSR implementation in Afghanistan: lessons on context, lessons on process design, and lessons on program implementation. Taken together, they help explain the challenges to operationalizing the DDR–SSR nexus and the failure of the demilitarization and SSR processes to live up to expectations. In some cases, the failures of DDR and SSR programming can be attributed to wider political and security conditions outside the control of DDR and SSR strategists and practitioners. In other cases, flaws in program design or ineffective implementation—acts of omission and commission—were the reason for the failings. One of the wider conclusions of this analysis is that in some cases the environment is simply not conducive for DDR and SSR in their conventional forms, and in those cases more harm than good can be done by attempting to graft a demilitarization or SSR process onto an unsuitable or unripe situation.

Contextual Lessons

Political Settlement. There was no classical peace agreement to anchor the DDR and SSR processes in Afghanistan and tie the main power brokers to them. The Bonn Agreement was a strategy for political transition, not a peace agreement signed by all parties to the conflict. In the case of DDR, the lack of a grand bargain for peace had two impacts. First, it meant that the process could not access spoiler groups such as the Taliban and Hizb-i Islami. With the process unable to engage two of the main players in the conflict, others were unwilling to fully submit to it. Northern Alliance militias were understandably reticent to demobilize when their rivals remained armed. Second, the lack of a peace agreement explicitly requiring its various signatories to disarm gave the government and the international community little leverage with which to compel compliance. The lack of a grand bargain for peace meant that Afghan government and international stakeholders had to negotiate minibargains with Afghan commanders in the field to secure their compliance with DDR and SSR. Not only was this time-consuming and politically cumbersome, but it also undermined the integrity and uniformity of the process.

Political Will. Perhaps the most profound challenge to the demilitarization process has been the tepid and variable political commitment displayed toward it by key stakeholders. For instance, the Afghan government, despite publicly supporting the demilitarization of armed groups, has tolerated the presence of numerous government officials with links to armed elements. According to some sources, up to half of the parliament has links to illegal armed groups despite a clear provision in the electoral law barring such figures from candidacy in legislative elections.

On the part of the international community, the U.S.-led coalition has directly undermined demilitarization efforts through its patronage of subnational proxies in the south and east of the country. While NATO has made robust declarations supporting DIAG, issuing directives to its Provincial Reconstruction Teams (PRTs) mandating their support for the process, that has not translated into constructive engagement on the ground. Without the active support of both national and international stakeholders, the demilitarization and SSR processes will be hard-pressed to make tangible progress.

Local Ownership. Chronic shortages in human and institutional capacity in Afghanistan coupled with weak domestic political will for reform have hindered the emergence of genuine Afghan ownership over the reform process. This partially accounts for the lack of a coherent SSR strategy. Organizations such as the Office of the National Security Council have been in a position to assert a leadership role in the process but have not. This has left the security sector without an actor capable of coordinating and rationalizing the interests and agendas of a diverse set of stakeholders.

Insecurity. Perhaps the foremost challenge to the DDR and SSR processes is the adverse security environment in Afghanistan. As conditions deteriorate, the prospect of successful demilitarization and SSR diminishes. More than a third of the country was off limits to staff of the ANBP in early 2010. As more and more Afghans face a security dilemma, fewer are willing to submit their arms—perceived to be their main source of protection—to the state or external actors.

In the case of SSR, the process is ill-equipped to withstand the stresses and pressures of implementation during an ongoing conflict. It is a process of institutionalization that assumes a level of security, political stability, and institutional capacity presently absent. The current SSR process in Afghanistan can be likened, as U.S. General David Petraeus has remarked in reference to its Iraqi counterpart, to "repairing an aircraft while in flight—and while being shot at."[8]

Demilitarization is seen as a low priority in the context of an ongoing insurgency. In fact, a number of programs are being advanced in the security sector with both tacit and overt support from the international community that would roll back some of the limited gains made by the DDR program. For instance, international and domestic stakeholders supporting the Afghan Local Police program, an initiative to mobilize community defense forces to supplement the regular police, have given little consideration to the impact of the initiative on demilitarization activities or how the armed groups being mobilized will be disarmed in the future if the security situation stabilizes.

Process Design

Lead Nation System. Rather than imbuing the SSR process with stability, predictability, and coherence as intended, the lead-nation framework actually frustrated efforts at coordination. The system fostered donor competition rather than collaboration and joint programming. If an Afghan-owned national security strategy existed that situated DDR and SSR within a wider policy framework, outlined a coherent leadership structure, and mandated lines of communication and collaboration for the DDR and SSR processes, this problem would be overcome. However, there is none. While efforts have been undertaken under the auspices of the Office of the National Security Council to develop such a document, it has yet to be publicly released. Its absence has contributed to the "siloed," compartmentalized approach to security policy and programming that has blocked the emergence of creative thinking on how to integrate reforms and activities in different areas of the security sector.

Regional Dimensions. Conflict dynamics in Afghanistan are regional rather than national in character. For instance, one cannot understand the situation in Afghanistan without having an awareness of developments and currents in the Pakistani tribal areas. Although this reality is widely accepted, demilitarization and SSR initiatives tend to feature a narrow national focus. There are some limited cooperative programs with Afghanistan's neighbors, particularly Pakistan and Iran on border policing, but they are small and only scratch the surface of the wider problems. There is tremendous scope and need for cooperative arrangements and joint reform programs in areas such as counternarcotics, counterterrorism, and customs.

Thousands of small arms continue to flow unimpeded into Afghanistan from neighboring countries each month, mostly from Pakistan and Iran. While the ANBP and the Demobilization and Reintegration Commission are aware of this, their programming does not seek to address the problem. This is a point of convergence between the demilitarization and SSR processes that needs to be understood and operationalized. Programs addressing weapons smuggling in the border areas, integrated into border policing programs, could give a significant boost to demilitarization efforts, as it would stem the continuous flow of new arms into the country. Cracking down on unlicensed weapons development and distribution in the tribal areas on both sides of the Afghan-Pakistan border, something the Pakistani government has attempted to do in relation to the arms bazaars in the North-West Frontier Province, could be a good entry point for further action on more thorny issues of border management.

Financial Sustainability. Surprisingly little attention is being dedicated to issues of reform sustainability. The SSR process is being driven by short-term imperatives of addressing the insurgency and creating security conditions conducive to international military disengagement, rather than fostering the creation of a self-sufficient security apparatus attuned to meeting domestic threats. Donor funding programs have reinforced Afghanistan's historic position as a rentier client state, dependent on external revenue flows to maintain the integrity of central state structures. Demonstrating the unsustainability of current security spending, in 2007 security expenditures were equivalent to more than 300 percent of domestic revenue. Given the planned expansion of the ANSF in 2010 and 2011, this sustainability gap will only grow. Even with the most optimistic revenue projections over the next 5 years, Afghanistan will not be capable of financing even a significant portion of its security budget, a reality that has dangerous long-term consequences given that the international commitment will not be indefinite.

In the area of demilitarization, there has been a similar failure to consider the long-term dimension of demilitarization programming. For instance, it is widely accepted that Afghanistan's thousands of former combatants will require some kind of continuing assistance. This can take the form of psychosocial support, assistance to the disabled, and employment services. This is central to the overarching goal of keeping ex-combatants out of militia structures. Plans were introduced during the early phases of the DDR program to establish a veteran's administration within the Afghan government, perhaps as a part of the Ministry of Labor and Social Affairs. By the beginning of 2009, all such plans had been discarded, leaving no framework for the government to provide long-term, ongoing support to its war veterans.

Program Implementation

Needs Assessments. Designing effective SSR and demilitarization programs requires a comprehensive understanding of the historical, sociocultural, economic, political, and security dimensions of the local context.

The Afghanistan case demonstrates the deleterious implications of failing to undertake an adequate needs assessment to inform program design. In the case of SSR, programming failed to comprehend the dominance of informal security structures across much of the country, the depth of corruption and clientelism in the security forces, and the challenges of establishing Afghan ownership of the process. In the case of demilitarization, programming failed to reflect the central role played by commanders in militia networks, the challenges of gathering accurate data on militia numbers and weapons holdings, and the problem of weak political will for the process.

The penchant for rapid and poorly conducted donor assessments, of which there have been many in Afghanistan, is even more dangerous than failing to conduct an assessment at all. In such cases, policy and program designers are not just operating in the dark, but can actually be misled by tainted data and faulty analysis. Had rigorous preprogram assessments for both the demilitarization and SSR processes been conducted in Afghanistan, the programs designed may have anticipated and adapted better to emergent security problems and more effectively gauged the resource needs of the process. Perhaps most importantly, a competent assessment could have alerted stakeholders of the need to manage expectations and recognize the long-term nature of the process.

Monitoring and Evaluation. There is a conspicuous lack of robust monitoring and evaluation instruments in the demilitarization and SSR processes. Donors have tended to rely on statistics to gauge progress. However, such statistics are notoriously unreliable and potentially deceptive in the Afghan case, as the number of confirmed ghost soldiers—those on the payroll but not serving in the ranks—clearly attests. The measures and benchmarks that exist tend to be more supply- than results-oriented, focusing largely on the resource levels disbursed by donors rather than their actual impact on the ground. The lack of good qualitative measures assessing short-, medium-, and long-term progress has undercut the ability of donors to effectively plan and adjust their programs during implementation. More nuanced and textured metrics assessing evolving attitudes toward the security environment and the state are needed.

The ANBP was seemingly slow to recognize the importance of developing monitoring and evaluation tools. It did not establish a process to track DDR program beneficiaries after the completion of reintegration assistance. The ANBP did launch a series of client evaluation surveys by 2007 to assess beneficiary attitudes. The surveys revealed positive feelings toward the program but were not designed in a sufficiently rigorous and comprehensive manner to identify long-term trends and employment prospects for ex-combatants.

The lack of effective monitoring and evaluation instruments for the demilitarization and SSR processes have made it difficult for donors to adequately measure progress and define a viable endstate. Part of the problem lies in the fact that no baseline data was collected under the auspices of a needs assessment at the beginning of the process, leaving little to measure the current situation against. Nonetheless, tens of millions of dollars have been squandered on programs that were ill-designed and achieved little, but continued for months and even years due to the lack of monitoring and evaluation mechanisms to alert donors of their poor performance. Deep problems of corruption in Afghanistan make monitoring and evaluation infrastructure even more indispensible, as donor funds have been the victim of malfeasance by both Afghan actors and international contractors.

Conclusions

One must be cautious in drawing lessons from the Afghan DDR and SSR experience for the implementation of the model in other conflict-affected states. While every conflict setting has its own complexities, the Afghan case has faced some particularly challenging conditions for both DDR and SSR. Paramount is the adverse security environment that in many ways defies classification as a postconflict context. With an active conflict raging in large parts of the country, DDR and other demilitarization activities have been increasingly viewed as unfeasible and impractical by most national and international actors, both logistically in terms of the actual challenges of implementation in an insecure environment, and sociopolitically, with most elites and average citizens unwilling to relinquish their primary means of protection until the broader security dilemma is resolved. The Afghan case shows that SSR can take on new meaning during conflict when viewed as a weapon of counterinsurgents and beleaguered governments rather than as a broader process of democratic reform and good governance promotion. This distortion of the classical SSR model—tilting it toward hard security interventions over soft civilian activities—undercuts the long-term objectives of SSR. For instance, a singular focus on training and equipping military forces without considering oversight and management structures can lead to the emergence of unaccountable and repressive security institutions prone to violating the principle of democratic civilian control, the bedrock of the SSR model. This type of reform process is not SSR at all, but something else altogether.

In a conflict-affected environment where both DDR and SSR initiatives are either unviable or prone to distortion, it is unsurprising that reformers fail to adequately develop cross-program synergies. In contexts like Afghanistan, a new typology of interventions that stands apart from the traditional menu of projects under the auspices of DDR and SSR, should be developed. Nat Colletta and Robert Muggah have dubbed these *interim security promotion mechanisms*, initiatives that are politically viable and logistically feasible in volatile postconflict environments.[9] They should be aimed to build trust among local actors, improve security, and perhaps most importantly, to buy time for reconciliation to gain traction and political will to materialize. Rigid adherence to traditional formulas of postconflict reconstruction, particularly in contexts where insecurity and political instability are acute, is a losing proposition. The viability of DDR and SSR is dependent on a set of specific preconditions, like a base level of security, human and institutional capital for reform implementation, stable funding structures, and domestic and external political will. In the absence of one or more of these factors, SSR programs are unlikely to be successful. In such circumstances, it is advisable to build those conditions before launching conventional security interventions such as DDR and SSR programming. The Afghan case demonstrates the critical interconnections between DDR and SSR and their importance for long-term peace and stability, but the conditions are not yet in place for that nexus to be actualized in policy or practice. This accounts for the many setbacks encountered by the DDR and SSR processes over the past 8 years and the failure to exploit seeming windows of opportunities to integrate DDR and SSR initiatives.

Notes

[1] The lead nation framework was created at a series of G8 security donor meetings in Geneva in the spring of 2002. It identified five pillars in the Afghan SSR process and assigned a G8 donor to oversee reforms in each. The pillars and lead donors were military reform (U.S.), police reform (Germany), judicial reform (Italy), counternarcotics (UK), and DDR (Japan).

[2] After almost 3 decades of war, Afghanistan is littered with weaponry—from 500,000 to 1.5 million small arms and light weapons, according to the Small Arms Survey—and a significant proportion of the male population is affiliated with nonstate armed groups.

[3] Interview with Senior ANBP official, Kabul, January 12, 2009.

[4] Islamic Republic of Afghanistan, *Millennium Development Goals Islamic Republic of Afghanistan Country Report 2005: Vision 2020* (Kabul: Islamic Republic of Afghanistan and the United Nations Development Programme [UNDP], 2005), 105.

[5] UNDP, *Afghanistan, Disbandment of Illegal Armed Groups (DIAG): Second Quarter Project Progress Report—2009* (Kabul: UNDP, 2009), 9.

[6] Quoted in Centre for International Governance Innovation (CIGI), *Security Sector Monitor: Afghanistan*, no. 1 (Waterloo, Ontario: CIGI, July 2009).

[7] Michael Bhatia and Mark Sedra, *Afghanistan, Arms and Conflict: Armed Groups, Disarmament and Security in a Post-war Society* (London: Routledge, 2008).

[8] David Petraeus, "Battling for Iraq," *The Washington Post*, September 26, 2004, B7.

[9] Nat J. Colletta and Robert Muggah, "Rethinking Post-war Security Promotion," *Journal of Security Sector Management* 7, no. 1 (February 2009), 1–25.

Chapter 15

Monopoly, Legitimacy, Force: DDR–SSR Liberia

By Josef Teboho Ansorge and Nana Akua Antwi-Ansorge

The peace process interprets the conflicts from their understanding. They are not interpreting the conflict from the grassroots, from the actual happening. . . . They have come and collected those same people who were bosses over us and refused to go to the grassroots. Most of the guys you see who got the scholarships, DDRR scholarships, some of them did not even shoot gun.

—Joshua Milton Blahyi (aka General Butt Naked)

Introduction

Security matters a great deal, especially to the most vulnerable members of a society. Yet the measures or processes that can most effectively achieve security are valid points of contention. The Disarmament, Demobilization, and Reintegration (DDR) and Security Sector Reform (SSR) programs in Liberia pose rich cases for the delineation of lessons learned as well as the identification of curious contradictions and potential paradoxes in the way these kinds of large-scale, postconflict reconstruction initiatives are designed, implemented, and measured. This chapter is a candid, down-range assessment by two practitioner-scholars who were closely involved with different aspects of the programs. While the DDR–SSR efforts in Liberia could be regarded as a success simply because they have persisted and there has not been a renewed outbreak of violence, at this stage it is safe to surmise that they have consolidated peace and security as well as contributed to the reconstruction of that country. This chapter describes the programs, highlights best practices, and identifies a number of areas for improvement, as well as important lessons and observations relevant to similar efforts in other countries.

A foremost lesson to be learned from Liberia is the danger inherent in placing emphasis on product at the expense of process. Attaching overbearing importance to outputs and tangible metrics—combatants demobilized, ex-combatants educated, applicants vetted, and recruits trained—may miss opportunities to strengthen long-term desired outcomes such as the improved capacity and legitimacy of the Liberian state. A second lesson is to emphasize that these kinds of reconstruction interventions need to be understood within the context of the countries they occur in. This means that politics, culture, and, crucially, the history of the country must be considered when constructing, executing, and evaluating such programs. Previous U.S. intervention and assistance were deeply ingrained in Liberia's political and military institutions, laws, and cultures. Finally, it is important to recall that for state rule to be effective and deliver basic human security to its citizenry it needs to be legitimate in the eyes of its population. A monopoly on military force is necessary but not sufficient for achieving such lasting gains in state-building. DDR–SSR programs should therefore be used as opportunities to construct sustainable legitimate processes and avenues through which citizens can interact with and build trust in their *own* governments.

Liberia—Historical Background

The Republic of Liberia is situated on the West African coast. The territory is 43,000 square miles and is bordered by Guinea, Côte d'Ivoire, and Sierra Leone. According to 2009 estimates, it has a population just shy of 4 million. Founded in 1847 by remitted and "repatriated" African-American slaves, the history of the country has been marred by corruption as well as cyclical and endemic conflict. The climate is tropical; the rainy season takes place during the summer and features frequent heavy showers. Liberia's main national resources are rubber, iron ore, timber, and diamonds, with oil on the horizon. The country is divided into 15 counties and has three main language groups and 19 major ethnic categories.

Those who have traveled and worked in Liberia report a terrain difficult to navigate both geographically and politically. Most roads are not passable during the rainy season, so large swathes of territory can only be reached from the capital by helicopter. While this presents obvious operational difficulties to any actor attempting to deploy and execute a program in the Liberian interior, it is also a symptom of the inability of the state to effectively project power, register its population, or levy taxes. This state weakness has, in turn, historically led military organizations and armed groups to pay themselves by plundering the countryside, inherently undermining the public's perception of the legitimacy of the state's use of force. The core operational concern of the road network and conditions is thus also an indication of the prevailing political and military structural circumstances that led to an intervention in the first place: weak state institutions with infrastructure and capital concentrated in Monrovia, having weak connections to the interior. This was part of the broader geographic and political background of the most recent and far-reaching DDR–SSR programs.

Arriving in the summer of 2005, we were not sufficiently aware of how we—along with other State Department contractors, UN officials, and the whole plethora of postconflict and stabilization actors—were part of a long chain of foreign intervention in Liberia. Indeed, the very construction of the airport where we touched down, as well as the genesis of the country, could be traced to U.S. involvement. An important insight lay in all of this: *Throughout the history of Liberia, previous attempts at a monopoly on the legitimate use of force in the given territory had always occurred through the support of foreign power or capital.* In this way, intervention was not the exception but already the case. It was part and parcel of the political system and situation, not simply a response to them. Overreliance on terms such as "reconstruction" and "reform" threaten to obscure the prevalence of previous projects and their role in shaping the political and military culture. The Liberian state's exercise of force in its territory amounts to a fascinating history featuring prominent U.S. involvement; to substantiate these points it is necessary to go on a short historical excursion.

Liberia was established and initially maintained with the assistance of the U.S. Navy. Liberia's original military organization was the colonial militia, formed in 1822. Its purpose was to defend the colonies from violent confrontations with indigenous Africans and Europeans, as well as to protect the interests of the settlers. Initially comprised of just 53 volunteers among the colonists, the militia was the origin of the Liberian army and remained the primary defensive institution of the state after it became independent in 1847. Due to the fact that Liberia was unable to maintain a large military organization, the U.S. Navy continued to provide support at the request of the Liberian government until 1915. It was around the same time that Washington, in response to what must be the first modern debt crisis of an African state, arranged for a temporary foreign oversight of the Liberian treasury and expenses.[1]

Following territorial disputes with both British and French colonial powers, the militia transformed into the Liberian Frontier Force (LFF) in 1908. To prevent further intervention and loss of territory, a 500-man force was created to establish effective control over the hinterland and its frontier. It was initially organized, trained, and commanded by a team of former British army officers and sergeants, who were expelled by the Liberian government a year later for meddling in politics. The force then came under the command of the settler elite, which staffed the enlisted ranks with indigenous inhabitants from the hinterland. The LFF became a notorious instrument of oppression against indigenous Liberians. In a familiar pattern, soldiers were not properly compensated or supplied by the government and paid themselves with what they could steal or extort. Liberian officials also used the LFF to forcibly recruit laborers to work on roads and government farms without pay, years later leading to a League of Nations investigation into accusations of slavery. In 1912 the Liberian government once again sought external assistance to reform its military. This time African-American officers from the U.S. Army were assigned to reorganize, train, and command the LFF from 1912 to 1922. While under U.S. command, the re-equipped LFF crushed the Kru revolt of 1915, thereby strengthening the state's grasp on its territory. With the advent of the Cold War, Liberia and the United States entered into formal defense pacts in 1942 and 1959, which involved Washington playing a larger role in the support of the military and being permitted to construct bases in Liberia. The LFF transformed into the Armed Forces of Liberia (AFL) in 1960, still under the command of the settler-elite. Recruitment and training in the new army was copied from the U.S. model. This even extended to the formal legal domain: a law in the Liberian military code of justice stated that for areas not covered by the code, the U.S. Code of Military Justice should be consulted. The composition of the AFL began to gradually change in the 1960s and 1970s, and by the 1980 coup the officer ranks were no longer the exclusive preserve of the settler-elite.

On April 12, 1980, the AFL directly intervened in Liberian politics when indigenous Liberian noncommissioned officers committed a coup led by Master Sergeant Samuel K. Doe, who turned 28 shortly after he assumed power. The coup replaced the settler-oligarchy with a military government. By 1984, it was estimated that about 300 of the nearly 500 officers of the AFL had been promoted from the enlisted ranks. Doe was self-promoted from master sergeant to general. Important civilian officials were also commissioned as officers during the military regime. From 1981 to 1985, Liberia received $402 million in aid from the U.S. Government, which was the highest per capita aid the United States gave at that time in sub-Saharan Africa. The official military component for that aid package was $15 million,[1] but the Doe government was notorious for mismanaging funds, making it difficult to figure how much money actually went to the AFL—a 1987 General Accounting Office audit revealed a misuse of U.S. aid funds, and Washington again arranged for financial experts to oversee Liberia's government spending. What is certain is that during Doe's reign the AFL received substantial external assistance in the form of training and supplies from U.S. military personnel. A Special Anti-Terrorist Unit was also established with assistance and training from Israeli security forces. The military government officially ended in 1984; however, it is widely accepted that Samuel Doe rigged elections in 1985 to remain president.

With the abrupt cessation of the Cold War, U.S. military assistance waned and the Doe government increasingly failed to project a monopoly on the legitimate use of force within the Liberian territory. By the time civil war broke out on December 24, 1989, the AFL had become Doe's personal army, disproportionately staffed and dominated by members of his ethnic group, the Krahn. The AFL was used to crush his opponents and oppress members of their ethnic groups, causing a loss of legitimacy for the projection of state force, leading to a loss on the monopoly of force itself and finally a gruesome civil war. In August 1990, Taylor's National Patriotic Front of Liberia (NPFL) and a breakaway faction called the Independent National Patriotic Front of Liberia (INPFL) were winning the upper hand against the AFL when the Economic Community of West African States Monitoring Group (ECOMOG) intervened on the side of the AFL to prevent the rebel factions from capturing Monrovia. However, ECOMOG was a peacekeeping force that had intervened without the consent of all the parties to the conflict and subsequently became embroiled as a faction. It failed to bring the warring factions to agreement and was accused of large-scale looting—Liberians sometimes say ECOMOG stands for Every Car Or Moving Object Gone. In September of 1990, the INPFL captured and publicly killed Doe and filmed him being tortured. After Doe's death, the AFL remained a central actor in the civil war and continued to serve as a staging ground for political and ethnic purges. When the first ceasefire agreement was signed in Bamako in November 1990, the AFL's scope of operations was restricted to Camp Schiefflin in the outskirts of Monrovia. As an institution, the AFL collapsed in the early 1990s, but it was not officially disbanded.

The civil war was characterized by a dizzying array of colorful local, regional, and international actors. At the local level there was an assortment of diverse rebel factions and state security forces sporting a multitude of acronyms and outfits. These included United Liberation Movement of Liberia for Democracy (ULIMO)—and the resulting Kromah (ULIMO–K) and Johnson (ULIMO–J) factions. Several peace accords were signed in the 1990s, giving government positions to each faction. However, fighting continued until August 1996. The first DDR program was attempted without success in 1996. More than 2,000 members of the AFL turned in their weapons in a mass disarmament at Camp Schiefflin barracks on December 31, 1996. However, only about 7,000 of the estimated 60,000 rebel fighters turned in their weapons. The factions were not reintegrated but were instead transformed into political groups, while the NPFL formed the National Patriotic Party (NPP). Upon winning the July 19, 1997, elections on the NPP ticket, Taylor drafted many former NPFL rebels into the AFL. He also organized private militias named the Anti-Terrorist Unit (ATU) and Special Security Services (SSS). The AFL and these private security forces were collectively known as "Government Forces" (GOL). Fighting began between the GOL and the reorganized former rebel groups in 1998, calling themselves Liberians United for Reconciliation and Democracy (LURD) and the Movement for Democracy in Liberia (MODEL). LURD, MODEL, and GOL engaged in several battles between 1999 and 2003 until Taylor relinquished power and went into exile in Nigeria.

None of these many state and nonstate armed groups survived the civil war with their reputation intact. In 2009, the Liberian Truth and Reconciliation Commission declared that:

> All factions to the Liberian conflict committed, and are responsible for the commission of egregious domestic law violations, and violations of international criminal law, international human rights law and international humanitarian law, including war crimes violations. . . . All factions engaged in the armed conflict, violated, degraded, abused and denigrated, committed sexual and gender based violence against women including rape, sexual slavery, forced marriages, and other dehumanizing forms of violations.[2]

The human toll of the 14-year civil war (1989–2003) is an estimated 270,000 dead, with at least 320,000 long-term internally displaced people and 75,000 refugees. Almost everybody in Liberia was affected by the war. A recent poll shows that 96 percent of respondents had some direct experience in the conflict and, of these, a shocking 90 percent were at one point or another displaced from their homes.[3] After the cessation of hostilities, complete generations of Liberians who spent their whole lives in or at war required demobilization, demilitarization, reintegration, and the establishment of holistic human security for peace to have a chance. Education opportunities needed to be provided to present young Liberians with prospects they were previously denied. Moreover, the national police (LNP) and the military (AFL) required radical reform, having suffered severe institutional damage and loss of legitimacy during the conflict.

DDR–SSR Liberia (2003–2010)

On August 18, 2003, not even a week after Charles Taylor resigned from the presidency following a condition set by the White House, the Comprehensive Peace Agreement (CPA) was signed by warring factions in Accra, Ghana. Through the signing of the CPA, Liberia emerged from its bloody civil war. It was now internationally associated with egregious human rights violations and the widespread use of child-soldiers, and was regarded as a major destabilizing force in the entire West African region. The civil war had pushed Liberia to the bottom of various health and development indexes. In 2009 it was ranked 169th out of 182 countries on the United Nations (UN) Development Programme (UNDP) Human Development Index. At 44.5 percent, the adult illiteracy rate is one of the highest in the world. Life expectancy at birth is 58 years. For 2000 to 2007, a staggering 83 percent of the population lived on less than U.S. $1.25 a day. Rates of education are low (combined gross enrollment is 57.6 percent, which means that close to half of Liberia's children and youth are out of school) and formal unemployment stands at a baffling 80 percent. The infrastructural legacy of the 14-year civil war is no central running water, telephone landline, or electricity grid. To this day, generators must be relied on for most electrical needs.[4]

The CPA was the core legal document for providing strong mandates for both the DDR and SSR programs. It required the signatory parties to establish "conditions for the initial stages of Disarmament, Demobilization and Reintegration activities" as well as to ensure "the prompt and efficient implementation of a national process of cantonment, disarmament, demobilization, rehabilitation and reintegration." The international community was called upon for the "provision of adequate financial and technical resources" to achieve these tasks. Demobilization of the rebel groups was designed to be final and lead to their disbanding: "LURD, MODEL, and all irregular forces of the GOL shall cease to exist as military forces, upon completion of disarmament." The United Nations Mission in Liberia (UNMIL) was established under chapter VII of the UN Charter and initially provided with 18,000 peacekeepers. Following the CPA, the United Nations passed a Security Council resolution on September 19, 2003 tasking UNMIL with the implementation of a comprehensive DDR program.

Due to the large amount of irregular troops, the number of fighters actually requiring the DDR process was unknown at the time. UNMIL would also take responsibility for the reform of the LNP. For the immediate future, the CPA mandated that the AFL "be confined to the barracks" and their "arms placed in armouries." In the long run, however:

> The Armed Forces of Liberia shall be restructured and will have a new command structure. The forces may be drawn from the ranks of the present GOL forces, the LURD, and the MODEL, as well as from civilians with appropriate background and experience. . . . The Parties also request that the United States of America play a lead role in organizing this restructuring program.[5]

Restructuring and vetting the AFL was thereby recognized as an integral part of facilitating security and contributing to stability, and the United States was once again identified as a key player in restructuring the AFL. Since 2003, the U.S. Government has spent around $2 billion on aid to Liberia and contributions towards UNMIL.[6]

It is of special significance to the issue of local ownership that the CPA mandated that the two main remaining rebel factions, the MODEL and the LURD, take places in the National Transitional Government of Liberia (NTGL) alongside members of the former Taylor regime. This caused the NTGL at times to be debilitated by infighting; subsequent indications have also surfaced of widespread corruption. Since the DDR–SSR process began with the Peacekeeping Operation, the host government representatives were at best transitional and not elected and at worst focused on personal short-term enrichment. By the time Ellen Johnson-Sirleaf was inaugurated on January 16, 2006, disarmament and demobilization of armed factions were completed, reintegration was ongoing, and the SSR process was well under way. One of the further key characteristics of DDR–SSR Liberia is that it mandated a split of responsibilities between two very different types of organizations, the United Nations and U.S. State Department contractors. This bifurcation was repeated when the State Department awarded a DDR–SSR contract that could have gone to one company to both DynCorp International and Pacific Architects and Engineers (PAE). DynCorp International was the State Department's implementation partner for the DDR of the regular AFL as well as the SSR of the new AFL.[7] PAE was tasked with providing further training and mentoring of the new AFL. Bearing in mind that DDR and SSR are ideally analyzed and planned in conjunction, in Liberia they were mainly treated as two separate endeavors. Hence, we will now turn to a more detailed discussion of the DDR processes before shifting to the specifics of SSR Liberia.

DDR

In 2003, 7 years after the failed demobilization of 1996, UN personnel were confronted by a complex logistical and political challenge. Tasked with the DDR of all fighting factions apart from the regular AFL, it was imperative that groups would disarm in separate locations and close to simultaneously. Yet due to the irregular nature of the fighting groups, no records existed indicating who was actually a combatant. The issue of identification was compounded by the widespread practice of fighters taking on different war names: memorable warlords included General Peanut-Butter, General Cobra, and General Mosquito.[8] Without being able to rely on rosters, the UN implemented a system in which arms would be submitted to qualify for the DDR process. Threshold amounts of bullets and qualifying weaponry were established: one combatant could be qualified through the submission of 150 rounds of ammunition or a rifle, two per light machine gun, four for an anti-aircraft gun, six for a Howitzer, and so on. This had the added advantage of incentivizing the physical disarmament of combatants, yet was especially vulnerable to misuse in an impoverished country awash with small arms.

Following a shaky start in December of 2003, which involved government soldiers and militias rioting at Camp Schiefflin, the rest of the DDR process was peaceful and successful; major disarmament and demobilization operations concluded in October 2004. Demobilization was conducted at specially designated sites spread throughout the country and timed to ensure that warring rebel factions would be giving up their weapons simultaneously or in quick succession. Due to the financial incentive and the promised educational opportunities, the DDR process was highly popular. Instead of having to coax individuals to demobilize, as in most other postconflict theaters, former rebels appeared to submit their weaponry gladly. The general attitude in the country was one of civil war fatigue. Taylor's departure and the arrival of the UN peacekeeping mission indicated a clear cessation of hostilities, which signaled to combatants that it was time to reorient themselves towards a peacetime existence. To be more specific, it was the combination of financial incentives and the nature of the political settlement which placed rebel factions in the government that led various leaders—"bossmen"—to encourage their troops—"boys"—to demobilize. It was not uncommon for bossmen to receive a percentage of their boys' demobilization benefits, further incentivizing the leadership to demobilize their forces.

Once the UN's disarmament and demobilization process was completed, the large number of processed combatants startled many observers. At 101,495 demobilized fighters, the figure was significantly larger than most had estimated. During the 2003 CPA talks with LURD and MODEL faction leaders, the number of combatants, including the AFL, had been put at approximately 38,000.[9] A look at the actual amounts of submitted weapons shows that fewer than 30,000 weapons were submitted, and the majority of DDR recipients qualified through the submission of ammunition.[10] Reviewing this data and considering the widespread references to DDR fraud encountered during vetting investigations for the new AFL, it appears the deception was committed on a massive scale.

Despite this, we argue that UN disarmament and demobilization need to be viewed as a success. Apart from disarming the factions at a crucial time, a whole host of positive unintended consequences can be attributed to the fact that not only combatants participated in the DDR process. First, it offered an immediate economic boost to Liberia and gave 100,000 people a concrete material stake in peace by providing them with stipends and offering educational opportunities. As a standard, U.S. $300, about 6 months of average salary, was being spent per demobilized fighter. At more than 100,000 demobilized individuals, this ~$30 million had a large impact on the crippled Liberian economy. Second, due to the inclusive nature of the DDR process, the stigma of being an ex-combatant was diluted from what it could have been. Third, the individual documentation produced through the DDR process provided a baseline which could be referred to during the recruiting and vetting of the new AFL. This last point was critical for conducting background checks in a country with no functioning records. Through recourse to the demobilization records, it became possible to verify whether an individual applicant had misinformed the background investigators about having demobilized. Table 1 shows demobilization totals.

Yet the real test of the DDR processes will take place in the long term, when reintegration becomes more important and it is increasingly apparent that there is a paucity of jobs for formerly violent youths, especially in the security sector. UN data shows that only 8 percent of ex-combatants currently enrolled in reintegration training programs experience an improvement in their socioeconomic situation compared to other categories of ex-combatants.[11] Furthermore, there was only a marginal difference between the socioeconomic situation of ex-combatants who had completed training and those who had only disarmed and demobilized.[12]

Table 1. Demobilization Numbers

Regular AFL	13,770
UN DDR	101,495
Women	22,370
Boys	8,523
Girls	2,440
Irregular Government Forces	60,900
LURD	28,400
MODEL	12,200
Total	134,833

Key: AFL = Armed Forces of Liberia; LURD = Liberians United for Reconciliation and Democracy; MODEL = Movement for Democracy in Liberia; UN DDR = United Nations Disarmament, Demobilization, and Reintegration

While civilians and fighters alike flocked to the UN DDR program, DynCorp International's efforts to demobilize government troops were met with minor resistance once it became apparent that the AFL's DDR would be total, retiring all forces. The Sirleaf and transitional governments remained committed to a wholly new AFL, thereby overcoming small-scale protests by individuals not wishing to be demobilized. It was possible to disarm the situation by emphasizing that nobody was de facto excluded from applying to the new AFL and therefore everybody could join as long as they met the criteria. Considering that the AFL DDR constituted the complete demobilization of a country's armed forces during peacetime, the process went smoothly. One of the main difficulties was logistical: ensuring that the correct funds for demobilization vouchers were at the right place at the right time. Establishing the correct size of the AFL was also difficult because the G-1 Section of the Ministry of Defense had suffered severe war damage. The Section had lost all its filing systems, including the 201 files of Military Personnel Record Jackets (MPRJ). Therefore, a large redocumentation exercise had to be launched. Personnel rosters were reconstituted through the assistance of the AFL leadership. Demobilization benefits were determined on a points system that took rank and duration of service into consideration. The minimal amount awarded to AFL soldiers was U.S. $540.

DynCorp International custom-built a demobilization site through which it processed 13,770 AFL soldiers; grievance committees were established with AFL officers and international observers which worked to establish identity in questionable cases. Individuals would be quizzed about their own biographical information as well as details of life in the AFL, such as the names of cooks at certain training camps. The demobilization and retirement process was completed smoothly by the end of 2005. During the subsequent recruitment and vetting process of the new AFL, threats were repeatedly made by former AFL soldiers demanding further recompense or opportunities. For instance, in 2006 the ex-soldiers claimed there would be "no Christmas" if their situation was not addressed. These threats were addressed by the Sirleaf government in a consistent and competent fashion—some were responded to and some were ignored. They lessened over time.

SSR

Guided by the CPA, an arrangement between the United States and the National Transitional Government of Liberia (NTGL) regarding SSR was undertaken on May 17, 2005. The arrangement specified that the parties would cooperate in the security sector reform of the AFL:

> [w]ith a view to establishing an effective, efficient and accountable military, which emphasizes democratic values and human rights, a non-partisan approach to duty and the avoidance of corrupt practices, and which also commands citizen respect and confidence and contributes towards maintaining and promoting respect for the rule of law, and peace and stability in Liberia.[13]

Under the same contract which determined the AFL's demobilization, DynCorp International was also selected as the implementation partner of the U.S. Department of State for recruiting, vetting, and training a new 2,000-strong AFL and 100-strong Ministry of Defense (MOD). A 2,000-strong AFL was agreed to by both the NTGL and the United States Government after extended discussions, based on an estimate of what size military the Liberian government could finance and sustain. This requirement was also unequivocally mandated by Liberian National Defense Law, which states that:

> The number of officers and enlisted men to be inducted each year for military training will be limited to the ability of the government to provide shelter, subsistence, uniform, arms and ammunition, and hospitalization.[14]

The creation of a civilian-controlled armed force in the Liberian theater of operations was no small task. It required a *de novo* reconstruction: complete from-scratch recruitment and training of the entire standing AFL. In regard to the composition of the new AFL, the SSR arrangement stipulated the following:

> Service in the reformed AFL shall be open to qualified citizens of Liberia. Applicants will be screened with respect to education, professional, medical and other fitness qualifications, including prior history with regard to human rights abuses. The AFL will reflect the national character of Liberia in terms of ethnicity, gender and religion.[15]

The gender balance requirements were later further specified at 20 percent women by the Sirleaf administration, which has yet to be achieved for the military. DynCorp International worked with the U.S. Embassy and the government of Liberia, in particular the Ministry of Defense, designing and implementing a complete recruiting and vetting process reflecting the requirements of the CPA and the SSR arrangement. During 2005, the Barclay Training Centre (BTC) was refurbished. It opened as the primary recruiting site for the new AFL on January 18, 2006, 2 days after Ellen Johnson-Sirleaf was inaugurated. Due to an unexpectedly large turnout for the first few weeks—the center had a capacity of 100 applicants a day but more than 500 arrived on the first day—a ticket system had to be implemented. One of the most sensitive and costly aspects of the process was the screening of applicants for human rights abuses and other unethical behavior not consistent with honorably serving Liberia. To achieve an AFL free of human rights abusers, tested investigative techniques were combined with international best practice to create a number of different vetting stages each applicant would have to pass through.[16] In this initial transitional phase, there was no AFL leadership apart from the Minister of Defense. U.S. drill instructors, under contract with DynCorp International, provided the training. As the training progressed, however, and classes began to graduate, some leadership positions were filled by experienced Liberians as well as regional transitional staff. It is worth noting that legal requirements for an AFL free of human rights abusers was also mandated by U.S. domestic law: "None of the funds made available by this act may be provided to any unit of the security forces of a foreign country if the Secretary of State has credible evidence that such unit has committed gross violations of human rights."[17]

Due to the expense and complexity of vetting operations—background investigation teams had to conduct neighborhood interviews to determine the character of individuals—they were the final hurdle an applicant would have to pass. The attrition rates shown in table 2 demonstrate how selective the process was: only 20 percent of the applicants were accepted for training.[18] What is of note is that great ethnic diversity was achieved without having to engage in any kind of affirmative action; the most qualified applicants to the AFL were inherently ethnically diverse. The question of educational requirements posed a more formidable problem. Due to the extensive civil war, formal education had all but collapsed in the country. Instead of having to rely on questionable transcripts, the SSR process created a custom-made aptitude exam which was used to measure educational equivalency. To ensure local ownership of the AFL, the final decision as to which applicants were eligible to enter AFL training was made on objective grounds by a Joint Personnel Board. Voting members of the board were a government representative, a representative of Liberian civil society, and a USG representative.

Table 2. SSR Attrition

Stage	Rate	Total
Pass Aptitude	59%	
Pass Physical Training	87%	51%
Pass Medical	80%	41%
Pass Vetting	59%	24%
Prepared for Class	83%	20%

A special characteristic of the training process was an emphasis on civics training. It was already recognized at the planning stage that the new AFL would require an entirely new organizational culture that respected civilian oversight and the rule of law. To provide an appropriate civics education, courses were custom-designed by local, regional, and international experts. The majority of the classroom instruction was conducted by qualified Liberians, including political figures who had in earlier decades been tortured by soldiers in the same barracks in which they were teaching ethics classes in 2006 and 2007. It is also important to note that due to the lack of educational opportunities, the new AFL recruits were highly motivated to actively participate in nonmilitary education.

Unfortunately, due to budget restraints, the civics component of the training program was cut in 2007.

Today, the U.S.-led recruitment, vetting, and training of the 2,000-strong AFL is complete, but the work of SSR remains. The goal of a sustainable and functioning security sector in Liberia has not yet been achieved. A fundamental problem, as ever, is the remuneration of soldiers and policemen. A private in the AFL makes a monthly salary of around $80. This is still more than the police make and the $1.25-a-day the majority of the population lives on, but not a lot of money to support a family in an economy subject to fluctuating food prices. With so little pay for policemen and soldiers, corruption becomes less an indication of poor character than of poverty. For the individuals in question, these aren't issues of morality, but of necessity and survival. What is delegitimized under these conditions is not the individual, but the system.

In 2010 the AFL has been the subject of alarming headlines in the Liberian press, such as "AFL Leaves Two Dead," "AFL Soldiers Storm New Kru Town Police Depot" (to secure the release of a brother of one of the soldiers), and "Defense Minister Appears Before House Today for Allegedly Mismanaging AFL." While the reliability of any postconflict press can be questioned, it is safe to say that these kinds of statements severely delegitimize the AFL and conjure up images of continuity with historic abuses in the eyes of the Liberian population. At the same time though, this order of statements also holds an important lesson for policymakers. It demonstrates the ease with which a new class of the AFL, the product of expensive SSR efforts, can be delegitimized once the international actors leave. What is far harder to delegitimize, however, would be a just and sustainable process. For us, having been a part of the DDR–SSR processes and having researched Liberia, this is the foremost lesson. Instead of focusing on the surface effects and immediate output of a DDR–SSR process—combatants demobilized and recruits trained—attention must be paid to the long-range political effects and emphasis placed on constructing a sustainable legitimate process from the first day of operations onwards. Ideally, this sustainable and legitimate process also enables the population to experience and engage with their own government as a capable and nonpredatory actor. Considering that the annual budget of the government of Liberia was around $100 million in the 7-year period during which the U.S. Government spent $2 billion on the country, well-resourced, jointly-run DDR–SSR processes are ideal avenues for the local population to encounter professional representatives of their own government as well as for the host government to foster a new culture of transparency and accountability.

Conclusion: Lessons Learned and Paradoxes of Intervention

DDR–SSR Liberia provides important lessons for similar programs of the future. A central lesson, when considering the peculiar history of Liberia, is that each case needs to be read in historical, political, and cultural context for specificity. In the case of Liberia, U.S. involvement actually played a pivotal role in the genesis and processes of host institutions. In this way, robust U.S. involvement legitimized, whereas it could well have delegitimized in other countries. Despite the historic evidence, it appears that in the imagination of the UN, DynCorp International, and other foreign political actors, Liberia was thought of as preintervention prior to their arrival. In fact, Liberia as an epistemological space and political territory was postintervention before the UN and DynCorp International ever arrived. The Liberian experience also reinforces the importance of the following factors.

Program Planning and Implementation Require Continuous Actors

The fact that civics training was scrapped points to two factors, since it was a key component of the initial planning phase and cost such a large amount of capital and resources to design and initially implement. The first is that the program leadership was sufficiently transient to realign its fundamental priorities. The second is that the training and political awareness of implementers were not adequate for grasping the importance of civics. This naturally leads to the second lesson.

Fewer Actors, More Accountability

The division of responsibilities, as it occurred between the United Nations and the United States, and between DynCorp International and PAE, is vulnerable to a lack of central planning and oversight and thereby also to a lack of accountability. In cases where such a diverse group of actors works on separate parts of a whole, we recommend the creation of a shared planning and monitoring group featuring prominent host government involvement.

No Appropriate Training or Formal Lessons Learned Mechanism

Unfortunately, there has not been a formal exercise or procedure to capture the experiences and lessons learned from SSR Liberia; the panoply of think tanks and international institutes publishing SSR Liberia lessons learned papers is no substitute for a good internal process. The lack of shared training of implementers also proved to be problematic at times. We recommend that training at institutions such as the United States Institute of Peace or the National Defense University should be attached as conditions to winning contracts. The same should go for requiring regular lessons learned reports and monitoring and evaluation processes.

DDR Is the Data Baseline for SSR

DDR should be understood as an opportunity to provide a data baseline for later SSR processes in countries with a paucity of reliable records. For this to succeed, biometric capacity and capability is a necessity. A key operational lesson learned is therefore to instate shared protocols early in processes with diverse actors.

Formal Conditions Should be Considered Requiring Host Government Involvement

Leaving a space for local ownership in program planning does not mean it will automatically occur; local political actors and stakeholders are not all always eager to be involved. If local participation is not forthcoming for the day-to-day implementation of a program, we recommend that conditions be attached that foster more extensive host nation involvement.

Living in a world of complexity that at times appears to manifest itself as a chain of unceasing contradictions, we now finish this chapter by proposing a number of especially fertile intellectual quandaries which could be of assistance to policymakers in planning and considering such interventions.

Intervention Is the Case, Not the Exception

This means that reconstruction may be attempted of a state that was never salient in the lives of most inhabitants, and was always sustained through external assistance. It is important to consider the historical development of a state before wholeheartedly buying into reconstruction discourses.

State-building Is Outsourced

This business practice goes hand-in-hand with a widespread ideological turn towards neoliberal statist approaches. It is useful to contrast the big government reconstruction initiatives undertaken after World War II in Japan and Germany, executed by states and committed to constructing powerful states,[19] with contemporary initiatives that are characterized by a multitude of private sector actors.

Human Security and Methodological Nationalism in One Approach

Interventions are framed in the universalist terms of human security but are always implemented in specific political contexts and state structures. This means that every general framework for DDR–SSR always needs to be adapted to local contexts.

Monopoly of the Legitimate Use of Force without Functional Bureaucracy or Rationalization

It is important to note that although Weber's definition of state capacity makes sense as a shorthand for representing DDR–SSR processes, none of his other usual markers of state power are present for most of the cases in which DDR–SSR would take place: sovereignty, territoriality, impersonal power, or efficient bureaucracy. In other words, DDR–SSR is not enough to reproduce the monopoly of force and to legitimize it. What is needed is an entire package of legal, political, and institutional reform.

In conclusion, it only remains to restate that security matters. Liberians deserve peace and stability as much as anybody, but how to achieve it remains a point of valid contention. It is a curious fact of DDR–SSR programs, however, that when they fail, the cause for failure is often sought in the way the program was designed. Silos weren't integrated enough, the database wasn't properly updated, the fingerprint scans weren't accurate, the program didn't sufficiently consider ex-combatants, the wives of deceased servicemen weren't adequately taken into account, etc. We always consider what was lacking and think that things would have worked out if the program had only addressed one or the other aspect. What this technical attitude potentially obscures is the deeply political nature of such interventions, and how there is a huge range of local political actors consciously shaping and influencing the programs.

This brings to mind the end of the movie *Green Zone*. In Paul Greengrass's 2010 adaptation of Rajiv Chandrasekaran's *Imperial Life in the Emerald City* (2006), Matt Damon plays Chief Warrant Officer Roy Miller. Much of the movie centers on Miller trying to get to an Iraqi general so that he can figure out why there was such bad intelligence on the weapons of mass destruction programs. In the climax, before he can fulfill the role Roy Miller wishes for him, the general is suddenly shot by Freddie, Miller's thitherto docile, marginal, helpful yet vulnerable Iraqi cab driver. When Matt Damon's exasperated character asks why he did this, Freddie says, "because what happens here is not up to you." In this instant the illegible interests of the host population appear to have outmaneuvered, disoriented, and overwhelmed Jason Bourne himself, the alter ego of the national security state. This is a poignant moment with wider possible interpretations. Whether we know it or not, we are always acting in the interests of a particular class or part of the population that has aligned its interests with the reconstruction programs. The ultimate outcome of a DDR–SSR program depends much more on local political dynamics than international technocratic processes.

Notes

[1] Amos Sawyer, *The Emergence of Autocracy in Liberia: Tragedy and Challenge* (San Francisco: Institute for Contemporary Studies, 1992), 181.

[2] Reed Kramer, "Liberia: A Casualty of the Cold War's End," *CSIS Africa Notes*, no. 174 (July 1995).

[3] Republic of Liberia Truth and Reconciliation Commission (TRC), "Consolidated Final Report" (Monrovia: TRC, 2009), 17.

[4] International Monetary Fund (IMF), "Liberia: Interim Poverty Reduction Strategy Paper" (Washington, DC: IMF, 2007), x; Neill Wright and Edna Savage, IDP (Internally Displaced Persons) Advisory Team and Vicky Tennant, PDES (Policy Development and Evaluation Service), "Real-Time Evaluation of UNHCR's IDP Operation in Liberia" (Geneva: United Nations High Commissioner for Refugees [UNHCR], 2007), 7; UNHCR, "Liberia: Regional Operations Profile–West Africa," available at <http://www.unhcr.org/cgi-bin/texis/vtx/page?page=49e484936#>; International Committe of the Red Cross (ICRC), "Liberia: Opinion Survey and in-Depth Research" (Geneva: ICRC, 2009), 1.

[5] Statistics compiled from United Nations Development Programme (UNDP), "Human Development Report" (New York: UNDP, 2009), 145; World Bank, "Liberia: Data and Statistics," World Bank, available at <http://web.worldbank.org/WBSITE/EXTERNAL/COUNTRIES/AFRICAEXT/LIBERIAEXTN/0,,menuPK:356220~pagePK:141132~piPK:141109~theSitePK:356194,00.html>.

[6] "Comprehensive Peace Agreement between the Government of Liberia and the Liberians United for Reconciliation and Democracy (LURD) and the Movement for Democracy in Liberia (MODEL) and Political Parties," (2003), Part Two, Article III, 2c; Part Three, Article VI, 1, 3, and 11; Part Four, Article VII, 1b; Part 8, Article XXI, 5.

[7] U.S. Department of State, "Liberia Background Notes," available at <http://www.state.gov/r/pa/ei/bgn/6618.htm>.

[8] For more on this, including detailed timelines, see Sean McFate, "Outsourcing the Making of Militaries: Dyncorp International as Sovereign Agent," *Review of African Political Economy* 35, no. 118 (2008).

[9] It would be of great interest to conduct a study of how rebel factions dealt with the problem of identification during the civil war. How did they verify and document the identity of individuals without modern bureaucratic machinery?

[10] Interview with DDRR Technical Coordinator, UNDP–Liberia, Monrovia, May 8, 2009.

[11] UNDDR, "Liberia Country Programme," United Nations Disarmament, Demobilization and Reintegration Center, available at <http://www.unddr.org/countryprogrammes.php?c=52#framework>.

[12] Similar findings exist for Sierra Leone: see Jeremy M. Weinstein and Macartan Humphreys, "Disentangling the Determinants of Successful Demobilization and Reintegration" (Washington, DC: Center for Global Development, 2005).

[13] UNDDR.

[14] "Arrangement between the Government of the United States of America and the National Transitional Government of Liberia Concerning Security Sector Reform in the Republic of Liberia," (2005), 1a.

[15] "Liberian Codes Revised: National Defense Law," Republic of Liberia, Vol. IV, 539, section 28.

[16] "Arrangement Concerning Security Sector Reform," Article 3a.

[17] For more on this see Sean McFate, "The Art and Aggravation of Vetting in Postconflict Environments," *Military Review* (July/August 2007).

[18] Public Law 107–115, Fiscal Year 2002, Foreign Operations Appropriations Bill, section 556.

[19] The number of accepted applicants should actually be lower due to a preadmittance literacy screen that was conducted. The statistics were not captured.

[20] See Francis Fukuyama, *State-Building: Governance and World Order in the 21st Century* (Ithaca, NY: Cornell University Press, 2004).

Appendix

DDR and SSR Based on UN Integrated DDR Standards

By Cornelis Steenken

Scope and Objectives

The United Nations (UN) Integrated Disarmament, Demobilization, and Reintegration Standards (IDDRS) of the UN Inter-Agency Working Group (IAWG) on Disarmament, Demobilization, and Reintegration (DDR) and Security Sector Reform (SSR), builds from shared principles to develop synergies between DDR and SSR and highlights potentially harmful contradictions in the design, implementation, and sequencing of different elements of DDR and SSR programs. Based on the lessons and best practices drawn from the experience of all the departments, agencies, funds, and programs involved, the IDDRS were developed to provide the UN system with a set of policies, guidelines, and procedures for the planning, implementation, and monitoring of DDR programs in a peacekeeping context. While the IDDRS were designed with peacekeeping contexts in mind, much of the guidance contained within these standards will also be applicable for nonpeacekeeping contexts.[1]

Background

In several texts and key documents, the UN has recognized that interlinkages exist between DDR and SSR.[2] This does not imply there is a linear relationship between these two different activities, since each activity has its distinct challenges. In the past there have even been cases in which DDR and SSR have contradicted each other. For this reason, it is essential to take into account the specific objectives, timelines, stakeholders and interests that affect these issues individually. Understanding the relationship between DDR and SSR, as well as drawing from lessons learned, can help identify synergies in policy and programming and provide ways of ensuring that short to medium-term activities associated with DDR are linked to broader efforts to support the development of an effective, well-managed and accountable security sector. Ignoring how DDR and SSR affect each other may result in missed opportunities or unintended consequences that undermine broader security and development goals.

While individual DDR and SSR activities can involve short-term goals, achieving broader SSR objectives requires a long-term perspective. In contrast, DDR timelines are projected to take place in a more short to medium-term period following the end of armed conflict, and the focus is narrowed on ex-combatants and their dependents. Relevant activities and actors are often more clearly defined and limited. But the distinctions between DDR and SSR are potentially less important than the convergences. Both sets of activities are preoccupied with enhancing the security of the state and its citizens. They advocate policies and programs that engage public and private security actors including the military and ex-combatants as well as groups responsible for their management and oversight. Decisions associated with DDR contribute to defining central elements of the size and composition of a country's security sector while the gains from carefully executed SSR programs can also generate positive consequences on DDR interventions. SSR may lead to downsizing and the consequent need for reintegration. DDR may also free resources for SSR. Most significantly, considering these issues together situates DDR within a developing security governance framework. If conducted sensitively, this can contribute to the legitimacy and sustainability of DDR programs by helping to ensure that decisions are based on a nationally-driven assessment of applicable capacities, objectives, and values.

Why Are DDR–SSR Dynamics Important?

DDR and SSR play an important role in postconflict efforts to prevent the resurgence of armed conflict and to create the conditions necessary for sustainable peace and longer term development.[3] They form part of a broader postconflict peace-building agenda that may include measures to address small arms and light weapons (SALW), mine action activities, or efforts to redress past crimes and promote reconciliation through transitional justice.[4] The security challenges that these measures seek to address are often the result of a state's loss of control over the legitimate use of force. DDR and SSR should therefore be understood as closely linked to processes of postconflict state-building that enhance the ability of the state to deliver security and reinforce the rule of law. The complex, interrelated nature of these challenges has been reflected by the development of whole-of-system (e.g. "one UN" or "whole-of-government") approaches to supporting states emerging from conflict. The increasing drive towards such integrated approaches reflects a clear need to bridge early areas of postconflict engagement with support to the consolidation of reconstruction and longer term development.

DDR/SSR Dynamics

- Disarmament—not just a short-term security measure of collecting weapons. It is an implicit part of a broader process of state regulation and control over the use of weapons.
- Demobilization—DDR decisions affect the future size, structure, and composition of the state security sector.
- Reintegration—Common goal of ensuring a well-managed transition of former combatants to civilian life, taking into account community needs.
- Successful DDR can free up resources for SSR activities that in turn may support the development of efficient, affordable security structures.
- A national vision of the security sector should provide the basis for decisions on force size and structure.
- SSR considerations—appropriate skill sets and past conduct should help determine criteria for the integration of ex-combatants in different parts of the formal/informal security sector.
- DDR and SSR offer complementary approaches that can link reintegration of ex-combatants to enhancing community security.
- Capacity-building for security management and oversight bodies provide a means to enhance the sustainability and legitimacy of DDR and SSR.

An important point of departure is the inherently political nature of DDR and SSR. *DDR and SSR processes will only be successful if they acknowledge the need to develop sufficient political will to drive and build synergies between them.* This reflects the sensitivity of issues that touch directly on internal power relations, sovereignty, and national security as well as the fact that decisions in both areas create "winners" and "losers." In order to avoid doing more harm than good, related policies and programs must be grounded in a close understanding of context-specific political, socio-economic and security factors. Understanding "what the market will bear" and ensuring that activities and how they are sequenced incorporate practical constraints are crucial considerations for assessments, program design, implementation, monitoring and evaluation.

The core objective of SSR is "the enhancement of effective and accountable security for the state and its peoples."[5] This underlines an emerging consensus that insists on the need to link effective and efficient provision of security to a framework of democratic governance and the rule of law.[6] If one legacy of conflict is mistrust between the state, security providers and citizens, supporting participative processes that enhance the oversight roles of actors such as parliament and civil society[7] can meet a common DDR/SSR goal of building trust in postconflict security governance institutions. Oversight mechanisms can provide necessary checks and balances to ensure that national decisions on DDR and SSR are appropriate, cost effective, and made in a transparent manner.

Challenges of Operationalizing the DDR–SSR Nexus

A number of DDR and SSR activities have been challenged for their lack of context-specificity and flexibility, leading to questions concerning their effectiveness when weighed against the major investments such activities entail.[8] The lack of coordination between bilateral and multilateral partners that support these activities is widely acknowledged as a contributing factor: stovepiped or contradictory approaches each present major obstacles to providing mutually reinforcing support to DDR and SSR. The UN's legitimacy, early presence on the ground, and scope of its activities points to an important coordinating role that can help to address challenges of coordination and coherence within the international community in these areas.

A lack of conceptual clarity on SSR has had negative consequences for the division of responsibilities, prioritization of tasks, and allocation of resources.[9] Understandings of the constituent activities within DDR are relatively well-established. On the other hand, while common definitions of SSR may be emerging at a policy level, these are often not reflected in programming. This situation is further complicated by the absence of clear indicators for success in both areas. Providing clarity on the scope of activities and linking these to a desired endstate provide an important starting point to better understanding the relationship between DDR and SSR.

Some of the dynamics between DDR and SSR are straightforward. Both sets of activities are preoccupied with enhancing security and stability and therefore sit within a broader security sector governance framework. They advocate policies and programs that engage public and private security actors including the military and ex-combatants as well as groups responsible for their management and oversight. Decisions associated with DDR contribute to defining central elements of the size and composition of a country's security sector. SSR may lead to the downsizing of security institutions and the consequent need for reintegration. Most significantly, considering these issues together can ensure that DDR programs reflect national capacities, objectives, and values as part of a broader vision for national security. Failing to consider these issues together may lead to the development of unsustainable and unaccountable security institutions that fail to address the security needs of the state and its citizens.

The issue of sequencing between DDR and SSR remains critical. Although there is a clear need to link the two processes, DDR programs often take place prior to SSR and too little attention is paid to the linkages between the two during the planning process. If SSR issues and perspectives are to be integrated at an early stage, assessments and their outputs must reflect a holistic SSR approach and not just partial elements that may be most applicable in terms of early deployment. Situational analysis of relevant political, economic, and security factors is essential in order to determine the type of SSR support that will best complement the DDR program as well as to identify local and regional implications of decisions that may be crafted at the national level. Moreover, specific elements of program design should be integrated within overall strategic objectives that reflect the endstate goals that DDR and SSR are seeking to achieve. Peace processes and agreements, transitional political arrangements, and elections all provide important entry points to ensure that DDR and SSR concerns are included on the national agenda and linked within a common framework.

There are several challenges to realizing synergies between DDR and SSR in practice. These include a lack of context-specificity, coordination and flexibility in DDR and SSR programming; weak or dysfunctional institutions; capacity gaps among national and international actors; and a lack of political will to support SSR. In order to avoid doing more harm than good, assessments, program design, implementation, monitoring and evaluation that address the nexus between DDR and SSR should therefore be grounded in a close understanding of context-specific political, socio-economic and security factors.

Dynamics to Consider Before and During Demobilization

Table 1 highlights synergies that may be realized between DDR and SSR activities prior to and during demobilization. An area of particular importance relates to the integration of ex-combatants into a reformed security sector. Communication and coordination between DDR and SSR stakeholders is a key theme in supporting the synergies identified in the table.

Table 1. DDR/SSR Considerations Prior and During Demobilization

Disarmament and longer term SSR	■ Consider disarmament as an entry-point for DDR/SSR coordination—define law enforcement support needed to support the disarmament process and communicate this to SSR-relevant authorities. ■ Support capacity-building to enhance national control over military/police/paramilitary armories and surplus stocks of weapons and ammunition.
Entry-criteria	■ Establish and apply clear and appropriate criteria for entry into the security forces based on an assessment of national security requirements to ensure that the security sector is capable of absorbing those ex-combatants who choose integration.
Rank Harmonization	■ Develop rank harmonization policies based on context-specific criteria for determining ranks, affirmative action for marginalized groups, and a clear formula for conversion from former armed groups to national armed forces. ■ Consider the potential consequences of rank harmonization on the defense budget as well as potential security risks created by perceived inequities.
Data collection and management	■ Identify and include SSR-relevant information requirements (for an indicative list see Operational Guide (OG) 6.10, Box 2) when designing a Management Information System (MIS) and establish mechanisms for sharing this information. ■ Include information collected in the MIS as a baseline for a future security sector census or vetting process.

Continued

Table 1 continued.

Vetting	■ Support vetting as part of a broader process of certification (including verification of age, education, relevant skills, criminal and human rights record). ■ Only conduct vetting if there is sufficient political will/national capacity to implement this process. ■ Define and apply minimum standards in relation to required skills and past conduct. ■ Vet all members of the security institution—not just ex-combatants—to avoid stigmatization and enhance the integrity of the security sector as a whole.
Support to ex-combatants integrating within the security sector	■ Provide psychosocial support and training/sensitization on behavior change for a successful transition to civilian life or into the security sector. ■ Engage in HIV/AIDS prevention at the outset of DDR to reduce new infections.
Balancing demobilization and security sector integration	■ Carefully consider incentives for demobilization and integration into the security sector to avoid the risk of unsustainable or disproportionate distribution of applicants between the two processes. ■ Develop a communications strategy to ensure that options are fully understood and avoid misperceptions.
Gender-responsive DDR and SSR	■ Ensure that women are informed of their options under the DDR and SSR processes and that integration opportunities are realistic. ■ Make adequate facilities available for women during disarmament and demobilization and provide specialized reinsertion kits and appropriate reintegration options. ■ Take into account the specific challenges faced by female ex-combatants (stigma, non-conventional skill sets, trauma) when considering their integration into the security sector. ■ IDDRS 5.60 for information on HIV/AIDS and DDR, and IDDRS 5.10 for information on Women, Gender and DDR.

Dynamics to Consider Before and During Reintegration and Repatriation

Table 2 highlights common DDR/SSR concerns before and during the reintegration phase. Security sector capacities that support the reintegration of ex-combatants will only be focused on this priority if support to the DDR process is factored into planning, training and resource allocation. Communication with SSR stakeholders is therefore of key importance.

Table 2. Potential DDR/SSR Synergies Prior to and During Reintegration

Planning and preparation in receiving communities	The DDR program should plan and budget for the following community initiatives: ■ *Reintegration planning:* ensure that reintegration planning is coordinated with the military, police, and other community level security providers. ■ *Community security:* Consider opportunities for confidence-building through joint community safety initiatives (e.g. weapons collection, community policing). ■ *Violence reduction:* support work with men and boys in violence reduction initiatives, including GBV.
Common DDR/SSR information requirements	■ Tracking returning ex-combatants: Assess the security dynamics of returning ex-combatants to facilitate reinsertion payments, highlight areas where employment opportunities exist, identify potential security risks and prioritize appropriate security sector responses. ■ Public information and dialogue: promote dialogue between communities and security providers to develop local security plans that address reintegration.
Sector-specific considerations	■ DDR and the private security sector: include the relationship between reintegration and the private security sector in evaluations of reintegration into rural and urban settings. Share this analysis with SSR counterparts. ■ DDR and border management: Assess flows of ex-combatants and weapons across borders in order to coordinate/prioritize responses with border security authorities. ■ DDR and SALW: include coordination with SALW initiatives in DDR/SSR planning; SALW availability and control measures should form part of joint assessments and inform subsequent program design.

Programming Considerations

Integrating relevant SSR concerns into DDR assessments, program design, monitoring, and evaluation is a way to build synergies into DDR and SSR programming (see table 3).[10]

Table 3.

SSR-sensitive assessments	■ Include the need to identify potential DDR/SSR synergies in terms of references (ToRs). ■ Disseminate draft ToRs among DDR and SSR focal points. ■ Include multisectoral SSR experts in assessment teams. For general assessments, expertise in the political and integrated nature of an SSR process may be more important than sector-specific experience. ■ Ensure host state/regional expertise as well as local language skills are available.
Program design	■ Clarify context-specific DDR/SSR dynamics relevant for program development and costing (see OG Box 6.10.3). ■ Map DDR/SSR capacities across UN, international community and national actors. ■ Seek to integrate different stakeholders within the DDR implementation plan.
Monitoring and evaluation	■ Collect and monitor baseline data on political and security dynamics to help planners adjust programming to changing conditions. ■ Review DDR and SSR programs jointly to ensure they are planned and implemented in a mutually supportive manner. Focus on actual versus intended impact to adjust programming objectives and priorities. ■ Conduct mid-term reviews to assess effectiveness and make necessary changes to programs.

National Ownership

Strong emphasis on national ownership is critical to addressing challenges of legitimacy and sustainability that are common to DDR and SSR and must be designed to fit the circumstances of each particular country.

However, the international community is routinely criticized for failing to apply these key principles in practice. SSR in particular is viewed by some as a vehicle for imposing externally driven objectives and approaches. In part, this reflects the particular challenges of postconflict environments, including weak or illegitimate institutions, shortage of capacity among national actors, a lack of political will, and the marginalization of civil society. There is a need to recognize these context-specific sensitivities and ensure that approaches are built around the contributions of a broad cross-section of national stakeholders. Prioritizing the strengthening of national capacities, so they are capable of developing effective, legitimate, and sustainable security institutions, is essential to meeting common DDR/SSR goals. Box 2 identifies different ways to enhance national ownership of DDR/SSR processes by promoting broad participation in decisionmaking and building national capacity in these areas.[11]

Box 2: Promoting National Ownership

- Support national dialogue processes that seek to identify security needs and values in order to foster common understandings of DDR/SSR challenges. Include transitional or elected authorities, security sector institutions, management and oversight bodies as well as civil society.
- Agree on a roadmap between national and international stakeholders for implementation of identified priorities.
- Jointly establish capacity-development strategies with national authorities (see IDDRS 3.30 on National Institutions for DDR) that support both DDR and SSR objectives.
- Prioritize the development of cross-cutting skills that will also be useful in future peacebuilding and development programs (human resources, financial management, building gender capacity, etc.).
- Identify and empower national reform "champions" that support reform principles. Such figures should be identified during the needs assessment phase.
- Support national level management and oversight bodies to lead and harmonize DDR and SSR activities.

(continued)

Box 2: Promoting National Ownership (continued)

- Consider twinning international experts with national counterparts in order to support skills transfer and thus support reform efforts which are driven from the inside.
- Support national DDR/SSR committees as a mechanism to coordinate implementation and evaluation of programs.

Supporting Coherent Approaches: Coordination

While DDR is characterized by a strong UN role, SSR activities (and funding) are frequently supported by a number of bilateral donors through specific arrangements with national authorities. This necessitates the establishment of effective coordination mechanisms. While it is recognized that national actors should play a key role in coordination, in cases where the political will or capacity to do this is lacking, Box 3 outlines some key considerations for ensuring international support to nationally-driven DDR and SSR processes in the areas of coordination, financial sustainability, and capacity-building.

Box 3: Key Considerations for Supporting Coherent Approaches

- Have opportunities been taken to engage with different bodies of the security sector on how they can support the DDR process?
- Are there national/international coordination mechanisms in place? Could the national commission on DDR fulfill this role by inviting a wider range of stakeholders to selected meetings? Beyond "core" DDR and SSR stakeholders, the membership of such a body should include representatives from health (including national HIV/AIDS Control Programs and strategies), gender, youth and child protection as well as the humanitarian community.
- Are the financial resource implications of DDR for the security sector considered, and vice versa?

(continued)

Box 3: Key Considerations for Supporting Coherent Approaches (continued)

- Are both DDR and SSR programs realistic and compatible with national budgets?
- Are DDR/SSR concerns reflected in the ToRs of UN personnel and in the profiles for different posts and in training considerations?
- Is cross-participation in DDR or SSR training encouraged in order to support knowledge transfer and confidence building?

Summary of Key Guidance on the Nexus Between DDR and SSR

- In order to build synergies between DDR and SSR, coherence across DDR and SSR activities is essential. Important issues include: rank harmonization; financial incentive packages for reintegration vs. integration; communication strategies designed to facilitate the transition from combatant to security provider, etc.
- Resource planning must seek to identify gaps, increase coherence and mitigate competition between DDR and SSR, and ensure sustainability in relation to national capacities. Financial resource implications of DDR for the security sector should be considered, and DDR and SSR programs should be realistic and compatible with national budgets.
- Efforts should be made to sensitize staff on the DDR/SSR nexus through training and sensitization activities. The need for personnel to link DDR and SSR concerns should be included in the ToRs of relevant personnel and cross-participation in DDR or SSR training encouraged to foster knowledge transfer and build relationships.

Box 4: Key Guidance on the Nexus between DDR & SSR

- DDR decisions should reflect and reinforce a nationally-driven vision of the roles, objectives and values of security institutions. Similarly, DDR considerations should be introduced into SSR decisionmaking to enable the security institutions to provide appropriate support to the DDR process.
- DDR affects SSR in the state concerned and given sensitivity of both processes, political will is essential. As they share objective to enhance objective of state, the ultimate goal is to create conditions necessary for sustainable peace. There are problems ranging from timing and sequencing, lack of resources and clarity to lack of coordination by national, bilateral and multilateral actors. Planning for DDR should take into account the relationship between DDR and its consequences for the security sector and its governance.
- Lastly, the IDDRS Module does not provide a blueprint because each DDR and SSR operation is different: hence they must be context specific. The module instead provides definitive guidance on these sets of processes to create synergies, not to undermine or create contradiction as it has happened in the past.
- Our knowledge and lessons learned are being accumulated, but it is clear that they affect one another and we are hoping to draw lessons from the past and apply them to future operations.

Notes

[1] UN Inter-Agency Working Group (IAWG) on Disarmament, Demobilization, and Reintegration (DDR) and Security Sector Reform (SSR), 1.10, Integrated Disarmament, Demobilization, and Reintegration Standards, August 1, 2006.

[2] See Statement by the President of the Security Council at the 5632[d] meeting of the Security Council, held on February 20, 2007, S/PRST/2007/3, February 21, 2007; Statement by the President of the Security Council, "The maintenance of international peace and security: the role of the Security Council in humanitarian crises: challenges, lessons learned and the way ahead," S/PRST/2005/30, July 12, 2005; United Nations Report of the Secretary-General, "Securing peace and development: the role of the United Nations in supporting security sector reform," S/2008/39, January 23, 2008; and United Nations General Assembly, "Report of the Special Committee on Peacekeeping Operations and its Working Group: 2008 substantive session," A/62/19, March 10–April 4, and July 3, 2008.

[3] All states periodically review and reform their security sectors. While recognizing that SSR is not only a postconflict challenge, this module focuses on these contexts as being most relevant to DDR and SSR concerns.

[4] For further information on the linkages between DDR and Transitional Justice, see IDDRS Module 6.20 on Transitional Justice and DDR, available at <www.unddr.org>.

[5] Report of the Secretary-General, *Securing Peace and Development*, paragraph 17.

[6] Organisation for Economic Co-operation and Development, "Security System Reform and Governance; A DAC Reference Document," 2005; Council of the European Union, "EU Concept for ESDP support to Security Sector Reform (SSR)," Council document 12566/4/05, October 13, 2005; Commission of the European Communities, "A Concept for European Community Support for Security Sector Reform," SEC (2006) 658, May 24, 2006; ECOWAS, "ECOWAS Conflict Prevention Framework (ECPF)," enacted by Regulation MSC/REG.1/01/08 of the Mediation and Security Council of ECOWAS, January 16, 2008; and UN Security Council, "Annex to the letter dated 20 November 2007 from the Permanent Representatives of Slovakia and South Africa to the United Nations addressed to the Secretary-General. Statement of the Co-Chairs of the International Workshop on Enhancing United Nations Support for Security Sector Reform in Africa: Towards an African Perspective," S/2007/687, November 29, 2007.

[7] For practical guidance on supporting parliamentary and civil society oversight of the security sector, see H. Born, P. Fluri, and A. Johnsson, eds., "Parliamentary Oversight of the Security Sector," DCAF/Inter-Parliamentary Union, 2003; E. Cole, K. Eppert, and K. Kinzelback, eds., "Public Oversight of the Security Sector," DCAF/UNDP, 2008.

[8] Robert Muggah, ed., "Security and Post-Conflict Reconstruction: Dealing with Fighters in the Aftermath of War," Routledge, 2009.

[9] H. Hänggi and V. Scherrer, eds., "Security Sector Reform and UN Integrated Missions: Experience from Burundi, the Democratic Republic of Congo, Haiti, and Kosovo," Münster: Lit Verlag, 2008.

[10] For more detailed information, see IDDRS 3.20 on DDR Programme Design and IDDRS 3.50 on Monitoring and Evaluation of DDR Programmes, available at <www.unddr.org>.

[11] See IDDRS 3.30 on National Institutions for DDR, available at <www.unddr.org>.

About the Contributors

Melanne A. Civic is the Special Advisor to the Center for Complex Operations (CCO), Institute for National Strategic Studies, at the National Defense University (NDU), seconded from the Secretary of State's Office of the Coordinator for Reconstruction and Stabilization (S/CRS). She is an international lawyer with a focus on rule of law and transitional justice. At CCO, she advises on issues related to civilian-military coordination in peace-building and stability operations and is the developmental editor of *PRISM*. She has trained military and civilian stabilization personnel at numerous military graduate schools and the Foreign Service Institute. At S/CRS, among other duties, she edited *DDR Lessons Learned 2006*. She has served in the State Department's Office of the Legal Advisor and policy bureaus, and as an intelligence officer. She was a Fellow to the Judiciary Committee to Senator Ted Kennedy and to the House Science Committee. Ms. Civic has worked for United Nations (UN) agencies, the World Bank, and international nongovernmental organizations (NGOs). She is the author of numerous law review and other scholarly articles and was an editor of the American Bar Association's *Year in Review*. She is the founder and cochair of the American Society of International Law's Transitional Justice and Rule of Law Interest Group and a steering committee member of the American Bar Association's Women in International Law and Women in International Security. Ms. Civic was a Presidential Management Fellow and holds a postgraduate LL.M. in international and comparative law from Georgetown University School of Law, where she earned her Juris Doctorate (J.D.). She studied at the René Cassin International Institute of Human Rights and earned her Bachelor's degree from Vassar College.

Michael Miklaucic is the Director of Research in CCO at NDU and the editor of *PRISM*. Prior to this assignment, he served in various positions at the U.S. Agency for International Development (USAID) and Department of State, including service on the Civilian Response Corps's interagency task force as the Senior Program Officer in the USAID Office of Democracy and Governance, and as the Deputy for War Crimes Issues at the Department of State. He has worked extensively on interagency collaboration, specifically in the rule of law and governance areas, and has published numerous articles related to transitional justice, democratization, civilian-military collaboration, and contemporary challenges to the state. Mr. Miklaucic received his formal education at the University of

California, London School of Economics, and the Paul H. Nitze School of Advanced International Studies (SAIS) at the Johns Hopkins University.

Josef Teboho Ansorge is completing his Ph.D. on the role of information technology in international relations at Jesus College, University of Cambridge, for which he is a recipient of a Cambridge Trusts scholarship. His research focuses on postconflict reconstruction, philosophy of technology, north-south dynamics, academic-military relations, and 19th- and 20th-century German political thought. He was recently the editor-in-chief of the *Cambridge Review of International Affairs* (2008–2010). He previously worked for a U.S. Department of State contractor in Liberia (2005–2007), where he was a human rights monitor and a member of the initial leadership team that designed and implemented the Security Sector Reform (SSR) of the Armed Forces of Liberia (AFL). Mr. Ansorge has experience in recruiting and vetting operations. He has given lectures at the University of Cambridge, London School of Economics and Political Science, and the United Kingdom's Joint Services Command and Staff College at Shrivenham, and he trained the first class of the AFL in international relations. Mr. Ansorge holds a Bachelor's degree in International Relations from the University of Aberystwyth and a Master's degree in International Relations from the University of Cambridge.

Nana Akua Antwi-Ansorge is a doctoral candidate at St. Antony's College, Oxford University, researching the Liberian civil war. She is an international lawyer with broad experience in postconflict reconstruction policy design and implementation. She was a member of the core team of human rights monitors and a coordinator in the U.S.-Liberia SSR program in Liberia. Ms. Ansorge previously investigated and decided human rights and administrative justice matters at the Ghana Commission on Human Rights and Administrative Justice, and managed criminal and immigration cases in the United Kingdom as a legal consultant. Ms. Ansorge is the recipient of Oxford University's 2009 Martin Lynn Scholarship for research in Africa, a St. Antony's College 2010 Warden's Scholarship, and a 2010 Wingate Scholarship for research. She received her Master's degree in African Studies from Oxford University, LL.M. from American University, and LL.B. from the London School of Economics and Political Science.

Judith Asuni is the Jennings Randolph Senior Fellow at the United States Institute of Peace (USIP). Dr. Asuni is an expert on conflict and development in the Niger Delta and is investigating the root causes of conflict there, particularly from the point of view of members of armed groups who are both victims of marginalization and perpetrators of violence. Dr. Asuni examines how similar projects have been managed elsewhere in Africa, particularly in resource-rich countries. Dr. Asuni is the founder and executive director of Academic Associates PeaceWorks, an NGO based in Warri, Delta State, Nigeria. She has extensive experience in conflict analysis, management, peace education, and development and has worked closely with varied stakeholders, including Nigerian federal and state governments, international oil companies, donors, community representatives, and members of the armed groups of the Niger Delta. In 2008, while a visiting scholar at SAIS, she founded the Niger Delta Working Group. Dr. Asuni holds a Ph.D. in Sociology from the University of Birmingham, United Kingdom, a Master's degree from the University of Ibadan, Nigeria, and a Bachelor's degree from Cornell University.

Alan Bryden is Deputy Head of the Division of Research at the Geneva Centre for the Democratic Control of Armed Forces (DCAF). He is responsible for conceptualizing, managing, and implementing programs. Dr. Bryden is widely published on issues relating to security sector governance in Africa and linkages between SSR and postconflict peace-building. Dr. Bryden executed a multistakeholder project on disarmament, demobilization, and reintegration (DDR) and SSR, which resulted in a new module and operational guide input for the UN Integrated Standards for DDR. He also works with African experts on policy research relating to security sector governance in Africa. Prior to joining DCAF, Dr. Bryden was a civil servant with the United Kingdom Ministry of Defense. He has held various policy and project management posts, including as a secondee to the United Kingdom Department for International Development, working as a project manager at the Geneva International Centre for Humanitarian Demining. Dr. Bryden earned his Ph.D. from the University of Bradford and holds degrees in Medieval History and International Relations. He is a graduate of the International Training Course at the Geneva Centre for Security Policy and is a member of the Advisory Board for the Geneva Peacebuilding Platform.

Véronique Dudouet works as the Senior Researcher at Berghof Conflict Research in Berlin, Germany. She coordinates a research program on nonstate armed groups in postwar security transition in collaboration with local research partners in South Africa, Sudan, Burundi, Colombia, El Salvador, Aceh (Indonesia), Nepal, Northern Ireland, and Kosovo. Dr.

Dudouet holds a Ph.D. and a Master's degree from Bradford University, as well as a postgraduate research diploma in International Relations and Security from the Institut d'Etudes Politiques, Toulouse, France.

Jennifer M. Hazen is a Research Fellow at the LBJ School of Public Affairs at the University of Texas at Austin. She is also a Research Fellow at the Center on Conflict, Development and Peacebuilding at The Graduate Institute, Geneva. Prior to joining the LBJ School in September 2010, she served as a Senior Researcher at the Small Arms Survey, Geneva. Previously, she worked with the United Nations Mission in Sierra Leone, International Crisis Group, and the U.S. Department of State and taught at Georgetown University and the University for Peace. Dr. Hazen's research interests include intrastate conflict, conflict dynamics, armed groups, peace processes, and postconflict reconstruction. She has conducted field research in numerous countries, and her research has been published in *International Peacekeeping* and *Contemporary Security Policy* and with the Small Arms Survey and International Crisis Group, among others. Dr. Hazen earned her Ph.D. in International Relations from Georgetown University.

Michelle Hughes serves as the Senior Rule of Law Advisor to Deputy Commander–Police, North Atlantic Treaty Organization (NATO) Training Mission–Afghanistan. She is on a leave of absence from U.S. Joint Forces Command, where she has been the Policy and Program Advisor for Rule of Law and SSR. Ms. Hughes was formerly the Principal Director, Rule of Law, for General Dynamics Information Technology. She participated in SSR-related activities in Ghana, Colombia, Kenya, Djibouti, Yemen, Ethiopia, Liberia, and Albania and mentored the U.S. interagency SSR assessment for Joint Task Force–435 (Afghanistan). She has worked extensively throughout the Department of Defense (DOD) and in collaboration with leading U.S. Government departments and agencies, including USAID, S/CRS, and the Department of Justice. Ms. Hughes was a commissioned second lieutenant in the U.S. Army, where she served as a military intelligence officer and was one of the first women to serve in the 82^{d} Airborne Division, the only female officer assigned to the U.S. Army Parachute Team (The Golden Knights), and the first woman to command an electronic warfare company in an armored division. She was honored by President Ronald Reagan as one of the "Top 10 Working Women of 1985." Ms. Hughes graduated at the top of her class from Regent University School of Law and earned her Bachelor's degree from the University of Florida.

Ambassador Jacques Paul Klein served as Special Representative of the Secretary-General and Coordinator of UN Operations in Liberia with the rank of Under-Secretary-General, selected by Secretary-General Kofi Annan in 2003. Previously, with the UN, Ambassador Klein served as Special Representative of the Secretary-General and Coordinator of UN Operations in Bosnia and Herzegovina and as Transitional Administrator for Eastern Slavonia, Baranja, and Western Sirmium. Ambassador Klein was a career member of the Senior Foreign Service and served multiple tours in the European region. He was seconded to DOD in 1982 to serve as Senior Advisor for International Affairs to the Secretary of the Air Force, with the rank of Deputy Assistant Secretary. When he returned to the Department of State, he served as the Director of the Office of Strategic Technology Matters in the Bureau of Politico-Military Affairs. In 1989, he was again seconded to DOD to serve as Assistant Deputy Under Secretary of the Air Force for International Affairs. Ambassador Klein also served as political advisor to the commander of U.S. European Command in Stuttgart, Germany. He has done postgraduate work in International Politics at The Catholic University of America and holds graduate and undergraduate degrees in History from Roosevelt University in Chicago. In recognition of his service to peace, he has been awarded an honorary Doctor of Laws degree by Elmhurst College.

Mark Knight is the Research and Analysis Officer with the PeaceNexus Foundation. He is responsible for the collection and application of best practices in peace-building. Mr. Knight has experience in undertaking research, analysis, and program evaluation and has implemented complex programs in conflict and postconflict environments. His geographic experience includes Sierra Leone, Indonesia, Afghanistan, Nepal, Albania, Nigeria, and the Philippines. Initially commissioned in the British army, Mr. Knight has subsequently worked for the UN, International Organization for Migration, Centre for Humanitarian Dialogue, the World Bank, the Organisation for Security and Co-operation in Europe (OSCE), and Department for International Development, as well as undertaking research for King's College London, Berghof Conflict Research, The Asia Foundation, and International Security Sector Advisory Team. Mr. Knight's experiences include implementing DDR programs in Sierra Leone and advising on peace processes in Nepal and the Philippines. Following his military service, Mr. Knight studied for a Bachelor's degree in International Disaster Engineering and Management at Coventry University and completed a Master's degree in Postwar Recovery and Development at the University of York.

G. Eugene Martin is an advisor at USIP. Previously, he was a Foreign Service Officer working on East Asia, with a focus on China and Southeast Asia. He served 11 years in Greater China: Taipei, Hong Kong, Guangzhou, Rangoon, and as Deputy Chief of Mission in Beijing and Manila. During postings in the Department of State, he was the Special Assistant to the Deputy Secretary, Special Assistant to the Assistant Secretary for East Asian Affairs, Deputy Director of the China desk, and a Congressional Fellow. Since leaving foreign service, Mr. Martin has taught Northeast and Southeast Asian area studies at the Foreign Service Institute and a course on China for Syracuse University graduate students and has directed the Washington office of the Hopkins-Nanjing Center for Chinese and American Studies. For 4 years, Mr. Martin directed the USIP Philippine Facilitation Project, which sought to advance the peace process between the Philippine government and Moro Islamic Liberation Front. Mr. Martin studied Mandarin and Cantonese. Raised in India, Mr. Martin graduated from Kalamazoo College and completed his graduate studies at the Maxwell School of Syracuse University.

General James N. Mattis, USMC, is Commander of U.S. Central Command. Previously, he commanded the United States Joint Forces Command and concurrently served as NATO's Supreme Allied Commander Transformation, from November 2007 to September 2009. Previously, General Mattis commanded the Marine Corps Combat Development Command and served as the Deputy Commandant for Combat Development. He commanded the 1st Marine Division during the initial attack and subsequent stability operations in Iraq during Operation *Iraqi Freedom*. General Mattis played a key role in the April 2004 battle of Fallujah, Operation *Vigilant Resolve*, by negotiating with the insurgent command inside of the city, as well as playing an important part in planning the subsequent Operation *Phantom Fury* in November 2004. He commanded the 1st Marine Expeditionary Brigade and then Task Force 58, during Operation *Enduring Freedom* in southern Afghanistan. General Mattis is a native of the Pacific Northwest and graduated from Central Washington State University. He is also a graduate of the Amphibious Warfare School, Marine Corps Command and Staff College, and the National War College. General Mattis was awarded the Defense Distinguished Service Medal, the Navy Distinguished Service Medal, the Defense Superior Service Medal, the Legion of Merit, and the Bronze Star.

Sean McFate is an Assistant Professor in the College of International Security Affairs at NDU. Previously, he worked in Africa, where he helped design and manage stabilization programs for the State Department, specifically in Liberia, Burundi, and Sudan. Prior to that, he was a policy advisor for Amnesty International USA, advising executive staff on human rights and armed conflict. He also served as an officer in the U.S. Army, primarily as a paratrooper in the 82^{d} Airborne Division. He serves on the editorial board of *Millennium: Journal of International Studies*. Mr. McFate holds double Bachelor's degrees from Brown University and a Master's degree from the John F. Kennedy School of Government at Harvard University, and is completing his doctorate in International Relations at the London School of Economics and Political Science.

Anne-Tyler Morgan is a third-year law student at the DePaul University College of Law where she has concentrated her J.D. studies in the field of international human rights law. Through her work with DePaul University's IHRLI, she has researched transitional justice issues and postconflict private development projects. Ms. Morgan studied European human rights at the University College Dublin School of Law and inter-American human rights at the Universidad Nacional in Heredia, Costa Rica. She currently serves as a congressional district leader for ONE, a bipartisan advocacy organization working toward the elimination of extreme poverty and preventable disease throughout Africa. Ms. Morgan holds a Bachelor's degree from Transylvania University in Lexington, Kentucky.

Jacqueline O'Neill is the Lead Advocacy Coordinator at the Institute for Inclusive Security, overseeing regional and thematic advocacy. She co-leads Inclusive Security's work in Africa, with a focus on Sudan. Seeking to increase the number and influence of women in peace and security operations around the world, Ms. O'Neill has trained military, police, and civilian personnel at organizations including NATO, UN, OSCE, Dutch Ministries of Defense and Foreign Affairs, U.S. Foreign Service Institute, and the Naval Postgraduate School. Ms. O'Neill has worked with women peace-builders from Afghanistan, Colombia, Kyrgyzstan, Liberia, Nepal, Sudan, and Uganda. Previously, she worked at the UN Mission in Sudan and Sudan's Ahfad University for Women. She was a policy advisor to Canada's secretary of state for Asia-Pacific and, along with retired Lieutenant General Roméo Dallaire, helped found an effort to bring together military, humanitarian, and human rights communities to address the issue of child soldiers. Ms. O'Neill holds a Master's degree from the Harvard Kennedy School and a Bachelor's of Commerce from the University of Alberta.

Courtney Rowe is a Master of Science candidate in Leadership and Policy Studies at DePaul University. While pursuing her degree, she advances her commitment to assisting diverse communities and supports the human rights program at DePaul University's IHRLI as a research intern. She specifically focuses on DDR as related to women and children in the transitional and postconflict environment. In 2009, Ms. Rowe was 1 of 30 students in the Chicago area to complete a workshop in international humanitarian law sponsored by the International Committee of the Red Cross. Ms. Rowe earned her Bachelor's degree in International Affairs from the University of Colorado at Boulder.

Mark Sedra is a Senior Fellow at the Centre for International Governance Innovation and teaches in the Department of Political Science at the University of Waterloo. His current research focuses on postconflict statebuilding with an emphasis on security issues. He has conducted research on a number of countries and regions, including Northern Ireland, Sudan, the Middle East, and the Balkans, and the bulk of his research has centered on Afghanistan. Mr. Sedra formerly was a research associate at the Bonn International Center for Conversion, a German-based independent think tank specializing in peace and security issues. He was also a visiting research fellow at the Defense Academy of the United Kingdom. Previously, Mr. Sedra served as the 2004–2005 Cadieux Léger Fellow in the Canadian Department of Foreign Affairs and International Trade. Mr. Sedra has provided consultant expertise to numerous organizations and governments on international security issues, including the UN, Canadian Department of Foreign Affairs and International Trade, and United Kingdom Department for International Development. He is currently completing his Ph.D. at the School of Oriental and African Studies at the University of London and holds a Master's degree from the London School of Economics and Political Science and a Bachelor's degree from the University of Toronto.

Matthew T. Simpson is an attorney specializing in public international law and international economic law. Currently, Mr. Simpson acts as one of two accredited legal advisors to the Darfurian delegation negotiating a peace agreement with the government of Sudan as part of the UN-African

Union Mission in Darfur Peace Process. In this position, Mr. Simpson advises Darfurians on the substance and strategy of negotiations, with particular focus on issues related to wealth-sharing, power-sharing, and security. Mr. Simpson acts as The Darfur Project director for the Public International Law and Policy Group (PILPG), a global, pro-bono law firm. With PILPG, Mr. Simpson manages The Darfur Project and advises on the development of sustainable solutions to armed conflict and the establishment of the rule of law in postconflict areas. Previously, Mr. Simpson was an associate with the international law firm Weil Gotshal and Manges, LLP, where he counseled clients in international trade remedies proceedings. He was a litigator before the U.S. Court of International Trade, U.S. Court of Appeals for the Federal Circuit, and the London Court of International Arbitration. Mr. Simpson holds a J.D. from American University, a Master's degree in International Affairs from American University, and a Bachelor's degree from Hobart College.

Cornelis Steenken is the first Coordinator of the UN Inter-Agency Working Group on DDR at the United Nations Development Programme. He helps coordinate 18 UN agencies working on DDR. Mr. Steenken is a retired Canadian naval lieutenant commander. After 27 years of service, Mr. Steenken left the service in 2002 to continue his specialization in peacekeeping and DDR. He served as the senior advisor on DDR at the Swedish National Defense College. Mr. Steenken worked at the Pearson Peacekeeping Centre, where he developed DDR training and coauthored the handbook *DDR: A Practical Field and Classroom Guide*. Additionally, he initiated the Integrated DDR Training Group, which helped to standardize global DDR training. Mr. Steenken graduated from the Royal Military College.

Jarad Vary is a graduate student in Lyon, France, pursuing a Master's degree from the Université Jean Moulin. His current research focuses on the metamorphosis of gender identity in the democratizing Middle East. Mr. Vary joined the Institute for Inclusive Security in 2010, investigating the diverse leadership structures of Burmese and Pakistani refugee camps. He helped organize Inclusive Security's annual colloquium, Women Moderating Extremism, with women peace-builders from Bosnia, Lebanon, Pakistan, and Rwanda. He earned a Bachelor's degree in Government from Cornell University.

Adriaan Verheul is the founder of Defense and Development Consultants, LLC, a not-for-profit consulting practice that provides support to fragile and postconflict states as well as advising developing countries on the consolidation of stability and growth. In 2010, Mr. Verheul served with the UN Stabilization Mission in Haiti as Senior Coordinator of the mission's input to the Post-Disaster Needs Assessment. Previously, Mr. Verheul served as the Chief of the Integrated UN DDR Unit in the UN Mission in the Sudan, leading the largest DDR operation worldwide. Additionally, Mr. Verheul served with the World Bank as a senior specialist in charge of the design, negotiation, processing, financing, and supervision of demobilization and reintegration programs in French-speaking Central Africa. Prior to the World Bank, Mr. Verheul worked in the Department of Peacekeeping Operations at UN Headquarters with responsibilities for the operational and political management of peacekeeping operations in the Middle East, Tajikistan, Central African Republic, Sierra Leone, and the Democratic Republic of the Congo. He also served as the secretary of the UN Special Committee on Peacekeeping Operations and as the special assistant to the Assistant Secretary-General for Peacekeeping Operations. Mr. Verheul has published in English and Dutch on SSR, peacekeeping, disarmament, and maritime affairs. He is a reserve officer in the Royal Netherlands Navy and holds a Master's degree in International Relations and a Bachelor's degree in Law from Leiden University, Netherlands.

Eric Wiebelhaus-Brahm is a Senior Research Fellow with DePaul University's IHRLI and an International Research Consultant at Hewitt Associates. He is an expert in human rights, transitional justice, and postconflict reconstruction. His current research focuses on the evaluation of transitional justice tools, DDR processes, and labor and welfare issues in the emerging economies of Asia and Africa. He is the author of several book chapters, and his articles have appeared in journals such as the *Journal of Human Rights* and *International Studies Perspectives*. Dr. Wiebelhaus-Brahm earned his Ph.D. in Political Science from the University of Colorado at Boulder.

Paul R. Williams holds the Rebecca I. Grazier Professorship in Law and International Relations at American University, teaches at the School of International Service and the Washington College of Law, and directs the joint program in international relations. Dr. Williams is the cofounder and executive director of the Public International Law and Policy Group, a nonprofit that provides pro bono legal assistance to states and governments involved in peace negotiations, postconflict constitution drafting, and war crimes prosecutions. During the course of his legal practice, Dr. Williams has assisted over a dozen states and governments in major international peace negotiations and has advised more than 15 governments across Europe, Africa, and Asia on issues of state recognition, self-determination, state succession, drafting and implementation of postconflict constitutions, and border and sea demarcation. Previously, Dr. Williams served in the Department of State's Office of the Legal Advisor for European and Canadian Affairs. He was also a senior associate with the Carnegie Endowment for International Peace. Dr. Williams received his Ph.D. from the University of Cambridge, where he was a Fulbright Research Scholar. He earned his J.D. from Stanford Law School, and his Bachelor's degree from the University of California, Davis.

www.ingramcontent.com/pod-product-compliance
Lightning Source LLC
Chambersburg PA
CBHW071014280326
41935CB00011B/1346

9781780399157